LABOR
&
VALUE

PETER LANG
New York • Washington, D.C./Baltimore • Bern
Frankfurt am Main • Berlin • Brussels • Vienna • Oxford

LAWRENCE KRADER

LABOR
&
VALUE

EDITED BY
CYRIL LEVITT & ROD HAY

PETER LANG
New York • Washington, D.C./Baltimore • Bern
Frankfurt am Main • Berlin • Brussels • Vienna • Oxford

Library of Congress Cataloging-in-Publication Data

Krader, Lawrence.
Labor and value / Lawrence Krader;
edited by Cyril Levitt, Rod Hay.
p. cm.
Includes bibliographical references and index.
1. Labor. 2. Value. I. Levitt, Cyril. II. Hay, Rod. III. Title.
HD4901.K658 331'.01'3—dc22 2003016535
ISBN 0-8204-6798-7

MIL

Bibliographic information published by **Die Deutsche Bibliothek**.
Die Deutsche Bibliothek lists this publication in the "Deutsche
Nationalbibliografie"; detailed bibliographic data is available
on the Internet at http://dnb.ddb.de/.

Cover design by Dutton & Sherman Design

The paper in this book meets the guidelines for permanence and durability
of the Committee on Production Guidelines for Book Longevity
of the Council of Library Resources.

Peter Lang Publishing, Inc., New York
275 Seventh Avenue, 28th Floor, New York, NY 10001
www.peterlangusa.com

Printed in Germany

Contents

Lawrence Krader *In Memoriam*

Lawrence Krader (1919–1998) studied philosophy at the City College of New York where he worked with the logician Alfred Tarski after having spent a year studying with Rudolf Carnap at the University of Chicago. At City College he was the winner of the prestigious Ketchum Award. Around this time he began his studies in anthropology with Franz Boas and Gene Weltfish at Columbia University. Serving in he United States Merchant Marine during World War II he participated in the run of the German blockade of the Soviet Union. After the war he studied linguistics with Roman Jakobson at Columbia University and began his long term research on the peoples of Central Asia. Completing his doctorate at Harvard University in 1954 under the supervision of Clyde Kluckhohn ("Kinship Systems of the Altaic-speaking Peoples of the Asiatic Steppes"), he continued in his position as Research Associate at the Bureau of Social Science Research at American University in Washington, D.C. In 1953 he married Dr. Barbara Lattimer whom he had met at the linguistics seminar of Roman Jakobson. at Columbia University. Barbara Krader who became a world renowned ethnomusicologist and co-founder and President of the Society for Ethnomusicology and the Executive Secretary of the International Folk Music Council, provided Lawrence with unwavering loyalty, scholarly support and comradeship throughout their long marriage.

In subsequent years Krader held several academic and extra-academic positions in the United States, Canada and Germany. In 1972 he was appointed Professor and Director of the Institut für Ethnologie at the Freie Universität Berlin, a position he held until his retirement. Fluent in the major European languages, he frequently lectured at several prestigious institutions of higher learning in the native language of his host academies. Over the years he had developed a special relationship with students and colleagues in Mexico through his friendship with the esteemed anthropoligist, the late Professor Angel Palerm. In addition to his work on Central Asia, Krader transcribed, edited and introduced the ethnological notebooks of Karl Marx, a labor which began as an idea developed in discussions with his friend Karl Korsch. Furthermore, Krader critically reworked the theoretical works of Marx and Hegel in a series of books in the 1970s and 1980s which included *Ethnologie und Anthropologie bei Marx*, *The Dialectic of Civil Society*, *The Asiatic Mode of Production*, and *A Treatise on Social Labor*. From 1989 until his death Krader produced 156 unpublished manuscripts which included works on labor and value, noetics, a theory of the Russian Revolution, mathematical logic, a critique of evolutionism, linguistics and many other topics reflecting his wide range of scholarship.

This volume, *Labor and Value*, is the first of Krader's many manuscripts to be published posthumously. He personally revised the draft of the work for publication, and wrote the Foreword to the book shortly before his death. Light editing was done to prepare the manuscript for publication by the two editors. A two volume collection of Krader's early writings in anthropology is in preparation as is the penultimate draft of his work on noetics. Other works will follow as part of an endowed research project at McMaster University which Krader was in the process of establishing at the time of his passing.

Cyril Levitt
Rod Hay

Editors' Introduction

The theories of labor and value have been closely related since their earliest formulations by the great thinkers of classical antiquity. Aristotle wrote about reciprocity between the farmer and the shoemaker in terms of the equation of the amount of work of each in relation to the other. According to Marx, it was also Aristotle who posed, but could not answer the problem of the value substance present in equal amount in two commodities exchanged for one another. The modern formulation of the theories of labor and objective value was accomplished by the classical school of political economy, William Petty to David Ricardo, and ended with the critique of Karl Marx.

A change in economic thinking occurred in 1871 when Menger and Jevons proclaimed the discovery of the law of diminishing marginal utilities.[1] Simply stated, the law maintained that the additional utility of increasing quantities of a good tends to decline. This gave them an apparent law of subjective valuation which would enable them to dispense with any objective theory of value. Economic psychology superceded the labor theory and moved economic thought away from the social theory of value in general to a theory founded entirely upon the behavior of the de-historicized and de-socialized individual.

This change in economic thinking, which was not limited to the economic sphere alone, could, in part, be viewed as a reaction to the development of the socially based theory of value which began with the Scottish School and was taken up by G. W. F. Hegel, and, following both, by Karl Marx. The Austrian and British Schools of marginal utility harkened back to the tradition of economic liberalism which continued to develop alongside of the social schools throughout the 19th century. One of the central points of contention between the social and individualist approaches concerns the relationship between the individual and the subjective. In viewing the development of the individual as an aspect of social development, the subjective could no longer be simply identified with the individual. Adam Smith, in his *Theory of the Moral Sentiments*, linked the development of the individual to the interactions with others. Invoking the concept of the mirror or looking glass he anticipated by more than a century developments in American social psychology. In Smith's view:

> Were it possible that a human creature could grow up to manhood in some solitary place, without any communication with his own species, he could no more think of his own character, of the propriety or demerit of his own sentiments and conduct, of the beauty or deformity of his own face. All of these are objects which he cannot easily see, which naturally he does not look at, and with regard to which he is provided with no mirror which can present them to his view. Bring him into society and he is immediately provided with the mirror which he wanted before.[2]

That the development of American social psychology should have been joined by neo-Hegelian thinkers only serves to illustrate Hegel's importance in developing the social nature of individuality itself in his own writings. The influence of Smith upon Hegel has been studied by a variety of authors who have shown that Hegel understood work as a mediate relation between human beings and nature.[3] The theory of the division of labor, which Hegel appropriated from Smith, represented the social mechanism linking the labor of one with that of the rest. As Lukács suggests:

> ...with his insight into the role of human activity in society Hegel attempted to overcome Kantian and Fichtian dualism of subjectivity and objectivity, inner and outer, morality and legality. His aim was to comprehend socialized man whole and undivided as he really is within the concrete totality of his activities in society... What enabled him to do so was the possibility of exploiting the conception of labor derived from Adam Smith.[4]

In his conception of labor which is derived from the work of Adam Smith, Hegel suggested that labor is social. Since the labor of the individual is part of a general social division of labor and the labor of one is dependent upon the labor of the rest, this labor is a collective power of the human species. According to Hegel social labor is the force by which the human species produces and reproduces itself. For Hegel the individual is not an isolated, atomic and abstract entity but an element of the society which finds its own expression through this elaborated individuality.[5] This is not a totalitarian formulation since the individual is not oppressed and manipulated by the social whole but reacts back upon the society which is changed in its substance by that individuality. Marx understood Hegel in this way.[6]

The consequences of this for value theory are significant. Methodological individualism, which is the premise of the marginal utility approach to value, is no longer tenable. This has long been recognized in the disciplines of anthropology, sociology, some schools of philosophy and in institutional economics.

Marx agreed with Hegel, as we have seen, on the social character of labor, on the mediate relation of the human kind to nature through labor, and on the self creation of the human species through this process. He also agreed with Hegel that the whole is the truth, but recognized that the constitution of the whole under existing conditions was contradictory in that society was divided into opposing social classes, viz., society, under existing conditions is divided against it-self. In terms of the theory of utility this implies that value judgments are a func-tion of the social divisions and thus divided societies produce multiple and con-flicting standards of value. In objective value terms, the class of social labor which produces the whole does not receive the whole of the value that it has produced. In addition, Hegel resolved the alienation of labor under the existing conditions only in thought since he grasped the alienation as an issue for the consciousness. From Smith, Marx took over the frame of reference of the classical school of political economy, including the theory of utility or use-value and the labor theory in the form of value in exchange, which he then subjected to logical and historical cri-tique. The historical critique which Marx brought to bear against Smith, indeed, against the entire classical school, concerned the historical specificity of systems and relations of production, a thought which Marx had found in the philosophy of Hegel and which led him to favour Hegel over Feuerbach.[7]

Krader on Labor and Value

In the following work, Lawrence Krader has reconceived and broadened the theory of value by expanding, deepening and systematizing its anthropological and his-torical basis. Krader's theories on labor and value are set within a larger naturalistic framework which he has developed elsewhere. In outline, Krader argues that we have become aware of three different orders of nature, although there may be other possible orders yet to be discovered. These orders are the material order, the human order and the quantum order. Each of these orders are part of the natural order as a whole, there being nothing beyond or above nature. Yet, none of these orders may be reduced one to the other since each has its own character and each stands in relation to the others by means of passage about which we know some but not all elements.[8] There is a close relation between the material and human orders of nature, since the human kind at the beginning of its evolution, had dirempted itself from the material order from which it remains in a primary state of alienation. We have dirempted ourselves from the material order in that we have interposed the grid of culture between ourselves and material nature which rests upon the organization and processes of human work and labor. In Krader's words

> Mediation and diremption are interconnected in the human order and in relations to external nature. The animal relations of age, sex, and the generations, are transformed into human relations by our labors. The human relation to the material world of matter and of life is complex, and permeated with hopeful gains, and regretful loss. All work and labor are dirempted by the human beings who engage in these activities by being distanced from the material order, and in this limited sense removed from a part of nature; we have other relations in nature, as a part of it, and to other parts of nature than those of material things. The diremption is a mediate connection to nature; mediation and diremption are

the natural relations of the human order. The distancing is effected by our work and by the use of our bodies, minds, and social relations, and their instruments. These uses are objective, the body, mind, social relations and instruments are objects on which we work and with which we work and labor.[9]

The material order of nature is concrete, thingly and direct. The human order of nature is concrete and abstract, subjective and objective, mediate and immediate. Our bodies are at once thingly and as such they are directly natural materials. But insofar as they are human bodies, they have become part of the human field of activity, and through the work of the body, have become objective to us.[10]

It is part of the human condition both in reality and in myth that we must labor to maintain ourselves as a species. But the organization, division and cooperation of labor has varied significantly across the epochs of human history as has the development of technology and science both practically and theoretically. Karl Marx identified four different economic formations as the Asiatic, classical-antique, feudal and capitalist. Krader has contrasted these four modes of production, all of which he considers to be constitutive of civil society, with primitive-communal collectivities.

Krader on Periodization, and Labor and Value

For Marx, the theory of value was developed largely in relation to the capitalist mode of production, indeed, to the capitalist mode of production during the few decades following the industrial revolution in Great Britain.[11] To be sure, he occasionally commented on the relations of labor and production in European feudalism, classical antiquity and on what he called the Asiatic Mode of Production.[12] On occasion, he even related aspects of the theory of value to these earlier economic formations. Yet, it cannot be denied that his primary concern was with the capitalist mode, which, as he argued in the Introduction to the *Grundrisse*, supplied the key to the understanding of the earlier epochs. Krader's focus is not specifically directed to the capitalist epoch. His theory of labor and value is derived from the relations and conditions which are common to all of civil society which stand in contrast to those of primitive-communal life.

Krader makes a distinction between the primitive-communal groupings and civil society along the following lines: in the former, the units of production and consumption coincide, the labor is communal and the communal product of labor is shared or shared out among the members of the group. The relations to nature are mediated by the communal relations of the group and thus the distinction between immediate and mediate relations is introduced and is a common feature of all human aggregation. There is no distinction between the form and substance of labor, nor is there a distinction between abstract and concrete labor. The objective and subjective elements of life pass into one another so that there is no disjunction between the two. Reification occurs only at the symbolic level, such as in myth, and is related to the primary mediate relation to nature.

The development of relations of exchange, first between communities, and later, within communities between different units of production and consumption, change the primitive-communal groups into communal-social organizations. The form of communal life is set forth in the village communities, kin and tribal groups, and the like, but the substance of the relations has become social on account of the introduction of the process of exchange. The process of exchange has a twofold effect. 1. It introduces a mediate relation between the concrete labor and its product, and 2. It effects a mediation between the processes of production and consumption. As a consequence, the product is alienated from the producer and the introduction of a class of people who engage in trade and commerce results. Furthermore, another class is developed which lives from unreciprocated exchange and thus the appropriation of the social surplus generated by those who labor.

It is precisely the mediation occasioned by the introduction of the exchange relation which is given social expression in value. The separation and opposition of abstract and concrete labor, of the labor form and substance, of the subjective and objective labor and of mediate and immediate production give rise to the value form and substance in the civil condition.

Karl Marx on Value Theory

The most systematic elaboration of Marx's theory of value (in his published writings) is found in *Capital*. Here, we find a discussion of use-value, exchange value, and value, and, at a later point in the text, Marx introduces the topic of surplus value.[13]

For Marx, a commodity as use value is indistinguishable from any other product of human labor capable of satisfying some human want. What differentiates a commodity from other products of human labor is the fact that the relations between the producers of commodities take the form of a relation between the products of their labor. This "topsy-turvy" (*verkehrtes*) relation is expressed in the form of exchange value. Exchange value is thus the form of value. Value is the "social substance."[14] (Note that Marx says that value is a social substance, whereas for Krader "value as such is not a substance, but has a substance.") Thus, exchange value is the invariant form of the value substance.

The relations of value are all objective for Marx. Value is nothing other than objective social value. Subjective elements are present in the case of use value, but they do not enter into the constitution of the value substance. That substance is determined qualitatively by the mediate relations between producers and quantitatively by the average labor time of society necessary for the production of any given commodity. Subjective elements come into play in the market in the creation of the demand for particular commodities, but if anything they serve to divert the price of the commodity from the expression of its true, objective value.

For Marx, value, being the "congelation of homogeneous human labor," "human labor in the abstract," is itself entirely abstract.[15] The concretion for Marx is work which is specific, discrete and differentiated according to skill, qualification, technique, instruments and tools, training, etc. This is not a true dialectic of the abstract and concrete, but a mere juxtaposition, for the concretion is posited as historically invariant in form and substance,[16] whereas the abstraction is introduced at a later point in history. Concrete labor, or work, producing use values is an invariant element of all human existence for Marx. From this point of view, there is no difference between commodity producing society and any other form of human society.

The surplus value for Marx represents that part of the value produced by social labor which does not accrue to social labor. Most of Marx's followers have understood surplus value as a unique feature of the capitalist mode of production. They refer to the booty of the exploiting classes in pre-capitalist societies as the surplus product.[17] Marx, himself, never systematically studied the forms of exploitation historically nor did he relate them to the theory of value except in passing. His central concern was indeed with the capitalist mode of production and its laws of motion. But there is a simple principle of logic which must be followed in scientific matters. If the defining characteristics of a phenomenon are present, then the phenomenon itself is present. In this case, if the defining characteristics of the relations of surplus value are present say, in classical Rome, then we are compelled to acknowledge the existence of surplus value in classical Rome.

As we have already suggested, these fundamentals of value theory have been largely unquestioned since the publication of *Capital* in 1867. It is precisely these building blocks of the theory which Krader has critically examined in his recent writings to which we now turn our attention.

Subjective and Objective Value

Karl Marx and his followers have developed and preserved the law of value as something wholly social and objective. Whenever Marx writes of value, he means objective social value. The Austrian economists hold to a purely subjective theory of value. Neither of these views is wrong; each has a valid part of the whole. Human relations are both subjective and objective; natural relations are thingly. To take the subject away from the object or the object from the subject is to make of the human being an angel or a beast.

For Krader, value is the expression of an estimation, of choice, of an evaluation in which both a subjective and objective process are operative. Objectively, we have creature needs and human wants which must be satisfied if we are to maintain ourselves at any given social level. For example, we have need of food and shelter from the elements, but whether we have a want for a cooked steak or raw fish, a condominium or a bungalow, is a subjective matter. We value raw fish or a bungalow or a red as opposed to a green automobile subjectively. The two elements in subjective valuation are will and desire.[18] Krader has brought the will and desire together into a common formula insofar as he sees the desire as the externalization of the expression of the will.[19] Subjective value is thus an expression of will and desire. This covers the voluntary, aesthetic and judgmental relations of the human kind. Marxism, especially political Marxism, has, for the most part, stressed the objective relations and processes, relegating the subjective to a wholly subordinate if not distorting role in history.[20] Krader emphasizes, however, that the human order is objective and subjective; both are equally constitutive of human being. The exclusion of the latter is a reification, just as the exclusion of the former is a mysticization of human being. And yet the subjective and objective are not symmetrical. In the expression of subjective value there is no diremption of the human form and substance, whereas objective value gives expression not only to the separation of form and substance, but to their opposition as well. Furthermore, the subjective processes are real only in a mediate way, i.e., through the objective human relations.

In primitive societies the subjective and objective sides of social life are interwoven such that there is no opposition between the two. This being the case, there is no practical difference between subjective and objective value. Hence, there is no actual value expression in primitive society, for the form and substance of value have not been elaborated. The separation and opposition of objective and subjective value is brought about by the development of social labor which is divided, combined, exploited and above all reckoned up in units of time.[21] It is social labor (both as a process and as product) which is the objective value substance. In fact, for all value expressions it is the social relation (especially of labor) which is the determinant. Value, being a form, is wholly passive.[22]

Objective value is an expression; it is not immediately a social substance. As an expression it is a form, i.e., the form of social labor which has as its substance the relations of human work and labor. Objective social value is the expression of relations of labor, abstract and concrete, in bourgeois and civil society actually, in some future society potentially.[23]

Value Form and Substance/Abstract and Concrete Value

With the development of the relations of labor in civil society, i.e., the growing division and combination of labor, the measuring, the development of exchange relations, abstract and concrete labor came to be differentiated from one another, and this in turn gave rise to the expression of an objective value substance, abstract and concrete.[24] The objective value expression is determined by the differentiation of form and substance of the human kind, which, essentially is the form and substance of human labor respectively.[25] Objective value is an expression of the relation of human social reproduction under specific conditions. Historically, the objective value expression was extruded by the civil conditions and relations of labor, but it will continue forward beyond the civil and bourgeois society because the measuring, reckoning up and accounting of labor will continue to be of central importance in any future society.

In the history of civil society, the abstract objective value form has been that of exchange value. And yet it is a mistake (one that Marx made) to identify the form of value with exchange value without historical specification. Exchange value gives expression to the exchange relation which is its determinant. The exchange relation in civil society is one of equal or equivalent reciprocity. But this equal or equivalent reciprocation is a wholly formal matter having to do with the juridical forms of freedom and equality. In this sense, exchange value, the expression of this formal relation, is a form of a form. There is an historical confluence of the abstract objective value form and exchange value; put simply, in practice the objective value form in civil society is exchange value. But the two are not the same theoretically or potentially in practice.[26]

This is so because the exchange value is the expression of the exchange relation whereas the value substance is the expression of the relations of social labor in the process of human reproduction whereby the needs, wants and desires of the human kind are met. Now in every human society production and consumption constitute the poles of the process of reproduction. That which mediates the process of production and human consumption is that of distribution. Exchange is one historically specific mode of distribution, namely, the predominant mode of distribution in civil society.[27] The exchange relation in society is a real relation and it is not the same as the relation of labor or production. Yet the relation itself is constituted by forms which are borne by the human beings engaging in the exchange process. They do not engage in the process of exchange because they are human, but because they are formal, juridical personalities, citizens, members of nation states, etc. It is because the exchange relation determines the relation of production of civil society in a mediate way that the value substance is given formal expression in exchange value. However, if and when the exchange process is superseded by the process of distributive reciprocation, then exchange value will cease to exist, its social basis having been destroyed. And yet, labor time and quality will continue to be of interest to society. Therefore, the objective value substance will be given expression in a new and as yet incomprehensible form.

Krader also argues that in addition to the abstract objective value substance there is a concrete objective value substance as well, since human labor is both abstract and concrete in civil society. The abstract, objective value substance is the expression of the (abstract) human labor expended in the process of social reproduction. The concrete objective value is the expression of the particular work expended in the meeting of needs, wants and desires. But there is an asymmetry here between the abstract and concrete value substance. The abstract value substance is the same expression as abstract labor, but the concrete value substance is not the same as the expression of concrete labor or work. This is so because the relations of abstract labor and the expression of the same in the objective value substance coincide historically, whereas the concrete labor relation arches over a greater variety of social formations than the expression of the concrete objective value substance.[28]

Just as exchange value and the form of the abstract objective labor substance coincide in civil society, so too does use value coincide with the expression of the concrete objective value substance in this historically determinate form of human society. And just as he erred in identifying exchange value and the abstract objective value form, in the same way Marx erred in identifying use value and the expression of the concrete labor substance.[29] According to Marx, the primitive hunter-gatherer produces use values. But Krader argues that the primitive laborer most decidedly does not produce use values; rather, he produces goods and products which satisfy his needs and wants.[30] Marx believed that the use value of a commodity was directly related to its physical properties whereby it is able to satisfy some human want or need. But according to Krader:

> Use value is not a physical property of a commodity... Water quenches thirst everywhere in the human condition, being generally a means of satisfying a particular want. On occasion, an exchange will take place to meet that want. The useful value that water provides is not inherent in the water itself but in the society wherein the exchange relations have been constituted and take place. The value in use is not in itself but outside itself, in the society of the social and political economy.[31]

According to Krader, the primitive hunters, gatherers and fishers produce nothing of value because they immediately consume what they produce. They have little by way of storage and accumulation plays even less of an economic role in their communities.[32] The labor of the one is immediately part of the labor of the others for labor is communal and reciprocal.[33] Labor is not reckoned up, abstracted, parsed, recorded, exchanged, rewarded, specialized, exploited, oppressed, or alienated in society. These are the relations of labor which give rise to the value expression (concrete and abstract, form and substance) in society. Concrete value is an expression of concrete labor or the work which people do in order to satisfy the wants and needs they have. It is the opposition between abstract and concrete labor which gives rise to the value substance and form. In primitive society the abstract and concrete labor are not opposed to or separated from one another and hence no value is produced. In civil society the form of concrete value is use value, where abstract value mediates the relation between the human being and the means of satisfaction of his or her wants. But use value is not the only possible form that concrete value may assume. It is an actual, historically specific form, namely, the form of concrete value in the civil condition of the human kind. Beyond that we can only say that the human kind would continue to reckon, parse, record, divide, specialize etc., its labor even if there were no exchange. In this case, concrete value would extrude a form different from that of use value.

Surplus Value and Fetishism

By means of the introduction of exchange relations mediately into the process of social reproduction, the archaic community is transformed into society, historically, into civil society. Through contractual exchange the social realization of the value form occurs; through the relations of exploitation, the anti-social realization of the value form occurs in civil society.[34] In the archaic, pre-civil condition of the human kind, an occasional surplus is produced. With the introduction of the exchange relations into the economy and society the surplus is socialized; it becomes a social surplus. At the same time the disposition over the social surplus is in the hands of the class of non-producers. Surplus value, according to Krader, is the expression of a relation of attribution without equal or equivalent retribution, which is alienation without equal or equivalent return in civil society, and is relative to exchange value mediately.[35]

The fetishism which Marx described in relation to the commodity form and in relation to capital has its roots in the separation and opposition of the subjective and objective, the abstract and concrete, and the formal and substantial relations in civil society. The fetishism of the commodity is an expression of the reification of human relations in the exchange relation. There are two aspects to this. First, the indirect relation of exchange is represented as a direct relation between human beings and the exchange process appears to generate itself, the products appear to have a life of their own. Second, the commodity relation is represented as being the whole of the social relation. "It is a substitution of a part for a whole, a form for the a form-plus-content, an object for an object-subject, an abstraction for an abstraction-concretion, a passivity, for an activity-passivity. It is then proclaimed that commodities are nothing but wholes, and that totalities have been exchanged. The commodity then appears to be a self-mover, with a life of its own."[36]

Now the fetishism of commodities is neither the thingly relations between persons, nor the social relations between things. That is so because this "topsy-turvy" relation is real and actual. The fetishism is the magical representation, the expression of real and actual relations as though it were real and actual itself. "It is the mysticization of the commodities in the exchange relation that constitutes their fetishism, which is neither a social relation between things, nor a thingly relation between persons, but a magical transposition of the things exchanged, as though they were living human beings endowed with a will and consciousness of their own. In the world of commodities, human beings stand to one another in a thingly relation, as persons bearing the character mask of commodities; they are human beings transformed into personifications of labor power and capital. These reified individuals are not a pure figment, for living social labor is embodied in those who in the wage labor transaction offer capacity labor for sale. The fetishism of the commodity of living labor takes the reified for the whole human being. The commodity, labor power, appears to have acquired a life of its own, independent of the human being to whom it pertains.

The fetishism of capital, or any other fetishism in civil society is no different. Marx on occasion described capital as the self valorization of value. But this is not capital, it is the fetishism of capital. Only when the prestidigitator waves his wand do *Monsieur le Capital* and *Madame le Terre* do their ghostly dance. Value, being an expression, is wholly passive. The fetishism of capital, which is the fetishism of value, is the representation of the passivity as a whole which is both active and passive. It is the representation of a reified human process *as though* it were entirely thingly.

Labor and the Natural and Human Orders

Labor is the active relation whereby the human kind distances itself from nature. At the same time, labor is a relation in society, one relation among several which together constitute the social whole. These two relations of labor are objective in the first place and they constitute the ground out of which all other human social relations are generated.[37] Labor is the means whereby the wants and needs of the human kind are met, and as such it is the active element in human self-reproduction.

By means of its labor, present and past, the human kind mediates between itself and nature. In so doing, the objective relation is introduced into the thingly order of nature. But this distancing of the human kind is a self distancing or diremption, the self-relation of humanity introducing the subjective relation into the natural order. Human labor, by transforming part of the natural field into the human field, objectifies part of the natural field as it creates the objective-subjective relation of the human order. The result of the transformative/self-transformative process from the human standpoint is the primary alienation of the human kind from nature. Human labor, present and past, theoretical and practical, active and passive, constitutes the grid which the human kind interposes between its own objective and subjective order and the thingly order of nature.

From the position of the human kind, the transformation of nature is viewed as a macrocosmic process; yet from the standpoint of the natural order, the reorganization of the natural (thingly) material by making it human (objective/subjective) is minuscule in scope and extent. The human order is but a limited sub-order of nature, from which it never takes its leave. The projection of the categories of the human kind (in all its historically specific forms) onto nature is an act of human self-aggrandizement.

Human labor, being objective and subjective, is thus the mediately instrumental relation of the human kind to nature. In other words, labor as a human process is discontinuous with nature, even though as a concrete process in the natural order it is wholly continuous with it. Labor as mediate process is objective-subjective relation, the grid established thereby mediating between the thingly and human orders. As a relation in society, i.e., within the human order, labor is both immediately and mediately social. It is in immediate relation to the practical and theoretical instruments and techniques of production in the process of meeting human wants and needs. All other labor in society is mediate.[38] At the same time, the labor process in society is abstract and concrete; concrete insofar as natural and human materials are transformed to meet specific wants and needs, abstract insofar as the process is an ongoing one and includes the labor of organizing, preparing, storing, transmitting and distributing the product of concrete labor.[39]

The Form and Substance of Labor

The problem of form and substance and of their interrelation has been central in the history of philosophical thought. Invariably, one or both have been understood as "eternal categories" or "timeless essences." Krader not only attempts to historicize these trans-temporal and spatial mystications, he develops their "rational kernel" in terms of the relations of the form and substance of labor.

The substance of labor is the set of internal and external relations which make up the process of its self-reproduction. These are the relations to nature and in society respectively.[40] The form of labor is an expression of the substance, but it is not reducible to it. Specifically, the form of labor is opposed to the substance with respect to the matter of labor's bondage and freedom and to the opposition between human and social labor as we shall see below. Both the form and substance of labor have their histories, yet the course of their historical developments are not the same.[41] In the natural order, form is not separated from substance, the relation between the two being concrete and direct. In the human order, the separation and opposition of form and substance is generated abstractly and concretely by means of human making (*poesis*) as opposed to natural doing (*praxis*). Although the form and substance are separated and opposed to one another and have their separate histories, they are nevertheless interdependent. The substance is the determinant of the form, the latter being passive, the former being both active and passive. The form, however, is internalized by the substantive relations and becomes a part of the substance in this mediate way.[42] Abstractly and concretely, substance is the internal constituent of human being, form is its external relation and expression. Form is an extrusion of the temporal process of substantive relation and activity.

The human substance is the set of relations to nature and in society. It is constituted by the interrelations of the labor substance and the social substance, and, in civil society, of the value substance as well.[43] The labor substance is constituted by the relations and activities of labor externally to nature and internally to society. The human social substance encompasses the labor substance and is the "set of internal relations of human beings to one another and the relations of the groups thus formed to other human groups." The value substance is not constitutive of human being from the beginning, but enters into the human substance mediately as a particular development of the social substance in the transition to civil society.

The labor substance and form together make up the active factor in the history of the human kind. that history is potentially and abstractly one, in actuality it is several, the different histories of different peoples having no synthesis and the social whole in civil society being greater than the class of social labor. In primitive societies the separation of the form and substance of labor is weakly developed and their opposition exists only as a potentiality, for the unity of production and consumption is not disrupted and the labor substance is in practice identical to the social substance. Objective and subjective relations are distinguished, but tightly interwoven so that they pass back and forth in the process of life without disruption and without impediment. Objectification in the labor process here is self-objectification, the subjective and objective sides passing into one another. Labor in the primitive condition is both abstract and concrete, but here too, the one is not separated from the other. All production being immediate, there is no division of "hand" and "head" labor. The value substance exists only as a potentiality of the labor substance since the units of production and consumption coincide and there is no difference in practice between the labor substance and the social substance. Exploitation may exist between individuals, for example in the slave relation among individual Chukchees, but this is a sporadic and ephemeral condition, the slave of yesteryear becoming the master of his former master this year. Without opposed social classes, primitive society is without an ongoing, systematic organization of economic exploitation. Labor in the primitive community was a necessity, for primitive wants and needs had to be met. However, primitive labor was neither bound nor free. The freedom or bondage of labor is a relation of social labor, i.e., the class of labor in civil society. In primitive communities, the class of labor is identical to the social whole and all that labor produces returns to labor by means of sharing, sharing out or some such practice of distribution within the community. The relations of labor were in form and substance communal relations in archaic times.

The Form and Substance of Labor Power

In his didactic piece of the late 1840s, *Wage Labor and Capital*, Marx had not yet made the distinction between "labor" and "labor power."[44] According to Engels' later introduction to the work, in drawing this distinction between the two, Marx was able to avoid falling into the same tautological trap which had ensnared the classical political economists—i.e., explaining the value of labor by the value of labor. For Marx, the laborer did not sell his labor, but his labor power or capacity to labor. Labor power, not labor, was a commodity. Only in the slave did labor and labor power coincide, for the slave himself was bought and sold and hence his labor and capacity to labor were bought and sold as well. The wage laborer, on the other hand, sold only a portion of his capacity to labor to the capitalist. It was this portion of his labor capacity which assumed the commodity form.

For Krader, it is important to maintain the distinction between the form and substance of labor power. Labor time and labor capacity are substantial relations in society. Labor power as the externality of labor capacity is the process of its reproduction is both a formal and substantial matter. The labor power substance is the labor time expended in the actualization of the labor capacity. The labor power form is the right of disposition over the labor time. As such, it is a juridical expression of legal power over the sale of the labor substance. According to Krader, the wage laborer does not sell his labor power (form) which is the right to dispose freely over his labor time. To do so would be to sell himself into slavery. The wage laborer is free *pro forma* only insofar as the right of disposition over his labor substance rests in his own hands and not in the hands of another. What is sold to the capitalist by the wage laborer is not his labor power, but his labor substance, i.e., the labor capacity and labor time. In modern civil society, the labor power form is not a commodity; the labor power substance (labor capacity and labor time) is. As Krader has recently written: "Labor power as a formal right of disposition over the social labor time and capacity, rests in the hands of wage labor in modern society, bourgeois and civil. The substantive power to dispose over that time and capacity rests in the hands of another class, which has the right of disposition over the means of production, whether by private or public control over it." When the trade unions bargain with the agents of capital, they are dealing with matters of labor power substance. The legitimacy of the bargaining process itself is proof that the formality is not called into question and not subject to debate.

Krader's work has reopened the qualitative side of the labor theory of value. If his ideas are absorbed it may be possible once again to make progress in this tradition of thought.

Cyril Levitt
Rod Hay

Notes

1. Carl Menger, *Principles of Economics*, (trans. James Dingwall and Bert F. Hoselitz), The Free Press, New York, 1950 (1871). W. Stanley Jevons, *Theory of Political Economy*, Macmillan, London, 1871.

2. Adam Smith, *Theory of the Moral Sentiments*, (ed. R. Meek, D. Raphael, P. Stein), Oxford University Press, New York, 1978, p. 204. Marx criticized Fichtean philosophy in *Capital* when he suggested that human beings are not born with a mirror in their hands knowing thus that I = I. Karl Marx, *Capital*, volume one, New York, International Publishers, 1967, p. 52n.

3. In his *Philosophy of History*, Hegel wrote: "Der Mensch... geht ... vermittelnd zu werke," [Man goes mediatingly to work]. G.W.F. Hegel, *Philosophie der Geschichte*, Frankfurt-am-Main, Suhrkamp Verlag, 1970, Bd 12, p. 295.

4. G. Lukács, *The Young Hegel: Studies in the Relations Between Dialectics and Economics*, tr. Rodney Livingstone, London: Merlin Press, 1975, pp. 321–22.

5. G.W.F. Hegel, *The Phenomenology of Mind*, tr. J.B.Baillie, London: George Allen and Unwin, 1931, pp. 413–438.

6. "The great achievement of Hegel's *Phenomenology* and its final outcome—of the dialectic of negativity as the moving creative principle—is thus first that Hegel grasps conceives the self-generation of man as a process, objectification as de-objectification, as alienation and as overcoming (*Aufhebung*) of this alienation; that he thus grasps the essence of *labor* and understands objective man, the true man because actual man as the result of his *own labor*. The *actual, active* orientation of man to himself as species being, or the activation of his essence as an actual species being, i.e., as human being, is only possible insofar as he actually develops (*herausschaft*) all his *species forces*—which is again only possible through the collective effect of all men, only as the result of history—relates to them as objects, which to being with again is only possible in the form of alienation." Karl Marx, *Ökonomisch-philosophisch Manuskripte* (1844), *Marx-Engles Werke*, Berlin, Dietz Verlag, 1973, Ergänzungsband erster Teil, s. 574.

7. "Verglichen mit Hegel ist Feuerbach durchaus arm." [Compared with Hegel Feuerbach is thoroughly poor.] Karl Marx to J. B. v. Schweitzer, 24 January 1865. MEW, Bd. 16, s. 25.

8. Leibniz, *Monadology* §15.

9. Krader below, p. 101.

10. On the work of the body see John Locke, *Two Treatises on Government*, Second Treatise. (ed. Peter Laslett), Cambridge University Press, 1960.

11. On the limitations of scope in both Smith and Marx see Krader's unpublished lectures compiled by Maria Lucía Muñoz.

12. See Krader's introduction to *The Ethnological Notebooks of Karl Marx*, Assen: Van Gorcum, 1972 and his *The Asiatic Mode of Production*, Assen: Van Gorcum, 1976.

13. Marx begins chapter one with the systematic elaboration of exchange value, use value and value expression in his analysis of the commodity. Surplus value is not treated in a systematic fashion until section two of chapter seven. Marx did not take up the question of the historical and logical relationship between exchange and surplus relations and their value expression.

14. Marx's explanation of the social basis of the value substance leaves something to be desired. At one point in the presentation he advances the thought that the basis of value is physiological. This contradicts his statement that value is a "wholly social substance." See *Capital*, volume one, pp. 46–47.

15. See *Capital*, volume one, page 38.

16. See, for example, the description of the peasant family in *Capital*, volume one, page 78.

17. See a criticism of this position in Cyril Levitt, "Dialectica y Sociedad Civil," *Comunicación e Informática*, primera parte, volume 2, number 8, agosto 1981, pp. 3–4, n.2.

18. Krader has noted that the matter of will has been brought out in the writings of Nietzsche and Schopenhauer. Aristotle advanced desire as the basis of the subjective. Hegel brought the two sides together as *Wille* and *Begierde*. In this he developed a thought already introduced by Spinoza.

19. The desire is the internal subjectivity which is then externalized as an expression of will. Lawrence Krader, lecture delivered at McMaster University, 1983.

20. This point is not unrelated to the reflection theory of the consciousness which has been a constant element in dogmatic Marxism since its inception.

21. By social labor we mean that labor which is carried on by producing units which are different from the units of consumption. See Krader, *Treatise on Social Labor*, p.136.

22. This is not to say that labor and labor time are not a matter of interest in primitive society. And yet the mode of estimation of labor and labor time is different in the primitive condition, there being no systematic reckoning up of the time of labor. See Marx, *Capital*, Volume I, p. 71.

23. At this level Krader draws no distinction between the capitalist societies and those within the former Soviet system.

24. See Krader, *Treatise on Social Labor*, p. 234.

25. The separation and opposition of subjective and objective, formal and substantial and abstract and concrete relations and their value expressions proceed *pari passu* with one another historically and are related to one another in the system of value as indicated here.

26. *Treatise on Social Labor*, p. 6.

27. Aristotle has drawn the distinction between distributive and commutative justice. Krader has interpreted this in such a way as to differentiate between the expression of distributive reciprocity and equal (and equivalent) reciprocity respectively. *Treatise on Social Labor*, chapter 4, pp. 397–491.

28. See Krader, below, p. 172.

29. In Marx's terms, use values are produced by concrete labor in all forms of human society. It is this notion which Krader submits to historical and systematic criticism.

30. "Value in exchange is produced because value in use has been socially produced, and conversely, use value is produced because exchange value has been produced. These two constituents of value are mutually determinants, one of the other. Without use value no exchange value, without exchange value no use value. In the primitive condition of economy and society there is neither exchange·value nor use value, nor is value in general produced. Useful things are produced in the primitive condition, but not as a general rule values of use and exchange." Krader, *Dialectic of Civil Society*, Van Gorcum, Assen, 1976, p. 197.

31. *Dialectic of Civil Society*, p. 198.

32. *Treatise of Social Labor*, p. 117.

33. *Treatise on Social Labor*, p.118.

34. *Treatise on Social Labor*, pp.129–130, 308.

35. Krader, below, p. 97.

36. Krader, *Treatise on Social Labor*, p.203.

37. Krader writes: "The active relation of the human kind to the natural environment is a mediate one, the medium or means being that of labor. Labor is complex, being constituted of the relation of the human kind to nature and the relation thereof in society." *Treatise on Social Labor*, p. 65. In this connection, Krader contrasts the role of labor and culture in human history and in the study of human history. "The relation of the human kind to nature is effected through the totality of culture critically. (In Greek the etymon of critic means sifting, sieve.) The culture in its variability is the selecting or sifting medium, and as such is an instrument abstractly taken. The instrument is activated or worked by labor concretely... The culture is solely the object, being the handed down, having no relation to itself, for it constitutes only the field of human activity. The

relation of labor to its past production is the relation of labor to its past self, and thereby to its present self. Labor in this sense is the prime mover of human history, the *nec plus ultra* in the inquiry into the source of historical activity in relation to nature and in society." *Treatise on Social Labor*, pp. 65–6.

38. Krader writes: "Concealed in the metaphor of hand and head labor is the relation between immediate and mediate labor; the immediate relation of labor is the relation to the technics and instruments of production, both practical and theoretical, in the process of reproduction of the human kind, and to the meeting of human wants. All other labor is mediate. Organization of labor by its division and combination in society, in human reproduction, distribution and consumption is mediate labor. Immediate and mediate labor are relative, some labor being more mediate than another. Immediate labor is generally more practical, concrete, and technical than mediate labor." Below, p. 9.

39. All human labor involves the use of "hand" and "brain" in different ways and in varying degrees. In civil society, however, "hand" and "head" labor come into opposition to one another, the former becoming the monopoly of the mediate producers. Krader describes the mediate producers as "... those who are not directly engaged in material production, the material interchange with nature and the transformation of the natural material, but undertake instead the labor of planning, administration, financing and regulation of the process of production, distribution, and exchange in society." *Treatise on Social Labor*, p.172. Thus, the organization, planning, control of production and the scientific and technological apparatus have been removed from the process of immediate production and from the immediate producers.

40. The labor substance, for Krader, "is the relation of self-reproduction undertaken by the combination of individuals in society. This relation of self-reproduction is... the relation of labor to nature and in society." *Treatise on Social Labor*, p. 489.

41. In the pre-civil condition of the human kind, there was no practical opposition of the form and substance of labor. In the history of civil society the form and substance of labor have come into opposition through the separation and the non-congruency of the class of social labor and the social whole.

42. For Krader the relation of form and substance is a truer dialectic than that of base and superstructure. The form can only become an active factor in history insofar as it is internalized by the substance and enters mediately into it.

43. In non-civil society the human substance and the labor substance are not the same in theory; in practice they are one. In civil society the human substance and the labor substance are different both in theory and practice. Here the human substance encompasses the labor substance, the value substance and the social substance.

44. *Wage Labor and Capital* was based on a series of lectures which Marx gave to a German workingmen's association in Brussels in 1847.

Introduction

The two parts, on Labor and Value, that follow, are the outcome of lectures given at the Freie Universität Berlin, and at the Centro de Investigaciones Superiores in Mexico from 1977 to 1992. Brief talks on the same subjects were given at Uppsala, New Delhi, Turin, Milan, Leyden, London, Michoacán, Hamilton, Ontario and Budapest. To those who organized and attended these lectures and informal talks, especially to Dr. Angel Palerm, and Dr. Guillermo Bonfil of Mexico, and Dr. S. N. Mishra of New Delhi, I express my profound gratitude for their kind reception and warm hospitality. The two parts of the present publication are further elaborations of earlier works, *Dialectic of Civil Society*, ch. 3 and ch. 4, which were translated by Lucía Muñoz, and *Treatise of Social Labor*, ch. 1 and ch. 2, which were translated by Dr. Brigida von Mentz. They both received thorough and friendly reviews, by Dr. P. Skalnik, then in The Netherlands, and by N. B. Ter-Akopian in Moscow. They have recently been summed and presented to the world again by Dr. Cyril Levitt and Rod Hay, of Canada, and Dr. D. N. Smith of Kansas.

There is another reason for returning to these themes beside their intrinsic importance. Since the downfall of the Soviet system, it is necessary to reconsider the work of Marx, its historical place, and the theories of economy and society generated by him, or imputed to him. The USSR called itself socialist, but was not. Its founding principles proclaim descent from those of Marx, but they do not trace back to his. Marx contributed to the theories of labor and of value, as part of a line which proceeds from Aristotle to Locke, Adam Smith, Ricardo and Hegel. To these I add Thomas Hobbes with regard to the social and historical meaning of contract, and Marcel Mauss with regard to the theory of symbolic exchange. Marx developed certain aspects of value theory; others are to be added to it. He was a significant figure in its development, not the sole figure. He set forth the theory of exchange value, not the theory of value in production in relation to exchange, and he did not grasp the theory of subjective value put forward by the Austrian school. Hence he omitted a part of the relation between value, market and price. His theory of society focussed on classes and class struggle, ignoring the factors of the public and private spheres of civil society, as well as the factors of nation, national identity, national freedom and national sovereignty.

With regard to the conflict between the public and private spheres, here the theory is set forth that the public power and sphere exert their influence on the market, which is to that extent unfree; the idea of a free market in which only private interests confront each other is a utopian ideal. The USSR during its history, and China from about 1950 to 1990, constituted national economies in which capital and wage labor predominated, as they do in Western Europe and America, In the Soviet system, capital was in the public hand, not in the private hand; prices and wages were controlled by the agencies of the state.

The intent of these two interrelated parts is not historical but theoretical. A theory of labor is set forth, the form and substance of labor power, labor in relation to nature and to society. A theory of objective and subjective value, the form and substance of value, value quantity and quality, abstract and concrete value, economic and symbolic exchange, and the theory of the market are here explored.

Part I: Labor

Labor, the Process of Human Reproduction

The human kind has an objective relation to the material-order of nature, transforming external matter into the processes and objects of the human order, thus reproducing our kind. The relation between the material and human orders is asymmetrical in that it is mediate from the human side, whereas the material-relations are direct, and thus the relation of the materials to the human labors on them is direct. By its labors the human kind meets its wants, which are human and objective, and its needs, which are animal, in the process of human reproduction. Labor is the human-relation to the material order, and is both material and non-material, abstract and concrete, whereas the material relation to the human kind is concrete, direct and material alone, which is a second asymmetrical relation between the two sides. A third asymmetry is this: human relations are objective and subjective, whereas the material relations are those of things, not those of objects or of subjects. By our labors we turn the things into objects; our interaction with them is an objectification of ourselves, our relation to the thing is objective on our part. This relation is a symmetrical one in that it is orderly on both sides, but the order which is the outcome of our labors is not the order which we find in external nature, the latter being the order in which we are generated. This is the sense in which we understand Thomas Campanella, when he wrote that mankind breaks the laws of nature. The objective relation of the human kind to the material order does not exhaust our relations to it, for we also undertake subjective relations to matter; these subjective relations are non-material, they do not have the effect of a material transformation, for thereby we will have wrought a change in the materials in the fantasy. We separate the subjective from the objective relations of the human kind by intussuscepting a mediate process between them, and then join what we have separated.

The material and non-material, objective and subjective processes of the human kind are real, being in nature. Thus, whereas labor is the objective relation of the human kind to the material order of nature, the human processes are both

objective and subjective, and therefore our labors have an objective and a subjective constituent in them. Objectively, our relations of labor are both material and
non-material, for we work out what we are going to do in our minds, and then
proceed to our labors with the various organs of the body. There is a subjective and
fantastic element in our minds and hence in our objective and material labors.
They are nevertheless objective in that we have matter as part of the means and the
object of our labors; we are bound to the material order for our sustenance.

Labor is the mediate human process in the interrelation between the human
and material orders of nature; it is the human contribution to the interaction
between them. The process has a formal and substantive side to it. Labor is the
common substance in the process between the human and material orders, but
this substantial relation is an asymmetrical one. The relation between form and
substance in the human order is mediate and separable, for while human form and
substance vary, they do not always vary together. The human substance in a particular process of labor takes on various forms. As we shall see, sometimes the
labor substance has a price put on it, as one of its forms, and sometimes it is
without a price; at other times the labor substance in a given form is beyond price.
The same price, as a form, has many substances. Thereby exchange is made possible. The labor form and substance, while they are variable, vary in a different
way from that in which the material relation between form and substance vary, for
form and substance of matter vary directly with one another. The human substance is variable concretely in the history of the human kind, abstractly and potentially it is variable as a unity, actually it is manifold in its constitution and
variation. The forms of labor are diverse both actually and potentially, apart from
the substance. The transformation of the material order by the human kind is a
macrocosmic process from the standpoint of the latter, a minuscule one in the
material order. Form and substance of matter are otherwise undirempted in their
mutual relations, varying together. Some relations of matter having relations of
form and substance, are to this extent inseparable; they are then mechanically
separated in civil society by human means.

The relation of labor to matter is a process of reorganization of material things
which are made into objects of the human order. The things are orderly in a mechanical way, and we apply their order to our own, transforming the one into a
human, objective order. The human relation to the material processes is active and
passive, each side transmitting and receiving the processes of the other. In this
sense the relation of the material and human orders is symmetrical. The material
things have forces and motions which partake in the human process of their transformation. We generate in the process of our labor a mediate relation between
ourselves and the materials on which we work. The mediate and objective relations of human labors are thus interactive.

We create a medium through which and on which we labor; the medium through which we labor is a means, and our relation in this case is an instrumental one; both we through our labors and the medium we create and shape to our purposes are agents. The medium is at the same time a field, and is the passive object which receives our laboring actions. We proceed in this way from the mediate to the objective relation to nature, to matter and to ourselves.

By means of the relation of labor, the past is brought into the present, and the passive relation of the past undertakings is made active in the present. These past undertakings are a potentiality of the human medium, and are brought into the present, being made into an actuality by our mediate relation to them. The past labor processes are in a mediate relation to us, the memory being the medium through which they are made active; the present relations of labor are both potential and actual, and are both mediate and immediate. The mediate relations of labor are active and reactivating, acting on the past in the present; they are variable as activity and passivity, as potentiality and actuality.

Labor in its process is mediate in a number of ways:

1. We are mediate in our relation to material nature by setting a tool of our manufacture between ourselves and the object of our labors, whereby we go mediatingly to work. This mediate relation is multiplied and potentiated, for we make tool-making tools. We shape the object worked on to our purposes, making the clay into a tool for potmaking; the mine is a tool for the mining of coal; pot and coal are further tools in the process of labor in food production and consumption.

2. Our relation to the tools themselves is a mediate one, for we work on them, thus making them into a medium in and through which we labor.

3. The mediate process of labor is variously complicated and simplified, and is variously organized, combined and divided in our social history. The organization is itself a mediate process, which is an abstract instrument of labor, and is made into the object of our plan and construction.

4. The concrete work tools are those we hold in our hands, and are transformed into abstract designs, sketches and formulas of artisans, craftsmen, engineers, chemists, physicists, mathematicians, and the combinations of the concretions and abstractions of the arts, trades, crafts, and professions.

The relations of labor in transforming the material order are mediate and objective, and these are the same relations of labor in the transformation of the human order. The technics are the practical activities and concrete relations of labor to the tools of work in the process of human reproduction of the human kind, and these activities and relations proceed through an internal development in the human order. The body's organs, senses, hand, brain are developed as instruments of labor and work, and the materials outside the body are developed in the same way. The processes of the senses in the living organism, of the muscles, and digestive tract are in their healthy and normal state orderly; the materials of the natural order with and on which we work and labor are orderly in the same way, materially, concretely and cyclically. Thus the sun shines and plants grow in daily, seasonal and annual cycles; the human labors in plant gathering and in agriculture are therewith determined as cyclical, which is a kind of order. The human order in this sense is the organization of the relations between the one order and the other, between the one cyclicity and the other, the one direct and the other mediate. The technics are introduced on the human side in this complex of orderly processes.

The medium in and through which we labor on our tools, and on the materials around and in us is culturally, socially and historically variable. Through this medium we select and screen out the works and things which we transform into the objects for our sustenance; the objects then become part of our human medium.

The technics are the combination of organs of the body with the materials, which are the expanded and varied means of labor, both practical and theoretical, for the bodies' organs are those of senses, hand and brain. The technics are therefore both practical, as those of the hands and other organs of the body, and theoretical, as those of the brain and mind. The technics, therewith the arts and sciences of the human kind are a part of the process of labor, but not the whole of it, for the technics are organized by the twofold relation of labor, in the past and in the present, the latter being the combination and division of labor in a particular social whole, under given conditions of its history; the relation of labor to the given technics are in this way organized by the relation of labor in society. (See Appendix I.)

Labor is thus defined as the mediate relation of the human kind to the material order, and the mediate and immediate relation of our kind to the human order; the relations to both orders are mediated by the organization and technics of labor. Labor is the active factor in the transformation of matter by means of the orderly processes of both, and by its own organization and technics. In transforming matter, by our labors, we transform ourselves; by mediating in our relation to the material world we mediate in relation to ourselves, and by objectifying our relation to the material things, we objectify our relation to ourselves. By means of the orderly, mediate and objective relations of our labors we create the relation to the self of the human kind. The self-relation is variably social and individual.

The theoretical and practical interaction of labor with the material order is a mediate process whereby human reality and actuality are constituted; by this process, the natural thing is transformed into the human object, the human kind is separated from the material order, and the human order brought into existence. The condition of labor is the self-mediatizing, self-objectifying relation to the natural order which is characterized by a metaphor, labor of hand and head. The practical activity of the human kind is that of both head and hand, and of other body organs, the theoretical activity is that of hand and head, etc., but all these organs are first humanized. Labor is the combination of the abstract and concrete relations, and of the practical and theoretical activities of the human kind, which are socially organized, combined, and divided. The division of labor in civil society has led to the separation of tasks which have then been called labor of hand and head.

Labor is the act of human parturition from the material condition of our existence. The parturition of which we speak is not a figure of speech, but diremption, violent change, and a great saltation in the order of nature. It is the act of human reproduction of the human kind, and is therefore a nexus to our natural surroundings.

The relations of labor to the technics are the practical ones of applying them, and the theoretical ones of planning, storing up the skills, accumulating them, choosing among them, and reworking them. The human instrumentality of hand and brain cooperates in varying the stored up skills in their application in the present; the variation is in this case the immediate relation of labor to an instrument, whereby it is applied in the work upon the thing transformed into the object of labor. The technics are therefore practical and theoretical, being the instruments and the skills in applying them; the skills are at once abstract and concrete, objectified and objectifying relations of labor; the objectified relations of labor are those of the past borne upon the present, and are the reworking, in this sense the reactualization of past objective relations; the objectifying relations are those of labor in the present on its object, but the object is labor in its self-relation whereby it applies the instrument to its tasks in transforming the natural materials, draws upon its stored up skills, plans its work and carries it through. The objective relation of labor in the process of its reproduction is therefore the objectifying and self-objectifying relation.

We make the things in the outside world into objects by our labors, and by the same process make ourselves into the laboring subject. The self is both subject and object, and we are the object of our own labors, thus becoming the subject-object, and the human self on which we work the object-subject. The self-relation of labor being both objective and subjective, therefore the self-objectification of labor is both objective and subjective. The relations of labor to the instrument applied in the process of transformation are objective. (See below.)

The relation of labor to the past process of labor and its results is variable, for labor works upon the past process as the active stored up skills of the living and on the past results of labor as its mediate, passive product. This activity and passivity of the past in relation to the present and the active relation of labor to the mediating and mediatized past is the means of reactivating and reactualizing the past. But also the objectification of the past in the stored-up memory, and in concrete products is a variable process, whereby the abstract and concrete past is reworked, varied, and repotentialized in the present, for new potentialities are seen in the past processes, and in the past and present processes of others. The self-objectification is therefore both a relation of self-transformation and transformation of the objective world by labor, whereby the self-transformation is the process of transformation of the stored-up skills and qualities of labor into a means of accumulation, reworking and repotentializing the skills and qualities. The stored-up skill is a cumulative process, and is extended, varied, drawn upon, and reworked.

Labor is in this sense the object of its own practical and theoretical effort; this is said in reference both to the technics and to the organization of the labor process. The practical relation of the human kind to all the material order is the means whereby both sides are transformed; the transformation of the human kind, however is a self-relation which is at once practical and theoretical. The labor of the head in the relation to the material and human orders is at once an objective relation to the technics themselves, whereby they are reworked both practically and theoretically, and thereby varied in the labor process itself. In theory this relation in the process of transformation of the material is a conjoint activity of head labor and hand labor, both in respect of the technics of transformation processes and in respect of the organization of the labor process as a whole, in society. In practice this conjoint activity is divided and as an organizing function is separated from the process of hand labor in industrial society of the present; and throughout the history of civil society the organization of the labor process has not been in the hands of the immediate producers. Thus the critical reworking of the technics has been separated from the labor relation, and is assigned in industry to specialists in management of private and public concerns. The technics of production, as well as the organization thereof, are the matter of hand and head labor, and of the immediate and mediate producers in the process of reproduction of the social whole. The study, control, critical examination, variation, and experimentation, in the technical and organizational relations of production and reproduction are made a matter of the sciences and are regulated by means set apart from the labor of the immediate producers; these are the sciences of technology, industrial management, and the like.

The study of the technics, or technology, is thus a practical relation of variation of the labor process, thereupon the theoretical activity of work upon the instruments of labor, their variation, and the theoretical activity of labor upon the skills and qualities thereof developed in the process of reproduction. The objectification of the technics is the mediate relation to them and their technological developments, which proceeds together with their immediate variation and application in the labor process. This is a simple process of objectification, which is made complex by reintroduction of new technics into variant processes, variant technics into old processes and their recombination in feedback systems. This objective relation is made more complex by the social reorganization of labor through a new combination and division, which is then combined with the technics. The self-objectification of labor bears both upon the technical skill and the organization and reorganization of labor in its combination and division. The distribution of labor tasks, specializations of function, and cooperation in the processes of combination, the division of labor, rationalization of work, productivity are inseparable from the mastery of the technics. The technology is the practical art of objectification, critical evaluation, and variation of relation to the instruments of labor in the labor process itself, then the comparison with other technics both contemporary and past and the introduction of new variations of the instruments and the skills in their use. The science of technology is the record of these variant practices in their historical development.

Concealed in the metaphor of hand and head labor is the relation between immediate and mediate labor; the immediate relation of labor is the relation to the technics and instruments of production, both practical and theoretical, in the process of reproduction of the human kind, and to the meeting of human wants. All other labor is mediate. Organization of labor by its division and combination in society, in human reproduction, distribution and consumption is mediate labor. Immediate and mediate labor are relative, some labor being more mediate than another. Immediate labor is generally more practical, concrete, and technical than mediate labor.

The reference to labor of the head or hand, or to work of the body is a biological metaphor which obfuscates as much as it illuminates the human process in the natural order. The head does not labor, but is set to labor by human relation and activity, which work upon the ganglia and neurons, forming thoughts, connecting them, drawing upon the unconscious, upon memory, bringing them to the consciousness, discriminating illusions from the real, filling in gaps, predicting, repotentializing past concrescences. The hand does not labor, but instead human being has the hand as an instrument whereby human work and labor is carried through.

It was once thought that the practical activity of slaves is the work of the social body, and that the head directs the other parts of that body. Plato and Aristotle held opinions of this kind. John Locke wrote of the labor of the body and the work of the hand. The hand is the artisan's organ; G. W. F. Hegel, D. Urquhart and Karl Marx were all opposed to the division of labor which makes for an industrial pathology.

Labor, mental and physical, is abstract, ongoing; the concrete labor is work. The work is the finished product of labor, ready for consumption. Labor is thus abstract and concrete, work is concrete. The work is organized, combined and divided into labor which is in immediate and mediate relations to the production process and the end product in human reproduction. In the production process of the modern factory system, the immediate producers work on the materials with the hand, and are separated from the design, plan and organization of the production process as a whole in the factory. Variations of technic are introduced by those who have charge of design, planning, etc., and these responsibilities are excluded from the area of activity of the immediate producers. Hand labor is here the continuation of the labor of the human being within the social whole. The immediate producers in the factory labor with their human being, which is their skills and capacities acquired during their working lives; that a part of our human being is dirempted from planning, organizing and regulating the work process has the result of the alienation of social labor in the process of production and in society; this diremption and estrangement is the source of the subjective feelings of frustration and resentment, as well as the sentiment of objective oppression. The division in the labor process of head from hand labor is an expression of the alienation of the consciousness of social labor and of the social whole.

The process of perception and the process of labor are both kinds of objectification whereby the external is internalized, and the internal externalized. The perception of the sense-datum is at once a taking in and a going out; it is a projection of that which is internalized onto the object perceived. Labor is an externalization in another sense, for the human kind, in objectification of the other objectifies itself, in objectifying itself objectifies the natural processes which are transformed thereby. The externalization of human relation by labor is the means of internalizing, appropriating and transforming natural processes.

The labor of the human kind combines within itself practical and theoretical activities; in a first alienation the practical are being divided from the theoretical not under human but under inhuman conditions, which have objectively disrupted and subjectively perturbed the process of interaction of the human and natural order. The separation, division and opposition between the organized and organizing, practical and theoretical tasks of the labor process constitute a second alienation of human beings in society. A third alienation derives from the sale of labor time and capacity by wage labor, and a fourth from the anomy, diremption, individualization and the resulting isolation of human beings in urban society.

Production and Consumption
Concrete and Abstract Work and Labor

Human reproduction is effected by work and labor, whereby the materials of the natural and human orders are transformed in the process of meeting human wants and material needs. The process of meeting them is concrete, for the physiology of air supply, body movement, food, water and biological reproduction of the species *homo sapiens* is ongoing, and is in one sense continuous, for interruption of these processes would bring the life of the species to an end. The physical relation of the human species in the process of its reproduction is two-fold: In its external relation it is the material interchange with the natural order which is its environment and constitution; in this way the external relation is an articulated system of external and internal processes. In its internal relation the process of reproduction is a metabolism, or building up and breaking down the biological organisms of which the species is constituted. In ancient Greek, as in Aristotle's Physics, *metabolein* meant change of all kinds; metabolism now means interchange. The building up, or anabolism, and the breaking down, or catabolism, are together the internal metabolic process which is an interchange with the materials of the environment in the external relations of the organism, and of the species. This is the primary interchange between the human and the material orders of nature.

The process of physiological reproduction is converted into human reproduction by human means, which are those of work and labor. Work is the concrete process whereby the materials are mediately and the human materials mediately and immediately transformed into the products which meet our wants and needs. The work comes to an end in the bringing forth of the product. The labor of planning further work is ongoing. The wants and needs are in a dual relation in the human order; as to the species, *homo sapiens*, there are only the physiological needs of food, warmth, etc.; these material needs are transformed into human wants, which are variable accordingly as the human kind is variable in the process of its work and labor, its organization, the social organization of the human kind, and the transmission of these human wants and organizing practices by traditional and novel means.

The processes of labor are abstract and concrete, not concrete alone. The labor is concrete in that non-human and human materials are thereby transformed; it is abstract in that it is not brought to an end by bringing forth the product. The labor is an abstract process in that it is ongoing, being the means of organizing, preparing, storing, transmitting and distributing the practical and theoretical effort of concrete work and labor; the process of labor is in this sense abstracted from the immediate relations of work and labor, which are concrete. Thereby we differentiate between two processes of abstract labor, the one immediate, and the other mediate.

The relations of mediate and immediate labor are relative, for in another sense all labor, both concrete and abstract, and all work, are mediate, for the human kind is not in a direct relation to the natural materials which surround and constitute it. Between the human being and the natural materials the human kind introduces the instruments of work and labor, which are both organic and inorganic, and of the organic kind, both living and dead. The hand, fingers, teeth, etc., are instruments which are controlled and instructed to perform tasks and functions not of an animal but of a human kind. Cudgels are shaped to perform these same tasks, with animal bones, claws and teeth inserted to cut and tear as our fingernails and teeth have done. The immediate and concrete relation of the human kind to these various instruments is that of production, whereby the material surroundings and human materials are transformed. We work on the human materials, which are the body's organs, muscular and nervous systems, etc.; they have been transformed and to that degree are no longer biotic materials as such; the means of their transformation are the human processes of mediation, internalization, abstraction and concretion, objectification, relation and reference, self-relation, mediate communication and expression.

The process of work and labor is distributed in the relation of human reproduction through the cycle of production and consumption. Thus there is the work of production and consumption concretely and the labor in the cycle of production and consumption, abstractly and concretely. Production is a part of the process of work and labor, work and labor are the means of human reproduction in the concrete process of production and consumption. Work is the concrete, immediate, practical, material process of producing useful objects to meet our wants and needs. Labor is the concrete and abstract, mediate and immediate, practical and theoretical, material and non-material process whereby the work of human reproduction is organized, carried through, transmitted, maintained, controlled, varied, and articulated with other processes, human and natural. Therefore we refer to the process of labor in the various relations of work, in production and consumption, in the process of human reproduction.

These processes are organized in different ways in the history of the human kind. In the communal relation of human reproduction, which is the primitive, archaic condition of the human kind, the relation of production and consumption is an immediate one, in that the unit of production approximately coincides with the unit of consumption, and insofar as the product of the given community is consumed therein; the archaic and primitive communities are in this sense virtually, or practically self-sufficient. They are not entirely so, and a small amount of external interchange between the communities is carried on. Within the primitive communities the relation between production and consumption is effected by sharing between the producers, and sharing out between producers and consumers. There is in this case no difference between the mediate and immediate processes of labor, none between mediate and immediate producers, or between mediate and immediate distribution. Mediate and immediate distribution is concrete in the relation of sharing and sharing out between producers and consumers in the community. Labor in this case is communal, and is communally organized; production is the same, and the social organization of the human kind is in the form of communal relations thereof. Social relations of the human kind are in this case the communal relations.

The communal relations of society, of labor, of human reproduction, hence of production and consumption are broken up, and transformed into social relations by the diremption of the relations between the units of production and consumption. The relation of production to consumption is thereby converted from an immediate to a mediate one. The product consumed is in this case not shared out, or communally shared, but the interchange between the communities, which has already been noted, is expanded and formalized. The relation of human reproduction by production and consumption, which was intermediated by the process of communal distribution, is now transformed and complicated by various internal and external relations, mediate and immediate, of articulation and concatenation, differentiation and mutual dependence between the units of production and consumption.

The process of production is separated from the process of consumption by the diremption between the unit of production and the unit of consumption. The product is thus dirempted and therewith separated from its immediate producer; the first diremption is the determinant of the second. The means whereby these diremptive processes are generated is the expansion and development of exchange between the different communities. By this development, distribution is formally commuted into equal and equivalent exchange, and the exchange is formalized as contract, purchase and sale. Money is introduced, and exchange in kind or barter gives way to the system of markets, commodities, pricing of goods, and factors of supply and demand in these processes.

The unities in the exchange process are made increasingly dependent on one another, and technical specializations of labor are developed thereby. The exchange process between the communities is then developed by an exchange process within the communities. The mutual dependency within the communities is reorganized, and the communal organization of labor is transformed into the social labor thereof. The society is now constituted of the different, mutually interdependent and reciprocally interchanging communities. These communities retain their primitive, archaic form at first, whereas their substantive relations of interdependence and interchange determine their conversion from communal to social unities. The labor is communal in form in this condition, but social in substance, being organized by the combination and division thereof, by technical specialization and mutual dependence. The primitive self-sufficiency and autarchy is developed as a social process of labor. Exchange between the communities is differentiated from exchange within the community.

The social process of labor is that of production and consumption in the reproduction of the human kind. But the relation of production and consumption is intermediated in society by the process of exchange. There is then no difference in civil society between internal and external exchange, for the exchange is generalized according to the principle of adversary juridical practice, formalized in the system of contract, market, commodity, money and price.

Labor is now distributed in this social form, which is that of civil society, in the different processes of production, consumption, exchange and distribution. In consequence of these moments of separation and diremption between labor and its product, labor has a mediate relation to itself and to the social whole. Out of this mediate relation the alienation of labor in relation to society and to itself in the civil social condition is brought about.

Labor in society of any kind is organized by combining and dividing it. Our minds are shaped and our bodies formed and transformed by the organization of our labors in the process of reproduction. The beginnings of the diremption of the labor process by its separation into tasks of immediate and mediate production were already apparent in the ancient practices of astronomy and geometry; the antecedent unity of the work process in the ancient village communities, whereby the needful observations of the heavenly bodies and land measurements for control of river flow according to the seasons, irrigation and allocation of ground for tillage was then disrupted, and specialist functions of prediction of rains and floods, and cadastral surveys apart from the village practices were developed in mysticized form. The astrologers and geometers were organized as castes, cults, sects, and guilds in the service of the state and separated from the process of immediate production; these ancient specialists, Brahmins, priests, mandarins or Pythagoreans, had mastered the abstract sciences of arithmetic and geometry, which are mediate processes in the relations of reproduction and production in the social whole, and which had been formerly conjoined with the immediate processes within the villages, then separated from them. Mediate and immediate relations of reproduction and production are now opposed to one another, the mediate relations being undertakings of head labor, immediate relations those of hand labor. The division of labor thus has come to be the tearing of the sciences, which are regarded as abstract and theoretical, from the practical and immediate tasks in the process of reproduction of the social whole, and the technology has been separated from the technics.

The concrete labor is the means whereby the abstract continuum of human reproduction is interrelated with the work process; the abstraction is the expression of the means whereby the continuity in the process of the human order is effected. This continuity presupposes the space-time continuum of the material and sensory order of nature, and is built on it. The expression is the adjunct in the human order that is made mediatively necessary for human continuity; it is the abstraction which is added, by intussusception, into the continuum of the material order by the intervention of the human kind. The continuum is the substance of this process in the given natural order, it is transformed into an abstract continuity and discontinuity by the human kind; the material continuity is at the same time continuous with human concrete continuity by labor, which is made into a concrete discontinuity of work. The expression of the human kind is the form thereof in the human order; form is given expression there, the human substance being given a momentaneous form, and absorbed into the natural process of reproduction. The continuum, which is a concrete relation in the material order, is transformed into an abstract relation in the human order, the formal relation being abstracted from its concrete state and made into the expression of the substantial relation. The expression is the diremption of the continuum in relation to itself within the human order, and is the mediate relation between form and substance, whereby each is made into a different object.

The relation of the human to the material order is the conjoint process of work and labor; the orderly process of nature indirectly and of matter directly determines the orderly process of labor. The relation of the present to the past is an orderly process of time, whereby the human past is recalled, readapted, varied and reworked in the present. The present acts of work and labor are a repotentialization by the human kind of the past, which is stored and reconstructed in the memory. Work is the practical process which has the product as its concretization, the labor is the abstract and concrete process which has its continuation as its materialization. The process as labor is the means of connecting the abstract, continuative process to the concrete product, which meets a concrete and practical human want and need; the same process that is materialized in the product is the recipient of the reorganization of the human material in its abstract, continuative mode. The process of work is the intermediate relation between the labor process and the means of meeting the wants and needs, the process of abstract labor is the intermediate relation between the concrete work process, that interrupts the continuous process of labor in the meeting of wants and needs, such as is necessary for the continuum of the social whole, which is both abstract and concrete. The concrete social whole sets itself forth materially, the abstraction constituting the means of relating production to consumption in the human reproductive process.

Objective and Subjective Relations of Labor

Science is the means of expansion of our theoretical knowledge of the natural order of all kinds, and therewith of the human order; conversely, it is the practical medium of our modest control of the material through the human order; historically the theory of the natural order was worked on by scientists, and only thereafter was it elaborated with respect to the human process and order. The natural potentiality in general determines and delimits the human, being the container, in which the human is contained. The human potentiality is at once a self-relation and therewith a self-expanding process, by means of its own activity of self-objectification. We proceed within the human order from variation within the natural order to transformation of natural thing into human object, which is the act of conjoint objectification and self-objectification of the human kind.

Labor is objective and subjective. Objective labor is the process of transformation of the materials of the material and human orders by material and non-material means. Objective labor is concrete and abstract, practical and theoretical, for the materials of both orders and the material means of their human transformation are practical and concrete, the non-material means are abstract and theoretical. The process of objective labor in that it is material, concrete and practical is continuous with that of the natural order, but is discontinuous with it in that it is abstract and theoretical. In the latter case our objective labor is in relation to the material order, to natural order generally, and to nature, mediately and indirectly. Subjective labor on the one hand is part of labor which is subjective and objective; there is no objective labor without a subjective constituent. Subjective labor as such is that of the will, desire and fantasy; it may, through objective labor, mediately, transform the material and human orders. The theory of labor in relation to the material order was brought out by Aristotle, thereafter in modern bourgeois society by Machiavelli, Locke, Smith, Hegel, and Marx, among others. Labor in this theory is practical and theoretical, abstract and concrete; the mediative activity of the human kind to the material order is effected thereby, for labor is a mediate and self-mediatizing relation and act. Labor, however, although it is the means of self-relation, self-objectification, self-concretization and self-expansion of the human kind is nothing other than social labor, labor in combination with others, which implies that the potentiality of self-expansion thereof is diminished by the extent to which the labor is less than the human social whole. This is a proposition concerning the nature of human society, and is generalized upon the observation of the historical record of civil society and its spokesmen, ancient and modern. It is an ontological and not a moral judgment, which follows from the antecedent, that labor being social activity of the human kind in relation to the material and human orders cannot exceed the social whole in its extent, for it is determined both in its organization and activity by the latter.

To the extent that the process of the human kind is mediate and self-objectifying it is labor; to the extent that the process of the human kind is passive, without self-objectification, it is thingly. The theory of history of the human kind is objective to the degree in which its canon is that of the process of objectification of the natural order and the objectification and self-objectification of the human kind.

Processes of matter are without necessity as such, necessity being a human construction. The human processes participate in these natural relations; necessity is introduced not in the natural processes directly, but in our judgments and statements pertaining to them. The material and human orders are in a process of change, without necessary stages of development in either. Natural processes, being without necessity as such, are nevertheless the conditions of human processes, to which they stand as the determinant and constituent relations.

The subjectified is opposed to the objectified existence of labor, and is non-objectified, or unobjective labor; the objectivity of labor is in this concept the means of production and of subsistence. This labor, which objectifies itself is a subjectivity, accordingly, and can be present only as the living subject, as capability, hence as the laborer.

Objectified labor is the form of which self-objectifying labor is the substance. The process of objectification presupposes the relations of mediation, materialization, self-concretion, and therewith self-abstraction of labor, for labor made into the object is both concrete and abstract, and therewith objectifies itself. Labor concrete, socializing and self-socializing, objective, objectifying, self-objectifying, objectifying the other, which is the natural material, and being objectified in the relation of present labor to past concrete labor, is the substance of human life. The activities of present living labor are abstract and concrete in relation to the object thereof, and subjective and objective in self-relation. Labor is the self-object and therewith the subject, but it cannot be the subjectivity, or the historical subject, alone, for that would be the hypostasis of the human being, living labor, the diremption of the subject from the object, and the abstraction of labor from its object, which is in the first place itself. This hypostasis of labor arises from the consideration of labor as the subject of the history that is predicated of it. But the subject and the historical agent are not the same; labor is the historical agent which is both subjective and objective.

It is sometimes averred that labor is the active subject and agent of human history. This is potentially the case, in that labor and the human kind are abstractly and potentially one, but is not the case in actuality. In the potential unity of the humankind with its labor the subject is then one with the object, and the agent with the patient, the producer with the product, and autopia is brought forth, in view of the immediate relation between the different sides in these oppositive processes. Labor in civil and bourgeois society is dirempted and alienated; insofar as it has not identified its own interest as such, it has false consciousness of its place in the social whole, and in that it has internalized this false consciousness, labor is the self-diremptive and self-dirempted, self-alienating subject. It is not the active subject, but the patient acted upon; it is activated as the product of directions and conditions which it does not control. The human kind is the subject-object in potentiality and possibility; in the human kind the process of constitution of the subject-object relation is generated, and further developed. This subject-object is the agent and patient; and labor insofar as it is able, consciously active strives and tends toward these states. The striving is in our control, and the tendency is subject to our regulation; that we strive is a qualitative relation of the subject to the object.

Labor as the passive factor in its own relations, in civil society, to the controlling agencies over the means of production and subsistence, is a commodity, selling its time and capacity as such. Labor is the passive factor in that the commodity is a passivity. The potentiality of unity between agent and patient, thus the abolishment of the commodity, market, exchange and contractual relations, brings with it the potentiality of unity of subject and object, and producer and product, therewith the potentiality of unity of labor and the human kind, in a mediate relation between these oppositive processes.—The subject thus is not the immediate human relation in the process of objectification and self-objectification by labor; it is part of the self-relation therein, the object being its opposite and complement. The self which is a process of the human and of no other natural order is the subject-object. Labor as the subject alone does not objectify itself, but is objectified. (See below, *Labor Form and Substance*.)

The human order as object becomes a means, just as the natural field is constituted as the means to the end of the one. This is the case of various forms of social labor in the history of civil society, of servile labor, unfree labor generally, and wage labor. The relation of the human subject to the field is not possible without the human object; the relation of labor in which the humankind stands to the field is an objectifying and self-objectifying process. This relation is subjective in the self-object relation, and objective in the relation of the social and individual self to medium and field of our labor processes. The relation of subject to object and of object to subject is the means of completing either, for there is no subject without the object, and no object without the subject; it is superfluous to mention the human subject, for there is no other subject, whether human being, social class, social whole or the human kind as a whole. We distinguish that which is actually from that which is potentially active and existent. The object is twofold, the process and the field of human activity. The active factor in this case is the relation of subject-object to the field, the object in immediate relation to the subject being human, or the self-objectifying subject-object, the object as the field being the non-human part of the human order. The human one alienates itself from the human other in the relations of estrangement, exploitation, social opposition, the alienation being the externalizing process of an internal diremptive relation. Both external and internal oppositions are at once subjective and objective, both passive and active relations. The present relations express more fully the potentialities of the given oppositions than do the past relations. The relations as a commodity of social labor are objective, and are the expression of a relation in which human beings stand to themselves as objects, which are falsely represented as things. The social relation which is expressed is that of the means to the objective relation of production in society, whereby the living individual, living social labor, excises a part of its labor time by the exercise of its power over it, by its labor power, and excises an aspect of its quality and skill, in the exchange relation. (See Section 6, below.)

The commodity relation of social labor is an objective relation, but is cut off from the human subject, the subject in the commodity transaction in turn being cut away from the object in the hypostasis of both. The human subject is potentially the social whole, in actuality it is social labor. The human subject is active in its own history, being the product of the incomplete combination and imperfect suppression of the separation of subject from object. The separation is partially effectuated in history by the relation of living labor to itself as a commodity, which is the realization of all the past possibility of dehumanization of the human subject and at once of desubjectification of the human object. The human subject separated from the human object is then treated as though it were a thing, an inanimate entity without will or consciousness, activated by the external forces of capital production and commodity exchange. The treatment of the human relation, as though it were a thing, is the reification of the process of social labor in the production of capital.

The relation of human work and labor is in itself a process of self-objectification. The self-relation is the active process of production, distribution and consumption, whereby social reproduction is carried through; the object is not labor itself but the product, whereby labor relates mediately to itself in the process of its reproduction. The mediation is an activity, the relation to itself is the activation of labor in the process of its reproduction. The self-objectification is the means whereby human work and labor transform the natural thing into the object, the product of work in its concrete form, and of labor as both the abstract and concrete relations of production. The object is the medium in the process of production, the subject is the expression of the self-relation whereby labor is activated, by activating itself. The subjective expression of the self-relation lies in the variability of labor past and present. The subjective substance, as we have seen, is the concrete consciousness, will, desire and fantasy applied in the process of social production, new production and reproduction, whereby past practices are abstracted from their erstwhile context, and varied purposefully and wilfully with respect to changing conditions of the natural and human environments. This conscious variation is distinct from natural, thingly variation, as human variation is distinct from natural adaptation. The abstraction made from past practice is brought about in conjunction with the arts of generalization, discrimination, judgment, estimation and valuation, which are of the objective, in part the subjective substance of the human kind. This subjective substance is developed in different levels or stages of the history of production, in the history of language, and of the arts generally, whereby the human kind has reproduced and expressed itself in human reproduction, human variation and natural adaptation and readaptation. The human aspect is the combined labor of hand and head, the natural aspect is the thingly doing of nature, both carried forward in the process of human reproduction.

The separation of subject from object is the consequence of the positing of the subject and object in the human order. The separation is implicit in the early history of civil society, and is effected more fully in the current history thereof, being made explicit in the relation of labor power and labor capacity, or the juridical power and right of social labor to sell its labor time and skill as a commodity against a wage, whereby it gains the means of meeting its social wants and needs, and assuring its existence as a social class. Meeting these wants and needs it achieves the means of its reproduction. The separation of subject from object is a diremption in the organization of social labor which is practically carried through in the oppositions between the social classes of civil society, between hand and head labor, and between living labor and its labor time and capacity, in that these are alienated in commodity form in the process of production. The living subject is excised from the production process, in that living hand labor has neither will nor consciousness, these being taken over by the mediate producers, managers, "head labor." To the extent that the immediate producers are deprived of will and consciousness, all of social labor, mediate and immediate, hand and head, has a false subjectivity in the production process. The objective conditions of the commodity relation fill in the abyss formed by the excision of the subjectivity, will, consciousness, fantasy and judgment. These objective conditions are then falsified, for they are transformed into a relation as though to a thing, that appears to have a life, will, consciousness, fantasy and judgment of its own.

Social Labor and the Class of Social Labor
Social labor is the means of human reproduction; production in a common process with consumption is the organization of this reproduction, being interrelated by the process of distribution. Labor is organized in its combination and division;

the specialization of function and the division of hand and head labor are means of the technical organization of production by combination and division of labor. Specialization of function and division of hand and head labor are a part, not all, of the organization of the reproduction process; the diremption internal to the production process is an active relation of labor which then alienates its product in the relations comprised under the laws of exchange and surplus value. The alienating relation in the exchange process is both active and passive, in regard to social labor; it is a social relation in that exchange is a relation of equal reciprocation. It is wholly objective, without affect or affection, and is to that extent inhuman. It is human insofar as it is an equal reciprocation, subject to the principle of commutative justice; it is inhuman insofar as it diverges from the practice of reciprocal distribution of the social product and from the principle of distributive justice.

The form of alienation is expressed by the passive role of social labor in production. The social surplus produced is alienated from its immediate producer, without reciprocation, in abrogation of the laws of commutative and distributive justice alike, and the rupture of the relations of equal and distributive reciprocation. The process of reproduction of the social whole is then submitted to the economic relations of exchange and alienation of the surplus from those who have produced it, of transformation of the class in society which has alienated the surplus into an exploiting class, the political transformation of that exploiting class into the ruling class by the concentration of the social power in its hands, and the juridical formalization and ceremonial celebration of these relations of diremption, alienation, exploitation, and concentration of power in the formation of the state.

The concentration of ownership and control over the means of production in the hands of the ruling class reproduces the process, in the history of civil society, whereby the diremption of social production from its control by social labor itself, and the formation of an alienating and non-laboring sector on the one hand, and a laboring and alienated sector in society on the other. It is reproduced again in the history of modern bourgeois society by the concentration of the control of capital in all its forms in the hands of a few. This historical formulation is subject to some variation which we will now examine, in bringing out the distinction between the process and the class of social labor, and the connection between the two.

Social labor is a process of which the class of social labor is an expression; the expression is not identical with the process, nor is the process identical with the class. The human kind reproduces itself humanly by its labors in common and apart, but social labor is not as such a process of the working class alone. In modern bourgeois society, the working class is paid a wage or salary in exchange for its participation in the process of reproduction of the social whole. A wealthier class in society takes part in this process as well, extracting not only a wage or salary but also an unearned surplus, and in sum a disproportionately large amount of goods and services to meet its wants and needs, desires and delights. The latter class is the heir of the bygone rulers and priests, slave owners and feudalists who performed no useful work or productive labor at all. The working class throughout its history, past and present, is exploited by those who take an unearned surplus from it. The working class is the class of immediate producers in society, the wealthy perform some managerial and planning services and have a mediate role in production. Few today perform absolutely no useful work at some time in their lives.—In part the unearned surplus goes to the rulers and priests as of old, in part to the political representatives of the ruling class, in part to the civil and military bureaucracies in the service of the state, in part to the political parties and trade union bureaucracies who represent the working class, and in part to the world of learning and its bureaucracy.

The process of human reproduction is complicated by the fact that on a global scale the unearned surplus produced is unevenly distributed among the various countries, some rich, and some poor. The working class in the poor countries is exploited by the wealthy and powerful in their own lands, and all these peoples, rich and poor, are exploited by the public and private agencies of the wealthy countries; the ruling class in the latter case profits in a major way, but the working class in these lands also participate in the common exploitation of the poor ones, in accordance with the practices of modern colonialism.

Labor is an ongoing process of the human kind, and constitutes the substance of human reproduction by human means. That process is variable in its historical forms; the social classes, and the nations, rich and poor, are such forms which come and go, according to objective human acts, and subjective will and desire. It is not essential in history that social labor and productive work be given formal expression in classes and nations, and the state, the military might, the political, civil, religious, educational professional, and union bureaucracies are not eternal but ephemeral and accidental social forms. Social labor itself is not an essential but a general human condition. We do not free ourselves from that condition, but deepen and extend it. There are no essences and accidents in history, for all processes interact with all others and each is the condition of the other. If we eliminate labor in society, we alter ourselves and our place in nature; our nature is changed. Our emancipation is not the freedom from the onus of labor, but the liberation from the burden of producing for others without remuneration. Working for ourselves is not burdensome or onerous labor. Exploitation is an inhuman condition for both the exploiter and the exploited as a class or nation, and is antisocial. Labor as such is neither free nor unfree but is the human, social and material condition of our existence.

We here refer only to the formal freedom of labor, its extension or reduction. There is no sense in which labor achieves the substance of freedom, either in civil or in any other form of human society, for we do not emancipate ourselves from the requirement to meet our material wants and needs for our sustenance in our labors by abolishing exploitation, or by shortening the working day. Formal liberation of labor is a juridical and political process, labor as such an economic and material one.

Labor Form and Substance

The substance of labor is labor time and capacity in the relations of reproduction of the social whole. The relations of labor are not the crude, unworked time, however, but the conjunction of all the technics, skills and qualities of labor. The substance of labor is therefore the mediate and immediate relations both active and passive, of human reproduction. The immediate active relation of labor is the time expended in the transformation of the natural material by the application of technics, skills and instruments, in the process of human reproduction; the relation to nature is reciprocally active and passive in this process, the human agent suffering the natural activity directly, the material agent suffering the human activity mediately; the reciprocal relation is thus asymmetrical. The labor substance in its immediate temporal relation is the present time of the process, the labor substance in its mediate temporal relation is the past and present time of the process of labor, the process of reproduction as a whole by the social organization thereof being a temporal-spatial relation. The mediate relation of the substance within the labor process is the relation between present and past skills, whereby technics are accumulated, critically treated and varied. The past skill and product are objectified, the one abstractly, the other concretely, both in their separation and combination. The past is introduced into the human substance anew, being made active again, but in a changed way. The mediation is the active relation of present labor both to the past and to the present task, the labor in the present changes that which is handed down and handed over actively, and mediates thereby in the relation to the transmitted materials. The organization in society mediately enters into the labor process, and thereby into the labor substance, by controlling the process of production; therewith the active relation of mediation by labor in the production process is alienated from the immediate producers.

The form of labor is determined by the form of the given social whole, the labor process being organized communally if the whole is communally organized, and socially if the whole is socially organized. The determinant of the substance of labor is the social and anti-social relation of wage labor in civil society at present, in which the formal relation of labor is social and anti-social.

Labor is variable in relation to the means of production and to the materials which are thereby worked upon; these materials are the concrete product of past labor and have the active relation to the human workman in their properties, which are variable; the human variability of living labor, the variability of the means of production, and that of the material of nature are interactive with one another, for each of the processes, material and human, are interactive. Labor in the present has the capacity to reactivate, reactualize and repotentialize past processes of objectified labor; the condition under which the past, objectified labor is brought into an active relation in the present process of reproduction of living labor is a complex one: the past concretion is brought into an interrelation with the present theoretical and practical activity of labor; the living labor in the present concretizes and thereby objectifies itself; the past concretum is dead, and is activated only by present living labor; being dead it is inactive, but has a potential to be worked upon by living labor. The past is a form which has a concrete substance contained within it; the form, which is the past substantive relation of living labor concretized in the product, is not a substance as such, but enters into a reproductive relation with living labor, which applies its formal and substantial human being in the present to the activation of the form out of the past; the concrete work instrument is the realization of past labors in the present act of labor.

Labor in the present act is a variation of the relations of labor, past and present. Innovation is a conscious variation of the labor process by the mediate and immediate producers in society; it is a kind of critical selection. Human variation is both conscious and unconscious, critical and not. Subjectively we may vary past processes for the sake of variation, out of boredom with routine. Objectively, critique is a mediate and conscious process of labor, a manifold process, with many directions. In one sense, and in one concrete direction, from past to present, it is a relation of means and ends, past and present. There are means of our labors in reality, with and without ends; ends without means exist in the fantasy. By our labors, human potentialities are converted into actualities, and actualities into potentialities. We repotentialize old actualities, and not only the old, but also the new; and we reactualize old potentialities and new ones. We raise the probability of actualization of the potentialities of our human being, our powers of labor, its organization, combination and division in society, and of our technics, material, practical and theoretical. We grasp new ways of solving old problems, and bring forward old solutions to new ones. The moving of the potentialities of our human activities and organization thereof from a higher to a lower probability, or from a lower to a higher, is an abstract system of reference; the change of the potentialities in their relation to actualities is both concrete and abstract, material and nonmaterial, practical and theoretical.

The labor form and substance are a condition of all human society and life; They are in a mediate and dirempted relation to one another in our society, civil and bourgeois; it is doubtful whether, once dirempted, the labor form and substance will return to an immediate, internal and undirempted relation. The return to an immediate, undirempted, unalienated relation of labor in society has long been a utopian dream.

There is a mutual adaptation between the human self and the material field, which is in this case the concrete instrument of our work and labor, the medium through which we labor, and its object. The instrument is abstract or concrete in its further development or both, so is the medium in which we apply it, and the object to which it is applied. The tool, process, and product are adapted to variable conditions, material and human. The adaptation is twofold, on the one hand, the adaptation of the self to the field of labor, and on the other, the adaptation of field of labor to the varying processes of human history. The adaptation of the self to the new circumstances of the human order is shaped by the process of critical selection, which is shaped by the adaptation between the self and the field of our activities. The process of adaptation of the field is mediate and objective; the process of adaptation of the self is objective and subjective; there is in this case an asymmetrical relation between self and field in their mutual adaptation. Each side changes as the other changes, but not in the same way; each side brings a change about in the other by the change of the one, but it is not the same change. The selection is a process between the self and the field of labors. The critical selection by ourselves is asymmetrical relative to the field in which the selection takes place and is carried through. The process of selection on the part of the field is not that of the field as such, but of human factors and material conditions active in the field. The field of labor is both an abstract and concrete construction, and lies within the human order of nature.

We select that which is adaptable to our lives, material and non-material. We are adapted and selected by agencies in nature which are internal and external to us. The process of mutual adaptation and selection is formulated in the cosmological and evolutionary principles.

The relations of labor form and substance, being in space and time, are made into historical categories. Substance, which was treated as the timeless and absolute constituent of being, is temporal and relative, and this is said of form; for that which is a form in relation to a substance is a substance in another relation, and that which is a substance in relation to a given form is a form in relation to another substance. The substance is not active as such, but is active only through and in a particular form whereby both are real. Substance is only potential or possible without a form. The form is the passive relation of the substance, the substance the active relation of the form; but without the activity there is no passivity, and without the passivity no activity. The activity and passivity, form and substance are relative; the substance is a form, and hence passive in relation to another substance, and the form is a substance, which is active, in relation to another form. Activity and passivity are in direct, indirect and transitive relations in the material order, they are in mediate relations through the separable and oppositive relations of form and substance in the human order. The human order has a common substance, and many historical forms and expressions. The relation between form and substance is variable in the material and in the human order, but that relation is not variable in the two orders in the same way, for whereas the relation in the natural order is direct, in the human it is mediate. The relations of the human kind both within the human order and to the material order are concrete and abstract; they are both abstracted from concrete mediate and immediate relation and generalized abstractly. On being abstracted from the particular, concrete relations they are sometimes hypostasized according to the conception that the abstraction is independent of the concretion; this hypostasis is sometimes made the object of veneration in the belief that it has a life of its own. Commodities, the commodity form of production relations, the abstraction of capital and labor, the subjectivity of capital and labor, and the hypostasis of capital and labor have been venerated and fetishized in modern civil society.

The concretion is relative, as is the abstraction, for that which is concrete in one relation is abstract in another. This is explained in terms of value theory. Concrete labor is in a mediate sense the value substance, abstract labor is in an immediate sense the value substance; abstract labor is in immediate relation to concrete labor and therewith in a mediate relation to concrete value, or use value, concrete labor is in an immediate relation to abstract labor and in a mediate relation to abstract value. Concrete and abstract labor, their separation, and the opposition between them are substantial processes which are given historical form in the development of the relation of exchange between unities of social production and consumption. The act of positing the existence of concrete labor arises out of these processes of separation and unfolding, of concrete exchange in relation to abstract exchange and of value and abstract value. Concrete labor stands in a mediate relation to the value form, and is in a mediate sense the value substance. Concrete labor comes forth in that value form and value substance are separated and opposed to one another; thus it is not the first term in the expression, but is mediately introduced, both historically and in the system of value. (See *Value*, below.)

Labor objectifies itself concretely by meeting human wants and needs; in this process the human substance is constituted in various forms. These forms are mediately bound to the labor substance in human society; we say mediately, for the reason that the form is severable from the substance, and undergoes a temporarily separate historical process. However variable the relation between human form and substance, yet the substance has some given form, and the form a substance. An abstraction may be hypothetically made of the substance, but the abstraction is returned to the concretion, the substance to the form; the alternative to this is the hypostases of the abstraction apart from the concretion and of the substance apart from the form. These hypostases are introduced, whereby labor is presented as the historical subject, under particular historical conditions, which has as its consequences the further hypostasis, which is that of the historical conditions as such apart from a human agency; the first hypostasis is that of a system divorced from the historical process: for labor is not a force in history directly or immediately, but is the substance of human life which acts through particular human historical forms; those are the given social whole, community, tribe, society, or the given social class, the peasantry, the class of slaves, or the industrial working class; the trade unions and working class parties are the personifications and representations of labor, the instrumentalities serving the historically concrete agencies. These agencies become the self-appointed subjects, but they are not the same as labor, nor are they the same as the subjective relation of labor. The instrumentalities serving these agencies are the hypostasis of the labor process when divorced from the human substance, which is labor itself. Labor in civil society is the object dirempted from the subject. The first hypostasis has the second as its consequence. It is not the relation of labor as a class which determines the relation of labor to material nature and in human society; on the contrary, it is the relation of labor as a class which is determined by the mediate-natural and social relation of labor. The political, associational and juridical relations of labor are in turn determined by the class relations; to begin the analysis of labor by its abstract, personified, representative relations is to begin in the middle, both in respect of civil or any other human society and its history. The human object is at once the self-objectifying subject, the subject is the object. Both subjective and objective relations are socialized and self-socializing, self-maintaining and varying relations, which are the *differentia specifica* of human labor. The labor substance is none of these, however, but is the mediate relation of the humankind to nature and the organization in society of this natural relation; the form thereof is variable, the organizational substantive relation of labor in society is both mediate and immediate.

The objective relations of labor are separated from the labor relation in civil society, and appear to have a life of their own. This appearance is associated with an interest in ownership by a class of human beings, and is protected and promulgated by means of coercion. These objectified relations are not the same as the objectifying relations of the human kind, which are the human self-objectifying relations at the same time. The objectified relation is the externality, concrescence, materialization of a subject-object relation which is social to begin with, then expropriated and rendered unto an anti-social relation. The consciousness of this objectifying and self-objectifying relation is hypostasized in the conditions of modern civil society; the consciousness as a state is reified, and the reference to the object is made out to have a life of its own, the objectified dirempted from the object immediately, and from the subject mediately. This product of thinking is made possible only by opposing the effect of objectified relations of society, of labor, and by submitting them to critique. The fiction of the objectified relation is then seen to be what it is, the product of the hypostasis which is introduced in the given civil society, ancient and modern, and presented as though it were a living being, the labor as objectified apart from the self-objectifying relation of the human kind.

The same error, in its inversion, is made in reference to relations of capital both in the private and public spheres of modern society. Capital is here supposed to have the capacity for self-valorization, which implies that it is capable of the active valorizing relation, and of the self-relation of that activity. Capital, however, is the expression of certain relations of labor in production, exchange, distribution and consumption in the form of a commodity; it is as such therefore in no way the materialized, concretized and objectified labor, and is neither the means of production nor the substance of value. Capital is a form without substance, without self, and without self-relation; it is therefore a passive entity which is activated by an effort external to it. Hence it is not self-valorizing or self-valuating, self-appreciating, etc. It is the objectified form without subjectivity; the labor of which it is the expression is the form of labor as a commodity, which sells its labor time and capacity and surrenders the control over that which it sells, being thereby self-diremptive in respect of self, subjectivity and objectifying activity. The self-relation and subjectivity of the process of social reproduction lie elsewhere in civil and bourgeois society, in the hands of the private owners under capitalism, and in those of the public sphere in the Soviet system. The relation of labor under the condition of wage labor in civil society is the objectified substance of labor, which is sometimes referred to as the reified form; the relation of capital produced under this condition is the objectified form of the same. The direction and control of the process of labor and capital rest not with labor, *a fortiori* they do not rest with capital, but with those who have a passive relation in production and an active relation in the direction and control of the social whole. Capital being a form separated from the human substance, which is labor, is made into an animistic creature, treated as though it had a life of its own, which is capable of self-valorization and is then made into a fetish object.

Abstract labor, in an immediate relation to concrete labor, and in an immediate relation to abstract value, is the substance of the latter and the form of the first. Abstract labor is the mediate development out of exchange relations, and the immediate expression of these relations, making them possible to begin with.

The exchange relation in civil society has the commodity as its expression, the commodity constituting the form, and the exchange relation in question the substance thereof. This exchange relation is an abstract process, constituting a form which has labor, abstract and concrete, as its substance; abstract labor is a form, the substance of which is concrete labor, the latter being the means, and the sole means, whereby human wants and needs are met. This labor, which is the only meaning in which it is employed, is therefore subjective and objective; labor in its external relation to the material order and in its internal relation in the human order is object and subject.

Several basic processes of modern civil society are determined in their substance and form by relations of wage labor and capital. Wage labor is human labor which sells its time and capacity against the means of subsistence; labor in this case is not as such a commodity, but its time and capacity, or quantity and quality, are converted into a commodity, which is sold and bought in a market relation, as any other; the wage then is the price for the labor time and capacity. The product of wage labor is another commodity in the abstract sense; concretely, the product is a part of the means whereby the human kind reproduces itself humanly; the other part of the process of human reproduction is our labor, mediate and immediate, as such. Labor is in part concretized and materialized in its product which is either immediately or mediately used up, and thus consumed. Some of these products are applied in the making of further products; labor in this case is both concrete, material, abstract and non-material. The products of labor which are applied in the making of further products are means of production, which are concretizations of the labor which has been expended in their production. If the labor is wage labor, that is if the labor time and capacity is converted into a commodity, then the product, which is in this case the means of production, is converted into a commodity. Capital, we have said, is the means of production in commodity form. As a form, capital is passive, without substance; it is an expression, an outcome and product, not a process of human labor. Capital increases in value expression as the value of labor, and thus the value of the national economy, or of any other workable economic unit, increases in value in civil society. Conversely, if the quantity and quality of labor is diminished, then the value thereof decreases. In a word, valorization is the expression of the process of increase or decrease of the value of some unit of the economy of modern society, such as a nation, or the like. The value is value of labor in production, and increases as the quantity and quality of labor increase, decreasing as the quantity and quality of labor decrease. We read in Marx that capital has a self-valorization or *Selbstverwertung*; this is not the case, for capital is an object which does not objectify itself, but is objectified by our labors. Capital is represented and personified by human actors who are self-activating, self-objectifying, self-mediating, and self-diremptive. The human labors of various kinds thereupon activate the means of production in a substantive relation to them, and therewith activate or set in motion their commodity form and capital, bringing about its increase or decrease in objective social value.

The acts of representing and personifying capital are undertaken in modern society not by the class of social labor, but by another class in society. Labor in this case relates not to the means of reproduction as a commodity, but relates instead to the means of production immediately as such, that is, to the means of our human reproduction by human means. This is accounted for as follows:

By labor is meant social labor, which is the human means of our reproduction. Labor as such is not a commodity under any circumstance, but is converted into a commodity in modern society, under particular circumstances of exchange, market and price relations and expressions. Under these circumstances it is transformed and transforms itself into a commodity, a transformation process which bears not on the relations of labor themselves but on the time and capacity thereof. That is, the transformation in question does not bear on the self-relation, self-activation and self-objectification of labor in its inner process, but only on the external relations of labor; moreover, it does not bear on the external relations of labor to the material order, but only on the external relation of labor in a particular social circumstance, which is that of modern society. The modern bourgeois society, formally regarded, is capitalist society. Civil society is the society which is divided, combined and organized in economic classes; it is the society which has brought forth the state in all its forms, and the society in which the several laws of value, exchange value, use value, and surplus value are applicable. Modern society is the society of the formation of capital in the private and public domains.

Labor in modern as well as in ancient society has a substantive relation to the means of production, and therewith a substantive relation to the process of human reproduction. The relation of labor to the means of production is active and immediate, whereas the relation thereof to capital is passive and mediate. Labor in modern society internalizes this mediate and passive relation to capital, to commodity exchange, therewith to the means of production, and thus maintains a passive and mediate relation to itself. The objective relation of self-diremption whereby the human kind transforms its material being and constitutes itself as human being is converted into a self-alienating process; thus we account for the rise of false consciousness and self-alienation of labor in modern society.

The representatives and personification of capital have a formal, not a substantial relation to the means of production, which is handled by them as a commodity, not as a means of our human reproduction. The representatives and personification of capital have not an immediate but a mediate relation to the means of production; they themselves are not active but passive in the process of our human reproduction; they have an activity *pro forma* in another social relation to the means of production, a relation which all the social classes have internalized uncritically, and which conduces to the false consciousness mentioned.

The representatives and personification of capital in modern society are divided into two mutually antagonistic spheres, the one private, the other public. The opposition between these spheres, each with its respective interest, means of self-promotion and means of self-defense, is a formal one. The process of representation of capital, although formal, is socially real; the process of personification of capital is the expression of the representation thereof in mystified form. In the private sphere, capital is represented and personified by the capitalists, whereas in the public sphere, capital is represented and personified by concrete agencies of the state, e.g., the bureaucracy, the political party, also the juridical and religious institutions. The false consciousness which we have referred to is generated when the representatives and personifiers of capital offer themselves as the representatives and personifiers of social labor and of the social whole.

The opposition of social labor to the private and public representatives and personifications of capital in modern society is a substantive process, not a formal one.

The representatives of capital, whether private or public, do not participate as such in the process of social production and of human reproduction, for they have a formal, not a substantial relation to this process. They are not the ruling class in society, but are transformed into the ruling class in consequence of their control and regulation over the means of production as a commodity, that is, over capital. This transformation process is a complex one. The representation of capital is a formalization of the economic relations of the means of production, of the production and market processes in both the private and the public spheres. By the transformation of the economic relation in its formal side into a political relation, the representatives of capital transform themselves into the ruling class of society. The formal economic relation is in this case the relation of ownership, control and regulation of capital, its formation, valorization, and alienation; the political relation in question is another formal one, being the control and regulation by the ruling class over civil and bourgeois society as a whole. We proceed in our analysis from the first sort of control and regulation to the second, and not vice versa. Modern society is the society of capital formation, both private and public.

Capital is defined as the means of production in commodity form; the means of production are the objectification of living labor time and capacity, in form and substance in the process of reproduction of the human kind. The means of production are the instruments, technics, and skills of social labor, which are applied in the process of human reproduction; they are both material and non-material, both practical and theoretical, and both concrete and abstract.—The commodities are property of various kinds, whether communal, private, public, or their combinations.

A commodity is a good which is sold and bought; the transaction of selling and buying is an economic exchange in reciprocity between buyer and seller; the reciprocation is in various forms, equal, equivalent, or else in an exchange in which a surplus is provided by one side, without an equal or equivalent being returned by the other. The exchange takes place in markets which together with the goods exchanged are concrete and abstract, material and non-material, but formal in any case. Barter is a kind of concrete exchange; other exchange is abstract, of which varieties are exchange by means of price and money.

The goods exchanged are abstract or concrete, material or non-material; they are formal and substantial. The price is an abstraction, and the commodity is the same; the market, in which goods having a price are exchanged as commodities, is likewise an abstract market, even though it is visible, audible, and tangible in its effects. The good is at the same time concrete in meeting and satisfying our wants, needs, and desires. Being human means of meeting these, they are mediate and not direct. The mediate relations of these goods are relative, some being more immediate, and some more mediate than others in the process of meeting our wants. Some of the goods are consumed in the human process of reproduction immediately, and some mediately; there is no absolute division between them. Those goods which are not consumed immediately are or may be applied and reapplied in the process of reproduction of the human kind by production and reproduction. The goods are both practical and theoretical. A human skill or capacity, a technic or a scientific formula, are all non-material goods, which are both practical and theoretical. They are means of production, albeit abstract. A tilled field, a factory floor, and the machinery on or in it are material goods of a concrete, practical kind; they materialize, embody and concretize past labors of the human kind. The labors are transformed into the abstraction and formality thereof in the exchange, commodity and market process; labor time and capacity is sold and bought, in the process of capital formation. The labor is therefore not a commodity as such, but by the abstraction and formalization of its time and skills in the capital relations it is made into a commodity and potentially into capital. The labor form in question is wage labor. There are conditions of slave and serf societies in which a small amount of capital is formed, and the labor, although *pro forma* unfree, is embodied as capital therein.

Capital is a formal and abstract process; it is non-material. Yet the labor time and capacity therein are concrete and material processes. They are not material in capital but in the means of production, which are the means of our human reproduction. Labor in these forms, but not in all its forms, is the concretization and materialization of the living labor form and the living labor substance. Commodities are abstract and formal expressions in the process of economic exchange in general; capital is an abstract, formal expression of the exchange relation under particular social circumstances. The commodity form is not universal in human history, but is particular to the relations of civil society, and of certain others like it.

Alfred Marshall attributed to Marx the following definition of capital: "... Only that is capital which is a means of production owned by one person (or group of persons) and used to produce things for the benefit of another, generally by means of the hired labour of a third; in such wise that the first has the opportunity of plundering or exploiting the others."—The means of production are converted into capital by virtue of being owned, of being sold and bought in a market transaction, and of a contract to fulfill a transaction of this kind. The means of production are objects in these relations of society, and our relation to them as civil persons is objective; they are as such not subjects, nor are they subject-objects; they therefore have no self-relation, which is a relation of the subject-object. The products mentioned are the products of human labor, in relation to the means of production; they are not the products of capital, for capital is not an agent in the relations of production even though it may appear to be so. Capital is a form without substance, save that which we attribute to it. The labor in question is social labor, in the form of wage labor, in modern civil society. The labor is hired and remunerated by wages or salary, in a contract; it is in a formal exchange relation of labor in social production, and is in the condition in which the labor, the means of production and the social product are converted into commodities. Those commodities which are means of production are converted into capital. It is not the ownership relation which is operative in this connection, but the relation of exchange in the market which determines the process of conversion of the means of production into capital. Ownership is a precondition for this process, but is too general, being found not only in capitalist society, or in society in which capital plays a vital role in the economy, but in many others as well. Marshall made some errors of omission in his statement.

The means of production and the product are the objectifications, materializations and concretizations of labor, past and present; the relations of labor as a commodity, being hired for a wage or salary, determine that the means of production and the product are commodities, in the latter case, capital. Not the formal but the substantive labor power is made into a commodity; the formal labor powers, as we shall see, are not relinquished by labor, which is hired for a wage. In this case the determination of the commodity and capital formation is made by working forward from the moment of sale of labor time and quality by labor which is *pro forma* free; the substantive labor power is then formally determined as a commodity.

There is a connection between the commodity form of exchange, the hiring of labor for a wage or salary in exchange for the supply to it of the means of subsistence, and the plundering and exploitative relation in which labor is held, in the process of capital formation. Marshall pointed out that there is a relation between wage labor, exchange, and capital; exchange value, and surplus value are expressions of this process in Marxian terms, not in Marshallian. But although Marshall pointed to the process and its system, he did not say what it is, and thus left the thought hanging.

The human kind has the substantive power, in its labor time and capacity, to produce more than it consumes. This statement bears on a fact of observation of the human reproductive and variational process from the Paleolithic times to our own; the historical purview of the statement is paired with its systematic exposition; the production of a surplus is a generic condition of the relations of labor to the means of production, of the relations of the humankind to the material order of nature, and of the mediate process and system of the human kind. By our relation in production we convert both material and non-material processes in our human reproduction. We apply not only our present, living labor in the reproduction process, but apply this labor in interaction with the past, materialized and objectified labors in this process. Our present, concrete labors, or work, are means to supply our needs for our biological reproduction; this presupposes a mutual adaptation between the species *homo sapiens* and the environment external to it. The systematic and widespread use of the means of production prepared in the past, in cooperation with our present work and labors augments our productive capacities; the product of these labors is in excess of our concrete and direct needs, and our immediate wants. The animal needs are met by work, the human wants are met by human labors. The production of the excess over our immediate wants and needs is further augmented by working on the medium of our labors, our concrete and abstract work tools and labor instruments, and on the means of production and reproduction of the human kind generally. The variation of our labors, organization and technics, the increasingly complex combinations, divisions, and technical specializations further assure the acceleration of the rate of increase of the excess of production over that which meets our immediate wants. The productivity is then increased, and the rate of increase of the productivity is increased. Historically, the rate of productivity is variable; it is more rapidly increased at present than in the past, such that the rate of change in the past appears to us to have stagnated; this is not the case, but is the result of an uncritical comparison between the two states.

In civil society, the formal labor power is separated from the substantive power of labor; the substantive labor power and the relations thereof to the means of production are controlled in this form of society by various means. The social product and the labor time and quality or capacity expended in bringing it forth are divided into two parts, one which is applied immediately in the reproduction of social labor and mediately in the reproduction of the social whole, and another part, which is in excess of the first. The excess over the first may then be applied to the augmentation of the reproductive capacities of the human kind, and a part of it is so applied. Once the relations of labor, its powers and capacities are removed from the control of social labor, then the control of the social product, of its distribution and redistribution is taken away as well. Moreover, the determination of what is required for the human reproduction of social labor is taken away from it as well. The matter of ownership is formally relevant to this process, but is only one means to control, among others. The substantive redistribution of the surplus part of the social process and the internal proportion between the sum of the product and the surplus part are matters of control, and not of ownership, save as a formality, either public or private. The formality is a juridical issue, and not an economic or social one. The surplus is unproductive when alienated from the class of social labor by the exploitative class in civil society.

Exchange relations are a precondition for the exploitative alienation of the social surplus from the class of social labor; exchange value as the precondition of the extraction of social surplus value is the formal expression of this relation. In this way, the formation of capital and the social exploitation of labor in society, civil and bourgeois, have a connection, historical and systematic, for the means of production as a commodity is subject to exchange, and has exchange value.

We do not distinguish, in the present context, between fixed and circulating, or between constant and variable capital; these categories are derived, perhaps, from the mechanical image of the means of production on the factory floor, and the further processing of products. The movement of such an abstract object as capital is only in part analyzed as a mechanical act with fixed and moving parts. The processes of capital are both linear and non-linear, and its movements are or may be in time abstracted from space, and in space abstracted from time. The means of production and the goods as such may be fixed in place, circulating, constant or variable. Capital is in any case not a constant and fixed but a circulating and variable entity, which is a commodity; the rates of its variability are themselves variable. Circulation is a kind of variability of capital.

Relations of Social Labor

Labor is the process between the human kind and the human and material orders whereby the material objects accessible to our senses and other objects, which are not, are organized and transformed, and the human kind and being are organized, combined and divided into given human social wholes. Labor is a temporal process between past and present, in the meeting of present and anticipation of future wants and needs, by which the human is maintained and varied. It is the process of self-reproduction.

Labor in all its forms, communal, social or individual is a human process, which is constituted of a number of substantive relations of the material and human orders. These relations, being of either order, and of both, are at once relations to and in either order, and both. The relation of labor to the material order of nature is that of the human kind, being a diremption, distancing and mediation with respect to the natural order, while at the same time it is generated and constituted continuously in the material order of nature; relations of the material order generate, and are continuously present in, human relations.

Labor Quantity and Quality. Labor Time and Capacity

The system of quantity and quality is brought forth in the human order; quantification and qualification are then projected onto the other natural orders. The relation of the human kind to the material order is a mediate one. It constitutes a medium which is at once the process and product of work and labor in society; the concrete work is represented in the social organization of production and of exchange; each of these processes is an abstract means of quantification of labor by reference to labor time.

The relation of labor time in this connection is qualitative and quantitative. Qualitatively, the relations of labor are more mediate in one process and more immediate in another. Thus production is a labor process, which is conducted by immediate and mediate producers. The producers are more immediate in their labor relations in production if they have less time in training, skill, qualification and preparation, and more mediate in their relations of labor in production as the amount of time expended in their training and preparation, qualification and skill is increased. In this process, the amount of concrete labor time decreases in proportion as the amount of abstract labor increases both in preparation, or in potentiality, and in actual production.

The immediate relation of labor has by virtue of the low degree of preparation, the small amount of time in training, education, a high degree of participation in concrete and material processes of production; yet it is mediate in its relation to the material order of nature. There is no absolute difference between human and other natural processes, for the natural material of the conformation and properties of the human eye and hand take part in the production process and those of the body in consumption.

The time in social reproduction is objectively and concretely valued and quantified, the quantification following the valuation; in order to be expressed as a quantity, the time is measured. The quantity is in this case an objective datum; it is abstractly expressed in relation to the concrete factum, which is the product of the labor.

The labor of the hand has reference to concrete labor of all kinds. The head stands for abstract labor, which, under particular historical conditions is self-diremptive and thereupon alienated from the concrete labor of hand and body. From the standpoint of the human order, the process of social labor is constituted of the relations of the human kind to the material order and the relations thereof as they are organized within the many social wholes. The labor of the head is in this sense mediate, the medium being abstract; the labor of hand and body is both mediate and immediate in relation to the material world, the medium being abstract and concrete. The whole is activity, the parts, abstractor concrete in their separation being incapable of activity. The quality of labor is realized only in the quantification thereof, the quantity has reality and actuality only in the quality thereof.

The quality in question is the collective skill of the social process of labor. This process is the activation of past by present, living labor. The quality of the labor implies mastery of relations and technics, and the planning of both, in the present social combination and division of labor, immediate and mediate labor, and present with past labor. The combination of the present with the past bears upon the transmission of the labor skills, organization of labor, and the variation thereof. The mastery and organization of labor and labor skills is objective, the technics are likewise objective; the variation of the skills and the organization thereof by present living labor is both objective and subjective. The quality of labor is the past that is borne upon the present, whereby it is mastered, varied and practically applied in the process of social reproduction, for mastery and variation are the same; thus mastery is both objective and subjective, whereby the past potentiality which is objective alone, is made actual in the present. The quality of labor is the process of giving new potentialities to labor of the past and the self-mediatization of living labor at present; whereas the process of repotentialization of the past is objective, the self-mediatization is at once subjective and objective. Labor, both quantitative and qualitative, transforms the natural field mediately by its skills, organization and technics. Production by rote and mechanical repetition is not mastery, but implies skill of a lesser degree. The past has two processes in the given human historical sequence, the one is the past as past, which is social, objective, concrete in a discontinuous temporal sequence; the other is the past which is in a temporal continuum at once objective and subjective with the present. The objectivity of the discontinuity and the continuity of the sequences of time process lies in the human social relation of both; they are the resultant of the embodiment of social organization in the practical combination and division of human beings in relation to one another in the process of reproduction in the social whole by their labor. The product of the social organization of the humankind is concrete, the organization is both abstract and concrete. The matter and field which are transformed in the process of self-reproduction of the human kind have an existence and determinate being independent of their human makers and users; they are transformed into an object by human means, and surrender their independent existence and determinate being. The natural thing, being made into a human object becomes a product, endowed with a new determination of its being, the object being the human determination of the thing and human relation to and of it. The objective relation of labor is its usefulness in meeting wants and needs in the process of human reproduction, of socialization of the biological being in the process of becoming human. We internalize the objective relation of labor, which is objective again in the sense of being the object of human activity of perception, internalization, mastery, appropriation and variation. The variational process of labor is at once objective and subjective, and is a part of the human continuum, in which the objective, as given in either sense is submitted to human judgment, consciousness and will.

The process of time is, in its human social relation, at once abstract and concrete. It is abstract in that it is abstracted from the particular temporal process, and continues in abstract process along with the same process, both abstract and concrete, from which it has been abstracted; the inherent abstraction of the human process continues undiminished by this abstraction. The concrete product is abstracted in another sense, being alienated from the original process, abstract and concrete, that has produced it; the concrete aspect of the process is diminished by this alienation, which now will meet the want and need of another. The diminution is made good if an exchange or a redistribution is thereby effected. The abstract process in the human temporal relation has the quality of the past that is activated in the present, and varied, the past having first to be abstracted from its objective sequence and replaced in the present, new one. The original natural time is thereby reordered, and the human order of time is constituted by the transformation of the objective, natural time. The latter continues in being regardless of human activity, it is the continuum which is varied and modulated by the human social relations of abstraction and concretion, subjectivity and objectivity.

Labor is a process of objectification whereby a thing is transformed into an object; the human order is constituted by this transformation process turned inward and outward. The practical consummation of objectification is the process of meeting human wants and needs, or the sustenance of concrete existence of the human kind by labor. Abstractly, the objectification of the world of nature is the relation to it whereby the human kind is constituted as the agent and matter is transformed as the object upon which the human kind labors, the natural object of human work and labor ceasing its thingly existence. The making of the world into the object is a temporal process of human making which is continuous with the ongoing natural temporal process, which is its practical doing. The making of the world into the object by the human kind is the primary relation of abstraction, and the establishment of a new quality of temporal continuum. The human agent at the same time turns inward, bringing the self-relation of objectification into being, constituting the self-object, and therewith the subject. These relations of objectification, self-objectification and subjectification, however, are not a temporal sequence of events, but a quality borne upon and borne by human temporal process in its active relation to the material order of nature and to the self. The human temporal continuity is a manifold in actuality which is potentially one; the manifold is both abstract and concrete, the potential unity is abstract alone, the abstract unity being the potentiality of the concrete manifold.

Labor in the human temporal sequence has manifold relations and states, the quality of abstraction being its unifying character; concretely the quality of labor is undiminished by the potentiality of its abstract unity. Labor is the means of transforming itself and thereby its temporal sequence, the movement being abstractly constituted by the labor relation, abstractly measured, concretely activated and expressed, concretely alienated and practically applied in the process of human social reproduction. The quality of mastery, variation and reconstitution of the human process in time is not independent of the original temporal process of matter, but is an objective character in relation to the latter. Although the human temporal quality is objective, yet it is not independent of the temporal process; timeless sphere or event, a backward flow of time, and an independent, parallel, recurred flow are all abstract temporal relations, whether hypothetical, speculative, theoretical, useful, or fantastic. Subjective time is time in respect of individual reference, and enters into the objective continuity by its relation in the given human substance and form. Time in human relation is made abstract and concrete by human activity, labor is the expression of human temporal quality, as opposed to concrete natural temporal relation. Human space is concretization of time by labor; labor is motion in the human order, which is at once the quantitative relation of time and space and the qualitative relation of the particular human process of time and space.

The quantitative relation of time and space in the human order, being manifold, is varied in the human historical process by the several social wholes concretely, by human being, social or individual, both abstractly and concretely. The quantitative relation is in this case objective in the sense of being independent of the human individual subjectivity, the quantitative relation being a simple, concrete, unidirectional process. The qualitative relation of time and space is a burden of the past that is placed on the present temporal-spatial relation, whereby the continuum is submitted to human variation. The potentialities of the past are reactivated, being made actual anew to different human processes, active and passive. The potentiality is therefore plural, various, and the actualization thereof likewise manifold within the particular human historical sequence; the potentiality of the abstract human historical continuum as a whole is a manifold. Labor bears within itself the quality of its own variation and therefore the qualitative temporal relation that is opposed to the quantitative human spatial-temporal relation. The quality of labor is in this respect both objective and subjective, abstract and concrete.

The skill and capacity of labor are the realizations of its potentiality, in a temporal continuity with matter. The capacity is at once new potentiality in another temporal sequence. The capacity and skill are both capability and achievement, the latter being a mastery of a past relation that is embodied, internalized and varied, being thereby further developed. The labor capacity is the qualitative expression of that which labor time expresses quantitatively. The two expressions are theoretically separate, practically they are inseparable. The labor capacity is separable from labor time, by making either into an abstraction. Labor time is not made into a commodity that is sold separately from labor capacity; on the contrary, they are bought and sold together.

The relation of labor capacity in the wage labor is no different, the quantity of labor time being inseparable from quality in the wage relation of living labor. Wage labor sells its labor capacity and time conjointly in the process of social reproduction in modern society, bourgeois and civil. This is the exchange relation of social labor which falls within its juridical power to transact on its own behalf. The exchange relation has a formal moment, which is the establishment of the labor contract as the condition of onset of the wage labor process; the exchange has a substantive moment, whereby wage labor continuously, throughout the process of social reproduction exchanges its time and capacity against the means of its self-reproduction. The socialization of labor has two moments in its historical process, both mediate, one substantial and active, the other formal and passive. The substantial moment in the process is the organization of labor by its combination and division in the relations of production, distribution and reproduction in society. The formal moment is that of exchange. The passivity and formality of the moment of exchange lies in the act whereby the product of labor is alienated from its immediate producers; labor then acquires the equivalent of what is produced by a reciprocation in the exchange relation. The product is made into a commodity, labor is itself made into a commodity, in its formally unfree condition, and its labor time and capacity are made into a commodity in its condition of formal freedom. Labor is acted upon in the exchange process throughout the history of civil society, hence the formal moment in socialization is a passive one.

The relations of class-divided society posit the production of a social surplus and its alienation from its immediate producers as a social class by another social class which may or may not be engaged in the process of social production; whether it is so engaged or not is irrelevant to the judgment and calculation of the social surplus. The production of this surplus is not a moral or political issue, but an economic process. The relations of exchange are predominant in modern civil society; these relations, and the relation of alienation of a social surplus mutually undergird one another in the history of that society; neither these relations nor the social formations that bear them out are identical.

The exchange relation is in and of itself mediate, the act whereby one production unit consumes the product of another which the one has acquired by an equal reciprocation. The substantial moment is doubly mediative in that it is determined by the relations of organization of social relations in the present and by the transmission and variation of skills and relations in society as temporal process. The abstract expression of the formal and substantial moments is that of labor time and capacity, or of quantity and quality, which is the same in this case.

The exchange relation in the process of human reproduction is a condition of the organization and division of social labor, and the organization and division of social labor is a condition of the exchange relation.

The quantitative relations of concrete work are variable in an immediate sense as they proceed from the past to the present. The abstract relations of labor are in a mediate sense relative to the concrete, in their constitution in the actual process of reproduction of the human kind, and relative as well in the process of preparation, training and transmission of labor skills, technics and science as they proceed from the past to the present. Qualitatively, the mediate relations of labor are variable in the process between the past and the present; the relations in this case proceed in both directions, from past to present, and from the present to the past. We reach into the past by our labors, and reactivate bygone potentiality, both of the concrete and abstract instrumentalities of human work and labor. Both the immediate and the mediate producers are engaged in discovery, renovation and innovation in respect of the past processes in the present; practically, this is the activity of grasping and applying the old processes in a new way, and is a new instrumental relation to past labors, both material and non-material. In this case, the reactivation is in the form of a repotentialization of the old, in the process of its human variation.

We turn to the question of the relations of quantity and quality in the process of training, preparation and education of those engaged in the human reproduction of the human kind. In this process, the relations of quality and quantity are in an immediate sense at first combined and there is no opposition between them. The process is the skill or qualification, whereby the labor in its result is better qualified and trained, but this has at the same time reference to the quantification thereof as well. There is no transition or transformation of quantity into quality, or of quality into quantity in this process. In the relation of labor in civil society in general, and in modern bourgeois society above all, the mediate producers and the immediate producers are separated, and this is referred to as the division of labor in society. The two kinds of producers are opposed to one another, and the former are advantaged at the expense of the latter, receiving more, and more advanced, training and education, higher pay and other emoluments. This separation and opposition is not a general but a particular condition, and the opposition between quality and quantity, i.e., the transformation of the one into the other in this case, is an ethnocentric and artificial one, being falsely projected onto the human condition beyond the limits of modern society, civil and bourgeois; it is then by further falsification projected onto the order of matter. The relations of qualification and quantification in the training, preparation and education of labor are immediate, but are immediate in social production; they are mediately separated and opposed to one another insofar as the relations of mediate and immediate producers in civil society, in the social division of labor, are separated and opposed to one another; such a separation of the processes of labor and the opposition which is developed from it bespeak an interest from which some profit materially, applying the differences to their advantage, at the expense of others. The oppositions between hand labor and head labor, and between workers with the body and the mind represent the separation of the immediate from the mediate labor processes, whereby the advantaged are reinforced in their advantages. There is no basis in this case for opposing quantity to quality in the relations of labor in society. In theory, the basis for making the distinction between immediate and mediate relations of labor lies in the degree of qualification by preparation and training of those engaged in immediate and mediate production. The quality is in this case a quantitative relation, which is applied to the system of concrete work and concrete and abstract labor, the work being more immediate in relation to human reproduction, the abstract labor more mediate. In practice, the work is more immediately the abstract labor more mediately related to the product of consumption. The concrete product of our work has no immediate relation to its abstract expression in the formal sense of its objective value; the abstract labor has a greater potentiality for its abstract and formal expression as objective social value, and this potentiality is realized in modern bourgeois society, and is projected backward onto ancient times, in the age of classical antiquity, and is projected forward onto other theoretical conditions than those which are connected with wage labor and the formation of capital.

Labor Quality, or Capacity

Labor is a twofold process, immediate and mediate, of the human kind. In its immediate relation it is a process between the labor quantity, or time expenditure, and quality, or capacity on the one hand, and the instruments of work and labor on the other; in its mediate relation it is a process between the humankind and the materials of nature. Both the capacities of labor and the instruments thereof are a twofold process in another sense, being abstract and concrete. Both the capacities and the instruments of labor are brought forward from the past to the present, but they are brought forward in different ways, the one as agent, and the other as the object acted upon. Capacities and instruments have a form and substance, which, being human, are mediate in their relation to one another, and diremptible, or provisionally separable from one another. The material objects of our activities, insofar as they are material, have a formal and substantial process which is in theory separable into parts, but in practice is not. The separability of the material object into formal and substantial relations is, however, a potentiality thereof which is actualized by our labor and work on them, in the process of our human reproduction.

The capacities of labor are the skills, the mediate relations of human beings to the instruments, the co-workers and to the self, the objectification of these relations, and the organization of labor in society. The labor capacities are potentially infinite but actually finite. The only self-starter which the human kind has produced in all its history is its labor capacity. The capacities of labor are not the amount of time but the quality of the labor expended in the human reproduction of the human kind. The capacities include the preparation and training of labor; these capacities have limits which are practical and theoretical.

Tools are concrete and are found in the activities of animal species, among them the mammals, ants, and bees, hence in the material and organic order of nature. The use of tools has been observed among the primates as well as the human kind, together with problem-solving by the use of these tools; hence we infer a quantitative difference, and a continuity between the natural and human processes in this regard as well as in the others which have been mentioned. There is at the same time a discontinuity, for whereas the tools are concrete, practical, both direct and indirect processes of the organic kind in the material order, the human kind has generated and continues to develop a different relation to these, and to the work process in which they are introduced. The work process is common ground between the human and the other organic processes of the material order, and is in a continuity with work, both organic and inorganic, of that order. This work, and the tools which are organic parts thereof, are varied by the human kind, the relations of human work being a mediate process, and not direct. The human relations of work, and the use of tools therein, are transformed into relations of labor, abstract and concrete, immediate and mediate, and the tools are transformed into instruments, both practical and theoretical, of the human kind. The process of labor, and the instruments developed in this process, are variable, but they are not varied as are the work process and tools out of which they are evolved. The evolutionary process is transformed by the human kind, and it is subject to change of another kind than that of evolution; variation of the human kind is both formal and substantial, but the form and substance vary in a mediate relation to one another, and not in a direct relation, such as is the case among the concrete, thingly, natural processes, including those of work and tool use therein. Thereby the human kind is differentiated twofold from the material order and organic process of nature, out of which is evolved our place therein; we differentiate ourselves, a), by our productive and practical relation to the natural materials, the productive being both practical and theoretical, and b), by our self-diremptive, mediated and mediative relations in the material order.

The instruments of human work and labor are concretizations of past labor in the meeting of our wants, needs and desires, thus in the process of our human reproduction. The instruments are both material and non-material, both abstract and concrete, and the concretizations thereof are both objective. Since the labor which has brought forth these instruments is both practical and theoretical, the concretization thereof is the same. The processes of past labor are thus varied in a way whereby the form is separated from the substance thereof, and a mediate relation is introduced between the two. It often appears to be that the old form remains, but is applied in new ways, or that old functions and applications of the labor process are reintroduced by new forms. In the former case we may apply a beast of burden or a wheeled vehicle to transport not only goods but human beings; in the latter case, the substance of the art of reckoning is made more exact, and applied with greater speed than it had been before the use of the computer, without change of the said substance.—The process between the past and the present is concrete and practical, in the case of the human order, in that and insofar as our wants are met, and the material and non-material reproduction of the human kind is brought about. The wants are not rubbed out, but are met and satisfied temporarily, to be met again when they reappear. The wants are objective, and are independent of our consciousness and will; thingly needs are transformed into objective wants; the desires are subjective, and are not independent of our will and subjective consciousness, but are one with them. The objective wants and creature needs return tomorrow, whether we desire them to or not, however well we have met them today by eating or warming ourselves before the fire. Our human wants and the material, organic, animal needs of gravitational attraction and electric charge, sunlight and rain, are met by interactions, human, organic and inorganic. Labor and its concretizations in the instruments are the means whereby we are related, distanced and dirempted from the natural processes in and by which we are generated and reproduced. The distancing is at once a connection, hence we do not leave nature, but transform and in this way leave the material order thereof, by the generation of the non-material, self-diremptive relations of the human kind. In this process of diremption, variation, and self-generation, the relations of past and present labor constitute the medium of our interaction with nature and with the material order of nature.

The non-material processes are abstract, non-sensory, practical and theoretical. They are generated in space-time, and are in their generation natural, concrete, material, and objective to the human kind. They are in their further development natural, but by the mediation of the human processes are both concrete and abstract, as we have said; we work on the medium, which is our human order, and make it into the means of our continuous-discontinuous relations in nature and to matter. The relation of the continuum is a material process of the sensory order, whereas the discontinuity is a process of discrete interactions, which are measured by quantum differences. This is a mesocosmic process of the human order, which is a part of the macrocosmic system of the sensory universe and the material order of nature, being generated within the latter. The mesocosmic process in this case is greater than the microcosmic process of the atomic nuclei, but does not contain the latter, for they are in a different space-time system; nor does the macrocosmos of the material order contain the quantum space-time and its processes and for the same reason; yet all these processes are natural, in space-time, but not in the same space-time. Hence the human kind has an asymmetrical relation to these processes, and these are generated and constituted by the relations of labor. We are internal to the macrocosmos of matter, but the quantum process is not internal to the human mesocosmos, nor to the macrocosmos, for the quantum space-time is of another order than the material and sensory.—Human work and labor, and our relations to their tools and instruments are both continuous and discrete, sensory and quantum processes of nature.

Hegel wrote that the human kind is related to external nature in a practical way, through its needs, and in that it meets and erases these, goes mediatively to work. He further averred that in order to constrain nature, we set natural things against the natural in the work process, and invent tools to this end. If we translate this insight into the system which is here set forth, we see that we go mediatively to our work and labor, and in this way meet our wants and needs. The tools are the past labor processes made concrete and varied in the present; they are concrescences of the past, as we have seen, which are abstract and concrete, sensory and non-sensory further developments of the past natural, therewith material and human processes. We objectify the natural processes, and introduce them into the human order, hence they are no longer natural things, but human and humanized, humanizing, mediatized and mediatizing objects. We work on the natural practically and in an orderly way in that it is materially constituted, and practically and theoretically, in an orderly and non-orderly way, but in either case objectively, in that it is naturally, materially and non-materially constituted.

Figure 1

The work process of the human order[1]	The work process of the material order
Concrete	Concrete
Practical	Practical
Material	Material
Immediate	Direct, indirect
Productive	
Objective, self-objectifying	Thingly
Discontinuous; completed in the product	

The labor process [1]

Concrete	Abstract	Potentiating
Material	Non-material	Repotentiating
Sensory	Non-sensory	Organizing
Practical	Theoretical	Self-relative
	Productive	
Objective, Self-objectifying	Mediative, Mediated	Continuous
		Immediate

1. Potential, repotentialized, organizing, self-organizing, self-repotentializing and varying, mediate and objective processes are qualities of work and labor; they are active and passive, potential and actual, as such. The variation is direct and indirect in the material order, and mediate in relations of form and substance, and past and present, of the human order.

The instruments of labor are processes and expressions of processes of the human kind. They are not self-active. They are concretized, materialized, and made into the human medium by its relation to the natural and human processes with which we are interactive. In this respect, the instruments of labor are in the same natural relation as is the human kind, which is no more self-concretizing, nor self-materializing than is the instrumentality which it produces. The human kind differs from its instrument concretely and its instrumentality abstractly in that we are our own self-relation and generate our own self-medium; hence we are a self-mediatizing and self-objectifying factor in nature, in the human order, and, in part, in the material order of nature.

The human kind bears material processes of nature within itself. By internal material nature, is meant the organs of our bodies and the body as such, to which our human relations are both immediate and mediate. At first our relations to the human physical organism are indiscriminately subjective and objective, but as we grow into youth and adulthood we distinguish the objective and the subjective processes of our selves, and the immediate from the mediate processes in our human acts. We develop the organs of the body as concrete instruments of which our work tools are extensions and projections, whereupon our mental and physical parts are developed abstractly and concretely both as means to further ends and as ends in themselves. Both means and ends are of various kinds, practical, theoretical, aesthetic. We later develop non-material, abstract instruments for our theoretical labors, which have no immediate relation to the organs of the body and the concrete tools of work.

Our relations to external nature are more mediate than those to the internal nature. The nature with which we are concerned is apart of being in space-time, another part of which is the non-material world of the human order; there are other parts of nature beside these. The material instruments of work and labor are a part of our instrumental assemblage which has non-material parts, in our plans and consciousness, designs and theories. The material instruments of work together with the non-material instruments are as tools and instruments the external results of past labor, in forms abstract and concrete, and are thus an opposed moment to the process whereby the capacities of present labor are made actual. This capacity, actual and potential, is a process of internalization, mediation, objectification and variation of the relation between past and present of labor; the self-relation of the human kind is thereby generated phylogenetically; the process of ontogeny of the self is opposed to this. The instruments constitute mediate relations and a medium of activation of the skills and capacities of labor. In that they are concrete, material, external relations of the human to the natural order they are objectified; they are not objectified and therewith material, external and concrete. On the contrary, they are material things which are then made into objects; they are external and concrete in that they are of the natural order to begin with, and are thereupon objectified by the human kind. The primary material which is objectified is the human body, hence the human kind in humanizing itself makes the body, *homo sapiens*, into the primary instrument of work and labor, and thereby undertakes its self-objectification. The instruments of work are concrete, alien, material objects, the use of which is mastered and varied; they are the materialization and concretization, externalization and objectification of past labor time and capacity. They are varying, impermanent, submitted to natural degeneration, oxidation, material loss and organic decay; they are varied, being repotentialized and actualized anew by the human relation to them; living labor in the present maintains and varies the relations to the work instruments; the relations of human labor to the instruments are at once abstract and concrete, theoretical and practical; they are subjective and objective, mediate and immediate. The instruments as such are passive objects; the hammer and the computer do not think; they do not start up of their own, but are programmed to do so.

Work tools are produced by the skills, capacities and technics of past labor and are given a substance and form accessible to the senses. The skills, capacities and instruments are applied in the reproduction of the human kind. The instruments of work are old labor processes reduced to material form, which has a separate relation to current labor processes from the substance. The form of past labor, materialized in the labor instruments is passive, concrete, the past borne upon the present. Being passive, it is activated, being concrete it is without abstract relation as such, in actuality, for the activity and abstract relation of the form of the material lies in the past. This form is passive, inert, either organic or inorganic, a wooden boat or a metal knife; whether it is dead or not is irrelevant. The bygone activity and passivity, concretion and abstraction, potentiality and actuality are reduced to passivity, concretion, potentiality of activation and application in the labor process. The labor instruments are matter, objective in form and substance, organized, ordered by the human kind. They are not thingly, natural matter, but humanized material relation. The act of picking up a tree branch from the forest floor transforms the surface of the earth in the forest into a field of human action, the sphere of the forest into a human sphere, and the tree branch into a shovel, hoe or cudgel. The natural material is thingly, accessible to the human kind, and enters into the work process.

The instruments of labor are the product of transformation of the natural materials, their motion and change, by living labor to a human end. An end is therewith introduced into the material relations, therewith indirectly into natural relation. The past is materialized by human work and labor; it is a process in space and time which is passive, hence does not materialize itself. it is not self-materializing for another reason, for there is no self-relation save that which is generated by living labor in the present.

The labor substance which is materialized in the instruments of present labor is of the past and has a different potentiality from the labor substance of the present. Past labor substance is the materialization of relations to natural processes and relations in the human order which is a variation of a previous labor process, present labor substance is a variation of the foregoing. They are not active as such, but are activated in relation to a given form, for the substance of labor has a potentiality of activation, is active through the given form in general, and is activated by living labor in the present. The potentiality of the substance of past labor has a variable relation, the relation of present labor to that potentiality being different from the relation of past labor to the materialization of it in the instruments. The form of the materialization is not variable but has various relations to the activities of present labor, to which it stands in a passive relation. The potentiality of variation and the varying potentialities of the instruments of labor lie in the relations between present labor, the form and substance thereof, and the substance of past labor in material process, realized and made actual in a given form. The form of the past is then made into the object of further labor in the present, and transformed. The potentialities of the past, materialized relations of labor are transformed, for they are not the potentialities of present labor.

The instruments of work are materialized, visible, tangible, generally sensory records of past labor, the processes of which are discovered, mastered and repotentialized by present labor. They are not the memory, but a memorandum of the history of labor in it relations to the natural order and in the human order. Labor in the present by its relations to the instruments thereof materializes itself, as substance and as subject, as form and object. The concrete work instruments are passive in the process of potentialization and repotentialization of the labor process. The labor skills, technics, and science, or capacities of labor, and the instruments, both practical and theoretical thereof, are made concrete in the product of labor; in combination with the natural matter of these instruments, they are transformed in their form and substance, and materialized by human labor. (See Appendix I, *On the Theory of Technics.*)

The second relation of labor capacity which we will take up is its self-objectification. This relation is a part of the more general self-relation of the human labor capacity, several other parts of which have been mentioned; these are the self-starting capacity of labor, self-mediation, or the mediate relation to the self and to its product; labor has the capacity for a self-finishing relation as well. These are several aspects of the self-capacitation of labor. By the act of self-objectification we literally and not figuratively make ourselves into the object of our labors.

The self-objectification of the human kind is in its system the relation of labor in the human and to the other natural orders; the process of self-objectification is in its generation a relation which is wholly within the human order. The self-objectification is a mediate relation of the human kind to the natural order; thus, by objectifying itself the human kind mediatively objectifies other parts of nature, which is the human relation of the human order. From the human standpoint, the human order is constituted in nature thereby, the field of human activity is alienated from the natural order, and constituted within the human order; the human order is therewith constituted within the natural order. The relation of the natural order to nature and to the human order is independent of the activities upon it of the human kind. The objectification of the self presupposes the relation whereby the field of the material order is objectified, being made into the field of human activity. The material thing is thus transformed into the human object; *homo sapiens* is to begin with a natural determinate being, a material thing which is transformed by human labor into the object of human activity. The humanization of the species *homo sapiens* and the institution of the self-relation proceed in step with one another; each is a part of the other, but they are not made out of nothing. They presuppose that within the material processes a variation has occurred, in which an internal relation is differentiated from that which is external to it. This internality has dirempted its inward relation within the material processes, and has concatenated these inward relations in an organized way. The variant process within the material order is alienated from the latter, and stands to it as an externality, having internal relations which are linked together, and are at once continuous and discontinuous with the processes of the external material world. The organization of the relations are those of inward and outward processes, and the differentiation and nexus of relations between the one and the other; the differentiation of the relations of internality as reflexive from those of externality, as diremptive, is made from the standpoint of the inwardly articulated relations; these are diremptive with respect to the outward relation. The relation of the inward to the outward is not that of the latter to the former; the human kind is mediate, objective and opposed in relation to the material surrounding, and has converted it into the human field and order. The organization of the environment is introduced and developed by living beings, and the relations of being alive, wakeful, attentive and aware are found in this organization of the environment. The development of inward differentiation in the human processes of relation and reference, asymmetrical relation in the reflexive relation, asymmetry in the relations of internality and externality, and in the processes of diremption and alienation, brings forth the transformation of natural life processes and their conversion into human processes. The relations of thingly determinate being are converted into relations of objective determinate being, the object is then differentiated both from the thing and from the subject by the development of the relation from reference, the reflexive relation is transformed into the self-relation, and awareness is transformed into consciousness, in the process of transformation of the living matter into human living matter. No new material, and no other existent being is introduced in this process, but that which is already existent is reordered and reorganized, constituting the human kind and order, human being and organization. The relations of human being become the medium of humanization of the natural order.

The process of self-objectification is at once the result and the means of conversion of a material into a human being. This process presupposes a self-relation which is the concretization of the process of humanization. The natural determinate being which internalizes the human relation makes the processes of internalization into a concrete process, differentiating form from substance. The process as substance is externalized as the form, form and substance become the medium of the human relation. The self is the subject of reference, and the object as the subject of relation and reference; the system of relation and reference of the human kind is not direct but mediate, the human relation to nature is thus not direct but mediative within the natural order which is thereby constituted. The medium is variously worked upon by the human kind; out of this medium the human order is constituted, and the human relation to the material order, therewith to nature, mediated in and through these fields of human activity.

These relations of the human kind are natural, but not material. Head, hand, body as such do not labor in the human order, but rather the human being labors, having the head, hand, body and sense organs as parts of the human instrumental assemblage.

The self-objectification of the human kind in substance is unique and is abstractly and potentially one, whereas concretely and actually it is variable, and historically manifold in its expression. The process of self-objectification is at once abstractly and concretely manifold; the history of the substance of self-objectification differs from the many forms of self-objectification. By self-objectification the human kind transforms nature, making both self and nature into the object that is transformed, internalizing a particular field of the natural order in the objectification and transformation of the field and of itself; the reflexive and objective transformation of the human and material orders thus is a twofold historical process. The natural order is concretely worked upon, being the concrete object of human labor as a mediate process; this process is the activity of human production and the social reproduction of the human kind. The unit of variation in this historical process is the social whole.

The mutual objectification within the process of work and labor presupposes the mediatization thereof, transforming the parts into members of the human medium, and readapting the combination of the parts of the natural order, by the actions of the human kind. The past adaptation and readaptation thereof within the human order is the process of human variation under new conditions of objectification, concretization, and mediation in the process of self-reproduction of the human kind. The readaptation is turned upon the instrumental assemblage of internal bodily organ and external tool; it is the externalization of the organ and the internalization of the tool, such that the latter becomes an organ and the body's organ a tool; it is not like a tool, but is a tool; the processes of internalization and externalization of the human order complement each other. This conjoint process of mutual complementation is carried out in objectification of the human self and of its field. It is an activity, of which the transformation of the natural material worked upon is the active and passive complement. The self-objectification is the internalization of the relation whereby the human kind assimilates its world unto itself and itself into its world.

The self-objectification is a threefold process in history; first, it is objectification by work and labor of the natural order; objectification of work and labor and their transformation into the object divorced from the subject, which is a condition of unfreedom of labor; and objectification of labor time and capacity, which is wage labor. Second, the self as object has the power over itself alienated from it in the history of civil society, has placed this power into the hands of another, and has regained it *pro forma* only in the course of its exchange of labor time and capacity against a wage. The process of bending back and forward of the relation of production and reproduction is incomplete, the anfractuosity of labor being the process of working itself, and of being worked upon in the market relations; labor is personified by formal act in the history of civil society. The self-objectification of human labor and the distribution of the product thereof by reciprocation is a potential development of the same relation, in theory, as socialism.

The organization of labor in society is the third aspect of labor capacity which we will mention. It is an aspect of the self-relation of labor, to which reference has been made. The organization of labor is its active relation to itself; the self-relation in this case is not the individual but all of labor in its various forms, collective, communal, social and individual. The organization is a twofold process in the system of the social combination and division of labor. The organization of social labor in its history proceeds from the communal combination and division to a more complex organization having relations within it which are collaborative and antagonistic.

Labor Power and Capacity

Labor is a human relation to the various orders of nature, which are transformed by our labors. It is not our only relation to nature, for we have others which are not laborious, and do not transform anything. The object of our labors is the order of nature. The object of our labor is orderly, and this orderliness determines our relation to it, which is orderly and not chaotic, being organized, combined, divided, connected and differentiated. The transformative process is a kind of natural variation, and labor is a kind of change. The variation, transformation and change are not direct but mediate processes of the human kind. Labor has time as its constituent, but labor time is not time unqualified; it is a natural temporal relation which is transformed by human activity, and labor time is a constituent of that activity. Labor time is not simple but complex, being an immediate, concrete, substantive, and an abstract, mediate and formal relation of labor. Time is at once a natural relation which is measured by labor. Conversely, the temporal relation is the means whereby productive labor and its product are measured; it is the container in which the amount of labor is expressed; the temporal relation is measured in its substantive aspect. Another relation of labor time is measured beside that of time expended in the determination of the total human process of social reproduction, and that is the quality, skill or capacity of labor. This second temporal relation differs from the first by virtue of its mediate character; the first relation is both container and object contained, the means of measurement and the quantity measured. The first relation is that of active beings and the expression of that relation which is denoted as time in the relation. Here it is time in the immediate sense in the human order and as the direct natural relation carried over into the objects of human perception; these are astronomical objects, the sun, moon, other heavenly bodies, and terrestrial objects. Of late, more precise measurement of the temporal process than before has been undertaken by observation of decay of atomic particles of cesium, chemically purified. The second human relation of time differs from the first by virtue of its being an actively mediative relation, to which the first stands in passive opposition. A great degree of quality or skill of labor is required for the measurement of time; labor quality, skill or capacity is the concretion of past labor time embodied in the present. It is not only the past in objectified form, however, it is at once living labor time as an active, mediative, objectifying process in relation to other human beings and to the self. The past labor time is objectified, transmitted, internalized, appropriated, mastered, practically and theoretically developed and applied in the present labors. By mastering the skills of the past, present living labor varies the forerunner by its development under new and changing conditions. The variation is not natural adaptation, but is a part of the history we make both consciously and unconsciously in a natural continuity and variation. The quality of labor in the second meaning of temporal process was intimated by Francis Bacon, *The Masculine Birth of Time*. Parturition is borne by the transmission of science from a master to a disciple; it is the 'human transmission, which is indifferently womanly and manly, for it is no respecter of the relation between male and female sex. The transmission process is at once that of the master to the disciple and the further development by the new master; "the disciples do owe unto masters only a temporary belief and a suspension of their own judgement until they be fully instructed."

The past in its relation to the present labors is in an abstract temporal continuum, which is disrupted by our concrete labors and is embodied in a concrete product. The continual temporal process of labor is accompanied by the continued existence of the past product; the temporal process of labor is both abstract and concrete, the continued existence of the product is concrete alone; they are objectively joined in the same time-space continuum. The product is the finished work, which has objective existence, the labor, both the abstract and concrete, has objective and subjective existence alike. Production leads to the objectification of the labor in the work, and meets a concrete human social want and need, insofar as it is social production, it is an objectification in any case, whether private, individual, public or social, or any combination thereof.

See Francis Bacon, *Temporis Partus Masculus*, On the Masculine Birth of Time, B. Farrington, transl. Bacon, *Advancement of Learning*, Part I, I. IV, 12. Here the dictum, the disciple should believe what he is told, is coupled with another dictum, once taught, the disciple should judge for himself. Labor is variable in the hands of the learner and the master. The suspension of judgement is the activity of the master; it is not a settled quiescence, *epokhé*. We consider, on the contrary, that if the disciples do not question and begin to judge for themselves as disciples, then it is doubtful if they will judge for themselves when they become masters. Aristotle (*On Sophistical Refutations* II. 165b) wrote, Didactic arguments are those which reason from the principles appropriate to each branch of learning, and not from the opinions of the answerer (for he who is learning must take things on trust.) (For *Temporis partus masculus*, read, the human generation of time, or its non-physiological origin.) To this we add, as above, that criticism begins in the process of learning, and not after mastery has been achieved.

Labor is transmitted from the past to the present and from one place to another by means of its embodiment in living people who have mastered the arts, technics, skills and sciences. Thus labor is transmitted from its internalized form and substance in one body of living labor, externalized in the process of transmission, and internalized by another body. The body is a social body, a process of social relations; it is incorporated by the human kind and thereupon by human individuals. The mastery and variation, however slight, are bound together in the arts and sciences of the human relation to the natural and human order. Labor is transmitted as a capacity which is actually or potentially mastered; it is not transmitted as labor time but as human process in space and time, that is, the labor process is transmitted concretely, both practically and theoretically. Labor is transmitted in a process of variable form and substance to be activated in the relation between the transmitter thereof and those to whom it is transmitted, the potentiality of the relation being variable. This bears upon the transmission of labor in materialized form as well, as we have seen. These skills, arts, technics, crafts and sciences, and the time expended in their mastery, variation and practical application are expressed by their abstraction, quantification and measurement; they are both potentialities and actualities of labor. The potentiality of labor to reproduce the human kind by its science and technics, practical and theoretical, is its capacity. In its actuality, labor by its general substance and through its particular form is the process of human production as such. The time is in the past which is made actual in the present; it is borne upon the present from the past, and by the present relation of present time with respect to the possible future. The relation to the past is at once variable, for the past is not a fixed relation but is capable of being reopened, and old potentialities therein are reworked and repotentialized, for which memory, records, consciousness serve as the material and practical instruments. The past is thus changed with respect to the human order, and is not fixed in its relation between actuality and potentiality. The relation to the past of the human kind is in reality unchanged. Thus in its temporal process, the human kind differentiates between actuality and reality, between the many potentialities of the past and its one past actuality, which is finished, and between actuality and potentiality. The actuality of human temporal process is variable in that its potentiality is variable, and conversely, the potentiality is variable in that the human relation to and in present actuality is variable. This variability is a multiple relation of human past to present and of present to past, and is opposed to the singularity of past human reality in its relation to the present. The human reality is a temporal process which is objective alone, the human actuality is objective and subjective. The human temporal relation is asymmetrical in respect of potentiality and actuality and in respect of our objective and subjective relations. The past reality is potential to us, whereas the present reality is actuality and potentiality.

Labor is a human capacity and its realization; it differs from other natural power in that it is a mediate relation which is itself worked upon by the human kind to its own ends. These ends are human ends, for there are no other natural ends than these. Our labor is the medium and object on which we work; it is thus the self as medium and object of the human kind.

The capacity of the human kind to meet its wants by its labors is made actual in society in various ways. It is a substantive relation which is made concrete, concrete wants thus being met by concrete labors, the substance having a variety of forms. The forms of the substantive relations are indispensible, for the substance either has a given form, whereby it is realized, or else it remains an abstraction, existing only in the realms of possibility. The capacity of the human kind to meet its wants is the potentiality which is developed by its labors, and is the substance of labor, varying as the relation of labor to the material order and in human society varies. The labor capacity is a social substance which remains a potentiality until it is combined with a given form, whereby its potentiality is realized. It is realized in a particular way under given social circumstances; the form is variable in human society, for those social circumstances under which the potentiality of the labor substance is actualized are not everywhere the same. There is not one particular form of the labor substance, but many. The labor capacity as such is variable in human society, but it does not vary as the form varies. The labor capacity varies as the relations of the human kind to the natural order vary, which is a process of mediative relation and variation from the standpoint of the human order; the labor capacity varies as the relations of the human kind vary in the different human social wholes, which is a process of mediate and immediate relation and variation; the mediate relation in the latter case is both active and passive, the mediate relation in the former case is active and objective. Nature stands to the human kind in an interactive relation. In modern civil society the form of the labor substance, whereby its potentiality is actualized, is an expression of a social relation which is external to the laboring human beings. We internalize the expression, and its formality enters into the social substance of the human being in a given social condition, and constitutes a part of that substance; it is the reified part in this case. The form of the labor capacity is the power of disposition over it, which is a right resting in the hands of those who have control over the social labor time.

Labor capacity is the combination of the potentialities of labor and their differentiation. However, the degree of availability and practical applicability of the potentialities is variable, hence labor capacity is not the same as the sum of those potentialities. The capacity of labor therefore is not one, for one skill may block out another, a third may be forgotten, and a fourth known to some, but not to others, who may have use for it. Labor capacity is a relation between the past and the present, wherein labor in the past transmits what has been acquired to the present, but labor in the present is not determined by these past relations alone; the relations of labor are determined by the reception, mastery and variation of past relations of labor as well. Labor capacity in a given social whole is both subjective and objective, being constituted of the objective relations of the past transmitted to present labor, and the subjective and objective relations of present labor to the process of reproduction of the human social whole. Labor capacity is mediate and concrete in relation to the past processes and products of labor; it is both mediate and immediate in relations of present labor processes, and both concrete and abstract in its relations. The labor capacity is both mediate and immediate in its present relations in that it is actively varied by labor, it is passive in its past relations as they bear upon the present, hence these past relations are concrete, objective and mediate. Both present and past labor capacity has a present potentiality, for the past does not lose its potentiality by being past. That potentiality is inactive without the intermediation of living labor in the present. Having retained its old capacity, past labor is both abstract and concrete, practical and theoretical.

Labor capacity is not a product but a process, which is measured by a rate of production and of productivity, or rate of a rate. It is not a result but a relation. At the same time, it is a result of past potentialization of labor, for the productivity is determined by a skill and a means of organizing the skill, activating and realizing it. The skill, science, technics, art are results of past labor, concretized in the present, where they are received, varied, and further developed. Being past and hence passive potentialities, the capacities of labor have not lost their abstract and theoretical content. They do not enter into the present substance of labor, however, until activated and actualized by present living labor. Labor capacity is therefore a rate and a rate of a rate, which is measured by ration and proportion, and by differential and integral calculus. It is the combination of past and present labor, the past being the labor process which has been mastered and internalized, the present being the practice and theory of the labor process as they have been taken over and varied by living labor.

The value expression is the measure of the product of labor, which is determined by the labor capacity in relation to the past and the present. The relation of labor in the present to the past is actual and potential, being both abstract and concrete, and variable. The relation of present living labor to the past being in actuality concrete is therefore constant, the variation in this relation being introduced mediately, by means of the variation in the potentiality of the past in relation to the present. The given labor capacity is a limit which is not reached by the labor process, but is only approached. It is the activation of potentialities, past and present, in changing combinations, immediately and mediately, and thereby the activation of the past actuality and reality of the concrete product of labor, which is passive in its relation to the activity of living labor. The capacity of labor in this relation is potential alone, the activity of living labor in the present is the sole means of actualization of its capacity and the sole means of activating the past product in its concrete form.

It is not the labor process but the labor capacity that is learned, appropriated, mastered, varied, reorganized, and reshaped under new conditions by living labor in the present. The labor process is the combination of the old capacity with the present capacity, which is taken over, varied and thus changed by living labor. The value form is the expression of the amount of labor which is expended and thus realized in social production; the amount of labor is measured in units of labor time, in hours, days or years. The expression of the amount of labor time which is expended in this way is a conjunction of past and present labor, the capacity thereof and its actualization. The process of production and of reproduction are in this case the same; it is the reproduction of the given social whole that is at issue. Past labor is both the concrete product thereof which is activated by present living labor and past labor capacity which is borne upon the present and there made actual and real. The value expression is therefore the value form, which is the product of past labor form as it is realized and made actual by the present living labor in the combination of form and substance. The past labor form is the concretization of past labor substance, and is thus the means whereby present living labor reaches back to what was acquired in the past, stored up there and made available to the present activity of labor. The past is in its appearance the form of memory that is available to the senses and hands, and is combined with the mental processes of consciousness, understanding, and reason. The past made concrete is the product of past labor, as it is produced and reproduced, applied and consumed in the process of social reproduction. It is only by means of its concretization that the past is stored and made available to the senses in the present, its potentiality being made actual in this way. The past is at the same time realized in the present abstractly by means of mental construction, memory, reorganization of the past in relation to the past and present; and the past is realized and made actual by the combination of the abstract and concrete processes in time. The abstract process of labor is both mediate and immediate, the concrete process is mediate alone. Labor capacity is the abstract side of the labor process, which is incompletely realized in the process of social reproduction.

The human reproductive process is variational. The unit of variation in the labor process has been the social group, whose industries are identified by locality, from the Upper Palaeolithic times and on. The variations in this process are shown both in location and over time. We infer that critical intelligence is part of the variational process, whereby the traditional workmanship varies from group to group and from generation to generation. The process is slow at first, and is accelerated in recent centuries; it is the same critical process throughout.

Labor power has been represented as a natural force by analogy to a waterfall and to the hydro-electric power which it generates. This is an illuminating analogy, but no more than that, for labor power differs fundamentally from the natural force and the power it generates. Labor power has this in common with the hydro-electric power, that both are generated by the human kind. Labor power has several aspects, which we will consider in turn. It is the power of labor to transform our material surroundings, for instance, in the case of the waterfall by means of which we generate electric power; it is the power of labor to transform our selves. By introjecting instruments of various kinds, from cudgels and knives, to electric turbines and generators, into our relations to our surroundings, we create a medium and a mediate relation through which we act on the surroundings and on our selves. We transform ourselves into a medium of plans and actions, and potentiate ourselves and our labor powers.

Labor in its form and substance is the human capacity to meet its wants, to sustain and reproduce itself. That capacity is conditioned by particular social relations, and is thus determined in a specific and not a general way. The human kind has a relation to the natural order that is asymmetrical, being continuous and discontinuous with the latter, whereas the relations of the natural order are continuous with those of the human kind. For the latter is a part of the natural order, and interacts with it, as a natural force in interrelation with other natural forces. The human kind has a burden which is placed on this process of interaction with nature, for whereas the relation of nature is direct and therewith also the relation of the human kind, the human kind is a variant of natural processes, and in this variant, the relation of the human kind to nature is not direct but mediate. The human kind reproduces itself through a medium upon which it labors and develops the medium which it acts upon in interaction with the material order. It is not nature as such which is the object of human interaction but the material order, the orderly in nature which is concretely worked upon, transformed, and abstractly constructed by the human kind. The human order is the mediate development out of this relation of and to the material order. Both orders are relational in their substance, the human order having a multiplicity of forms which are mediately related to the human substance.

The control by social labor over the labor time and capacity thereof is formally expressed in the relations of modern civil society. The control over labor time and capacity is given juridical expression throughout the history of civil society, ancient and modern alike, as labor power, which is the right of disposition over the time and capacity of living labor in society. We will consider this topic within the framework of European history. The control by right over labor time and capacity rested predominantly with the slave owners in the ancient history of Europe, and with the feudal lords in medieval European history; this formal labor power then accrued to the class of social labor in the history of modern civil society, as the concrete condition of its equality *de jure* and its freedom *pro forma*, both conditions being necessary for acknowledgment of the validity of contracts in that society. The labor power stands in opposition to labor capacity as a formal to a substantial relation. The formal labor power is a necessary relation within civil society, in the relations of contract, wage labor, exchange and commodity form, and in the social condition of commutative justice and right. Labor capacity arches over these relations; it extends over the expression of these relations as distributive reciprocity, as opposed to equal reciprocity, and of distributive justice and right, as opposed to commutative justice and right.

The relations of labor capacity in this sense stand in opposition to those of labor power as substance to form; the substance has a wider set of historical and theoretical relations than those of the form. The labor quantum in this case is applied without difference to both; in this case, the quantitative relation is not opposed to the qualitative relation, whereas the formal and substantial moments are opposed to one another in their abstract expression. To overcome this opposition calls for the reorganization of human society.

Labor power has both formal and substantial relations, the formal relations being abstract, the substantial abstract and concrete.

The abstract expression of labor power is a system of rights to which obligations are opposed. The abstract expression, labor power, is the actually existent and realized potentiality of labor as abstraction. The abstraction, labor, has two expressions, as an equivalence between different forms or as an equality of different distributions of the same form of concrete labor on the one hand, and on the other as a system of rights and obligations. These abstractions come together in civil society; they do not have a necessary combination therefore, only a contingent one, that is historically limited, and in this sense determined, for they come together in no other human historical conditions than these. It is not necessary to speak of social labor in this case, for if it is abstract in form, and thus separated from its concretion in relation to use in meeting wants and needs, then it is socialized and it is already social labor. The abstraction is universally abstract in the first expression, for it participates in the universally human capacity of abstraction, which is potentially self-diremptive and separable together with subjective alienation from its concretion.

The abstraction of labor power is a set of opposed rights and obligations and this abstraction differs from the abstract expression of labor relative to the value substance in the process of reproduction of the human order. The abstraction of labor power is limited to the exchange process of civil society, in which relation of equal or equivalent reciprocation is given objective expression as quantifiable and quantified rights and obligations. These rights and obligations are quantifiable for they have been made concrete and objectified. They are objectifiable because man stands to the matter that has been alienated from the natural order, and appropriated and transformed in the human order in a mediate relation, at once objective and subjective. They are concrete in relation to human wants, needs and desires.

Relations of labor are variable historically and systematically; formally, labor is voluntary and involuntary, associative, bound and free. These relations are not fixed but variable relative to the conditions in history of a particular social whole. The mediate and immediate relations of labor are not absolute but relative to one another, and are variable, and so are their abstract and concrete relations.

The living labor time and skill is given an abstract expression, as exchange value, and is sold as a commodity in the production process in society. The society in question is not the whole of human society, but a historically determinate form of the society; it is not class divided society in general but a determinate historical form of class divided society, in which the market, exchange and surplus value and the commodity relation of social labor come to predominance historically. In the current condition of social labor it has achieved the power over its own time and productive capacity, being able to sell these as commodities. The relations of production and exchange are social relations; the relation of social labor to its own time and skill is a juridical power expressed as a right. It is labor power, owned as a property by social labor in the society in which the formation dominates our relations of economy and society.

The right of disposition over labor time is a form in civil society whereby the labor capacity and the social substance are controlled. Labor power in the case of unfree labor rests in the hands of the master of the unfree labor, whether that unfree labor be formally communal, collective, slave or servile. This was the case in the history of ancient civil society, in the conditions of the antique and feudal modes of production. Labor in this condition was unfree both in form and in substance, but the relations of its unfreedom therein were not in all cases the same.

In ancient Asia the relations of labor were social in substance, but communal in form. The social substance of the labor relations was determined by the exchange process on the one hand, and by the production of an unremunerated surplus, which was alienated from those who produced it. The social substance is thereby determined as a relation which is at once social and antisocial, and this relation is further developed as a determinant relation throughout the history of civil society. Labor in ancient Asia was formally under the control of the village community and of the state, which was the village community magnified; labor was in substance determined by the opposition between the communal form and the social substance, hence it was unfree in its substance. In the servile condition of labor in classical antiquity, the slaves were unfree both in form and substance. The difference between the conditions of formal unfreedom in ancient Asia and in ancient classical times lies in this, that the communal labor in the former was implicitly unfree, the slave labor in the latter was explicitly unfree.

The right of disposition over wage labor rests in the hands of wage labor itself. This is the predominant condition of labor in modern civil society, and signifies that wage labor is *pro forma* free. The power over the labor time, as a right of disposition over it, rests with social labor itself. That right is in general a formal expression of civil social relation, and is brought out as a power over the labor time and capacity, varying accordingly as that power rests in the hands of the community, the slave owners, the feudal lords, or of labor as such. The form of the labor relation varied in the history of unfree labor, the substance of the unfreedom underwent a different historical course in the different times and places during the ancient history of civil society.

The formal right of disposition over labor time and capacity rests in the hands of wage labor in modern civil society, and this labor is therefore *pro forma* freed by its ownership of that power. The labor power is the juridical expression of a social capacity in a given form to produce socially useful goods, services, objects. The capacity is bought and sold in units of labor time, in which it is presupposed that the time is socially determined, having certain skills, arts, capacities which constitute its substance, being contained in it, or associated with it. The power over labor is the same in the various historical conditions of civil society, being the right of disposition over labor time; that right is differentially assigned in society, resting here in the hands of the workers themselves, there in the hands of others who are the masters over the workers. In the first case the workers are *pro forma* free, in the second they are *pro forma* bound. In either case those who labor, work, in civil society are bound in their substance, for there is no way to gain the means of subsistence other than by labor, but these means are not owned by labor in civil society; they are owned by another.

Labor power is in one sense therefore the form of the labor capacity, being the right of disposition over labor time. This form is variable in the history of society, the relation between form and substance being variable. The labor power is the externality of the reproductive capacity of social labor, which is a self-relation and a self-development thereof. Both form and substance enter into the process of social reproduction, but the form is not sold, the substance is. The substance, labor time and capacity, is given the form of a commodity; labor power is not, but is instead a juridical right of disposition over the labor time and capacity; and this right is inalienable, given that social labor as wage labor is *pro forma* free. In its internal relation, wage relation is bound, for it is required to sell its substance for its sustenance. Labor power and labor capacity together, as formal right and substantive process constitute the means of social reproduction of the human kind in the civil condition. In this way it is implied that the relations of capacity and power over labor in society are separate, their ligature being an external relation of the two sides to one another. The capacity of labor is the relation of labor to nature and in society; it is a formal and substantial relation, a potentiality which is realized and made actual in the process of human reproduction. Labor power as a formal right of disposition over the social labor time and capacity, rests in the hands of wage labor in modern society. The substantive power to dispose over that time and capacity rests in the hands of another class in civil society, which has the right of disposition over the means of production, whether by private or public control over it.

Labor power in modern society has the form of wage labor, which sells its substance against a livelihood; the substantive process of labor, or its time and quality, and the means of subsistence are commodities, the form is not. The substance of labor is thus exchanged, the form thereof is not, in the mutual, nonreciprocal process between wage labor and capital. The substance of labor and the substance of labor power being the same, the term power in this relation is superfluous; the term, power, in the formality of the process between wage labor and capital is not. The term labor power in its substantial moment has been introduced in order to distinguish between the natural force and the human power.

By transforming the waterfall into a hydro-electric power source, we change the shape of the landscape, and out of the natural materials, produce hydroelectric power; the labor power of the human kind is then distinguished from the natural force of the waterfall. The labor power is a human power with a separable and separately modifiable form and substance, as we have seen. The distinction between the natural force of matter and the human power has been introduced in another way, by making the distinction between the praxis and human poiesis, or between a direct and a mediate process. Wage labor sells its time and quality against a wage which it then exchanges against the practical means of its subsistence in a money economy. The quality is a potentiality which is realized in units of time, the working day or year. The temporal unit is both an abstract entity, a unit of reckoning and account, and a concrete element in the working space of the production process. The productive quality, time and capacity, of labor is expended in production, distribution and consumption and is therefore the same as the labor capacity of the human kind, by which is meant its reproductive capacity; therefore the term, productive capacity can be taken only as an abstract unit of reckoning, in answer to the question, how many of these products in a given time have been produced? The answer is expressed as a rate. It is human space and time that is reckoned up, and it is only for convenience that we reckon up the labor by units of time alone. The space is the mediate, objective and concrete product of the expenditure of the labor capacity. Time and space are in this case considered as abstractions, and dealt with separately from one another, and from the laborer. The quality of labor is determined by the amount of time spent in its preparation, training and education, and is brought out in the expression of the amount of skill thereof. The quality of the labor is realized in its relation to the past objectified labor, which is the work tool in particular, and the means of production in general. The labor time is of different qualities, greater or lesser, depending on its capacity for production, distribution and consumption; in civil society we are accustomed to think of the quality as high or low, and the wage and salary scale accordingly as high or low.

The formal labor power is not sold or exchanged. but is retained; since the abolition of slavery in the 19th century, the sale of the right of disposition over labor time and quality has been forbidden by law in bourgeois society. First we consider what this is not: The right of disposition over the slave labor is retained by the slave owner; the product and the slave are then sold as commodities, but the slave owner does not sell his formal labor power; he does not, that is to say, sell his right of disposition over the time, quality and product of the slave mode of production, but sells only that which rests in this slave. The two sides, form and substance, are combined in a different way in the case of wage labor. The slave is formally unfree, wage labor formally free. Labor is neither free nor unfree in its substance, for we are bound to the matter of life in its concrete animal existence, clothing ourselves against the cold, and cleansing our bodies against disease. This is the condition of our material life, for we are not free spirits. The value of freedom in this case is the expression not of our material condition, but of our human relation to it; we oppose that unfreedom by our mediative and objective powers, directed by our consciousness and the subjective will and desire. The escape from matter is neither of us nor for us, nor is it generally wanted or desired.

The objectification of the material order is constituted by distancing, alienation, mediate relation and transformation on the part of the human kind. Distancing and alienation of labor are practical and theoretical, its mediate relation is active and passive; its self-transformation is effected by abstract and concrete labor. The objective relation to nature is at the same time the self-relation of objectification, the human organs, hand, nervous system, sensory system, body, being objectified, mastered and developed. The means for the objectification, mastery and further development is the internalization of precept and example, making it one's own, varying it in and by adapting to changing conditions that which is learned. Learning is opposed to imitation, and the former enters into the process of human relation to nature. Learning is a social relation to other, to many others, to the natural order mediately and to self-immediately.

Human labor in the transformation of the physical body constitutes a self-relation that is objective to begin with, thereupon it is made into a subjective relation. The subjective relation is social, being the relation of self to social whole, self to other and to self. The self is cognized as a subject by the relation of others to self. The social field in its difference from other fields becomes the human social field; therein the self is constituted in the relation of the one to the field. The relation of the one and the field is that of the individual to the social whole. The field is in a mediate relation to the one, being mediated by the relation of many to one. The many human social fields are differentiated and mediately related to the human one, who thereupon enters into the self-relation by means of the general relation of one to the field, and to many fields.

The work process consists in producing a concrete good which meets a human want. By meeting the want we do not cancel it forever, but postpone its exigency. The process of production, insofar as it is immediately connected to that of consumption, is not quantified; the wants and needs that are met are quantified, but production that is immediately related to consumption admits of no intervening process whereby the amount of effort is measured. The quantity is measured in the wants and needs that are met. The immediacy of the satisfaction precludes any measurement or quantification other than the process of goods made available for the meeting of the wants and needs. The relation of wants and needs to meeting them is the process of production and consumption. This process, being human, is mediated by the relation of distribution in sharing and sharing out. The relation is social, and is thereupon reduced to the relation within the family. The unit of production and the unit of consumption are the same.

Form and Substance of Labor Power

The separation between form and substance in the history of the human order is the act which enables the development of formal relations quasi independently of the substantial. This development is self-limiting, for the form has but a restricted potentiality apart from the substance; it is not necessary to dwell on the artificiality of formal apart from substantial relations, which appear to have a life of their own; this gives the form a cultlike existence by observance of social relations without the substance, whereas the substantive foundation of the form continues to be active, albeit in a hidden way. The effect of the separation of the form from the substance in the process of self-objectification has been to make the human being into the object in the process of social production and reproduction, and to make the objective and self-objectifying relation of labor into a formal property relation. The separation of the formal from the substantive relation of social labor has led to the formal ownership by labor of its social substance and value substance; this process is developed over the entire history of civil society. The social substance is separated from the value substance, and opposition is generated between them in this circumstance, the opposition having the potentiality to be overcome, subject to the tendency to unification of social labor with the social whole, and with all of the human kind.

Wage labor is *pro forma* free, and alienates its living labor time and substantive power to other persons, getting in return the capacity, which it does not own, to reproduce itself. The living labor time and substantive power are thus transformed by the exchange into a capacitation of labor, having form and substance; only the substance of the human being is alienated in the process of earning a living. The formal and substantial labor power in the condition of unfree social labor is in the hands of the other person who is the owner of the formal property in the slave; this is a mediate relation of labor power. Wage labor stands in an immediate relation to its labor time and substantive power, which it alienates in the process of commodity production, and earning a wage and living, thus reproducing the social whole. The formal property is sold by social labor which is *pro forma* free in the condition of wage labor; before, in the condition of formally unfree labor, it was sold, the difference between the two being that the unfree labor itself does not alienate the living labor time, but is alienated by the slave owner. The formal power is the right of disposition over living labor in the case of social labor whether it is *pro forma* unfree or *pro forma* free; the labor power is a formal property in either case, in the hands of its owner whether that owner is another juridical person, or is wage labor as such. In either case it is the substantive property which is alienated; the formal property of labor power is inalienable as a right in modern bourgeois society.

Living labor and living labor time are the same. The labor space measured in reckoning the value of living labor is the concrescence of past time expended in the production process. The time in question is an expression of motion, which is in time and space; the labor is a formal and substantial relation of the humankind in the process of self-reproduction as a whole; it is abstract and concrete, its activity is practical and theoretical. Labor is the relation of human beings to one another in the transformation of determinate things into objects whereby the reproduction of the human kind is effected, as opposed to the biological reproduction of the species *homo sapiens*. Labor is in this sense the small scale teleological activity of the human kind. The labor is abstract as the expression of an ongoing process, and is concrete as the effort in producing a consumable good, which is useful in the process of human production under a given condition of society. As labor the effort is abstract and concrete, concretely it is work which is directed toward the good produced in a consumable form, which is the end product of the particular labor process. The labor is both mediate and immediate; to the material order it stands in a mediate relation, to the human order labor stands in a relation which is mediate and immediate.

Labor in this sense is the mediate relation to the natural order of the human kind, and the mediate and immediate relation thereof in the human order to the end of transforming both in the process of reproduction of the human kind. Labor is organized by its combination and division in given social wholes, the mediation, transformation, and organization by combination and division are both active and passive relations of labor. The form is separated from the substance by virtue of the mediative, active relation of the social whole in the organization of social labor; the value form is therewith separated from the value substance in the process of human social reproduction in civil society.

Labor power is formally a right of alienation by a juridical person over living labor time in its external relation; labor power has a mediate relation to the labor substance, or the human substance in its relation of labor in society. Living labor motion and time are constituted of formal and substantial properties, and labor power bears on the former, not the latter. The labor power bears on the human substance in its relation of social labor mediately by transforming it into a form, which then may be alienated as any other commodity in civil society. Living labor is in this condition constituted as form and as substance, the form being alienated by right of property; that form is the formal labor power. The substance of labor is the living labor time and quality, the qualifications and skills of the past that are borne upon the present. The past is in this sense a potential which is drawn upon in the present and made actual, the past potentiality being variable, the present actuality and potentiality variable internally, both in relation to itself and in relation to the past. The present time and quality of living labor as the substance of the human kind is transformed into a labor form which is alienated; the labor substance is subject to the formal right of alienation in virtue of the labor power, in two senses, the first of which is the labor power as the right of alienation of the formal property of labor time. The second sense of labor power in this case is that which is actually alienated by living wage labor in the sale of living labor time and quality.

Labor power is both concrete and abstract, for labor itself is both concrete and abstract. The abstraction of labor as such and as process is univocal, being the relation of mental and physical activity and interactivity of self-reproduction of the human kind. The concreteness of labor as such and as process is twofold, being the embodiment of labor in human being, and the embodiment thereof in the product of the labor, the two concretions being interactive in the self-reproductive process, as the action of the hand which is mediated by the tool in the process of transformation of self-and object in the relation of the human kind in the human and natural order. The labor power and labor itself are transformed by the relations of reproduction in civil society, the abstract relation being separated from the concrete. The abstract relation of labor in this condition is that of labor power, which is a twofold abstract relation, one formal, external and passive, the other substantial, internal and external, and active. Labor power is the power over labor as a right of use and using up, *jus utendi et abutendi*, of the labor time, capacity, and concrete substantive productive power of labor; the location of this right is variable in the history of civil society, being determined by the state of formal freedom and unfreedom, and of substantive freedom and unfreedom of social labor; the process of concrete productive power is that of self-reproduction of the human kind, not in general in this case, but under particular historical and determinate circumstances.

The formal abstraction of labor power as a right is opposed to the substantive concretion of labor power as productive quality, skill and capacity, the abstraction in this sense being an abstracting, tearing away, of the given amount of time, skill and capacity from the process of reproduction of the human kind by itself. This is the secondary abstraction of labor power in human society, and presupposes a primary abstraction of labor power, which is the abstract power of the human kind to plan the labor process. The conscious relation of labor is the objectification thereof in the process of self-reproduction, and is an abstract relation, which is variably joined to its concretion and separate from it. The relation of labor in its quality of abstract labor power pertains to the substantive property of labor to objectify itself, vary and repotentialize itself both in relation to the past, which is objectified in the human beings and in their instrumental assemblage, and in relation to the future, which is submitted to the planning of the act of transforming the natural and human orders. This primary abstraction of labor power is a self-diremptive relation of the human kind, whereby the practical process of mediation relative to both orders is separated from the theoretical, and is the accidental, historical condition whereby the second abstraction of labor power is brought forth.

The formal labor power is exploited by its owner, whether that owner be mediately another person in the case of unfree labor, or immediately the one person in the case of wage labor; the labor power in this relation is the formal property over the capacity for self-objectification of the human kind. This capacity is at once an active and a passive relation, the active relation being the formal power to alienate the labor power substance as a matter of right, and the substantive power to engage in the process of social reproduction; the passive relation in civil society is that of being exploited by another, and is mediate, the active relation is that of self-exploitation in the process of self-alienation, and is an immediate relation of production in civil society.

The conflicts between the substantive power of social reproduction of the human kind and the formal property over living labor power, time and quality, and between the present productive power and past objectified form of labor are historically determined, but are not necessarily given in the relations of the human kind to nature and in society. Such conflicts are developed out of the separation of the object from the subject and of the form from the substance in the history of the human kind. The self-objectifying subject, in view of the conflicts, is not the self-object, but is the object of another person's activity; in opposition to this state of affairs, the subject becomes the object in relation to the self; the self as an object is separated from the subject, which is falsely objectified. The self-objectifying subject, having been transformed into the object as unfree labor, becomes the self-object which alienates living labor time and substantive labor power to another in its capacity as free labor; this labor is free *pro forma* but in its substance unfree, for it is an object in relation to itself. The separation and opposition which is developed through the separation between the form of self-objectification and its substance and between the substantive property of social reproduction and the formal property of the same is historically determined, not of necessity. These conflicts, diremptions and oppositions determine the condition of the human kind in civil society, which is free *pro forma* and unfree in its substance; the human kind then stands in a formal relation, which is separated from the substantive relation to itself.

In a positive sense the right of labor to sell its time and capacity, the substance of its labor power, to another person in exchange for the means of subsistence is a formal process in which we are empowered to alienate parts of our human substance. This alienation is made in view of an equal return in the exchange relation, but without due and equal return in the exploitative process. The positive right is a formality of labor power. Negatively, wage labor gains two rights; one, it cannot be deprived of its formal labor power, which is the right of disposition over its substantive labor power; wage labor alone has the right to sell its time and skills. Two, no one can rightly or legally take away the entire substantive labor power; wage labor can sell only parts and not the whole of its time and skills in one act. The two negative rights bear in the one case on a formal, in the other on a substantial labor power. The negative formal power has a qualitative expression, the negative substantial power of labor a quantitative one.

The relations of human labor in the process of transforming the material order are variable in their productive quality, which is subject to internal development in the process of self-objectification. Such objectification is developed in respect of the productive power of labor, which is the system of reference to the relation in social reproduction of the substantive labor power. The productive power comes into conflict with the formal property, the substantive labor power comes into conflict with the formal labor power in civil society. The productive power of labor is a substantive relation, which is developed both abstractly and concretely as the capacity for self-objectification of the human kind in the mediate relation to the natural order. The capacity for self-objectification is developed mediately in the human order by the organization of the given social whole, whether unitary or diremptive, whether complex or simple, combined and divided, free or unfree; the capacity for self-objectification is developed immediately in the relations whereby skills are transmitted, varied, and variably exploited in the process of social reproduction; the capacity for self-objectification is developed in the process of mediate and immediate organization and transmission of the substantive power of labor by being differentially internally, practically and theoretically varied, and variously exploited and applied.

The human kind relates by its labor to the material order, whereby matter and the human kind are transformed, but not in the same way. By transforming the natural material, the human kind constitutes, transforms and reproduces itself. The process of human reproduction is that of production and consumption of the materials which are shaped and transformed by labor in a durative process of potentialization, actualization, repotentialization and reactualization by labor in the present of past products. This relation between past and present labor is the means of self-reproduction of the human kind, whereby that which is produced is consumed, reproduced and varied in its reproduction.

The instruments are the mediate and objectified form of human labor which is reproduced and consumed in its substance.

The unit of reproduction of the human kind is non-differentiated in its form and substance, and the unit of biological and of human reproduction are without difference with respect to one another. This is variously expressed in the family, band, clan, tribe, lineage, in its units of bilateral, unilateral, ambilateral descent. In this archaic process of human reproduction, the unit of production closely coincides with the unit of consumption; the relations between production and consumption in this condition are those of distribution by sharing, sharing out, by attribution and reciprocation without accounting for return. The distribution is made by substantive and particular right which is recognized and acknowledged through membership in the given social group, and this right is articulated with a substantive and general obligation of reciprocative contribution by those participating in the reproductive process. The given group constitutes a social whole which is self-diremptive in relations to the human others. The right of participation in the process of reproduction, production, distribution, and consumption of the given social whole is an informal, particular right, in that it is established by mutual recognition and acknowledgment, objective and subjective, of membership in the whole; it is informal and particular in that it is not established by an accounting of the labors by the individual in social reproduction; it is informal, moreover, in that it is established implicitly, by tradition, and not by explicit legislation. It is thus an immediate right of use and consumption which is joined to a general and mediate obligation to contribute the labor and product to the social whole.

The things of the material order are transformed into objects of the human order by our labors in production, consumption and distribution.

The relation of production and consumption is transformed from informal sharing, sharing out and distribution into a formally equal and proportionate reciprocation by development of the relation of exchange. Equal and proportionate reciprocation in exchange is constituted by combining the moment of archaic symbolic exchange with that of measurement of the amount of labor time expended in the process of social reproduction. The unit of production is now separated from the unit of consumption, but the separation is a relation which is internal to the social whole which comprises the producing and consuming unities.

Between these unities there is a mediate relation of equal reciprocity in exchange; the process of self-diremption is not that of the producing or consuming unit but that of the given social whole in which the exchange process takes place. Social labor is at the same time increasingly combined, separated and specialized in the process of reproduction.

A third diremption is developed in the process of intermediation between production and consumption by equal reciprocity in exchange, which bears upon the relation of labor in production to its product. (See Appendix II.)

The process of reproduction in the archaic primitive condition is disrupted by the relations of exchange, whereby the product is dirempted from the producers and the producers are self-dirempted from the product in exchanging it against another. The relation of self-diremption between producer and product is an internal one; externally, the producers alienate the product of their labor to another. The rights and obligations of equal reciprocation in exchange constitute a system which is formal, general, mediate, and is summed up generally in the principle of commutative justice, and particularly in the formal right and obligation of contract, of civil society.

The diremption enters abstractly into the self-relation of the human kind;

concretely it is the process of separation and distancing of the human kind from the other natural orders, the division of the unit of production from the unit of consumption in the human order, and the alienation of the product from the producers reciprocally, whether by immediate or mediate equalization; the consumer in both cases is the producer; the immediate equalization is a process between the two producing units, which are consumers, whereby no distinction is made between like and unlike products exchanged. Thus, exchanger *A* provided a bushel of wheat yesterday, to exchanger *B*, which is returned in like kind and equal amount today; or the same bushel is exchanged against a basket, or a healer's service. The exchange of like products in like amounts at the same time and place appears to be what it is, to wit, a process of symbolic exchange, for there is no difference between the wants, needs and functions fulfilled between the exchangers. Therefore there is no substantive difference in the exchange, which has only a formal meaning, and a symbolic communication is then to be explored.

System of Labor Power and Capacity in Outline
Labor capacity is the expression of the quantity and quality of labor, hence is the expression of the labor substance in this respect.

Labor quantity, time and therewith working conditions, having reference to external conditions of safety and internal conditions of health, are the subject matter of negotiations in the sale and purchase of labor time in social reproduction.

Labor power is expressed in the law of economic relations, pertaining to the productivity of labor. Labor power in the formal sense is expressed in the juridical relation of labor in the process of social reproduction and production.

Labor power in the formal sense is a civil right, or a right of persons in civil society to dispose of an object, good, human capacity; in this case we do not distinguish between a civil and a juridical right; the civil right has the juridical right or formal power of disposition of its capacity as its expression. The civil right in question cannot be alienated by a citizen of modern bourgeois and civil society to anyone else, nor can that right be alienated from wage labor. Only the labor time and capacity, the substance of the power of wage labor, is alienable. The alienation in this case is juridical right of contract, explicit or implicit.

Labor power is a social power, having a form and a substance. In its form, the power is the right of disposition by those who have a juridical power in civil society over the labor time and capacity of labor in the process of social reproduction of the human kind. The formal power of labor to contract for the sale and purchase of the time and capacity in the process of social production and reproduction is expressed as objective value in general, and as exchange value of labor in modern civil and bourgeois society. This is a formal right of wage and salaried labor as a juridical person in this condition. The substance of the labor power is none other than the labor time and capacity to reproduce the social whole; the control over this substantive power rests with the dominant or ruling political power in society.

Wage labor as a social class has the formal power, which is its civil right, to sell its labor time and capacity, or labor quantity and quality in its substance against the means of subsistence. Wage labor cannot be deprived nor can it deprive itself by right or by law of the power to sell the formal labor power, or to make over under any circumstance to any other person the right to sell and buy the labor time and capacity, in modern bourgeois society. Thus wage labor cannot divest itself of its freedom *pro forma*, or its right as a juridical person over its substantive labor power.

The productive force of labor is the productive power of society. The productive force is both abstract and concrete. The abstract productive force is productivity, which is a rate at which work is carried on, at which labor is materialized and concretized in the product thereof; it is expressed as so many products, such as needles per hour.

Increased productive power or productivity is expressed in abstracto as an augmentation of the number of products in the given time period by the same quantity of laborers. There is an increase in the productive force but not an increase of the labor qualifications; in fact the increase in productivity is often an expression of the simplification of the labor tasks, requiring less training, less qualification, etc.

The concrete productive force is the productive power of social labor. This is a substantive force which is formalized in the production relations of wage labor in modern society. The concrete productive force is measured by the abstract force, and not conversely.

Labor and the Periodization of Human History

Primitive and Civil Society

Human history, as a matter of convenience for our mental grasp, since it is too great to be comprehended as a whole, is divided into periods; these periods are schemata, and as such are constructions, which are objective and subjective in their constitution. Attempts at periodization of human history, to the extent that they are objective, have the relations and organization, and changes in the relations and organization of social labor, at their basis. The relations of social labor are those of the human kind to the material order, whereby matter is transformed in the meeting of human wants; by the transformations of matter and the meeting of our wants the human kind reproduces itself in a human way; the reproduction process is variable according to the relations, internal and external, of the different human social wholes. By the organization of social labor is meant its combination and division. The relation of the human kind to the material order is mediated by the various traditions of technics, arts, crafts, skills and their invention and innovation; these relations constitute a material interaction with the natural order, and a material and immaterial interaction between stability and change, between tradition and innovation in the economic formation of society, and in the processes between the different economic social formations. Organization and reorganization of the relations of social labor in the reproduction of the human kind are another immaterial process in this formation.

Human history in its objective determination is divided into two major periods, of primitive and of civil society; the transition from the one to the other is not a period as such. The connection between them is the process of transforming the primitive communal into the social labor. The history is recorded as a matter of convenience in terms of the divisions of civil society into political segments, from the times of the Egyptian, Chinese or Roman empires to the modern nation states. The economic formations of these various political unities constitute social wholes which correspond in an imprecise way to political divisions of civil society in ancient and modern times. The relations of these economic formations are the determinants of the processes of stability and change in the histories of the social wholes and the political entities established therein. The relations of labor, communal and social, productive and exploited, mediate and immediate, private and public, and the distribution of the labor product, whether by reciprocity, alienation by force, or by exchange and contract for its purchase and sale are the objective determinants of the units of our observation in the delineation of the historical record, which are usually the political entities already referred to, and of the transitions from one period to the next, in the processes whereby these entities are constituted and go under.

Human relations throughout the history of the archaic condition are social; society in this condition, however, is the communal unity, consanguineal and vicinal.

The relations of labor are throughout human history social, being brought forth in the form of communal labor under archaic conditions; these relations, which in their substance are the means whereby the given social whole is maintained and reproduced, have the form of relations of kin (family, sib, clan, gens, lineage) and of neighbors (band, group, village) or of their conjunction (kin-village, etc.). The relations of labor in the archaic primitive condition are cooperative, but the extent and variety of cooperation by combination and division of labor and specialization of technics in production are relatively low by comparison with the extent and variety in modern bourgeois society. The relations of labor in modern civil society are formally free, in ancient civil society formally unfree, and in both conditions they were and are in their substance bound. The formal freedom of labor in modern society is socially determined, by the relation of wage labor, by the relation of equality *pro forma*, universality of law, by the public relation of citizenship, by contractual relations of rights and obligations. The substantive relation of unfreedom of social labor in civil society, ancient and modern alike, is determined mediately by relations of society to external nature through its labors, mediatively by the relations of production, of the concrete agencies of the state and of civil society, and is determined immediately by the relations to one another of the social classes. The relations of labor are not those of individuals, but are constituted of and determined by the formal and substantive relations, in their historical variation, of the given social whole within the human order, and thereby to the material order.

The human individual is the product of the relations to one another of the human kind and of the relations of the human kind to the material order. Therefore the human kind in its social and natural relations is the starting point, both as a systematic process and as a historical course, in the analysis of the relations and activities of labor. The human kind, however, is an abstraction, the mediative relations in the human and natural orders are concretely realized in a historically determinate social whole; this realization is at once abstract, and within the numerous social wholes the potentiality of unity is abstractly set forth. The social wholes bear names; they are the primitive bands, clans, village communities, tribes and nations, on the one side, and the states and empires of civil society, ancient and modern, on the other. The processes of labor are concretely carried out, transmitted, varied, and maintained by the combination and division of labor, in which the individual human being is but a dependent and subordinate part. The individual in this process is the concrete and objective means whereby the instrumental relations of the human kind in the process of its self-reproduction are developed. The human kind, as the abstraction, relates to the individual human being abstractly and concretely by the interaction of the given social whole with the human kind and with the individual human being. The interactive process is practical and theoretical, and both of these as activity and passivity; this process is internalized by the individual human beings in their combination and interrelation. The isolated individual as the starting point in the relations of labor, or as the starting point with reference to those relations, is a fantasy on the one hand and a reification of the human kind on the other. As a fantastic device it is the representation of the human as superhuman, as a reification it is the representation of the human as infrahuman.

Labor in the primitive social condition is communal in its organization, combination and division; there is little difference in this condition between mediate and immediate labor, between individual, communal and social labor, between objective and subjective labor, or between labor form and substance. Labor in the primitive condition is communal in that the means of production, such as the territories of gathering wild plants or larvae of insects, hunting grounds and fishing banks, are collectively controlled. It is a primitive work process in that food, clothing and housing materials are produced by gathering, hunting and fishing, in the main; and it is a primitive process of social reproduction in that the unit of production and the unit of consumption tend to coincide. The primitive village community produces all, or nearly all, that it consumes, and all who are able take part in this process. Thus, social production and consumption in the reproduction process are in an immediate relation to one another, in an immediate relation between the producers and their product, and in an immediate relation between concrete work and the product consumed. The transformation of primitive society is brought about by the generation of a mediate relation between the concrete labor and the product, on the one side, and between the process of production and consumption on the other. The producers then alienate their product to one who has not produced it, and receive in exchange the product of the other. The unit of production is not the same as the unit of consumption, but imports a part of what it consumes, and produces another part. The mediation between the producers is the exchange process between them, and this mediation enters into the relation between producer and product, being the condition for its alienation to another. The process of distribution, which was the relation of immediacy between production and consumption in the primitive condition, is made into the mediate relation of distribution by exchange.

By the disruption of the immediate and close relation between concrete labor and its product by the systematic development of the exchange relation, the ground is prepared for the alienation of the product in a bifurcate manner, to and by another, or with and without an equal or equivalent reciprocation in exchange. In the first case, a group of specialists in exchange, trade and commercial practices is developed in society, whereby the alienation to another is mediated; in the second case, an exploiting group is brought forth in society, which lives by the extraction and alienation of the product in the form of a surplus alienated by them without reciprocation in exchange.

The division of society into economic classes is effected by the process of alienation of the social product from its producers without equal or equivalent reciprocation in exchange. These classes are then joined by the systematic, durative and oppositive relation between them; their difference and juncture issue forth as one condition in their class formation, the systematization and duration of these relations is the other. The relations of the classes to one another is the substantive process in the formation of civil society; the formal condition therein is the unification of the society into a whole, the concentration of the social power into one hand, whereby the exploiting class is transformed into the ruling class in society, and the conforming reorganization of the institutions of juridical, political and ceremonial life. The substantive process is then formalized as civil society, or the society in which the state is formed. In this early stage of civil society, the class of specialists in commerce do not constitute a social class, but serve the interests of the ruling class, and therewith of the society as a whole. The societies of civil life are divided into urban centers and rural clusters, with the beginnings of market, commodity and manufacturing relations throughout. Labor in the early period of the history of civil society is communal in form, dispersed in the rural parts of the society, it is social in its substance, for it produces not only the means of its subsistence, but also a surplus which is alienated from it, by means of which the ruling class subsists. The social labor is unfree, being bound to the soil by traditional practices, and is unfree in its form, in this sense; it is unfree in its substantive relations, for it is bound to produce the social surplus whereby the ruling class is maintained. Labor in a servile condition is unfree in its form and substance, the substantive relations remaining as before, whereas the formal condition of unfreedom is now changed. The village labor in the earlier period of the history of civil society was bound to the community in concreto, and to the community abstractly magnified and represented as the state. The servile labor of the later periods of civil society, e.g., in ancient Greece, Rome and feudal Europe, was bound to the person of the slave owner, or to the soil.

Wage and salaried labor in bourgeois society is free *pro forma*; it is free to contract as an equal party with the employer; it is unfree in its substance, for it is obligated to produce and maintain itself and to produce a surplus for the maintenance of its rulers. The two products are respectively measured by the value and the surplus value of social labor; they represent the formal social and the formal antisocial constituents of the process of social labor. Labor which is *pro forma* free exchanges its time and skillful capacities against the means of subsistence and reproduction.

The class of specialists in commerce and urban manufacture does not constitute to begin with a social class, but in the period of liberation *pro forma* of social labor joins the ruling class and constitutes a new form thereof, in the process of generation of urban centers of production, and of commodity and capital formation and exchange. The means of production are then concentrated in private hands, in the cities in the societies in which capital reproduction is predominant.

Social labor, its form and substance, freedom and unfreedom, capital, commodity and social production, are defined generally, and not with respect to a given period; on the contrary, the periods are defined acccordingly as these relations come to predominance or disappear. The formal freedom and substantial unfreedom of social labor is a predominant and determinant condition of life in society in which capital is brought forth, but is not found only in the society in which capital predominates over all other social relations. The laws of value, exchange, and surplus are valid for all periods of civil society, just as the laws of labor, labor substance, exchange, and of objective and subjective value are valid for all conditions of human society and for no other; the conditions are variable in their existence and relative predominance, *in concreto*; the laws are variable otherwise, as abstract formulations. Commodities, wage labor and capital existed in ancient and modern periods of civil society, hence the laws of exchange value, surplus value and of value existed and exist, without restriction to modern society, bourgeois and capitalist.

The determination of the periodization of human history is made by the consideration of the relations of labor, whether communal or social, whether free or unfree, in form and substance. Thereby the formation of primitive society, the transition to civil society, the constitution thereof, and the condition of its dissolution are objectively determined. To these objective judgments, the subjective value judgments of progress and regress are then associated.

The historical limits of society and the limitation on science which is connected therewith do not prevent us from eliminating the ambiguous role that was assigned to nature in the production process, by the materialists of the 19th century. The relation of the human kind to the material order of nature is uninterrupted, but is not direct, being mediated by the process of self-objectification of labor in the present; by this process, labor activates itself, and the objectified and materialized relations in the past of the human kind as a whole. The objectified is the product of past labor which is then taken up as an instrument of labor; the instrument is abstract and immaterial, concrete, material and practical, either separately or in their combination. The objectification is externalized, the outcome of the inward and outward relation of mediation of the human kind in relation to itself and to the field of its activity; the self-objectification is carried through by an immediate inward process, and thereupon by an external relation to the objectified past. This process of self-objectification is the primary diremption of the human kind from the material order of nature. It is an active relation, concrete and abstract, which is at once a passive relation. The active factor is the potentiality that is made actual and real by the human kind, which is thereby brought into concrete existence; from which it follows that the natural order is dirempted implicitly and concretely by the process of human transformation of thing into object, whereupon the human kind dirempts itself from the material order, the diremption being the process of formation of the human kind. Neither in the system of matter nor in the human system is the process absolute, for the barrier between the two orders, while general is mobile both in its internal and external relations. The transformed field of nature is the medium, means and object of humanization; the internal nature by the genetic process has been formulated in the 20th century as the object of scientific research, and brought within the human ken, both in theory and in practice. The natural material is, from the standpoint of social labor the object of the human self-relation, for by objectification of a field within the natural order the human kind has within it made itself into the object of its own labors, whereby we reproduce ourselves by our relations to nature mediately and in human society both mediately and immediately. The natural material is therefore the dirempted and at once the alienated and necessary means of self-reproduction of the human kind by its labors. From this standpoint, the labor time and skill expended in social production is mediately natural, being the mediative relation of the humankind in the natural order, and is in this sense required for the purpose of social reproduction. From the standpoint of the humankind, however, that which is required for human social reproduction is not a material process, either immediately or mediately, but is the process of alienating from the material world the means for the maintenance of the human kind, transforming those means by objectifying them, and submitting them to human ends. That which is called the material interchange with nature is not an exchange relation, because the parties in the interchange process do not have the same relation from the standpoint of the human order. The relation of the human kind to the material order is alienative, self-diremptive, mediate, objective, reflexive, oppositive, complex and immediate, particular and limited. The relation of the material to the human order is direct, indirect, and far more complex than the theory of matter. The standpoint of social labor is potentially that of the human kind as a totality, hence the human interchange with material nature is the process of the human whole in the economy of reproduction of its kind. In the long run the human species will die out, but the records of the human kind will not die with our bodies. The interchange with material nature will have then been brought about by natural processes of stability and change, but the interchange will be other by virtue of the mediate and localized reorganization of the natural matter from the standpoint of the human kind. The process of interchange with material nature is not exchange in the trivial sense that exchange is the relation of equal or equivalent reciprocation, which is a localized relation, developed within a given epoch of human history; it is an interchange that is not reciprocal in the sense that the material and the human standpoints are not equatable, as we have seen. For if we return our deposed bodies to the ground, that is the end of us directly. Beyond this is a mediative process in opposition to which we bring forth our embryon atoms; this opposition is the diremptive and asymmetrical relation of the human kind to matter.

The opposition between the doctrines of struggle and attraction in civil society, modern and ancient, is projected onto the entirety of human and thereupon onto the entirety of natural history; it is an anthropocentric concept on the one hand and the error of taking the particular for the universal on the other; in the latter case it is an ethnocentric error of taking one cultural model to be valid for all cultures. Hegel thought that the opposition of the human parts of nature are universal oppositions of nature; he assumed what was to have been proven in this case.

In ancient civil society, the limitation placed on the human order was that of unfreedom, both formal and substantial, of social labor, hence the inequality, both formal and substantial, of the social whole. From the standpoint of modern civil society, the limitation placed on the human order is the contradiction between the formal freedom of social labor, and the formal equality in the social whole, on the one side, and the substantive unfreedom and inequality of the relations that obtain within the social whole. From the standpoint of ancient civil society, the relation of the part determines that of the whole for the reason that the part in question bears within itself the potentiality of becoming the whole. From the standpoint of modern civil society, the contradiction that runs through the whole determines the contradiction of all the parts, in that the organization of the whole is the determinant of the relations of labor in society in the modern condition. The reason for this is that the immediate determinant of the relations of ancient civil society was the relation of the substantively unfree social labor in the social whole, and its formally unfree condition. Therefore all were unfree, in the ancient civil society, both master and slave, for the unfreedom of the one determines the unfreedom *pro forma* of the other, the substantive inequality of the one determines the substantive inequality of the other. In modern civil society the movement of social labor to be free and equal has been realized *pro forma*, and the potentiality of the ancient slaves to that degree has been achieved. The mediate realization is the passivity of social labor in history, for the initiative in the formal expression of the equality of the social whole lies in the active relation of the social whole, the freedom *pro forma* of social labor being mediately the determinate thereof, or its mediated determinate. The reason for this is that the exchange relation which is developed in the history of civil society is made universal throughout the system of that society, whereby social labor has the right of free disposition over its time and capacity in production, or the power to dispose of its labor time and capacity as a commodity. This labor power is the universalization of the commodity relation that was first developed in ancient civil society in respect of past, dead and objectified labor as the object of exchange, and of the whole of social labor insofar as it was unfree. Aristotle in summing up the relation of economic exchange in ancient civil society made exchange dependent on the combination and division of labor in various segments, such as bakers, shoemakers, carpenters and physicians. These exchanged their goods and services in relations of equivalence. Aristotle did not ask how the system of equivalence in the exchange was achieved. (See *Value*, Appendix I.) The system of equivalence of the goods and services presupposes that there is difference and nexus between the labors of various kinds; these are social labors, which, together with their products, such as bread, shoes, chairs and healing services, are offered and taken in exchange. The combination and division of labor are the foundation for the exchange, and their theory accounts for the fact that an exchange will take place. The fact of the exchange is not the basis for the equivalence in exchange, for we then have to establish a fair exchange, and offer so many loaves of bread against a pair of shoes, a pair or more of shoes against a chair, so many loaves, or chairs or shoes against the cure for an ailment, and translate these goods and services into money; the circulation of money is as such a good, which is a service. The money as such is neither a good nor a service, but is a formal expression of the good in the process of circulation. Aristotle propounded the basis for exchange, not of fair exchange, by his theory of the combination and division of labor. The exchange is the form in which the distribution of goods and services takes place under given social conditions. The fairness of the exchange has a substantive element, which is expressed as the value of the exchange. This relation of form and substance is examined in *Value*, (below) in which fair exchange and just price are distinguished.

Living labor, in a theory of classical antiquity which was made explicit in Roman jurisprudence, was insofar as it was unfree treated as a commodity. The living commodity of labor in this case was bought and sold in the same way as its animate or inanimate product. Living labor was unfree both in form and substance in ancient Asia, in the traditional African kingdoms, in the Inca and Mexican empires, and in the periods of European slavery and serfdom. These are all summed up in the category of the pre-capitalist formations of civil society. In these periods, foreign labor, the clientele of the patron, indentured labor, apprenticed labor were all in the condition of unfreedom, formal and substantial; the forms were more variable than the substance of the bondage.

Unfree labor has no formal property over its labor power, by definition; this formal unfreedom is either customary, unspoken, and unwritten, or it is explicit in the word. In one sense, the bound labor has no substantive property in the labor power, for the product is sold by the dominant civil power, whether the priest, the prince, slave owner, feudal lord, or the like. In another sense, the bound labor has the common human labor power, which is thought, fantasy, reason, cognition, memory, and language, dexterity, cooperativeness, foresight. The civil power over the process and product of the labor determines whether the labor is unfree or formally free. Unfree labor has no formal property in the sense of dominion over the labor power; ownership as a right of use and consumption over labor power exists in all conditions of civil society, and holds regardless of whether social labor is bound or free, and regardless of whether the freedom or unfreedom is a formal or substantial condition. If social labor is unfree *pro forma* and in its substance then the property over the labor power rests in the hands of those who keep social labor in bondage; if social labor is free *pro forma* then it has the property *pro forma* over its labor power. Slavery is the expression of the separation of form from the substance of the human kind, the slave being a formal property of another person. The slave, however, has a substantive property which is twofold; the product of the labor power substance is appropriated by the master, formally and substantially, but only in the first sense mentioned; in the second sense, the slave does not surrender to the master the substantive labor power. Hence the property of the master in the product of the slave is the outcome of a formal appropriation. The formal appropriation as a right is alienable, the substantive power is in one sense alienable, and in another it is not. It is presupposed thereby that the human form is separated from the human substance. Manumission was a form of emancipation of the slave from the owner or the offspring from the paterfamilias in ancient Rome.

The slave produces goods which are measured in terms of value, exchange value and surplus value; the slave is an expression of value in the same sense as the product, but this bears only upon the property *pro forma* of the slave; in his substance the slave is not a property, for it is the formal property of the slave which is bought and sold. Social labor, whether free or unfree, has a formal relation to labor power which is alienable; the alienable in the labor power relation is the formal, external property thereof, or its attribute, in the sense of that which is socially attributed to it under given conditions of the history of civil society. The goods produced are objects which are wholly alienable in form and substance, the objects being in this case alienable in respect of their formal and substantial properties; their value is measured in terms of the value substance expended in their production. These objects are commodities. The slave is a commodity in another sense, for while slaves are commodities they are self-objectifying commodities, and in this respect have a substance which is separable from the form. The human substance is not alienable in the sense in which the human form is alienable, the form having value which is determined by the substance. The form is the property which is bought and sold, the substance is the substantial property which is inalienable.

The bound condition of human labor, which is the formal and substantial want of freedom and equality, was predominant throughout the ancient history of civil society, in the Asiatic, classical antique, and medieval feudal economic formations of society. The ancient bondage is replaced in the societies of the production of capital by the condition of formal freedom and equality, while the condition of substantial unfreedom continues to be the regimen of the human kind; the unfree state and the relation of substantial inequality continue in being in the present organization of civil society. These relations will only be abolished when the conditions of society civil and bourgeois as a whole are eliminated. The slave has a voice, which is a human quality, the slave and his master being capable of human communication, which is the common property of all, slaves and their masters alike; it is mediate communication, and is opposed to the communication between animals and between human beings and animals.

The slave is not a thing but a human being, who is treated as an instrument with a voice, instrument being a human product, the result of human relations in society, hence object and not thing. Reification in this case is a fallacious conception, for the human being as slave is not made into a thing, *res*, but into a human instrument. The Roman *instrumentum vocale* was the slave, the speaking instrument, which is not real, but is a construction. The real and actual is the blood, sinew and vocal ability of the living being. That being lives in a particular human society, by the relations in which one is made into a slave. The slave is not a natural but a human condition, which is a natural datum only by an abstract human construction; it is not a natural datum but a human fact. The opposition between abstract and concrete is a human mediation in the natural, concrete and thingly process. Aristotle mistook the concrete condition of slavery for an abstract and universal condition of parts of the human kind; he further mistook a mediate, concrete and abstract human production for a concrete natural doing of things. The slave is not a thing any more than the instrument is a thing, both having been transformed into object. The slave is unlike the instrument, being a living subject and object, who is capable of self-objectification, both actively and passively. The product of the self-objectifying process in the case of the slave is the opposite of the human, living process, however, for it is the fixation of the process of production whereby it is separated from the self-determination by the human subject, which enters anew into the process of reproduction of the human kind. The slave is a part of the process, but has his freedom and equality taken away formally and substantially, and does not reproduce the human relation.

There have been many kinds of slave conditions in human history; among those which have been most intensively studied have been the condition of unfree labor in ancient Rome and in the south of the United States before the Civil War. There is little in common between these slave conditions; yet in both of them the slave has a master, and has no freedom to move about, to change place of employment or residence, save by the master's decision. Both were subject to another's necessity. In Roman jurisprudence, the slave was held to be a thing, *res*, an instrument (with a voice). The master is subject to another necessity, being dependent on the slave for his livelihood.

Discussion of necessity, freedom and bondage in antiquity made the assumptions, that there were some human beings who were slaves by nature, or in contradiction, that we are free by nature, which is to say that we are born free. Slavery is in the latter case a state of captivity by an act of war, which is a public act, or by a private act of raiding; to sell oneself into slavery, bondage, clientage or predial servitude is another private act. Those who sell themselves into slavery may be driven by hunger to do so. It is presupposed in all these conditions that there is a public law recognizing the status of slavery and acknowledging ownership of the slave by another person. Those to whom the slaves have sold themselves may be public or private persons.

There is no necessity in the relations of things, no freedom, and no bondage. Freedom and its opposites, necessity on the one side, slavery or bondage on the other, are human inventions and constructions. We have not discovered these relations in the natural conditions, but have invented and constructed them out of our human and inhuman, social and antisocial relations to one another, for social exploitation of one human group or class by another. What is necessary, what free, what bound is a matter of human acts and judgment of these acts. No human being is a slave by nature, for we have no nature; we are what we are by virtue of our social relations, of one to another, and these are variable; nor are we free by nature, save in a subjective sense, in our inner world of will and desire.

The bondage of the slave is a human act, and that bondage is transformed into a state of formal liberty by another human act. This is not one act but many, bearing on the human formal relations and on human substantial relations in another way. The acts bearing on the formal liberation are historically many, whereby the ancient peasants in the Orient, Mexico and Africa, and the slaves of antiquity and of modern times, and the serfs of medieval Europe were freed. There are many other states of formal bondage beside these; in all cases mentioned, the transformation is the overcoming of our bondage as the meeting of our radical want and need. The history of the transformation is not single but multiple; we are bound both *pro forma* and substantively; we first overcome our bondage in the civil condition *pro forma*; the substance of liberty still remains the radical want of the humankind, without distinction as to its parts.

The slave in ancient Greece and Rome was a human being, a juridical person in a limited sense, with rights of possession but not of ownership or citizenship, and a work tool in yet another sense. The right over the labor time and skill of the slave in social production rested with the master; hence the slave could be sold as a commodity, just as the product of the slave's labor time and skill could be sold as a commodity. The product of the slave was in part good in the process of production and in part a consumer good; the slave was as a good in the production process, an instrument of labor, who is at once a human being by natural and human, social development. The language is a human social property of the human kind as a whole, in all conditions and circumstances. This property is internal to the human kind, which has appropriated, internalized, made into a mediate process, and developed the animal voice of direct, concrete and thingly communication. The human vocal property is abstractly one, concretely it is many. The Roman slave, as an alien, had first to gain the Roman tongue, receive the communication, which was voiced, then reproduce it.

The freedom of wage labor, which is the universal condition, *de jure*, in the history of modern society is determined by historical factors: 1. The transformation of the commodity exchange relation into a relation of exchange of living labor time and capacity as a commodity relation; labor time and capacity has its expression as exchange value, and is subject to contractual right and obligation. 2. The contradiction between equality *pro forma*, expressed in the right of contract, and the substantive inequality. Formal labor power, or the right of disposition over labor time and productive capacity, passes from the hands of the slave owner to the hands of social labor in modern civil society. These are relations of the social whole that determine the relations of social labor.

Distribution is a part of the process of distributive justice; it is a system of right without obligation. Aristotle saw that exchange and reciprocity go together, and hold civil society together, whereby we are bound in one society to one another. He saw that justice is related to inequality under this condition, for an underling does not strike his superior. His theory has a bearing on other social forms than the unequal and unfree social conditions of ancient civil society; it is also abstracted from the condition of capitalism; and out of the opposition between the classes of civil society in ancient and modern times we abstract the principle which binds together the present social condition, arching over the opposition between the system of private ownership of the means of production and the system of public ownership thereof. The system of right without obligation is the human right, whereby the opposition between right and obligation in the civil social condition is overcome. To make of the system of distributive reciprocation a human universal, however, is a utopian vision. The principle of distributive justice is opposed to the principle of commutative justice; according to the latter a right is opposed to an obligation systematically. The system of distributive right and justice is opposed to the principle, from each according to his labor; it is an individualist doctrine in which each individual is made into the center of the formulation; on the contrary it is the social unity and not the individual that is in the center of the formulation. The doctrine, to each according to his wants or needs is likewise an individualistic doctrine which is opposed to the social wants. The distributive principle that is common ground in the system of Aristotle and the theory of socialism calls for the reorganization of human society.

The human kind is in its substance unfree, for it is bound by its wants and needs to the material order of nature; only by our labors do we transform the matter in the process of meeting our wants, and there is no other way to do so. Unfree labor is doubly bound, therefore, as the human kind is bound, and as the labor is bound in its civil condition in society. The first bondage is the general, substantive bondage of the human kind, the second is the formal and substantial bondage of unfree labor in the various modes of production in civil society. In modern bourgeois society, which is a form of civil society, the formal and the substantial relations of labor are separated from one another. Labor in the bourgeois condition is *pro forma* free, but in substance is doubly bound, in view of the general human condition, and, as labor, is in substance bound in civil society in particular. Throughout the history of civil society, labor, whether unfree or free, does not work for itself, but works for another. In modern bourgeois society, labor is free to work in this place or that, or for this employer or that, but is bound to work for someone other than itself. There are few exceptions to this rule, which is in effect in the various systems of modern civil society.

Labor in the modern civil condition has been freed, and frees itself, of the *jus abutendi*, or the right of another person to use it up, to consume it entirely, or to abuse it in the work process. The right to abuse and use up labor in former times lay with the exploiting class, the sovereign power, the social classes of slave owners and feudal lords. Labor legislation in modern society decrees against being worked to death, or to the point of sickness by overwork. These are formal matters of the law which enter thereupon into the human social substance. They are in part undertaken on the initiative of labor and in part by representatives of the social whole.

Labor in Civil Society

Slaves have a property of speech in common with the slave master, which is turned to the interest of the master by the labor of the slaves. In the idealized picture of life in ancient Rome which is afforded by Theodor Mommsen, it was proposed that the master and slave worked side by side in the family economy. This was perhaps the case in the countryside, but less so in the city; their labor is another property common to them. The slave was granted a good which was particular to him; a part of the increase of the animals he tended was his, but not as a right of property over it; it was attributed to the slave by the master, and taken away by him; the attribution was a *peculium*, the animal, *pecus*, he retained, a possession and not a property. Varro, *De re rustica*, On rural matters, wrote of the legal action, *adimere servis peculium*, to take the slave's peculium away. The property as a juridical expression of an exclusive interest was a right of the Roman citizen, who was a freeman, having membership in a gens, a nomen and a cognomen. The legal action was instituted in view of the extension of the same right to the slave, and the acknowledgment of this right in Roman jurisprudence. The common property is divided in civil society.

Wage labor has the right to the labor time and capacity, and this right is a further extension of the property right. The labor of the wage earners is alienated from them only with their consent; thereby the relation between slave labor and wage labor is relativized in the history of civil society. The slave is bound formally and substantively, the free labor is bound in its substantive relation alone; free wage labor is unfree in its substance, for it is bound in its labor to the means of subsistence; we earn our bread by our labor in exchange for wages. The latter is a formal change in modern bourgeois society from the relation between the villagers in the Asiatic mode of production, and of servile labor in ancient and medieval Europe, who had an immediate relation between their labors and their means of subsistence. The bondage of the slave is the form of the human being as a thing; in its substance the slave relation in civil society is the consequence of the transformation of a human being into an instrument with a voice. The instrument is that which has been mediately transformed from a natural thing into a human object, the instrument, as it is applied in the process of human work and labor, having been dirempted from the natural field; the given amount of human work is contained and determined in the instrument. The instrument is first an object, which is the product of human activity, being given a determinate form in the process of human production. The instrument is in the human field, and contains the amount of human work applied in its mediate transformation and alienation from the natural field. The instrument has an activity and reactivity of a material body which, as a human product, is activated and applied to human ends by human work and labor; it becomes a means of production by these direct and mediate processes, which are respectively natural and human. The mediation is the active relation of the human kind conjoined in this case with the passive relation of the product. The slave is a contradiction, being an instrument that is alive and a human being, living labor transformed into an instrument of production. The contradiction of the instrument lies in the recognition and expression of the vocal capability of the enslaved human being. The voice of the slave is the common human property, the product of the slave labor is not the common human property, but the property of the master. The slave is not an inert instrument but the human living labor treated in the law as an instrument.

The treatment of the slave as an instrument is a relation which is inhuman abstractly and anti-social concretely. The relation of production is a social relation which is both formally and substantially contradicted by the slave relation, the humanity of the production relation being negated mediately thereby. The relation of bondage of the slave is actual and real; the product of the slave process of work and labor contains concretely the actual and real time and quality, knowledge and skill of the slave; abstractly it is its expression. The product is alienated from the slave and is sold and bought on the market by the master as a commodity. The subjective will to alienate to another the product of slave industry is that of the master, and presupposes the prior alienation of the product by the master from the slave. The product is in the form of a commodity, being subject to exchange and is exchanged, but not by its immediate producer. There is a second alienation, which is conducted for the profit of the master, and not that of the slave, the profit being the expression of the surplus value in concrete form. The slave relation is a construction that is both practical and theoretical; in practice the slave relation is real, producing objects of value in civil society, the value having an objective expression as exchange value. The human construction is expressed in the juridical form of property over the slave. The slave then becomes a commodity, but that slave commodity is not the commodity in the same sense as the commodity of the product of human labor, whether slave or not. Living labor, free or unfree is the means of mediate activation of the means of production. The means of production do not activate themselves in any immediate sense; the self-actor is a contradiction, for the self-activating machine does not exist; neither the automobile nor the cosmos is a self-activating machine. The slave is an object in which the objectified relations of production are embodied, the embodiment not as physical containment but as substantiation; the slave is the unfree social substance or the bound social relations in the form of a human being. The unfree human being is deprived of subjectivity; the will and desire in the relations of production, exchange, and the extraction of the surplus in the slave society, are the will and desire of the master. The slave apart from these constraints has a subjective and an objective life as any human being, one that is not envisaged in the slave relations of the society; the subjective life of the slave is recorded in the folklore and in the slave revolts, in which the will and consciousness of the slave are brought to social expression. The slave in the slave society is an object which is engaged in the process of social production, having a determined relation in the economic formation, in the organization of which he is taken to be a passivity. He is not passive in his subjective and objective relations, but is dealt with as a passive instrument that is activated on the master's command. This passivity is indifferently that of the domesticated animal or the machine. The activity of the slave in its subjectivity and objectivity belies the passive and objective expression of the slave relation in the juridical system. The human being is opposed doubly to the slave, as activity, passivity to passivity, and as subject, object to object. The relation to the human being as the object by the human subject alone, as opposed to the subject, object, on either side and the relation as passivity alone, as opposed to mediative activity, passivity, is that as to a slave. The two relations are summed up in the notion of reification, the treatment of a human being, the relations of the human sphere, or the ideas, as an object, as though a thing. The difference between object and thing is disregarded in the term reification, which is an error both in theory and in nomenclature. The error is formal on the one-side, substantial on the other. The formal error lies in the disregard of the mediate relation of human beings to one another, which is opposed to the thingly relation, the latter being direct or indirect, and in either case non-mediate.

The treatment of a human being as an unfree being is the reduction of the human being to a relation that is as though it were thingly; the relation is not so, it is unfree and in this sense wholly objective from the formal standpoint. Yet the relation "as though" a thing, when applied to a human being is a reification; the human being is treated as an object. The objective relation alone is here at issue; it is a reduction of the human being to an object, in the process called reification, as opposed to objectification. The process of objectification is not a reduction; objectification of the natural world, objectification of the human world and self-objectification of human being are, on the contrary, means of potentializing, or of heightening the potential, of the human order, and proceed together with subjectification of the human kind, whereby the human kind and the human being are made into the active, conscious historical subject, which is the whole of human society as agent, the organization of the social whole; the objective relation is the necessary completion of the social whole, together with the subject; the order in which the terms are introduced into the system is significant; the relation of the human kind to the material order is mediated by the self-objectifying process. Reification is opposed to objectification, for the human being undergoes a loss in the former process, and a heightening of the potential in the latter. Subjectification, apart from the objectifying process, is a construction of the fantasy; subjectivity apart from objectivity exists only in the realm of possibility, not of reality.

The whole of human society, of the human kind, of human history and of the human individual are a factum, a construction by the self-objectifying mediation of human activity, whereby human determinate beings are transformed into objects. The reification of the human being is not a subjective figment but a further objective construction out of this human activity. It is part of the human product which knows that it has lost a part of its humanity; the slave knows that he is not his own master, having lost his will and subjective life in its external form. Reification has formal, but no substantive reality. The reification can be potentialized; it is a lessening of labor's potential, without its opposite, the increased potentialization of the human kind, and of human being. The formal reality of the human social datum in general and of the human reification in particular is passive; this is the case with the state, and the juridical, political and religious systems, which have no substantive reality; they are abstractions, without the capacity of self-objectification. Yet they form a part of the human social whole, entering mediately into the process of self-objectification of the human kind by its activity of self-production and self-reproduction; these are real systems of human society which take part in the organization of the social whole in history, whereby the process of self-objectification has been effected by the human kind. The organization of social labor in modern bourgeois society has been the most complex and productive that has hitherto been developed in the history of human society, for labor in this society is *pro forma* free and has achieved an equal status with all other legal persons. It has done so by conversion of social labor into wage labor, selling its labor time and capacity as a free contractor having equal status in the law with those who buy them. Notwithstanding, unfreedom and reification are actual relations of human society in the civil condition, and an expression at the same time of the separation of form from substance in the process of self-constitution of the human kind. The substance of the self-constitution is the relation of social reproduction and production; the process of human reproduction is the active relation of self-diremption and self-mediation in relation to the material order on the one hand and to the means of production and reproduction on the other. The mediation is effected by the social organization of work and labor in society, by its organization, combination and division. The organization of production is carried through by the social formation of the economy, and therewith by the economic formation of the society in general, and by the working class in civil society in particular. In this organization of labor, the process of reproduction is determined by the organization of the society as a whole in its combination and division of the social relations; the division in this case is an oppositive one.

The human substance is the sum of these mediate and immediate relations of human beings to one another, and their mediate relations to all of nature; the sum is variably additive and cumulative; it is at the same time a defective composition of elements which have in part an adequate fitness relative to one another, and in part do not go well together. We have parts which are at peace and parts which are at war with one another. The conation of the human kind is not a smooth forward progress either in its achievements or in its process; we subjectively evaluate the processes as progress or regress; elsewhere in this work we have given some indices for an objective evaluation of our progress; these indices bear on some not all parts of the human order, kind and being. The progress moves backward and forward by discontinuous stages at uneven rates.

The cumulative processes of social labors are systematic, and in theory all are summed up. In practice and in history, on the contrary, all is not summed up; ground is lost and gained, and is as often willfully destroyed as constructed. Only in the material universe is entropy posited in an objective theory; the laws of energy are applied to the fields of culture and labor by analogy and metaphor, as good or bad poetry. The human kind is, in its labors, only in a minor degree efficient; the time and energy lost in class antagonisms, lockouts, strikes, slow-downs, strikebreaking and protests are then measured against their amount applied in social production. The energy applied in conspicuous consumption is wasted. In the 18th century, Bernard Mandeville and Adam Smith thought that the accumulation and expenditure of wealth were a spur to production; thus they sought to oppose the thesis of mercantilism, which held that whereas the accumulation by the individual should be unrestrained, its expenditure should be guided by the state. The evaluations on both sides, on the part of the mercantilists who sought to strengthen the state power, and on the part of Adam Smith, who despised it, were subjectively grounded, whether by the application of sumptuary laws or by removing the bridle of law from the rich and idle.

The social substance of the human kind is not the same as the actual or potential energy applied in social production; the substance is summed up in the relations of society which have, on the contrary, another form than the form of the energetic system. The substance cannot be summed up by addition and cumulation, for the lines of development are too numerous to be given such simple formulations, and are of various qualities. We give the process of cumulation a quantitative formulation which is in part numerical, and in part non-numerical. This is the objective aspect of the account of human development. Subjectively, we are mindful of what we lose as well as what we gain in the process of addition and cumulation in social production.

The losses are summed up subjectively and irrationally in the myth of the golden age adversely, and in the myth of utopia advantageously. The myth of the golden age is adverse, if it expresses regret; the myth of utopia is on the contrary a subjective spur to reform and future orientation, not guidance, pointing not to what we have notionally lost but to what we might well win. Gifted thinkers, such as Dante and Pascal, have indicated the weakness of our powers of memory, expression and representation.

By the transformation of the material thing into human object, the natural order is to that extent humanized; this is a two way relation, for likewise thereby the human kind objectifies itself; the objectification is a mediative process. There are thus two processes of objectification, whose order of introduction is of moment. The one which is directed outward is prior to the inward, self-relation, for we first treat the self as an object, then discover that it is the subject, turning the outward inward. We are dependent on the outside world, before we assert our autonomy in relation to it. This is a novelty in nature, for there is no mediate, and hence no self-relation of the material order; there the relations are direct or indirect; the self-relation is of the human kind and is first the objectification of the world, then the assimilation of the self to the world, and the assertion of the self as existent. The objectification is twofold, systematic and developmental, the latter a concrete and chronological process, the former abstract and atemporal. The objectification is constituted in its system by the separation of the objective form from the substance which is to begin with unseparately and indifferently objective and subjective substance. The form and substance are parted from one another in history, the juridical and political, contractual form from the labor substance; the form is only objective, the substance objective and subjective.

The social whole, prior to the formation of civil society, is organized communally, in groups of kinfolk and neighbors; it is communal in both form and substance. The unit of production, which is the social whole, is the same as the unit of consumption; the local kin community is the social whole; form and substance are not clearly divided; the process of reproduction is that of the community and takes place by distribution of the product among those who have produced it; the labor of production and reproduction of the whole, and the organization of work and labor under these circumstances whereby production and consumption are linked by sharing and distribution of the product to its consumers, is communal and collective; the social unit which produces and reproduces itself by its own product is maintained thereby in the undirempted combination of its form and substance. Negatively, the social unit which is reproduced by its own efforts is maintained thereby without differentiation of social form from social substance, with but little alienation of the social product from its immediate producers either by exchange or exploitation, with the inequality which this twofold alienation generates, and without the unfreedom created by these means. These negative processes have both a systematic and historical connection.

So long as the relations of production and reproduction between human beings are without difference in the form and substance of their social equality, they remain without hierarchical difference. They are mediate relations in society, and as such are at once subjective and objective, but they are without abstract and concrete difference; the form and the substance of production are immediately related to one another and are non-different; the form and substance of the product are the same. By economic exchange the form is separated from the substance, their relations are mediated by the formal difference between the products exchanged. That which is intrinsically and internally non-different is now externally and extrinsically equal to another product, both being the concrete and externalized forms of the process of production. Being equal they are introduced into a reciprocal relation which is objectively an equivalence between the parties who are formally non-different, and thus are objectively equals. The exchange relation is therefore a social relation of formal equality, but in its substance it is not; abstractly it is an equal relation between equals, concretely it is not; objectively it is an equal relation, subjectively it is not. The exchange of products by reciprocation in equality or in equivalents is therefore the condition for the separation of form from substance, of abstract from concrete social relations, hence of the subject from the object in the given social whole, which set of conditions is expressed in the commodity relation and in the law of exchange value. This law has a bearing both on living labor and on the product thereof.

Living labor as a commodity in civil society is to begin within separable from the living human body in which it is incorporated, the two being bought and sold as one; later the two are separated from one another, and it is labor time and capacity which is alienated by exchange; wage labor replaces unfree labor. The communal relation of the village producer, in the early period of civil society, continued to exist *pro forma*, for the village as a unit was responsible for the collection and alienation of tax-rent; but the substance of the social relation, which is exchange and collection of rent-tax was no longer communal; form and substance of social relations were under these circumstances divided from one another. The new social substance in this condition of twofold alienation is an internally oppositive one, being that of formal equality and reciprocity in exchange, and of formal answerability before the law for the provision of a surplus produced in rent-tax. The opposition between form and substance in the exchange relation and in the socialization of the surplus and its alienation by collection of rent-tax in kind and in labor constituted the new social substance; it was a twofold opposition, each undergirding the other. These oppositions are constitutive elements in the formation of civil society, and are expressed in the society of classical antiquity, in ancient Rome and Greece, in the system of bondage, which was the predominant condition of social labor therein; in the ancient Oriental societies, the village community was the predominant form in which social labor was organized, whereas the relations of society, expressed in the system of exchange and collection of tax-rent were opposed to the village communal form. These oppositions are mediately related in civil society; the relation of formal equality is in turn twofold. The process of production is given expression as value, use value, exchange value and as surplus value; the form is concretely plural, the substance abstractly one. The form is separated as abstract exchange value and concrete use value. The historical subject remains what it was, the social whole as an abstraction, and as a potentiality; the historical subject is opposed to the self-objectification of the human kind by its work and labor.

The elementary form of this manifold process of separation and opposition is the mutually antagonistic relations of the class of social labor and the class that is formed in the process of extraction of a surplus and its expression in surplus value. This elementary social form is made historically manifest by the alienation suffered by labor; the alienation is the separation of the unit of production from that of consumption; by economic exchange in civil society as a reciprocal and equal relation between the parties to the exchange, an alienation of the product from its immediate producer takes place. This system has the moments of equality of exchange, reciprocity, alienation of the product; an abstract measure of the value of the product between exchangers who stand to each other as alienators is required and is introduced. The abstraction of exchange value for the measure is opposed to the concrete substance of the production process which is aggregated in the product; the immediate relation of production and consumption is replaced by the relation of discontinuity between communities; the unity within the community is transformed into a mediate relation between the communities. The relation of equality between communities and of mutual dependence in exchange is an abstract relation; concretely it is effected by the combination and the division of social labor. The communal organization is transformed into the social organization of work and labor. By exploitation of one class by another, social bondage and inequality are introduced, a social hierarchy is brought out, and the social relation of civil society is transformed into its opposite, an anti-social relation. Inequality is held in place by the form of ancient communal living; it is the form of life of the immediate producers, whereas the substance of the social life is under the new condition the unequal relation expressed in the form of surplus value and the equal relation expressed in the form of exchange value. The opposition between the two forms is the concretion of the abstract opposition between value form and value substance. Inequality is at once formal and substantial inequality; it is both abstract and concrete. The social inequality and social unfreedom are immediately connected, each being the condition of the other. Objectified labor in concrete form is mediately opposed to objectified labor in abstract form, the medium being the market, commodity exchange, and the treasure of the social surplus. The objectified labor is opposed dually, internally as concrete and abstract labor, and internally again to self-objectifying or living labor. In the latter opposition the objectified is opposed to the objectifying as passivity to activity, concrete to concrete and abstract, and as subject and object to that which is the object. The unfreedom is that of the past which is actually unseparated from the present *pro forma*, and actually and potentially separated from the present in substance. The new producing community is a community *pro forma*, it is a member of civil society in its substance. The unfreedom and inequality in society is internalized in the process of social production. The living labor capacity which until this point in its historical development is indifferently subjective and objective is now objectified, the subjective being systematically eliminated in the production process doubly: by transforming subject-object into object alone, and by transforming the activity of self-objectification into the passivity of being objectified. The ancient Oriental community and the slave of antiquity were the embodiment of living social labor, each in a different condition of unfreedom and inequality in the early periods of the history of civil society. They were like in that both pro-

duced that which is expressed by exchange value and surplus value, however modest the proportion of either may be in the total process of production of the respective societies; they both produced capital in a very modest amount compared
to the capital production of the modern bourgeois mode of production. They
were unlike in that the bondage of the Oriental communities was brought out by
the opposition between the social relations of exchange, alienation and exploitation on the one side and communal equality on the other; the bondage was en-
forced by tradition and implicit in the customary law. The bondage in the form of
slavery was explicitly brought out in ancient Rome and Athens, and was imposed
on the great majority of social labor in the ancient Oriental and Mediterranean
worlds. The processes of objectification and passivity in the production relations
of ancient civil society are carried forward and summed up in the relations of civil
social production both ancient and modern. The passive mode of objectifcation is
reification.

The object is the product of the human kind; it is not as such hierarchized,
but is made into the hierarchized object by virtue of its relation to and in a
hierarchized human order. This hierarchy of the human order does not come from
nature, as Aristotle thought; hierarchization of the human order and of the object
within it is developed by the relations between the social classes in civil society,
and is established by the opposition between rulers and ruled. This opposition is
represented by the former in their interest as the relation of higher and lower ranks
and strata in a subjective hierarchical ordering of the social classes. The hierarchized
relations are immediately present in civil society and are then projected uncritically
onto the sphere of natural and human relations. The fallacy in these projections
and retrojections is threefold; the hierarchy is introduced by the human kind into
nature, in an anthropomorphism, and into the various human societies, by the
relations of civil society, ancient and modern, in an ethnocentric act. A third fallacy assumes that hierarchy is an intrinsic relation of the social whole. On the
contrary, hierarchy is projected onto the social whole in the history of civil society,
and is an expression of its inequality.

Inequality in civil society is brought forth in the process of social production,
and is reinforced in the process of consumption. Here the immediate producers
are ranked lower than the mediate producers, who are the organizers, managers,
planners, and those who provide professional and educational services generally.
The mediate producers require more training for their tasks in production, and
are in turn ranked socially lower than the heads of state who have a ceremonial
role, and take no part in production. The consumption process of modern society
is full of inequalities, which are both formal and substantial, and both mediate
and immediate. Civil society as a whole is divided and mediately related, formally
and substantially, by the production process, which is an internal relation of the

social whole. Inequality is a formal and internal relation of that process and of the social whole. Exchange is a fundamental, mediate, formal relation of civil and bourgeois society; it is a relation between communities, societies and individuals who stand in an external relation to one another; the exchange relation is a relation between equals. The process of social reproduction therefore is in a contradiction in our society, for it has parts which are relations of inequality and of equality. The inequality is internal to the society and is internalized by the individuals of the society; it is both objective and substantial in and to us. The equality is a formal and mediate relation of the society which is an externality of our lives, and is internalized thereby. The contradictory moments of inequality and equality are related to the oppositions between form and substance, subject and object, self- and other, abstraction and concretion of social labor. The form of equality and the form of freedom of modern bourgeois society are interrelated.

Social labor throughout the history of civil society is mediately embodied in the class of social labor. The embodiment is a physical location, and at once an abstract expression. The abstract expression apart from its concrete location is a personification. The class of social labor is a corporate body which reproduces itself in society. Social labor is carried through mediately by the class of social labor in civil society; it is organized not as such but by the whole of society, the reproduction of which is effected by means of social labor, the class of social labor being its incorporation and embodiment. The community is the means of organization of social labor in the archaic primitive condition of social life. The self-objectification of the human kind is, throughout its history, archaic primitive or civil, mediated by the organization, combination and division of labor, which is the active principle and practical means whereby mankind objectifies itself and thus transforms itself into an object. The reification of the object is its secondary objectification, whereby the human being is rendered into the passive object. In theory the activation of the reified object is undertaken by the social organization as a whole. The dominant class in civil society takes over the active principle from the organization of the whole. This is the contradiction of whole and part in a twofold sense: the part has taken over the direction of the whole mediately, standing for the whole; secondly, the interest of the part is taken for the interest of the whole. The first contradiction is that of composition, the second that of the construction made upon the composition. The composition is an objective expression; it is the contradiction between the opposed social classes, and the further contradiction of the reproduction of society by labor and the organization of reproduction and of labor by the social whole. To take the interest of the part for the interest of the whole is a mere figment, a construction which is subjective.

The reification of the object makes its historical appearance as the reified subject. This is in turn a twofold process of separation of subject from object and the forcing into passivity of each side of the dirempted pair, subject and object. The reification of the object is effected by the socialization of the relations of production and their contradiction of the antisocial relations of society. Therewith the relations of formal equality in exchange and of substantive inequality in exploitation are introduced. The reification of the subject is the theoretical expression of the practical relation of unfreedom. The unfreedom is both formal and substantial at the beginning of the history of civil society, and substantial alone in the later periods. The reification of the historical subject is the consequence of the inequality in form and substance at the beginning of the history of civil society and of the substantial inequality in the later periods. The reification of the Roman slaves, of the Oriental community in antiquity, and of the serfs in the Middle Ages of European history, is the expression of the condition of their unfreedom in form and substance. The unfreedom of wage labor in the mode of production of the production of capital is a substantive unfreedom and at the same time a conjoint freedom and equality *pro forma.* Wage labor sells the labor time and capacity thereof as an equal in the law relative to its purchaser. The labor time of wage labor is sold and bought by means of the alienation of the labor capacity. The wage labor retains the power over the sale of the labor capacity thereof as a juridical right. The alienation of labor capacity and that of labor time are mediate social relations, the labor power is the juridical expression of both. The right to alienate labor time and capacity and take it unto itself is a social power that rests objectively, formally and in theory with the Oriental monarchy; it rests with the master of the slave and in the overlord of the serf, both practically and theoretically in either case. The right to alienate labor time and labor capacity separately and mediately is a power that rests with wage labor in theory; the right is a formal right and bears upon the power to limit the amount of labor time that is sold by wage labor, without reference to labor quality and capacity. The right is without substance, for wage labor sells its labor time in an amount necessary for the maintenance of the class of social labor and sufficient for the maintenance of the social whole, or else that whole will in its given historical form go under. It is a formal right of labor, for it cannot do otherwise and survive in modern bourgeois society; it must sell its labor time and skill to others. Its right to sell what it sells is asymmetrical, for it has no right to withhold its power, time and capacity as a whole. The right to sell is paired with the obligation to sell; it has, as Hegel said, as much right in this regard as it has obligation, or rights and obligations cancel each other out; it is in this sense a civil person, and is composed of a body of civil persons. These are formal rights and compositions. It is the formal and immediate embodiment of the social reproductive process; the social whole and other social classes are engaged in this process both substantively and mediately.

Social labor in civil society according to one expression is identified with the working class and is personified in the class of the immediate producers, who are subjected to the extreme of exploitation, and whose working and living conditions are the poorest of all in the history of that society.

The technocrats claim that the mediate producers in society, as the engineers, constitute a social class; most Marxists hold that the immediate producers alone constitute the class of social labor. Social labor, as we have seen, is constituted of immediate producers, mediate producers, and those who participate in the distribution process, including exchange and circulation of money and credit. Producers of all kinds are exchangers and consumers.

Social labor reproduces itself by its labors, and thereby reproduces the social whole. The process of self-reproduction by the human kind is social reproduction, constituted of the interaction of those who are engaged in the relations of social labor, and these constitute both the immediate and the mediate producers in society. Both the mediate and the immediate producers are engaged in practical and theoretical activity, and in abstract and concrete relations of labor. The idea is sometimes expressed that the immediate producers have no part in the theoretical activity and abstract relations of production, and this idea is internalized by a part of social labor, and believed by many of them. In consequence, the immediate producers are alienated in the production process, and the consciousness of the proletariat is therewith reified. The consciousness of the ruling class in civil society is reified not in this way, but in another, by its self-diremptive relation to the process of human self-reproduction, and by the fallacy whereby it is made out to be one with the social whole, making itself out to be the representative thereof.

The mediate producers, engineers, skilled technicians, scientists, specialists with advanced training, are a class, but they are not a social class, and the same is to be said of the immediate producers in civil society. The former engage in relatively more theoretical than practical activity, the latter relatively more practical than theoretical activity in their production relations, which are undertaken by both. The mediate producers are separated from the immediate by privilege and preference, better working conditions and pay within the class of social labor from the class of the immediate producers. In ancient civil society, the astronomers, mathematicians, physicians, agronomists, engineers, literates, chemists served the ruling class as priests, sacred scribes and archivists. When most people were illiterate, the services of predictions of the flooding of the great rivers in ancient times, managing the control of the flood waters, record-keeping, mathematical computation, healing, chemical experimentation, were mystifed by astrological and alchemistic phantasmagoria. By the play of subjective interest upon the mediate producers in civil society they were and are separated from the process of social labor, the unity of which was and is disrupted thereby. Objectively, however, there is little difference in the production process between the activities of the mediate and immediate producers therein, whereas by the alienation of the two from one another, and their reification, the productivity of the social whole is lowered, inventiveness and innovation are restricted and the process of production as a whole is to that extent deformed if not suppressed. The mediate producers are by preferential treatment made out to be as though members of the ruling class in civil society, and are cut off from interaction, by this token, with the class of immediate producers. The whole of the value expression is thereby reduced in its amount and rate of development.

Capital in modern civil society, whether publicly or privately owned, is inactive, until it is acted upon by a human agency. It is personified in its private form of ownership by the class of capitalists, and by the public form thereof by the concrete agencies of the state. Both forms of personification are mysticizations of the production process, which has many other potential forms relative to the substance thereof; that substance is the agency and relation of the mediate and immediate producers, both inclusive of the learning and teaching process, whereby social skills are extended, handed on over time and therewith varied from one place to another, from one group to another and from one generation to the next. The personification of social labor by the associations, unions, or political parties does not differ in kind from the personification of capital by private capitalists or by the public hand and concrete agencies of the state. All personification, whether by the ruling class or by the representatives of the working class, is a substitution of form for substance, both are mediated relations, which are passivities relative to the process of social reproduction, and are removed from it by one step in the case of the union and association representatives; political party leaders, capitalists and the agencies of the public hand are removed from the substantive process of social labor two steps or more; these are differences in degree of distancing by personification, not difference of kind. The phenomenon of personification in modern society is a mystical act which is not other than the representation of thunder by Zeus or Wotan.

The voluntary association of free workers is a means whereby the living standards and working conditions of social labor have been changed in modern civil society, particularly in the 19th and 20th centuries. These associations have less to do with the theory of socialist society than the association of free workers, which has been mentioned above; for the association of free workers is a representational body in capitalist society, and stands for the workers whom it represents in a *pro forma* relation, against the capitalist representative over the bargaining table. The free, voluntary association by virtue of the representative process is therefore the form of a form; the representative of capital is the formal personification of an inorganic object, the representative of the labor union is the formal personification of the form of a body of living social labor.

The association of human beings with one another in a voluntary union brought about by a rational process has been proposed as the principle of a just society. The members of this association expend their individual labor capacities in a self-conscious combination which is social labor capacity. The means of production are held in common by those who labor in this condition, but they are not socialized thereby; the means of production are socialized by being activated in such a way that their product is the product of the union of the freely associated individuals whose common property is thus transformed into social property. Labor in common, means of production as common property, and product in common are thus transformed by the act of free, voluntary association, and of distribution of the means of subsistence according to a plan. Labor in this condition is social labor, and is substantively free, its relations being formally and substantively socialized; society is free both *pro forma* and in its substance. The relations of labor are cooperative, being divided and combined socially, and the means of production are one with the relations of production.

The idea of a free, voluntary association of human beings who by their organization in society will assure the downfall of social inequality and exploitation is an appealing sentiment, but is a revival in fact of the already outmoded fallacy of the Robinsonade as the basis for social theory and planning; it depicts the conjunction of rational individuals benevolently cooperating toward a rational end. Notwithstanding the nobility of this image, we do not commence with the individual, rational or irrational, cooperative or competitive.

Equality in society is a formal, not a substantial relation between persons. We are in theory equal before the law, and in other formal relations; there is no other equality than this.

The unit with which we begin the analysis of social labor is not the individual in an association of free workers; we begin with the relations of the social whole, which is potentially the whole of social labor. The associated producers, the union of free men, or of free workers is a pleasing image perhaps for a society in which consciousness of unfreedom is deep and widespread. In civil society we are conscious of the contradiction between freedom *pro forma* and substantive unfreedom, and this contradiction is the condition under which all thought of freedom is expressed. The means to overcome this unfreedom, however, is not the advocacy of free union, by voluntary association of individual human beings. The opposition between individual and private property is eliminated not by "the cooperation of free workers and their common property." On the contrary, the cooperation of free workers will not eliminate this opposition, but will intensify it, for the starting point is still the individual human beings, their volition, freedom and reason. By starting with the process of social labor, the social whole, which is one with social labor, is set forth as the means of self-relation, therewith self-constitution, self-objectification, self-activation and self-mediation of the human kind. The individual human being is the object that is worked upon, by internalizing the social relations, by constituting out of these relations the means of transformation of the biological material into the human being, the human agent as the historical subject is brought into being. The abstract subject is the human kind, the concrete subject is the particular social whole in history; this concrete subject is at once abstract as agency, for it bears within it the potentiality of becoming one with the human kind as a whole; abstractly and concretely social labor bears within it the potentiality of becoming one with the social whole, and conversely, the social whole bears within it the potentiality of becoming one with labor. The social whole is therefore the mediate relation through which social labor becomes one with the human kind. The human agency is therefore the oppositive relation between the given, concrete social whole and abstract and concrete social labor.

The social whole is at once an abstract and concrete relation and a practical and theoretical activity, which is internalized by individuals. The social relation is at the same time a concrete, sensible relation and an abstraction of relation and reference. The human individual is not other than concrete to begin with, being the raw, inchoate mass of nascent flesh which is shaped into a human being by the combination and internalization of practical, concrete social relation by the new-born, practical, concrete product of the conjugation of *homo sapiens*. The product is a natural doing, the act of sexual coupling, and birth is a process of material nature; the humanization of this material now begins; however, the natural process does not therewith come to an end, for it cannot be ignored.

The labor process is represented by the class of social labor in civil society, but is not the whole of that process. The opposition between social labor and the whole of civil society is that between the part and the whole, and out of this general opposition many particular oppositions are brought forth. The social labor is performed for the social whole, but the labor is not reciprocated throughout civil society, for some labor for others, but the others do not labor in return for the reproduction of the whole. The product of this labor is not distributed in such a way that the wants and needs of all are met in an equitable way; some have more of the product than they want and need, which they then waste; some have less than they want and need. The equality of modern civil society is a formal expression of the juridical and political relations of that society; this is opposed by the substantive inequality whereby some labor for others, but this labor is not reciprocated; and the product of social labor as a whole is unequally distributed, some being poor and some rich. This substantive inequality and formal equality of civil society is developed *pari passu* with formal freedom and substantive unfreedom, the oppositions between freedom and unfreedom and between equality and inequality in this condition being mutually and reciprocally determinative.

Reification of Labor, Alienation and Objectification

The bondage of social labor, whether formal and substantial or substantial alone, is socially and objectively real. The bondage is a mediate and passive relation of labor in society. The reified condition is its result and causes nothing. It is a particular, and not a general or universal condition in human history, and follows from organization of society into classes, the exploitation and oppression of one class by another immediately; it follows mediately from social processes of diremption; it follows, however, not necessarily and automatically by a mechanical law, but contingently and conditionally.

Reification of labor follows from the mediate relation of the human kind to the natural field and to itself, from the use of the human body and brain as instruments, from our self-objectification and the objectification of the world around and in us, and from the alienation of our products and of ourselves in our society.

Mediation and diremption are interconnected in the human order and in relations to external nature. The animal relations of age, sex, and the generations, are transformed into human relations by our labors. The human relation to the material world of matter and of life is complex, and permeated with hopeful gains, and regretful loss. All work and labor are dirempted by the human beings who engage in these activities by being distanced from the material order, and in this limited sense removed from a part of nature; we have other relations in nature, as a part of it, and to other parts of nature than those of material things. The diremption is a mediate connection to nature; mediation and diremption are the natural relations of the human order. The distancing is effected by our work and by the use of our bodies, minds and social relations, and their instruments. These uses are objective, the body, mind, social relations and instruments are objects on which we work and with which we work and labor.

The organization by combination and division of the tasks of work and labor by human beings is the human relation to nature, in nature, and to one another. Some will sew and some will hunt. A tree branch found on the forest floor by its human prehension, by acts of lifting, bearing and striking is made into a cudgel; thus it is transformed from the world of matter to the human world, whereby it ceases to be a fallen branch and becomes an instrument of productive labor or of war.

The organization, combination and division of labor are acts of mediation and diremption; they are mediate and self-diremptive acts, for we act on ourselves, and are the passive recipients of our activities. The action of matter is direct, non-dirempted, the human act is internally dirempted; the human act is internally mediate in the material order. The mediative and diremptive acts are made into alienative processes, a primary alienation in history being the act of sale and purchase of useful goods between communities. By buying and selling in exchanges each side alienates to another its products or its labors, These alienative processes are external, reciprocal, mediate, objective and formal. A second alienation is the organization, combination and division of society into opposed classes; this alienation is external, nonreciprocal, mediate, objective, formal and substantial. A third kind of alienation is subjective, in which we feel unwanted and alone amid the wonders we have made; the studies of anomy and suicide have a bearing on the last mentioned alienation.

The diremptions, alienations, social, antisocial, relations are the result of the historical process whereby the human kind has converted a part of itself into the object of its labor. Laboring abstractly and working concretely upon itself, the object of this effort is then made into a false object, for it is severed from the subject, which is the one-sided object and the reified human subject.

Two sets of oppositions between human form and substance are to be distinguished in the history of the relations of labor in civil society, which are not found in the archaic, communal organization of social reproduction. In the beginnings of the history of civil society, the form of the archaic, communal organization of society and labor continue to exist, whereas in its substance, the social relations, the production relations and the relations of exchange and distribution are no longer communal, but social and at once antisocial, for they are unequal and unjust. The form of the relations, both in the community and the society is that of the archaic, primitive kind, in which the state was made to appear as a magnified community, existing in the abstract, as the juridical expression of the concrete village community of the Asiatic mode of production, and this opposition between the archaic form and the modern substance has endured over the greater part of the history of civil society and the state in many parts of the world. The second set of oppositions between form and substance in the relation of labor in civil society is that between formal and substantial freedom, and between formal and substantial equality, which are two aspects of the same oppositive relation. Labor was unfree in ancient Asia in that the opposition between the archaic equality of non-differentiation and the modern in equality *pro forma* in the relations between the social classes is developed. Formally, labor was bound in ancient times by the practices of the village, expressed in custom, habits and feelings; substantively, labor was bound by the relations of exploitation, rent-tax, obligation and debt. These two systems of formal and substantial unfreedom are not the same, but opposed to one another, for they arise in different historical conditions, and are related by particular local conditions. The form of this unfree condition disappears in the later history of civil society, whereas the substance of the unfreedom is further developed in the condition of industrial society in the present time.

The two oppositions between form and substance, whereby the unfree condition of labor is determined in the history of civil society, are related to one another.

The later history of unfreedom is brought out by the making explicit of bondage, which is expressed in the laws of servitude of slavery and serfdom. The opposition between the public and private spheres of civil society, which are expressed in the differentiation between public tax and private ground rent, is a further differentiation in the development of unfree relations already found in the beginnings of its history. Rent and tax, either undifferentiated or separated, are forms in which surplus labor and surplus product are alienated from their immediate producers throughout the history of civil society. The differentiation and opposition between relations of form and substance within the human order are not internally composed, but are projected onto new oppositions in the history of the human kind. The old is not synthesized, but is internalized by the new.

Diremption takes place in the human order; it is not directly a relation of the material order, but a variation within the latter, from which the human order is extruded, alienating the material order from itself and thereby constituting itself as a bit of the material order which is external to the latter. Once nature is externalized by the human kind, the latter then internalizes its alienated existence. This internalization presupposes, however, a distancing, hence, from the human side, an asymmetrical, at once mediate and reciprocally active relation between the two orders, material and human. Within the human order, the diremption is an internal division, for we bear the active factor in the diremption from nature within ourselves. Variation is a process common to both the material and human orders, the human order is the expression of a natural variation.

Variation in the material order is relative, practical, direct and concrete; our work and labor, which are constituted as a variation of the material processes, are made mediately and relatively self-dependent within the natural order; they are concrete, and are transformed into the abstract and concrete human object and subject. The relation of concretum is continuous between the material and the human orders, the thing is transformed into an object in the human order by human activity, whereby the thing in the material order is passive and active, being submitted to human variation. The object of the act is ourselves, our social relations and our material surroundings. The human object is converted into a subject-object by human activity. In its system, the transformation of the thing into the object is prior to the opposition of object to subject and to consciousness. The opposition between the abstract and the concrete object is a mediate relation which is posterior to the opposition in the human system between form and substance; the opposition between human form and human substance is a variation upon the direct relation of form and substance of matter, which is effected by the introjection of a human mediate relation between them. Such a variation is an overload upon the activity which has not taken leave of the material order of nature, but is a transformation of a natural process; in one respect the natural process is doubled upon itself, but this is a small part of the transformative process. The transformation is the totality of human effort, which is a natural process, a readaptation of natural means, and the organization of the natural materials in a natural variant; its reorganization is then developed further in interaction with the material order. The human kind is an evolutionary variant of the material order, adapting and selecting processes of the latter in its generation. The human kind, once constituted, is opposed to the order of nature in which it is generated, reorganizing and readapting the natural materials by human means. The opposition is an asymmetrical one, and is incomplete; it is not reciprocated by the processes of matter. The human process is a conative orientation which constitutes human change in the natural order; it achieves its fulfillment by the material interchange with nature, which is our mortal limit, and is not brought to completion. This fulfillment, however, is the return to the natural process, being the negative of human conation, the latter alone leading to objectification; the return to nature is literally thingification, in which we turn ourselves back into things.

The difference between reification and objectification rests in part on that between thing and object, and in part on that between the processes of reification and objectification. The thing is the starting point in relation to ground and surrounding in the natural order, and is not the object. The opposition between object and field, self, object and medium, self-objectification and objectification of the field are processes of the human order. To reduce an object and the self-object relation to a thing is a deterioration of the natural process, and a confusion of the human process with the process of the material order; we then take on the role of Leviathan. Those who seize control over human life and nourishment act in an inhuman way, without regard to common humanity. The relation between human beings, as within the human order generally, is both subjective and objective; to make the objective relation into a relation between things is to falsify the human relation as such. The results of the separation and diremption of the object from the subject, are reification, false objectification, false subjectification, false object and subject. Reification is the human recreation of the act of death; the mortality of the individual and of the species is not thus but the material interchange within the natural order. For some human beings take on the function of the mortal god, which is the civil power to hold all men in awe.

The self-relation of the human kind, whereby the human subject and the human object are brought into a mediate internal relation, a mediate relation to external nature, and into an objective relation to both constitute the human substance. The immediate natural environment is transformed into the field of human active relations. Reification is the deformation of this process, whereby some human beings are forced by others to act as though they were things in the process of objectification of the world. The self-objectification of the human kind is transposed into what it is not, in a common dehumanization of exploiter and exploited, oppressor and oppressed, which can be only eliminated by eradicating exploitation and oppression.

The objectification of matter, of the self, and of human society is carried through regardless of whether the reification takes place or not, and regardless of whether the power over its labor rests in the hands of social labor or not. Reification is the deterioration of the relations of human reproduction, for in it the power over itself is taken away from social labor in a process of false objectification.

In modern society, the reification of labor has been further developed in industry. The sciences, engineering, technology, the abstract art of industrial architecture and design, planning and management are separated from immediate production; rationalization, control of production and productivity are reduced to its routinization; variation by means of initiative in the production and hence reproduction process is taken away from labor, which is alienated in the process of industrial production, as the ancient peasants were alienated in the process of agricultural production. The alienation of the product from the immediate producers is a related alienation, but is not the same; the psychological and sociological alienations in modern society are processes related to the foregoing but differ from them.

The reification of labor is interactive with its alienation, first in the process of immediate production, and second in the exchange relation of labor; labor in this case is in substance unfree; wage labor is *pro forma* free. By alienation is meant the concrete exchange of the time and capacity of labor and its product for the means of subsistence. The alienation is thus the concrete relation of the double objectification, and the interaction with the latter, which is the abstraction of the same.

The reification of labor is in a common social process with the reification of self and of judgment. The reification of the self by the separation of objectification from subjectivity of judgment is a process of substitution of the false for the actual self, which is the social whole of the human kind. The reification is a process of falsification, and is objective, that is, it is external to the self-mediatizing and self-objectifying class of labor in civil society, and independent of that class. It is a relation of the social whole that varies according to the relation to the process of social reproduction by the class that labors and the class that does not. The relation of reification is a false objectification of the self-relation on the part of social labor; it is false in that a notion of passivity is set in place of the activity of social reproduction, as though social labor were acted upon and then active. The active reification of the social class that does not labor is a false objectification in another sense, for that class is represented, and represents itself as the initiative and active factor in the process of maintenance and reproduction of the social whole. Both processes of reification are pseudo processes, the false activity of the second relation being opposed to the false passivity of the first. But both falsities are internalized by either class. Thus the processes of pseudo-objectification become actual, although they have no relation to reality, that is, neither the material of the natural nor that of the human order is thereby transformed. By being internalized in this way the false self does not lose its false character, however faithfully the self-materializing subject and however interestedly the materialized social other, therewith the whole, have internalized it. The consciousness of social labor concretely and in particular, and the self-materializing capacity of the social whole abstractly and in general are therewith reified. They are not reduced to things, for they are not really alienated from the human order, but it as though they are things, the part which is as though a thing being determined by the pseudo-thingly relation of the whole. Value judgment, as the relation of the social whole, is an expression of the whole insofar as it is dependent, hence as a part; that which is not a whole is dependent, that which is dependent is a part. There is no whole of nature, but a relation of interdependent parts. Neither the material nor the human order is independent, both being parts of a greater, which is the relation of nature. The human social whole is therefore but a part, and the value judgment that is generated by the whole is the judgment by the part. It is sometimes the judgment by the part as though it were the whole; it is the expression of value of the dependent part, as though independent of the other parts of the human order, of matter, and of nature in general.

Labor, Productive and Unproductive

Learning is not restricted to the human kind, but is practiced in other parts of the animal kingdom. The learning processes of the mammals differ from those of other vertebrates, such as the birds and snakes. The learning processes of the humankind are more variable, having a longer duration, and occupying a greater proportion of the life cycle than those of the other animals. In modern civil society the learning process has been made into a formal and substantive part of the labor process. Throughout the history of civil society, ancient as well as modern, it has been a specialized relation between teacher and student. Thus in ancient Asia officials of government received specialized training; perhaps the best known cases were those of the mandarinate of China in classical times, and the caste of Brahmins in India. In the history of Asia, particularly in its later periods in the Middle East and Central Asia, as well as in East and South Asia, in the later European Middle Ages, and in the early period of capitalism, training in specialized trades was restricted to the guilds which regulated the relations between masters and apprentices.

The student in modern civil society has a place, which is one of preparation for employment, requiring some degree of qualification, the degree being relatively high if the student is the product of a university, when compared with the qualification of manual labor. While in the state of preparation for future employment, during one's student years, one may earn one's keep by working as a dish washer; the two processes, student and dishwasher, are not the same, however. The kind of employment which the students then undertake depends in a significant way on the type and length of their studies, whether in the way of practical professional training in engineering, industrial biology, chemistry, geology, physics, mathematical sciences, in medicine, accounting, law, social work, and teaching. Training in languages, music, design and architecture are not different from the foregoing in their relation to employment for the products of university instruction. The pay in these professions is variable, from middling to high, and well above that of dishwashers. There are yet other students who are not preparing for professional careers; either they have not yet decided on what they are going to do, or they have no intention to make such a decision. Yet the difference between the two kinds of students, who have, have not or have not yet, some practical or theoretical goal for their studies is subjective. By following these students along and observing what has become of them in their later lives, we then can make some objective judgment about the nature of their student days; until then, the classification of the students of the different kinds, purposeful or not, practical or not, is subjectively determined by their will and desire.

Students are defined as a class which is being prepared for some future activity. They come as a passive receptacle to an institution of teaching, such as an elementary school, a middle school, a university, or a technical school, and become more active as their training in practical and immediate terms, and also their training in study, and learning to read and write, proceeds. Some of those who had, and some who had not a particular goal, whether practical or theoretical, drop out, join the counterculture. Therefore the distinction between the different kinds of students, whether active or passive, is also a subjective one. We speak only of activity of students as students, not of their extracurricular activities. Most advanced students, in fact the great majority, have some profession of the sorts indicated, and most of their careers have some significant connection with their studies. The difference between men and women in these regards is wide, but is narrower in our society than it was a few generations back.

If we take the life earnings of those who have been students we see that by virtue of having been students, and to the extent of their studies, their total earnings are higher than those who began to earn a livelihood at a younger age, entering the labor force immediately after childhood, or as soon as the law allows. All these types of people, with and without some specialist or technical training, exchange their time and skills against the means for their subsistence. There is a mediative bond therefore between the student life and the subsequent acts of employment, and more widely, of the way of life, in relation to pay, capital and exchange.

There are some problems in theory which have arisen in connection with the definitions and theses advanced just now. We will consider two of them. The first is the problem of the student in relation to productive and unproductive labor. Imagine a shepherd watching sheep and playing on a flute while so engaged. The sheep watching is productive, for the sheep are sheared, the wool sold, the ewes are milked for cheese making, and the cheese and the lambs are brought to market, sold and eaten. The wool, cheese and lambs are products of productive labor in our society, for they are commodities, and so is the labor of their production, sale and purchase, and consumption. If the pastoral flautist sells his tunes in the market place, then this labor too is productive, and the flute an instrument of labor. Otherwise it is an instrument of pleasure, and the labor of playing it is unproductive. This is Marx's analysis. We see that the judgment in classifying the different kinds of labor, as to whether it is productive or not, is objectively determined only in relation to its outcome, that is, by its relation to the market, commodities and capital. Marx, however, went further, and particularized this analysis, listing a number of employments as productive, and a number as unproductive; among the latter he designated civil servants, physicians, lawyers and scholars in bourgeois society, together with cooks, tailors and gardeners, on the grounds that they exchange their services against revenues, private or public, without converting the revenues into capital. Labor for personal consumption is, according to this analysis, therefore not productive labor. This is an error. We first establish that our concern is not with individual relations but with all of social labor in our civil condition of the modern time. Let us consider the medical profession. Those who labor are not all in perfect health all the time, and require the services of physicians. These services, although relations between persons, bear on the capacity of the working class to labor as a class, whereby the ailing segment of that class is restored to health, and returns to work. The cure and the payment are linked; accordingly, no payment, no cure. The working class and the medical profession, together with others, are different parts of the process of social labor in our society, the working class having a more immediate relation to capital formation, the medical profession a more mediate one.

Marx took for his example the individual cook, tailor and surgeon, but could not see beyond the relations of their personal services in making the classification of productive and unproductive labor, and set them into the second category. This involves an anterior error, which is called a Robinsonade, in consideration of the isolated individual, for instance on a desert isle, in a one to one relation to another, as in the case of Robinson Crusoe and his man Friday. This may explain how Marx arrived at the error of classifying the personal services of the cook or physician as unproductive; the problem of the generation of an error is not the same as the problem of its constitution, which we will now consider. The class of physicians is not a social but an occupational class, performing productive labors in that the people whom they restore to health are productive, working in factories, fields and mines, exchange their labors against a wage, and converting both their labors and the product into capital. The physicians as a class add days and years to the sum of the labor time of their patients healed. Working back from the capital formed at the end of the process of labor to the labors in the factories, fields, mines and hospitals themselves, we see that some are more immediate, and some more mediate in relation to their products.

Scholars are included in the listing of unproductive labors of Marx. Some of these are ivory tower types; the occupational class of scholars also includes experimentalists, observers, and teachers who advance the various sciences, natural, social and human, exchanging their services against wages, salaries, royalties, and training students to follow in their way, for which they are paid. The function of the learned is determined in civil society by these social relations, and the ivory tower types are assimilated to the former in our analysis. That is one way of entry into the class of productive labor; the selling of the products of scientific investigation and of speculative writings on the market is another.

The students are not as such a class of productive labor, but are a preparatory step on the way to entering that class. The teachers at elementary, middle and higher schools of learning perform a personal service of instruction, but they are part of processes of preparing social labor in the skills of reading, writing, mathematics, thus enhancing the qualities of social labor in the future, when the students will enter the production process, commodity exchange and therewith capital formation. The employment of labor in society civil and bourgeois is a process in which labor converts itself and the materials of nature into capital by exchange of labor time, skills and qualifications against a wage. The class of wage labor retains over its time and qualities, a power which is expressed as a legal right of disposition over them. Labor in the form of wage labor has no right to sell or otherwise alienate to some one else the power to dispose over its labor time and capacity; in this way, labor differs from slave or servile labor, or any other unfree labor. Students are productive labor of a potential, not of an actual kind. Labor capacity is the skill, technical ability, or quality of labor generally, in production. The greater the degree of preparation for the eventual employment, the greater the productive capacity of labor generally, and of the students in particular. The greater the period of study or other preparation, the greater the potentiality of the students for production. This is the quantitative side of the question. There is a qualitative side to it as well, which is the intensification of the preparation, and therefore of the productivity, of labor.

Productive labor in our society is defined as labor which is sold in exchange for a living wage. It is social labor, but it is determined to be such not by its contribution to society, but by its conversion into a commodity, wages and the means of subsistence, as these are expressed by the exchange value of the labor. The definition of production, therefore, is not made in terms of labor's production relations, but in terms of its exchange relations. This is a strange matter, which is connected to the processes in our society, whereby labor sells its living and working time for wages. But the value which labor produces and the exchange value of the labor are not the same, for production and exchange are not the same. The two value expressions coincide in our society, in which exchange is a part of the production process. This led Marx to take labor value for exchange value, making a general law out of a particular social circumstance. (See *Value*, below)

The second matter bearing on the place of the student in the society and economy is the relation between mediate and immediate labor. The distribution of the immediate and mediate relations of labor in the oil industry serves to illustrate this problem. Social labor is constituted of productive, not of unproductive labors; some social labor is immediate, and some mediate in relation to production. Mediate labor tends to have more preparation and training and immediate labor tends to have less. The labors of those who actually drill for oil are more immediate in relation to production than are those of geologists, engineers, chemists and physicists, who explore for oil, or find new ways of drilling for it. Oil is a kind of capital in modern bourgeois society, but it is not capital as such; capital it is by virtue of what it becomes, or what is made out of it. It is converted into capital in that it is a means of production which is bought and sold as a commodity, and this fate which it endures then determines that the activity of the oilfield hands, the geologists and engineers is that of wage labor, respectively immediate and mediate in its relation to production. That which determines social labor as wage labor is first, the exchange of its time and capacity against the means of its subsistence, and second, the conversion of its product into a commodity, which then appears on the market as capital. Conversely, the sale of labor time and capacity against the means of subsistence is a condition of capital formation, the conversion of the product of that labor into the means of production, and the conversion of the latter into a commodity is a second condition of capital formation; these conditions in turn determine that labor is a commodity, which then appears in its social character as wage labor.

Social labor objectifies itself in the process of human reproduction by human means. Thus by our labors we make things into objects which are requisite and used in meeting our objective wants, material needs and subjective desires. Our labors are the means whereby we convert the body's organs and the capacities of *homo sapiens* into human organs and capacities, the social relations of the animal genera and species, of which the species *homo sapiens* is a part, into human social relations, and the work of physical things, inanimate and animate, into human work and labor. The objectification is self-objectification; this, however, is not the starting point in the process of transformation of animal matter into the human form and substance, material and immaterial. The process of mediation between the human kind and the material order of nature in which we are generated is the means for the self-diremption of the former in an asymmetrical and nonreciprocal relation to matter; the mediative process of differentiation and connection in and to nature are the conditions for our self-formation, self-objectification, objectification of our field of labor, and of things in that field. We make things, therewith ourselves in relation to the field, into objects by our labor, which is the mediate relation to all of them. Labor thus converts its object, and therewith itself into the means of self-reproduction and variation of the human kind. Our labor capacities are natural forces converted into human powers, formal and substantial, to humanize ourselves.

We objectify ourselves, we sell our labor time and capacities against the means of subsistence, as wage labor in modern society, bourgeois and civil. By the two processes, of self-objectification and the sale of its time and capacity as wage labor, which is self-reification, labor converts itself into capital. Capital does not convert itself into labor. Wage and salaried labor converts itself into capital in a mediate way, first making its time and capacity into a commodity, and thus into capital. The sale of labor time and capacity is a mediate process between the production of the means to meet the human wants and their actual consumption, whereby they are met. The sale is an objectified, passive process, and not active, thus it is an asymmetry which is referred to as reification.

Capital, we have said, is defined as the means of production in commodity form. In the capitalist system, these means of production were wholly or predominantly owned in private in England in the 18th century; there has been modification of this conception since then, but it is conceived that under the capitalist mode of production at present, the means of production, such as factories and other industrial centers, are in their predominance privately owned. In the recent past, the Soviet system held the means of production in commodity form, and thus as capital, with this difference, that they were predominantly publicly owned.

Labor is converted into capital where the means of production are wholly or predominantly in commodity form. The form is public or private. Labor is a living activity of living human beings, whereas capital, as all commodities, is nonliving, a form of labors and goods, which is animated only by our beliefs and superstitions. Thus whereas labor is converted into capital, capital does not convert itself into labor or value or any other process whatsoever. Labor converts itself into capital by selling its time, skills, capacities and knowledge, in the form of wage labor. Capital converts itself into labor, commodities, goods and values only by animistic, fetishistic, and magical acts.

Labor is converted into capital by selling its time and capacity for a wage. The capital relation of labor is determined by what becomes of its product when it is ready to be used and consumed. If the product is sold on the market, then it is converted into a commodity, and the labor which went into its production, if sold by the laborer for a wage, is a commodity. The wage laborers act as though they were capitalists, with this footnote, that they own no capital but their commodity relation to their time, skills and knowledge. The closer the laborer is to the end product, the more immediate it is; it is immediate labor. The further labor is from the end product, the more mediate it is, being active in the regulation, control, planning, distribution of tasks, divisions and combinations thereof in the production and distribution process; this is mediate labor. Modern industry has both immediate and mediate labor within it. Thus the different employments in the production process are classified as immediate or mediate in their relation to the commodity, which is the end result, and this end result then determines the production relation. This process of classification is the reverse of the process of production, which moves forward from the raw oil to the heating fuel and gasoline. In the classification of social labor as immediate or mediate, we move backward from the product to the process of production. We have seen how this reversal is applied in the objective classification of the students' preparatory studies as practical or theoretical, productive or unproductive, by moving backward from the end result to the training process. The classification of all the occupations and the preparations for them are determined by their relation in society, which in our period of history is a process of capital formation. The capital transactions in the market place differ from the exchange process in the production relations; these transactions are not relations of production, but relations of distribution, exchange and circulation of money. Thus they are mediate relations, but they are of another kind, which is relative to the process of distribution and exchange. The teachers of the engineers, physicists, geneticists, microbiologists, geologists, chemists, and the like are further removed from the production process than their erstwhile students, and hence enter into the class of social labor by several more steps of intermediation; yet they are a part of the process of productive labor for all that they are mediately and not immediately a part of it. We classify the labors in society as mediate or immediate, just as we classify them as productive or unproductive objectively by working back from the finished product, whereby we determine that it enters into the relations of commodities, exchange and capital.

Marx in listing the unproductive occupational classes included therein the servants of the state, or civil servants in a modern usage. The state in the 18th century had been investigated by Adam Smith, and in the 19th by Hegel and

Marx. In its concrete historical manifestation in England, the society which Smith observed was bourgeois, and the state was then expected to serve as no more than a nightwatchman. The state which Hegel observed in Germany differed from its English counterpart, for Germany was not as far advanced as England in the development of capitalism. Civil servants were in Germany more than nominally the servants of the crown. The English civil servants and the German crown servants of that time were alike in that neither class got its hands sullied in trade. These categories and functions were borne in mind by Marx, when he classified the servants of the state as unproductive. By the end of the 19th century, both England and Germany reached the height of capitalist development of that time. Marx had the model of the state set out by Smith and Hegel in his mind, and did not take into account the changes which it underwent during his lifetime. Thus the state in England at that time had concrete agencies which restricted the employment of child labor, and prohibited the employment of servile and slave labor. These agencies, moreover, supervised the Factory Acts, by which the length of the working day was fixed. Marx was conscious of all this, for he carefully examined reports prepared by inspectors employed for the supervision of the Factory Acts; they were among his source materials in the writing of *Capital*. The inspectorial activities were a considerable move beyond Adam Smith's ideal state, which did no more than chase off highwaymen, and keep pickpockets away from persons of property; Smith scorned the insidious and crafty statesmen who deprived the capitalist of his capital in the period of industrial capitalism's beginnings.

The civil servants of our time have many more functions than those of the factory inspectorate of Marx's time; since both enter into the production relations, the difference between them is one of degree and not of quality. In the advanced countries of civil society, the state enters not only into education, health, factory inspection and environmental control, but also into capital formation in industry and banking. The civil servants are in this connection a kind of mediate labor.

The students, we have said, are far from being a class of unproductive labor; they are on the contrary a class of potentially productive labor. Now consider their teachers, who are an occupational class of mediate productive labor; their labors are not potential but actual. The mediate productive actuality of the professorial labors in the economy of our bourgeois society is not determined by what they do, but is objectively productive in the light of what their students do with the preparatory studies, training and learning set out for them by their professors as professors. In this case again we work backward from the product to the producer; Given that the former students of the professor sell their labor time and capacities on the market as commodities, therefore the teaching activity of the professor is determined as productive; it is productive in actuality not in relation to the intercommunication with the students before them but in relation to the entire ambit of the post-university occupations of the students, and the capital relations of the society in which their employments are exercised. If the professors also serve as consultants to an industrial enterprise, private or public, such activity is apart from the relations in the classroom to their students.

The process of transformation of the educational institutions from the halls of gentlemen, such as Oxford once was thought to be, into places of occupational training, theoretical and practical, is not easy or simple. Much as been written about the transformation of the elite into the mass university. In this transformation there was another motive force, which was to make the university into a center for the useful arts in industry. Such was the ideal of Benjamin Franklin in the 18th century; it was applied to the development of chemistry in the German university by Justus Liebig in the 19th. Thomas Jefferson had previously conceived of the usefulness of state universities to mining and agricultural development.

The Poet and Unproductive Labor

Productive labor of the human kind is mediative in relation to the material order of nature, and both mediate and immediate in the human order. By productive labor we transform the natural materials to the end of meeting human wants, needs and desires. Thus, our labors are subjective and objective, since the wants and desires are subjective and objective, and the means to meet them are not otherwise. The alternative would be a thingly process in meeting the wants and desires, which is excluded. But the productive labor is a means between the processes of the given material order and the human processes of the human order; the means are not an end, save in the process of perfecting them, wherein we work on them. Labor, subjective and objective, is a process of human reproduction, in which the productive process participates and is mediately connected to the process of consumption. The mediation in society, civil, bourgeois and capitalist is dominated by the relations of equivalent reciprocation in exchange. The poet too is engaged in this mediated relation of getting paid for his poetry; yet the poet has an immediate relation to it, which is subjective and internal, and this relation is then objectified and externalized in the process of publishing, getting remuneration, retaining rights of authorship, etc., in the given status of society.

Milton got £5 for his *Paradise Lost*. The labor of the poet is productive in general, potentially, concretely, and actually. The actuality of the productive labors is human in general; it is particular in a given society; but given the predominance of exchange, money payment and contract in this society, the productive labor of the poet takes on a different form from that of the intervention of subjective, immediate and internal processes of the human kind in its self-reproduction in general. The proof that the labors of the poet are productive in the human order in general, as a part of the human labors, mediate and immediate, objective and subjective, internal and external, rests not in the relation of the poet to his poetry, nor in the relation of the audience or readership to the same, but in the process between the poet, the poetry and the reader or hearer of it. Under particular historical circumstances the act of contracting for publication of the poetry, getting paid in connection with the publication, and of paying out for a copy of the publication enters into the process of labor and self-reproduction between the poet and ourselves; the productivity of the labor is thereby determined not in general but in particular. But the productivity of the labor cannot be determined in its particularity with its determination in general, nor, conversely, can it be determined in general without its determination in particular. Since Milton got but a small sum of money for his poetic labors, there is some doubt about its productiveness under the given circumstances of its publication. The productivity of the poetic labors is relative, however, on the one side to the going rate for other poetic products as a particularity of the given social process, and on the other, relative to the poetic productivity in general. F. Leavis, in the 1930s, might have thought that the amount paid out by the publisher was a fair estimate of the worth of the poem. Aristotle, in the *Poetics*, judged that a poem is both useful and gives pleasure. A bad poem may be useful, but gives no pleasure. The pleasurable is subjectively useful. Had Milton been a poetaster, he most likely would have received many times that amount for his talent, for the going rate for hack work in the past seems to have been a penny a line, and there are over ten thousand lines in his masterpiece. But the poem as poetry is different from the poem as a commodity. In our society, the productiveness of a product, poetic or other, is expressed in its commodity form, but since the commodity is a formal and not a substantive process, the productiveness is not determined thereby; the determination and the expression are otherwise arrived at under other social circumstances. Thus under primitive conditions, the productiveness of the process and product of the human kind has another form than that of the commodity, and in our theory of socialism, the commodity form of the productiveness of labor disappears. It is false to regard the particular circumstances of the production alone as the determinant of the productiveness. We change the formal expression but not the substance of our productiveness by eliminating the commodity, exchange, contract, the market, and the principle of commutative justice and right, from our civil mode of production. Had Marx left the story of Milton and the £5 at this point, we would have only had to add the consideration of the general determination of the productivity, which has been done. The commodity is a form through which the substance comes into its process. The substance, human and natural, is active through a determinate form. The commodity form is the means whereby the human substance, which is labor, is active in modern society, civil and bourgeois, but this is not the only form of that substance known in human history and theory. Under other conditions, the substance and its productiveness, subjective and objective, has the same general determination, but another formal expression than that of the commodity. Productivity comes forth under other human conditions than those of commodity exchange. He did not leave the story at that point, but added that Milton produced *Paradise Lost* out of the same ground that the silkworm produces silk; it was the activity of his nature.

The silkworm produces nothing; its bringing forth of the secretion which is made into silk is a natural process, which is *praxis* or doing, and not a human one, which is making, *poiesis*, producing. The silk is, in the human order of nature, an object, and our relation to it is objective; as the spider's secretion it is a thing, in nature, as is the work which is active in a thingly way in this regard. The question of Milton's nature and natural action is another matter. Since Milton's poetry is under discussion, it is his art and not his nature that is at issue. He sold his poem, which is labor of another sort than the labor of producing it; and in this case it was the labor of making the sale that had a price, just or unjust, placed on it; the production as such had no price. The question of Milton's nature is a speculative matter, which lies outside the canon of science. The question of the value, objective and subjective, of the human product, is embedded in the answer to the problem concerning the relation between human form and substance, and therewith of the human kind and order to the material order, and the relation of these to the processes of nature.

Art is not nature directly, but is mediately a part of it. Art is human, the sensible process and product of our non-material nature; the material processes, which are another part of nature, are not art, but are the medium through which art is expressed by the human kind, communicated and lastingly recorded. By means of art, the human kind transforms the nonmaterial conceptions, affections and representations into work accessible to our senses. The artist has no nature, but it may appear that the work of art comes forth unwilling or unwilled, as though it were a work of nature, at which we who are not artists are filled with wonder. At the same time we consider that all of human work and labor, its productive process and its ongoing product, evoke the same wonder and awe. These are subjective feelings which in times of fear may make life appear to be worth living.

Here we distinguish art and technics. Art, as in the case of Milton's *Paradise Lost*, has technics of meter, rhythm, and figure as part of it; another part is some great Idea to which his figures rise, and from which the poem issues forth; the internal rhyme, alliteration, consonance and dissonance between meter and rhythm in Milton's *Paradise Lost* also pose a question of technics. In ancient times art and technics were held to be one. We see how in our usage they differ and are the same. We turn now to the general question of technics.

Appendix I. On the Theory of Technics

(This was originally published, in somewhat changed form, as Foreword to H.P. Müller, *Die technologisch-historischen Exzerpte von Karl Marx.* Ullstein 1982, and to Rainer Winkelmann, *Exzerpte über Arbeitsteilung, Maschinerie und Industrie von Karl Marx.* Ullstein 1982.)

The process of human reproduction, in opposition to the physiological process, comprises the labors of production, consumption, and the mediation between the two, which is realized in the labor of distribution. Distribution in turn is realized in concreto in our bourgeois society in exchange and commodity transactions, as well as in distribution without reciprocation in exchange; the latter process is carried through within the factory or firm, prior to putting up the product thereof for sale on the market for exchange, as a commodity. Exchange in the economic sense is defined as a process of equal or equivalent reciprocation between the various parties therein; it is a social relation for two or more who are capable to carry through the exchange on social, economic, juridical, moral, objective and subjective grounds. Distribution in our society is therefore both with and without reciprocation, as a process without reciprocation, it is distribution as such; as a process with reciprocation, whether equal or equivalent, in mutuality, it is economic exchange. That which is exchanged in the economic process by the one is recognized and acknowledged as a means of meeting a want and need or desire of the other, and conversely, that which is exchanged by the other is recognized and acknowledged to be a means of meeting a want, need or desire by the one. Exchange and commodity relations are an essential condition of capital and money circulation in our society.

In carrying through the labor process, the human kind goes mediatively to work, in order to meet its wants and needs, as Hegel expressed this, and to rub them out. The human mediative activity is generated, however, not only in the relation between the worker and the product, and not only between the producer and the gratification of the wants, but also between the processes of production and consumption, and within the mediate process as such, with production on the one side, and consumption on the other. The first mediation mentioned is between human labor and its internal and external surroundings in general, of which the process of our human reproduction by meeting of our human wants and physiological needs is a particularity. Labor consists of a material element, in that the human kind takes up and transforms the materials of its inner and outer surroundings, that we may carry on our lives, reproduce and vary our human conditions, and an immaterial element, in that we by a mediate process differentiate and connect, organize, combine, and divide our labors; the nonmaterial element of the human order is social and mental. Much has been written about the division of labor, which presupposes the relation between the human kind and the material world, the differentiation between the relatives, and the connection between the differentiae in this process; the differentiation and connection in the human order is not direct but diremptive, self-diremptive, dirempted and mediate; further presupposed is the social organization and social combination of labor. For that which is divided is first combined together, and then divided. The combination of labor is a communal process in primitive society; this combination is developed as a social process in our society. Thus the division of labor does not stand alone, but appears as a part of that which is greater, and this is the process of labor organization, which is a precondition of the exchange process.

In the organization of labor in the modern factory, the combination of labor is a presupposition of its division and specialization. The division is a social relation of labor, the specialization is a technical relation thereof. In its historical as well as its systematic process, the technics of labor are an essential part of its organization, in its material as well as in its non-material side. Thus the combination and division of labor in society, and the specialization of the technics in production have their concrete and abstract relations and aspects. Technic is defined as a concrete process of labor; it is the immediate relation of labor to the tools and instruments of labor and work. Technic is defined also as an abstract process of labor; it is the mediate relation of labor to the means of production. This technic is both an abstract and concrete relation of the human kind in the production and reproduction process. Technic as an abstraction enters into the sum of skills, capacities, preparations, arts and powers of labor in the process of human reproduction. The abstract side of the technics is brought out in the origin of the term, in ancient Greek *techne*, with the meaning, skill, art, industry, and also in the Latin term, *ars*, with approximately the same meanings. The practical side of the modern usage is closely related to the theoretical and abstract side of the ancient usage; the theoretical and abstract side of the modern usage is new, and is not differentiated from the history and science of technology, which has the development of the technics as its object.

Technics, as a part of the organization of labor in general, is not static but dynamic, and is furthered in connection with the opposition between the traditional, or the handed down, and the innovative according to the different social conditions, and is embedded in the different epochs of human history in different ways. Marx drew the attention to the role of invention in the development of technics, and made fun of the cult of personality in the process. Since everything in the last century was individualizing and individualized, there was a widespread interpretation of invention as an individual affair. Invention is a part of a more inclusive category, which is that of innovation, and the latter is a part of a greater, which is the technics; technics in turn is a part of the labor process in society. In practice, the technic is a part of the innovation process immediately as well, since labor is not fixed but variable, dynamic and innovative, save where it is subject to restrictions external and alien, placed on its dynamism. These restrictions are found not only in the ancient guilds but also in the modern factory.

Everything is in change and nothing is fixed, as Heraclitus said. Yet the technics changes and is varied at another rate and historical tempo than the social labor in the process of human reproduction, and does not proceed with the latter in a simple parade step. The technics and its change as material processes are doubtless more strikingly evident than the more abstract relations in human history; yet the technics is not the determinant factor in this history. The changes in technics are determinates of the changes and transformations in the organization of social labor, whether the latter is communal or social, and in the second case, the oppositive relations between the social classes are the determinant factor and motor of history. Nevertheless, the technics, in its function as the immediate relation of the worker to the tools and other means of production, concrete and abstract, takes part in all the other human processes. If in the Palaeolithic period the changes in the technics are measured in tens of thousands of years, the changes in the ancient Chinese, Indic, Egyptian technics and science stretch over thousands of years, which gives the impression of stagnation. On the contrary, we are certain that human life in the archaic primitive conditions, or the history of the Asian empires, was developed in a constant change which was in no way stagnant, and this is to be seen in the history of the technics, although these processes were slower in their development than the way they appear in our immediate historical experience. In either case, the twofold process of innovation and its social working out is in opposition to the traditions of the production process of a given society. Investigators of the history of technics and science in ancient China are concerned to show how that land has in practice a precedence over the same developments in the Occident. This may well be, for the human mind is everywhere wakeful and working. Yet the scholars in this field have set the question of the technics and of precedence in an imprecise way, having taken the form for the substance of the matter. The changes in social labor are the determinants of the changes of the technics and sciences; technics and science are parts of the social labor. The relations of labor determine both the retention and innovation of the sciences and technics; the relations of society determine the relations of labor, and the relations of labor determine the relations of human society. The technics and sciences, and their development and effect, their objective process and subjective importance are developed by the relations of social labor; hence the precedence of one country over another in the matter of technics and science is a determinate and not a determinant of economic and social development. In this connection, two matters are to be brought out: First, the social labor process is a complex of determinative factors in human history; second, technics are a part of this determinative process. It is not a matter of wonder that the ancient Chinese made great advances in technics and science; Aristotle had regarded the progress of mathematics in ancient Egypt with admiration, and held it to be in advance over the Greek. The same is to be said of the natural and mathematical sciences in ancient Mesopotamia. The greater development in technics and science made by the capitalist society in Europe at the beginning of the modern period in comparison to the societies of the Orient is not to be explained by the progress made in science and technology in Europe at that time; the advance of the Europeans over the science and industry of the Orient, after its less considerable beginnings in the west, is accounted for not by developments internal to technics and science, but by social processes of a greater intensity and extensiveness in the connection and working out of the production, exchange and distribution relations of the European economy than that of the Orient at the time of early capitalist developments, during the late 15th and 16th centuries. The advance of science and technics was realized by their closer connections to the European production processes than the Asian, whereby the technical and scientific advances were such that their potentialities were more rapidly realized in the former than in the latter. The Europeans, by more closely relating their own production and exploitation relations to the reproduction process, were able to incorporate and exploit their technical and scientific achievements on the one side, and to incorporate those of the Chinese, in the matters of paper manufacture, printing, and gunpowder. The interconnection and elaboration of the production relations were then and are determined by the labor and reproduction process, and these together determined the changes and rate of changes in science and technics.

Technic is primarily a practical process in human reproduction, in relation to our concrete tools of work and theoretical instruments of labor.

At the beginning of the capitalist age, and of the corresponding epoch of the modern bourgeois society, the developments in technics and science were prosecuted with increasing acceleration, which has in no way diminished since then, as in the petrochemical and electronic industries. At the time of Gutenberg and Henry the Navigator the innovatory processes in printing and navigation were developed relatively slowly, so that the effect and development of an invention or discovery are measured in centuries. At the time of Marx the effect of innovations in the iron and steel industry, and in electricity were worked out not in centuries but in human generations or decades. In our times, the length of time to work out a new process in computer technics is measured in months or weeks.

Marx stood in the middle of these historical developments, materially and mentally. Many matters were worked out by him thoroughly, others were taken up provisionally, without elaboration. He took over the differentiation between the history we make and do not make, as he conceived it, from Vico. We refer to all history as a record which we set down, and in this sense make; we further distinguish between inherited adaptations of the given species, in relation to its environment, on the one side, and the cumulation of human skill or labor quality on the other. In the current development of ecological science, the difference between species and environment is taken up as an adaptive process between them. The cumulation of skills and the accumulation of capital products are mutual in another sense than the foregoing; the human cumulation and accumulation are a mediating and mediated relation of labor in the oppositive process of innovation and stabilization in industry in particular and in the human order in general. This consideration indicates that the materialist interpretation of history, which was developed in relation to the Darwinian theory of organic evolution, could only be developed up to a certain point. The difference between the processes of living matter and those of the human kind in the processes of labor and in the organization of society were clear to Aristotle, and this difference is here taken up and set forth. Yet at his time the theory of evolution had not yet been developed. The connection between the human species and the other life processes, and the differences between them are accounted for by means of scientific contributions from ancient times down to the present; we do not arrest the process or the account, Aristotelian, Hegelian, Darwinian, Marxian, gene theory, or any other. The theory of variation brings together the material and human processes of change in nature; but we distinguish between biological change and human change, biological variation and human variation. Biological variation is an evolutionary process, carried through by the transmission and inheritance of vital properties in a direct natural process of the genes, and in an indirect natural process of the somatoplasm, from one generation of life to another. The cumulation of capacities, skills, technics and science on the one hand, and the accumulation of products of those skills, capacities, on the other, are a mediate process of the human kind. The mediation is both active and passive, objectifying and objectified. The mediative is the cumulation and application of the capacities and potencies, by the human kind in its labors, as an agency; we are the agent of our self-reproduction and self-alteration. The active mediation is opposed to the passive process of mediation by accumulation of goods and products, commodities and capital, which are the result of our agencies. We are in debt to Hegel, to the evolutionists and to Marx for this insight. Technics was understood in the past century as a historical process, natural and human, whereas its system, and the distinction between the animal and human process was left for a later time to be worked out, together with its definition in the human order, and its distinction from the material order of nature.

The relation of the human kind to the human order and thereby to the material order is the act of transformation of the two orders by our work and labor. The relation to both orders is exhausted by this relation, insofar as it is the human relation that is in question; in the material order what is being carried through is an interchange of natural materials. The human relation to nature is first the transformation of matter by the primary transformation of the human order, the mediate transformation of the human kind, the transformation of the field of nature in which we labor, and the transformation of both; the natural processes of these transformations are direct and indirect variations by adaptation and readaptation of the material elements. The human relation to nature is mediated by the relations of the human kind in the given social whole, there being no other way of relating to nature by the human kind than this. The relation to nature being exhausted by this process, it is evident therefore that the relations of mediation and labor are one, for they are the same relation in the opposed contexts, labor in relation to the process of reproduction of the human kind, mediation between the human kind and the natural order by the human order, labor abstractly expressed as mediation, mediation having labor as the abstract and concrete expression thereof.

The relation to nature is denoted as art, Latin *ars*, which is skill acquired by study, practice, technical knowledge both abstract and concrete; *techne* denotes craft in the material sense of workmanship, and in the spiritual sense alludes to what is crafty, cunning (see Alexander Pope, *The Works of Shakespeare*).

Technology is a Part of the Science of Human History

The *techne* is not the whole but a material part of the relation between the human and material orders; in the conceptions of old, the technical skills were a sort of cunning, whereby the materials were tricked into collaborating with men for human ends, which were other than the ends of the materials themselves; labor itself was conceived as cunning, personified in the craft of the workmen, from the standpoint of the ancient Greek literati, who were members of the class opposed to that of social labor. Art has in it the abstraction, and reference to craft, crafty reproduced the Greek practice. The banality of labor by rote, refers to the work by the oven, fireplace; *banausos*, laborer, *baunos*, oven; this was the expression of the craft of the laborer, the routine of work, and the place of the woman in the home; the craft has its trade secrets; the craftsman is the seller, by bargaining, *kapeliké*, in the marketplace in the conception of Aristotle.

The history of technics and arts is opposed to the science thereof; the history of any subject matter presupposes that it is not a system; science is the system of the relation to nature; the science of techne or of art is that of museology. Technology is the record of transmission and acquisition of skills, qualities of labor and of workmanship; in reality it is the record of concrete variation by discrete human traditions and groups, the particular mastery by appropriation and readaptation of the given skill by the apprentice, who takes unto himself by taking away the skill of the master, but by becoming the master renews, readapts, relearns, curves forward the mastery of the older one; alienating and appropriating the skill is the civil social process; redistributing it is the process of distributive reciprocation.

In tracing the history of technics from ancient to modern times, we see that several contradictions in its usage are overcome. The ancient Greeks separated *techne*, skill or craft, from banal labor, routine, and housework. Against this, which is a contradiction from our modern point of view, we see that there is a technic in work of all kinds, in and outside the house, and in both skilled and routine labor. There is, moreover, technic both in concrete work and abstract labor. The ancients applied the concepts, *techne*, or *ars*, to praxis, to practical and not to theoretical human undertakings, excluding theory from the medium and field of labor. Labor is still not a joyful but a laborious task, having pain associated with it in childbirth. Against this contradiction we see that there is a technic in labor of all kinds, the practical and the theoretical, the routine labor in the house and in the factory, the labor of the skilled crafts, the labor of engineering, applied and theoretical science, and in the arts; there is a technic of labor broken up into discrete tasks by rationalization of the production process, and technic of the skilled crafts which see the product through from start to finish. Figuratively, there is also joyful labor in the vineyard and in home gardening, with the technics which appertain to them.

We go not only actively and mediatingly but also passively and mediatedly to work. The order is indeed reversed. The material world acts on us, and we feel hunger, thirst, or fatigue. We act on the materials, gathering food, carrying the water and refresh ourselves. The materials by their gravitational pull, friction, density, chemical composition, and electrical effect, offer resistance, which we overcome in meeting our wants and needs, or fulfilling our desires. But first of all we go immediately and not directly to work.

The contradictions which have been set forth are in fact conflicts between Weltanschauungen. The ancients saw technics, *techne* or *ars*, in a limited way. Optimistically, Bacon, Milton, and Laplace saw the active relation of the human kind to the surrounding nature; we see the active relation of the surroundings to us, and our active relation to our surroundings; both sides are active and passive in these processes. Moreover, the material world is not only around but within us, and each side acts on the other in symmetry.

Our technics are applied not only to the material world, but to the human world; since nature is broader than both these worlds, and our technics are general, we speak of their application to nature generally, and not in a limited way to this world or the other. The technics begin with the use of the human organs as tools of work and the use of stone, wood, bone and clay as work tools which are the extensions of our organs. We think of both the organs and the tools as concrete, practical instruments, in interaction with the abstract and theoretical instruments. The technics are but a part of the process of work and labor, which are combined and divided, in their social organization. The concrete work and the concrete and abstract labors, the concrete and abstract technics and means of production are distributed in society; the exchange of the skills, technics, and the products by sale and purchase is a part of the distribution process in our society, in a local and temporary, not a universal and eternal condition of the human kind.

Instruments of labor and tools of work are not means of production as such, but are converted into means of production in the process of human reproduction; as such the work tools and the labor instruments are applied in the process of production, distribution and consumption. Work tools insofar as they are concrete and practical are shared by the human kind with many other mammal species, and with the bird and insect species as well. The work tools of the human kind are opposed to those of the animal world; the latter are not opposed to the human work tools, but are part of the process of evolution of the one into the other. The human work tools are converted into labor instruments, the practical tool into the practical and theoretical instrument; the labor instruments and work tools are converted into means of production, consumption and distribution in the process of human reproduction.

Appendix II. Diremption and Alienation of Labor

The diremption of the relation between labor and its product has generated the differentiation between like and unlike labor, between like and unlike qualification or capacity, between like and unlike product, and exchange of one against the other, for the exchangers meet not as kin or neighbor, ally or friend, but as contracting parties who are opposed and estranged from one another. The alienation of the product of the one, mediately, immediately, in equal, equivalent or proportionate reciprocation, is therefore a relation which is actually or potentially between antagonists.

In the process of diremption and alienation in exchange a difference is generated between like and unlike, and between the quantitative measure of difference and the qualitative affirmation or denial of difference in the objects, goods, matters and commodities exchanged.

Presupposed in this process is a quantification of the substance of the exchanged, and of the wants and needs which are thereby met.

Diremption and alienation constitute a mediate human process, a formalization of the medium is constituted thereby; this formalization bears on symbolic exchange and on economic exchange whereby wants and needs are met. The mediate relation is a substantive process whereby the human kind reproduces itself, its variability of reproduction having different formal modalities in human history. The product in the exchange process is both the materialized object of past labor, and the present material and immaterial labor time and capacity which is exchanged.

The product as a formality of the exchange is therewith objectified, but it is not an active relation of objectification. The exchange is the formality of the relation, in which labor in its activity is dirempted from its passivity, and the latter is objectified, being transformed into a good, or object, as the commodity exchanged. Being the passive object divided from the active subject, which is labor, the objectification is the reification of labor, whereby the formality and passivity of the social relation transforms the producer as though into a thing, but really into an object.

Labor in its unfree social condition is a commodity which is alienated by another to a third party. The producing community of labor in the Asiatic mode of production alienates the social product thereof. The product is materialized in the exchange relation, whereby the form of the product is separated from the substance, which is the labor of making it. The form is alienated as a commodity, by equal, proportionate, or equivalent reciprocation in exchange between concrete, modest communities; that class of product is then alienated by an agency of the state, which in the ancient Oriental society is the community magnified, and personified in the monarch; the sovereignty seizes a part of the village product, without reciprocation in exchange, which is exploitation. Servile labor is alienated not in a communal relation, as in the Asiatic mode of production, but in a relation between persons, slave and master, serf and lord, client and patron. The power over the labor in the unfree condition thereof rests with the community, concrete or magnified and sovereign, with the slave, master, patrons and lords. It is a formal right applied to the time and capacity of the class of social labor in the history of civil society during the pre-capitalist social formations, Asiatic, African, Andean, ancient Mexican, Graeco-Roman, feudal, or in the relations of guild bondage, race and colonial slavery in the capitalist social formation. The power over labor is bought and sold as a commodity, the labor time and capacity is the substance of which the power as a right is a social form. The form and substance coincide in the pre-capitalist periods of the history of civil society, for the labor power, time and capacity are controlled by an alien presence, the community magnified, the agencies of the state, the masters, patrons and overlords of the unfree labor. The form and substance of the unfree condition of social labor and the political and economic control over it coincide in this condition for the reason that social labor is there and then unfree in form and substance.

In the capitalist period of the history of civil society the predominant form of social labor is wage labor, which is free in form and unfree in substance. The formal power over labor passes over the labor itself, which is of like kind in its legal position relative to the capitalists as a social class, each side contracting as free and equal persons, the one for the sale, the other for the purchase of a stated quantity and quality of labor. The formal power of social labor over its time and capacity is not sold by the laboring persons or by the class of labor, but is retained as a right, which is the title of its condition of formal freedom and the term of its condition of formal equality to the representatives of capital in society.

Labor power as such is not a commodity, therefore, but is the expression in the hands of wage labor of its formal freedom and juridical equality with all other moral persons. The right of labor is socially acknowledged as the power of its disposition over its own time and capacity in production, which is its substantive labor power. Labor is in substance unfree in this social condition, for there is no way in which it can gain the means of its subsistence, thus no way that it can gain its living, no way that it can reproduce itself and all of society save by the sale of its time and capacity to produce the goods to meet the wants and needs of all. Thus the form of equality is dirempted from the substance, and the form of freedom is dirempted from the substance thereof. The labor form is dirempted from the labor substance in the history of civil society by the diremption of labor power from labor quality and quantity and by the alienation of labor quality and quantity in the wage labor relation

The quantification and social differentiation of qualities of labor are the preconditions of the equalization and liberation of labor. Thus, labor is equalized and liberated by the development of exchange relations, but this equalization and liberation, whereby the human kind passes from the primitive communal to the social condition is a formal process. This is the constitutive condition of formal equality and liberty of labor of the humankind. The substantive liberty and equality of labor is the condition of liberation and equalization of the human kind.

Equality in civil society, we have said, is a formal and objective relation alone, freedom a relation of all kinds, formal, substantial, objective, and subjective.

The diremption in the process of production recapitulates the diremption of the human kind in relation to the world of matter in which it is brought forth. It is in this sense a general human condition. The alienation of the product from the producer to another is not a general but a local and particular condition of the modern and bourgeois society, which has its beginnings in ancient epochs of civil society and earlier periods as well.

The opposition between the product of living capacity and the living labor capacity itself is that of the objectified relation, in relation to the particular natural field and to the particular human society, to the capacity of the human kind to objectify itself. The objectification of itself by living labor in the process of expenditure of its time and skill in social production is the active relation that is opposed to the passive relation embodied in its product. The objectification of the self by the living labor process in production is at once the constitution of the subject in relation to the object, the positing of the object in the history of the human order immediately, in the material order mediately, and thereby the positing of the subject as the active factor in history within the human order, actually, potentially and in reality. The product is objectified labor, labor past and dead, passive, without productive capacity until activated by new living labor that is applied to it in the process of social reproduction. The opposition within the labor process in this case becomes that between past and present, passive and active, potential and actual, objectified and objectifying, self-objectifying labor. The subjectivity of living labor in its relation in production, and of living labor capacity in its relation to use and to its expression in value is introduced mediately by the process of self-objectification of labor in production; living labor far from being a subjectivity in relation to the product is the means of objectifying the latter, that is transforming the natural thing into human object, for the reason that living labor objectifies itself. Living labor is not an object in itself, nor yet an object to begin with, but becomes the object in relation to itself by its motion, by activating itself, whereby it becomes the self-objectifying moment in the human order, the moment whereby the human order is opposed to, diremped within and alienated from the material order. The objectified product of that relation is not opposed immediately as living labor capacity as self-object and thereby as subject. Living labor is opposed as subject to its objectified product mediately, the objectified past labor is opposed to present labor, object as passivity is opposed to object as activity, object is opposed to object in self-relation, and thereby is opposed to the subject immediately.

Notes

Note 1

There are two theories of labor power. The first is given by Marx, *Kapital* (MEW 23, p. 192), as follows: 'The use of labor power is labor itself.' 'Labor is first of all a process between man and nature, a process in which man by his own act mediates, regulates and controls his material interchange with nature. He juxtaposes himself as a natural force to the natural materials. He sets in motion the natural powers belonging to his body, in order to appropriate the natural materials in a form useful for his own life.'—On labor power in this connection Marx wrote: 'The buyer of the labor power consumes it in that he allows its seller to labor.' 'A man brings his labor power to market for sale as a commodity.' This is wage labor.—In the first theory, labor is a force, among other forces over nature, not directly of nature; the natural powers of the body are not forces in the same sense that labor is a force. Labor in its beginnings is of the animal kind, and instinctive. The situation, wrote Marx, in which the worker comes forth as seller of his labor power on the commodity market is separated from the primeval situation in which human labor has not yet stripped off its first, instinctive forms. The second theory is the one that is here propounded. There are, according to this theory, two relations of labor power, formal and substantial, the one in which we have the formal right of disposition over it, and the other, in which we have the power to make, produce, to work, to meet our social, objective wants, and our material needs, and by which we reproduce our kind in and through our human activities. The second power is the substantive power of labor; in modern civil society, the substantive labor power has a particular form, the right of labor to dispose of it as a commodity which is sold and purchased.

In the history of the human kind, the animal forces of material nature are overcome and transformed by labor. These natural forces do not disappear, but remain in the pumping of the blood by the heart, the muscular forces and the energies of the nervous and glandular systems. They are converted into human powers by the natural evolution of the human kind in interaction with the human development of our relations to the material order and in the human order. We therefore speak of natural forces on the one side, and of human powers on the other. Of the human powers, the labor power is the one that converts all the others into human processes. Thus labor power is a continuation of the natural forces, for it is an outlay of muscular, nervous and other forces, but has a substantive difference from these, for it is organized in a human way, that is by processes of human society, and therein, of the mind and consciousness. Labor power is thus connected with and opposed to the natural forces in form and substance; the labor power in human society has different formal and substantial relations in the human and material orders; the substantive processes of human labor differ from the forces of nature, and are common throughout the human order, both in the primeval and civil conditions. The formal processes of labor differ from those of the material forces and from the substantive relations of labor. The history of the labor form differs from that of the labor substance, the histories of the labor form being many more than those of the substance, which can be summed up in one history.—Labor power in its form is not labor power in its substance, for its substance is the process whereby we transform the materials of nature, of the human order, and of ourselves in accordance with our human undertakings. Labor power in its form, we have said, is the power as a right of disposition over the labor time and quality, and over its product. If we sell our labor time and capacity to reproduce our lives, it ma be thought that we sell them as labor power; but in this case the words, labor power, are further to be analyzed. The substance of labor power is here in question. We do not sell the right of disposition over the labor substance as wage labor; hence we do not sell the formal relation of labor power. Yet the substance of labor is realized only in a given form, which is that of wage labor in modern civil society; the form is the contract for sale and purchase of our labor time and quality, for which we receive as wage labor a living wage. The wage is the means by which the human kind reproduces itself in that it is exchanged against the means of subsistence; the circulation of wages as money constitutes the medium in which the substance of labor and the goods whereby it subsists and reproduces itself and the human kind in the current period of its history are distributed. The right over the labor power substance is the formal labor power in civil society. The right of disposition over the time and quality of social labor varies, resting with the slave owner in one form of civil society, with the monarch in another, with the feudal lord in a third, and with wage labor itself in a fourth, which is that of modern bourgeois society; it rests with wage labor in any circumstance in which social labor exchanges its time and quality against the means of subsistence. This exchange takes place in various degrees during the different forms and periods of the history of civil society, but is the predominant form of labor in our modern period.

Labor is a natural force and a human power. In the natural force, the form and substance are in a direct relation, in the human power they are in a mediate relation to one another. Thus in the human condition they are separable, and vary separately from one historical epoch to another. The right of disposition over labor time and quality is a formal freedom of wage labor. Labor is in its substance neither free nor unfree in the human condition generally; its freedom rests poetically in the recognition of its bondage; the law does not give us our freedom, for the law of material existence is the condition of our lives, not of our freedom; the recognition of the law, its scope and limit, is the condition of our animal nature. Labor in civil society is in its form unfree, whatever the condition of its substantive freedom maybe, in that it works for another person in that society; this formal unfreedom can be eliminated. The substance of that unfreedom is variable, and is eliminated in another way.

Setting the question of the social surplus or excess labor aside, therewith the particular condition of bondage, there remains the question of the general condition of bondage; in this sense all labor is necessary, and is opposed in no respect in the human order. It is only outside the human order that labor opposes something else, but is without opposition in this case by that to which it opposes itself. Thus there is no condition of human life which is not laborious; the subjective likes and dislikes of the laborer do not alter this state of being. The alienation of the surplus labor and product in society by the exploiting class from the hands of its producers in the production of capital, has the form of surplus value; a part of the condition of human freedom, and therewith of socialism, is the liberation of this excess from the representatives of capital, who have appropriated it, and its return to its producers, who are now free to do with it what they will. It is the human power, according to Marx, true freedom. This concept, however, is the translation of the categories of capital formation to another system, which is not socialism, nor is it freedom. The division of production into the categories necessary and free in the production process rests on a misconception.

Social labor in the condition which is dominated by the formation of capital takes the form of wage labor, or contractual labor. In this condition the owners of all kinds, of labor time and capacity, and of capital, are legally bound by the terms of the contract for selling and buying what they own; the length of the working day is one of the terms of the contracts. Such a stipulation concerns work or labor done for others, not for ourselves. If we work for ourselves then our labor time and capacity have another quality, and another quantitative measure by shortening or lengthening it, setting aside sleep and mealtimes in meeting our wants and needs, desires and goals.

If we consider that labor is the human condition, then it is one with the social whole. All who are not infantile or old, weak or ill, work, as far as they are able, and in ways that they are able; learning is part of the labor process. Labor in this condition is not an external necessity, for it is the human potentiality, which is realized by the human kind in general, and by the human individual in particular. There is no division in this potential condition between necessity and surplus time, power or product, no division between basis and superstructure, and none between internality and externality.

Labor is the human process of interaction with material nature and within the human order of nature; it has many sides, practical, theoretical, abstract, concrete, rational, imaginative, conscious, unconscious, traditional and innovative. It is the objective relation of the human kind to the material order, and the objective relation to and in the human order, whereby matter is transformed, in the process of generation and reproduction of the human kind, and the human order constituted. The relation of the human kind within the human order and our relation to the material order is objective and subjective. From these relations a supreme end in itself is excluded, for it is a false teleology of human activity. Our ends are particular, not universal.

The relation of labor in and to the human order is that of an internality. There is an externality in these relations, but it is not that of labor. External are the physiological needs, which are internalized and therewith made human by the human kind. Thus the material order of nature is outside and inside the human being, and is in either case other than the latter. The externality, in this case, is there, as a potentiality to be humanized. It is opposed to another potentiality, which is that of the unity of the particular social whole with the human kind as a whole. The first potentiality is concrete and particular, the second abstract and general.

Labor is combined and divided, the combination in collectivities and communalities is objectively determined in the relation between the human kind and the process of its human reproduction. The directions of determination between human wants and physiological needs are in an interaction, each side determining the other. The system of labor determines and is determined by the relations of the social whole; the relation of the social whole to the process of human reproduction is that of labor, which is the mediate process between the two. The system of labor and that of wants and needs are in interaction, each side determining the other. Thus labor determines the wants and the latter determine the process of labor. The expansion of the one thus determines the expansion of the other.

Labor is applied in the given social whole and determines the latter as an internality; each side is a mediate and objective determinant of the other. The determination of labor as an external necessity is therefore a subjective evaluation; equally subjective is the determination of labor as an internal necessity; needs must when the devil drives. The determination of the organization, combination and division in society by an external necessity, and the determination of the same by an internal necessity are subjective. The determination of the organization, combination and division of labor in society as an objective necessity and as subjective necessity is external as well. Labor as an external necessity belies the labor of love. Comradely and friendly labors, collective and communal labor in this sense are not labor as an external necessity; but in that they contribute to the human reproduction of the human kind, they are not other than slave labor, wage labor, servile labor, in their substance; the differences between them are formal; the forms of labor, on being internalized enter into the substance of the human kind.

The process whereby labor determines and is determined by the relations of the social whole is immediately internal to the latter and therewith the latter is mediately internal to the former; for labor is determined in its organization by the relations of the social whole. It is a part of the social whole, internal to and contained within the latter, which is the greater in relation to labor, and labor the lesser in this relation. The relations of labor to the material order of nature and to the human order determine the relations of the social whole; in this respect labor is both internal and external in actuality to the given social whole, and in potentiality to the human order. Labor as such has no standpoint, the standpoint thereof is that of the mode of organization predominant in the given social whole, whereby the relations of labor are determined.

Labor as such is neither free nor unfree, but a part of our existence in the material and human worlds. Once we have left the Garden of Eden we live by our mental and manual labors, which constitute our human substance. In their form our labors are free or unfree; they are unfree as slave and servile labor; wage labor is *pro forma* free in the disposition of its labor power as a right. We have distinguished the formal labor power from the natural force, or the force in the material order of nature. The right of disposition over its time and capacity which wage labor has is its formal labor power. In modern civil society, we know only formal freedom; equality in our society is formal in all cases; there is no substantive equality in theory; there is substantive freedom in theory.

Note 2

Francis Bacon wrote of the Temporis Partus Masculus. It is a human act of parturition that is envisaged, which is effected by our labors. (Bacon, *Temporis Partus Masculus*, 1603.) Aristotle considered the theory of change in his *Physics*, principally in Books 5 and 6. In his *Politics* he wrote of change in Book 5, in which he took up the causes of violent change, or political revolutions, such as the acts of demagogues, poverty, or invasions of the liberty of citizens. These saltations are made within the human order of nature. We consider that this order is as such a great saltation in the natural order. Nature in the generation of the human kind, order and being made and underwent a great leap. The generation of the material universe and order of nature is another great saltation of nature. Contrary to Leibniz, nature makes leaps of various kinds. One of these kinds is the constitution of the human kind out of the material order; another is effected by our labors. Diremption and self-diremption are both saltations.

Note 3

The discussion of slavery in antiquity made assumptions pertaining to nature, to a so-called human nature, and to the nature of things. We will consider the last question first.

Things are natural, being of several kinds. They are in space-time, which changes, and is changed, the things changing and being changed. Things are in several relations in nature. Things change, and are changed; in changing, passing through change, and being changed, the thing becomes other. Thus, the one thing is one and becomes something else, being thus other. The thing is both one and other, the same thing and another; it changes, into a third. Thus it is 1, 2, 3... n things, and is the same thing. It changes hy acting on another thing, and is changed by virtue of the action of the other on the one. Both things are concrete in the same space-time system, which changes; in this way the things pass through change. No thing is without change *in concreto*, in space-time, in nature, that is, in being and becoming. There is no existent in particular, no existence in general, no individual, particular or general being that is not in nature, in space-time, in being and becoming.

Thus things are one, other and many, having relations of one, other, and many; they change and are changed. There are no things without relations, all being relative, one to another, and to many others, for it is changing and changed, thus one, other, and many. Some relations of nature have difference and nexus of one, other, and many others, with regularity and duration of these relations; such relations of things are orderly. The orders of nature are many, accordingly as they are variable, having continuous and discontinuous relations, concrete and abstract relations, and relations which are direct or mediate; there are many other relations beside these; none of these is more basic or fundamental than another, in their system, but some appear in evolution before others. The system of fundamentality is one kind of system, the system of evolution is of another kind.

There are several orders of nature, among the order which is called material, or the order of matter. In this order of nature, things are in a relation of one, other, and many, which is concrete, direct, continuous. The things are material particles or bodies. These things, and the material relations are not exhaustive of the relations of things, or of nature and the nature of things. There are other orders of nature than the material, and in these other orders, relations are linear, nonlinear, continuous, discontinuous, concrete, abstract, direct and mediate.

Thus far in our discussion, we have referred to things which are in relations of one and other, one and many, *ad infinitum*, with difference and nexus among them. The thing acts on another and is acted on by the other; their relations are active and passive, and actual and potential. There are many things, and they are of a particular kind, which changes and is changed. The thing is a henad; it is an orderly thing, having relations of regularity and duration of the occurrence of the relations. The orders of the thing are of several kinds, among them, the quantum, material and human orders of nature. There is an evolution from the one to the other, in a series which is an orderly variation of nature. The thing, being a henad, is one, other, and many; it is not a monad, which is one alone, or *solus ipse*.

The human kind has not a direct but a mediate relation to things. The mediate relation is such that we act both on the thing and on our relation to it. Our act is thus dual; the thing we act on acts on us, in interaction, but its act is single; thus there is an asymmetry between the human kind and the thing with which we interact. The relation of the thing to the human kind is direct, whereas our relation to it is mediate. The thing is a thing, and a thing it remains, whereas it is transformed by the human mediate relation to it into the object of our activity. The object is then transformed into the subject-object.

The human kind constitutes the relation of mediate activity and mediate passivity in nature, but not in nature in general; it constitutes this relation in the human order of nature, whereby the thing is transformed into the object. It does not cease to be a thing, for it has not taken leave of nature; inside the human order it is not a thing but an object; the human being is not a thing, but an object which is a subject.

In considering what is a thing, we have considered what nature is, and what the nature of things are. The thing has no nature as such, but is variable, according to the processes of the various orders of nature. We do not assume that all is orderly in nature. We do not assume that all relations of things are continuous, or that all relations are discontinous. We exist and we think. We cannot exist and cannot think without being and thinking in space-time. Our being is in space-time, and our thinking is in space-time; there is no thought and no thinking without an object, which is in space-time. Thus our being, and thinking are natural, but they are not thingly; by our acts of transformation of nature we are of a certain kind of nature, mediate, objective, human, subjective-objective, abstract and concrete.

Aristotle held that things have a nature; in particular, he thought that a slave has a nature; thus, some men are slaves by nature. In the *Institutes of Justinian* the assumption was made that all men are free by nature; thus; men have a nature, which is a state of innate freedom. We hold that all these assumptions are untenable. Human beings have no nature, save that which we make ourselves, and make of ourselves. Yet we are in nature, being in space-time, and have not left it; we are, however, of no particular nature. The particularity is what we make of ourselves. The distinction between the particular and the general we owe to Aristotle.

There is no necessity in the relations of things, and no freedom; freedom and its opposites, necessity on the one side, and bondage on the other, are human categories; they are objective and subjective. In evolution some things convert into others, but other things, which are of the same kind, retain their condition as before, or *status quo ante*. Thus some processes of matter have evolved into living processes, some have not. Some living processes have evolved into human processes, some have not.

The human process of transformation of matter and of ourselves is that of labor, concrete and abstract, practical and theoretical, mediate and objective.

Aristotle. *Politics*, Bks. 1 and 3. *Nicomachean Ethics*. Bk. 8. There he called a slave a living tool, and a tool an inanimate slave, making the same point in the *Politics*.
Institutes of Justinian. Bk. I, Tit. 2.

Aristotle and Marx have often introduced the concept of necessity in their writings. This has to be critically revised. We speak of necessity only when we have complete knowledge of a topic. But this is possible only in certain formal systems. George Boole, *Laws of Thought*, first began to relate necessity to completeness.

Note 4

"The capitalist mode of production and appropriation, hence capitalist private property, is the first negation of individual private property based on one's own labor. The negation of the capitalist process is produced by itself, with the necessity of a natural process. It is the negation of the negation. This reconstitutes individual property but on the basis of the achievements of the capitalist era, the cooperation of free workers and their common property in land and the means of production produced by labor itself."—Marx. *Kapital,* I, Ch. 24, sect. 7. (2nd ed.) In the 3rd ed. and on, the last sentence is changed to read: "This does not reconstitute private property, but instead the individual property on the basis of the achievements of the capitalist era, the cooperation of free workers and their common property in land and in the means of production produced by labor itself."

Setting aside the analogy to necessity of natural process, we take up the cooperation of free workers, their individual property, common property in land and the means of production. The common property is in this case social property; the cooperation of free workers is not the starting point but the middle of the process of socialization. This is put as follows by Marx:

> "With his i.e., civilized man's development, the realm of natural necessity expands because the realm of wants is expanded, but at the same time the productive powers are expanded which meet these wants. Freedom in this field can only consist in this, that socialized man, the associated producers, regulate their material interchange with nature rationally, bring it under their common control, instead of being mastered by it, as by a blind force; that they accomplish this with last expenditure of energy..." Marx, *Kapital,* vol. III, Ch. 48. MEW 25, p. 828.

The passages cited propose that the free individual is the end of the overturn of capitalism and hence the end of history.

Marx wrote, "The creation of much disposable time beside the necessary labor time for the society generally and for each member of it (i.e., the space for the development of the full productive power of the individual, hence also of society), this creation of non-labor time appears at the standpoint of capital, as of al learlier stages, non-labor time, free time for some." (*Grundrisse,* p. 595. "For the real wealth is the developed productive power of all the individuals." Ibid., p. 596.) "The saving of labor time equals increase of free time, i.e., time for the full development of the individual, which itself as the greatest productive power reacts upon the productive power of labor."(Ibid., p. 599). "The capacity for enjoyment is the condition for it, hence the first means to it, and this capacity is development of an individual pattern, productive power." (Loc. cit.) Throughout, the individual is the productive power, the center of further development, of enjoyment, the beginning and the end of production. This reaches its peak in the slogan of the *Critique of the Gotha Program,* "From each according to his capacities, to each according to each his needs." This is no less a caricature of socialism. It is pure individualism, in Marx's own term, a Robinsonade.

> "Finally let us conceive, by way of change, a union of free men who work with means of production in common, and expend their many individual labor powers self-consciously as a social labor power. All determinations of Robinson's labor are here repeated, only socially and not individually." Marx. *Kapital*, I. Ch. I, sect. 4.

Marx conceived that individual labor powers are transformed into social labor by the union of the free men who work with the means of production in common. To this it is opposed that the labor powers in civil society, bourgeois, capitalist, feudal or other, was social to begin with. It is falsely conceived to be individual according to the myths of the Robinsonade, of the practice of contract between individual capitalists and individual workers or individual representatives of labor. In terms of this conception, Marx held that the free men and women expend their individual labor powers with self-consciousness as social labor power. The consciousness of self is, however, not the means of transforming individual into social labor power, nor is the union of the free the means to do so. The expenditure of labor time and capacity in human reproduction is divided up into the different categories, necessary and surplus, mediate and immediate, but its social character is not destroyed in capitalist, civil or socialist society. The social process is converted into an individual process under capitalism only in the juridical, political and religious institutions of that society, whereby it is superficially modified. But the change of the relations of labor from socialism to capitalism is not a superficial change; it is a fundamental one, of which the free union and self-consciousness are but a small part; even work with means of production in common is a minor and not a major determinant of the transformation of labor from capitalist, civil into socialist labor. The main change is that of the elimination of capital, of commodities, of means of production as a commodity, of labor as a commodity, and the development instead of the distributive reciprocity in the process of human reproduction of all the human kind. The distributive reciprocity in this kind of reproduction is a process of production, distribution and consumption, not of any one, but of all parts of the process together, and not of any one individual, but of all the human kind working together. The elements of union by voluntary decision, consciousness and freedom enter into these processes as part of the process of human being; they are not instigators of these processes of reproduction, nor of the given processes of human being. The elements mentioned are rather the subjective side of these processes.

Marx, Karl, *Kapital*. 2nd ed. and on. Ch. I, sect. 4. Ch. 11, Ch. 24, sect. 7. MEW 23, pp. 92f., 789–791. *Kapital*, III. MEW 25, pp. 185, 197, 267ff., 400, 456, 828, 859, 883. *Theorien über den Mehrwert*. I. MEW 26.1., pp. 366f., 189.

II. MEW 26.2, pp. 522, 529, 97ff., 583. III. MEW 26.3, pp. 414f., 420f., 488, 495, 252f., 344ff., Beilagen 4, 5. *Kritik des Gothaer Programms*, I, 3. *Grundrisse.* 1953, pp. 596, 600.

Cf. David Ricardo. *Works and Correspondence.* P. Sraffa ed., Cambridge, Cambridge University Press, 1951– .

Note 5

On the classification of productive and unproductive labor, cf. Karl Marx, *Grundrisse der Kritik der politischen Oekonomie.* Berlin 1953, p. 372, = Marx Engles Gesamtausgabe, 2. Augabe. 2. Abt., Band I, Teile I, Teile 1–2.(MEGA²) Berlin, Dietz Verlag, 1976.

Idem. Resultate des unmittelbaren Produktionsprozesses. *Arkhiv Marksa i Engel'sa.* V. Adoratskij ed. Vol. II, 1933.

Idem. *Theorien über den Mehrwert*, vol. 3. (Marx Engels Werke, vol. 26.3, 1968.)

Smith, Adam, *The Wealth of Nations*, R. Campbell, A. Skinner and W. Todd (eds.) Oxford University Press, Oxford, 1976, Bk. I, ch. i.

On the state and statesmen, cf. Smith, op. cit., Bk. IV, ch. ii.

Hegel, G. W. F., *Grundlinien der Philosophie des Rechts.* Frommanns, Stuttgart, [1821], 1928.

Marx, Karl, *Kritik der Hegelschen Rechtsphilosophie. Marx-Engels Werke*, vol. 1. Dietz Verlag, Berlin, 1968.

On Reports of inspectors pursuant to provisions of the Factory Acts, cf. Marx, *Kapital*, vol. 1, 1867, and on.

On the theory of immediate and mediate relations of labor, cf. Lawrence Krader, *A Treatise of Social Labor*, Assen 1979, Ch. II, parts v, vi, vii; esp. pp. 160–175.

Note 6. Bibliography on Art and Labor

Plato, *Republic.* (On utility of art, and on assimilation.)
Aristotle,. *Metaphysics.* (On beauty.)
———, *Poetics.* (On mimesis.) Quoting Sophocles (on the distinction between real and ideal mimesis).
Leonardo da Vinci. *Notebooks.* (On imitation and similitude.)
Milton, John, *Samson Agonistes*, Proem. (On minesis.)
———, On Shakespear. (Sonnet.)
Pope, Alexander, *Works of Shakespear.* Preface.
Coleridge, Samuel, *Biographia Literaria.*

138 / Lawrence Krader

Hegel, G. W. F., *Phänomenologie des Geistes*. (On tragedy.)
————, *Vorlesungen über die Aesthetik*. (On tragedy.)
Krader, Lawrence *Treatise of Social Labor*. (On freedom.) (See *Human Being*, Part
   II.)

Note 7
Means of production are the products of past labors in society which are applied
in ongoing production processes. The products are of all kinds, practical and theoretical, concrete and abstract, material and immaterial, whereby our wants and
needs are met. Hence the means of production are practical and theoretical, concrete and abstract, material and immaterial. Work tools, hammer and nails, needle
and thread, spades, shovels, tractors, combine and harvesters in agriculture, machinery, an entire factory, a railroad or shipping line, a water canal, a draft horse,
skilled hands, a scientific or technical process, a mathematical or chemical formula are all means of production.

The past is immediately past, which can be one tenth of a second ago, or
mediately past, which is relatively longer ago, measured in hours, days or centuries.

By our labors we maintain, produce and apply the means of production; these
are the relations of production.

Production is a part of the process of human, social reproduction; this process
is constituted of parts, which are production, distribution and consumption of
social goods. Work *in concreto*, and labor, abstract and concrete are applied in the
process of human reproduction in its various parts.

Exchange, trade, and commerce are concrete forms of distribution in the society of market relations, commodity and capital formation. Exchange is further
concretized in money and credit.

A mode of production is the economic formation of society. The mode of
production is communal or social; the social mode of production is the economic
process of society in its several parts, production, distribution and consumption;
the mode of production is therefore an elliptical expression, whereby the part is
used to designate the totality, or the lesser the greater.

Part II: Value

Labor and Its Expression by Value, Quality and Quantity

Value has a qualitative and a quantitative expression. By its qualitative expression we bring out our relation to some part of the human world; a value is an expression of a judgment, objective or subjective, of our relations to our world. In evaluating our world or some element in it, we make a judgment of its worth. It is either relative to other parts of our world, in our objective judgment, or it has a unique place in it, as something absolutely great, immeasurable, an inordinate element, a xenolith, or a chaotic attribute of the world, in our subjective one. Of those elements in our world which are relative to others, some parts are systematic and orderly; these will be our chief concern in considering the problem of value, and we will have less to do with the qualities of value which are subjective. The quality of value is systematic or not; the systematic qualities are in some ways measurable, in which case we assign a quantitative expression, whether numerical or not, to them. The quantitative elements of our world have a negative or positive value, we assign a numerical expression to them, in answer to the question, how much?, or we assign a non-numerical quantitative expression to them, more or less, saying that we value this more than that, but do not say how much more or how much less in numerical terms. Not all values are quantitatively expressed. Of the values which are systematic and measurable, we will take up chiefly those which are given objective expression in their relation to work and labor.

Valuation, the value expressions, and the laws of value are mental processes, thus have a bearing on our conscious and unconscious activities and states, and on our thinking and cognitive processes and on our affective or emotional processes. Thought, cognition and emotion are factors in our judgments, including the value judgments of the objective as well as the subjective kinds. Not all value expressions are laws of value, but all the latter are value expressions. The expression of the unique, the absolute or inordinate as a value is subjective, and may fall outside the realm of law.

Work is an expenditure of energy both by material nature and by the human kind, its organization being transformed, together with the material processes to which it is applied, by labor. Labor is variable in human history, and thereby work is varied in its relation to the human and material orders of nature. Labor in its abstract form has social, objective, abstract value as one of its expressions. Work has not this expression, but another, which is, under given social conditions, concrete value, or use value.

Value, as objective, social value, is the expression of the amount of time, skill, ability and capacity which is expended under given conditions in the process of meeting human wants and needs, therewith in the reproduction of the human kind. Hitherto, the notion has been widespread that in human history, value has been brought forth in civil society, and is not brought forth elsewhere. We will examine this critically. Objective value is not all there is of value, for in addition there are individual, symbolic and subjective values. Subjective and symbolic values are brought forth in all conditions of human society, subjective value being the expression of our choice, will and desire.

Value is either objective or subjective, and is in either case a form which is connected to a human substance. The connection of form to substance in respect of objective value differs from that of subjective value; the substance of objective value differs from that of subjective value. The value form in either case is an expression which is an activation of a substantive process whether objective or subjective, by its external relation. Thus value, by virtue of the relation of the substance to form, is either objective or subjective but not both. The objective value form is a law, which, if it is valid is objectively so; there is a law of subjective value, but it is determined by other substantive relations, both internal and external, than those of the objective value, its form, expression and validation. Some subjective value has no law. The field of value of either sort is a human field, having reference by abstraction to relations of the human order which are concrete, taking place in space and time. Value is abstract as expression and as law, in its objective form, in space-time.

The value substance, in respect of objective value, is labor, but whereas labor is universal in the human order, hence in human society, its presence as value substance is not, for if there is no value expression or form, then labor cannot constitute its substance. Objective value is not universal in human society, but is constituted and determined only under the condition in which social labor is reckoned up in the amount of time expended in the different tasks of reproduction of the human order. Labor which is expended in social reproduction and production, in distribution, exchange and consumption of the human kind, and in the preparation and training for these tasks, has objective value, on the condition that its time is measured. Objective value of production and reproduction and social value in this sense are the same; they are the formal expression of social labor. The value form is expressed only where social labor is quantified in its temporal process; but since this is concrete labor, it is human work in space-time, and therefore it is a spatial-temporal process which is given abstract expression as value form. In respect of this value form and substance, a law is brought out which is not general with respect to all human societies, but only those in which labor is socialized and in which the social labor time is given a quantitative expression. The process of socialization is abstract and concrete, that of quantification is abstract labor expended in the reproduction of the human kind, which is socialized and quantitative, is objective, having the same relation to the natural order as labor of another kind, but is not objective value substance, and has no relation to objective value form. Labor expended in human reproduction, without socialization and quantification is of the same substance as social labor, for both are the process of transformation of the material and human orders to the end of meeting human wants and needs, but the labor which is socialized and, together with this, quantified, has objective value of production as its form. The other labor has been, in the history of the human order, labor in the archaic and primitive condition, collective and domestic labor in the same condition, private and subjective work under any conditions; this other labor does not have the value form, and hence is not submitted to the law of objective value.

Each of the relations of labor, to the material order, and within the human order, is the condition of the other, neither exists independently and each is the means of realization of the other. The human kind relates to the material order only through labor, which is the means whereby the human order is brought into existence to begin with, thus transformed from natural determinate being, and constituted as such. By our labors we relate to the various natural orders, material, human and others, and these are the chief relations of our labors of all kinds. Thus our labors are principally determined as orderly, and our relations to the material world, and in the human world are determined as being orderly. The value expressions of these relations are orderly.

Since the human kind comes into contact with the material order through labor, the relations to matter are mediate. The mediation is effected variably, being separable in form and substance. The medium constituted by labor is variable in relation to the material order, and is worked upon, being perfectible, destructible, augmented, diminished, organized, combined and separated in its form and in its substance, in the human order. The medium is not unitary in actuality, but is constituted of a number of fields, which are both abstract and concrete, of labor. Abstractly and potentially the medium from the standpoint of the human kind is unitary.

Objective value is a social form which has labor as its substance. Labor in turn has both form and substance, the form being the differential expressions of labor in society, the expressions being the activation of the substance in seeming independence of the latter. Labor in its history has been organized communally, and in this condition has been temporally organized but has not been objectively, abstractly measured. Labor is variable in its substance, for the relations of the humankind to natural order are variable, the wants which are met being variable from one social whole to another; labor is variable in its substance again, for the organization by its combination and division varies from one social whole to the next. Although the substance of labor varies in relation to nature and in society, yet these relations, in constituting the substance of labor, have one form or another. They have only an abstract existence apart from a concrete and actual form. There is no universal and concrete form of the labor substance in actuality, and the sole means for its activation is that of a particular form in a given social whole.

Objective value of production is not the labor substance, but the form; it is the condition in which labor, abstract and concrete, is abstractly reckoned up in units of labor time. Human wants are met by labor, but not all of labor is expended in this way, not all of labor that is expended in this process is differentiated into abstract and concrete relations thereof, and hence not all of labor is reckoned up in units of labor time. The value form of labor is therefore not distributed universally in human society, whereas the labor substance is universally distributed therein, being transformed into value substance by the processes of socialization, abstraction and quantification of labor, therewith the development of value form. It therefore follows that the form of the labor substance varies separately, accordingly as labor time is reckoned up in the process of meeting wants and needs, and this is the abstract form and the concrete variability of the form in relation to the substance. The labor substance is constituted of mediate relations, which are those of the human kind to the material order, and mediate and immediate relations, which are those of the human kind in society. The labor form is constituted of the social organization of labor, whereby the time expended in meeting human wants and needs is or is not abstracted and reckoned up. The labor substance in this sense is the human constant in relation to the form, the labor form the variable in relation to the social substance.

The labor time expended in meeting of wants and needs is concrete; the process of reckoning up of the amount, and its expression, are abstract. The abstract expression of the amount of time expended in the social reproduction of the human kind is objective, social value. Thus value is an expression of the means whereby the natural thing is transformed into the human object; there is no other means whereby this transformation is effected, and there is no other object than that which is constituted by the human labor process of transformation of the natural thing. By its transformation, thing is converted into object, but it does not cease thereby to be a thing. The transformation process is an activity which is both theoretical and practical; by observation, sense perception, abstraction, reference and by concrete body labor, the natural determinate being is transformed into a determinate being of the human order, which is the natural determinate being as the object.

The expression of the amount of time expended in the transformation of natural material, and in the organization of the process of transformation, enters into objective value; this value expression refers to the process of objectification of the material and human orders. This expression covers the entire amount of the value, but covers less than the total amount of labor, and is therefore less than the total process of objectification, which comes to the same. The expression of value is an abstraction which is in a determinate relation to abstract labor. Objective value, which is the expression of the form separate from the substance of labor, is thus distinct from subjective value, in which no separation and difference between form and substance is made out, the form and substance being in this case the same. Objective value has no bearing on labor in which the quantity of time expended in production and reproduction is not reckoned up, nor does it bear on labor in which nature is transformed, but not to the end of meeting concrete wants and needs.

The quantification of value is determined by the quantification of labor time and capacity, the quantification being conceived in this case as cumulative. All labor time is quantitative and quantifiable, but only that labor time which is social, objective and abstract is quantified cumulatively. Moreover, while value in the sense given is brought forth only as the expression of labor and that which comes from labor, not all of labor is expressed as value, but only social and abstract labor has this expression; excluded is communal, family, or individual labor, which is subjective and objective, but is concrete in its objectivity, and is abstract only in its subjectivity. For the process of socialization of labor is the means whereby labor is transformed into its own medium, both active and passive, and in this process the subjectively abstract labor is made objectively and subjectively abstract. The active mediation of labor in the process of transformation is that of objectification of self and other, the passive mediation of labor is the process of being objectified; the object of labor is made concrete in the commodity, the self as commodity is the concretization of living labor in this same process.

The theory of value thus yields up findings of experiments and conclusions that are objectively verifiable, as any other scientific theory. These findings are given qualitative expressions, which are abstractly similar, but concretely dissimilar. The single value expression of all industrial production, while it would not require the superior intelligence postulated by Laplace, is not practically ascertainable at present.

Objective and Subjective Value

Value is the expression of the worth of a human activity. It is found in all human social conditions, primitive, archaic, and civil. We distinguish between objective and subjective value, between abstract and concrete value, between value form and substance, and between quantity and quality of value. Whereas value expressions are found everywhere in human society, they are systematically developed and distinguished only in modern society; in ancient civil society, and in primitive society, they are or were present, but only sporadically differentiated and distinguished; thus the system of these distinctions and differentiations of value is a potentiality of those other societies, and an actuality of modern society. Value as an expression is not the same as the object of the expression; for the expression is a form, bringing out our estimation of the worth of a human process and/or its product, which constitutes its substance.

Value, being the expression of our estimation of the worth of the human substance, as a concrete or abstract process, is objectively other than that substance. An estimation leads to or leads from a choice, a selection, the choice being the practical side of the estimation. In the objective value process, the choosing is differentiated from the substance and from the estimation; in subjective value, the choosing, the choice, the expression and the substance are not so differentiated.

Value is thus the expression of a relation between the humankind and its activity, the relation being abstract and concrete, the activity practical and theoretical. Value, being an expression, has reference to an activity in which a passivity is presupposed in practice, but is not relevant to the system of theoretical reference; value is opposed in theory to the activity of estimation to which it refers, and of which it is the expression. The estimation is a mode of selection and judgment, critical and non-critical, in which variable human factors are at work. The expression of the act of estimation bears on a mediate relation between the human agent and the product of the agent's activity, hence on a human process, whereas the expression as estimation is an immediate relation, which bears on the process and the product, as it does on the undifferentiated relation between them and the estimation. The mediate relation between the value expression and the process is the result of a mediative relation between the human agent and the process and product of the agent's activity; the value is therefore in this sense an expression of a mediated relation between the product and the human agency. The immediate relation of value is without differentiation between the act of estimation and its expression, and without difference between process and product but with difference between the human agent on the one side, and product and process on the other. The mediate relation of value is a particularity of some human relations in society, but not of others, the immediate relation of value is a general human practice. Both the immediate and mediate value expressions are relative to the process of estimation, to the product thereof, to other value expressions, and to other products which have values as their expressions.

Value is the act of estimation, or the valuation of the worth of an object, and further, an expression of self-relation of the human subject. The difference between the two expressions is the result of the means whereby the value is arrived at, which is the two different processes of valuation. The expression is a deictic, having a form and a substance; the relation between expression, form and substance in the matter of value is variable, being mediate or immediate, general and particular, constituting and being determined by human relations. Value as the differential expression of valuation is mediate, objective and subjective, and particular to certain human social wholes. Value as the expression of an estimation without difference between process and product is without difference between subjectivity and objectivity of value; the estimation is immediate in its expression, for there is no difference between form and substance, in that the relation between them is immediate and not mediate. Since the form and substance of value in this case is without differentiation and mediation, the condition of non-difference between subjectivity and objectivity of valuation is met, and the non-difference of the product and process of value. Therefore the expression of value and its content are not opposed to one another. The abstract sequence in the order of development is that of diremption, differentiation, mediation and opposition; this abstraction is concrete in respect of human form and substance, the expression and content thereof, subjectivity and objectivity, and process of labor and its product.

Value is organized, combined and divided in human society once the relations of that society are organized, combined and divided; the social relations determine the value expressions, and not the converse. The social differences between human form and substance, between abstract and concrete relations, and between object and subject determine the distinctions between abstract and concrete value, objective and subjective value, and between the value form and substance. The relations of labor in particular, and not the social relation of the human kind in general determine the distinctions of the value forms. This organization of the relations of value as a system is brought out only on the condition that labor is socialized and reckoned up mediately and immediately. Labor by its social organization is brought to the consciousness as the object, and as the object and subject of the consciousness; the immediate condition of this process is that labor is combined and divided, exploited, managed, manipulated, externally directed, personified, dirempted and alienated. This condition is an insult to our human being in a mediate sense; cocaine, LSD and heroin are insults to our nervous system, and alcohol to the liver, directly. The social organization of labor is the condition without which value is not. Labor is the condition of life in primitive, archaic human society, as it is in the society of social classes, or civil society, that is, in the primitive social as well as in the social condition of human history. But primitive social labor is not objectively valued labor, for it is estimated otherwise than the way it is in civil society. Labor is immediately relative to its process of meeting our human wants, needs, and desires, whereby the human kind reproduces itself in the communal condition. Objective, production value is the expression of the mediate process of the labor relative to meeting our wants, needs and desires, whereby the human kind reproduces itself in the social condition of its history. The various forms of value are brought to our consciousness in view of their realization formally and socially, through contractual exchange, and in view of their realization formally and, antisocially, through exploitation for profit.

The ability of the human kind to make conscious judgments and to analyze the relations and expressions of value rests on the identification of labor as the substance of objective value, and of the desire and will as the process of subjective value form and substance. These relations are not symmetrical, for the value substance is not the same as the value process. The subjective value form and substance are non-dirempted, whereas the objective value is divided into the form and substance. The objective value form is often mystified by being made out to be a self-acting process. The objective value substance is constituted as a process in modern society, by having the form of exchange value attributed to it. There is no distinctive value expression in the primitive communal condition, for there the contractual, formal exchange and the social exploitation for profit are not the predominant relations of society.

A substance is realized, being made actual only in a given form, whereby it is constituted as a social process, natural or human. Labor in civil society is constituted as a process in a particular form, which is value, in its given, differential relations. The value expressions are historically variable; they are known to us concretely only in the history of civil society. Objective value is the form of the social labor process under socialism, human work and labor constituting the substance, for labor under socialism is social labor, with this difference, that the formal-contractual and the anti-social relations of labor have been eradicated; value is the form of social labor, but exchange value and surplus value are not; use value is the form of concrete value in civil society, and is converted into the latter under socialism; value is then objective, abstract social value.

Objective value is the formal expression of a quantum of social labor time, being quantifiable and actually quantified as exchange value in modern civil society. Subjective value and use value are quantifiable, but in another form. These forms are given mathematical expression, having been separated into distinctive quanta, each having a characteristic formalization. Values are expressions of different processes, objective and subjective, abstract and concrete. They are quantified as such for the reason that the object has been separated from the subject, and the abstract from the concrete. Thereby the substance of the objective value in a mediate way and the objective value form in an immediate way are quantified, and the subjective value expression is formalized quantitatively in another way.

Each expression, relative to the objective and subjective value forms, is a *characteristica specifica* of the human kind. There is no expression of all value, for the respective processes, abstract and concrete, objective and subjective, differ from one another. The abstract and objective processes are cumulative, aggregative, the subjective and concrete are a zero-sum process and expression. The formalization of the objective value expression is a qualitative process; the formalization of the subjective value is quantitative; the qualitative expression of the latter is without difference from the quantitative.

Objective value is externalized; as a form it is external to the labor process to begin with, wherever it is found; yet since it is not found everywhere in the relation of human reproduction by the human kind, therefore it is not its universal characteristic. The objective value expression is, however, the universal characteristic of social labor, or the specific characteristic of labor in society, as opposed to labor in the primitive community, on the one hand, or to subjective labor on the other. Objective value is an abstraction; it is abstracted from the labor process in society. Like intelligence, it is externalized and formalized. The formality thereof is the form of value, or intelligence, respectively, which is mistaken for the substance; however, form is neither process nor substance. This has been made clear with respect to value.—C. S. Peirce distinguished between form and process of mathematics; deduction is a formalism, and is distinct from the process whereby mathematical equations and other expressions are produced, which is a substantive one. Abstract value is expressed in mathematics; it is a form and is therefore one with its expression; its formal expression is its content, and its content is its substance as form. The generation of the expression is, however, not the expression as such. This is the case with value, as well.

Next, we turn to the relation between value and labor. Value is the abstract work of labor, for value, objective, subjective, or other, does not come forth of itself, nor does it descend from the heavens, as the rain, but is a human product. It is not a human product in general, or in universality, but is a product of the human kind under particular social conditions, and is the expression of the labor under these conditions. The expression is a kind of labor, and is the form; it is an externalized relation of the substance, being its expression, relative to the different kinds of value, in use, in exchange, in surplus, concretely, or abstractly. The paradox in this connection is that work is concrete, labor abstract and concrete. Value, we have said, is the abstract expression of labor; that is, estimation and expression are a kind of labor, in abstract form, which is expressed concretely, hence it is a work, as well as a labor. Value, being the product in this sense of labor, has no self-relation, for it is passive in relation to the agency, which is the labor process. Labor, however, has a self, an active and passive relation, and is its own form and substance; it has value as its form in particular, and has another form in general, where it is not found in conjunction with the value expression. The self-relation of labor is constituted of its relation to the general and the particular, to the one and to the other, and to the form and substance; these relations are diremptions, having separation and connection of the separate processes.

Objective value has an abstract substance which is opposed to the objective value form. It is thus opposed to subjective value in the genesis of either; objective value form is abstract and quantitative, and is opposed to the objective value substance. Subjective value has no separate substance, and is at once abstract and concrete. Without the opposition of abstraction and concretion there is no separate human substance; this opposition is developed in the relation denoted by the law of objective value.

Subjective value is at once abstract and concrete, and in this respect does not differ from objective value; moreover, both are expressions of some human relation. The difference between them lies in their provenience, and in the separability of the objective value form from the substance, and of the objective value expression from the content, and the mediate relation between form and substance, also between expression and content in this regard, whereas subjective value form and substance, and subjective expression and content have an immediate relation which is not separable in the same sense as it is in the case of objective value.

By separation of the form from the substance, the opposition between abstract and concrete objective value is brought about. The objective value expression is objective alone, without subjectivity, in its abstract modality; concretely it is at once subjective and objective. The objective value substance is both objective and subjective, being constituted of social labor, which is subjective and objective, abstract and concrete. The objective, concrete value form coincides with the objective, concrete value expression, whereas the objective, abstract value form does not immediately coincide with the expression; mediately the form and expression coincide, the form becoming the value expression in this respect, for it is determined by relations that the human kind has set in motion, but are no longer immediately submitted to control by its authors. In this matter, the objective value form stands to the human subject as the human kind stands to the natural order, which is as the lesser to the greater. The natural order in general is both active and passive; the value form is passive, and abstract. The value form is potentially a single expression, in actuality it is not; the human order and subject are potentially and actively the same, whereas the natural order is neither actually nor potentially one.

The subjective value expression is concrete. The form of subjective value is the act of will and fantasy in judgment, and consciousness, and its content is the subjective substance to which it stands in an immediate relation. It is evident that the form of subjective value is an active relation of the individual human being, in relation to the substance, which is the subjective relation of the human kind.

The expression is the external relation of subjective value, or the externality of the subjective relations of the human kind, and is accessible to the senses; the substance of subjective value is its expression. The subjective value, form and substance are opposed to objective value, but return to unity with the latter under the condition that the will of the human being is submitted to the control by objective relations of the human order.

In the study of objective value of production we separate the object, labor, from the subject, which is the will and desire of the human kind, and objective value from subjective forms of value. The subject is not the will and desire, but is so in respect of value. The potentiality is not the concrete possibility, but is so only with respect to the relation between concrete experience and the abstract mental act. With respect to value, no actual characteristic universal is presupposed, but only the *characteristica specifica* of objective value, exchange value, use value, surplus value, subjective value. Their reduction to a single value expression would be the characteristic universal of value.

The science of value is developed in civil society, throughout its history, from ancient to modern times, both with respect to objective and subjective value forms. Plato contributed to the grasp of subjective value of the True and the Good, Aristotle both to subjective and to objective value, and these contributions have been further developed down to our own times. The particular form of the value expressions is related to the consciousness of the conditions of society, civil and bourgeois, and is determined thereby. In this condition, labor is dirempted and alienated, quantified, sold and exploited; the subjectivity of will and desire is separated and distinguished clearly from the objectified and self-objectifying labor in meeting the human wants and needs.

In the primitive, archaic conditions of social life, there is no exploitation of one social class for the profit of another; there is no great deal of sale of labor, labor time, capacity or quality in economic exchange, hence there is no objectification of such processes, and no science of value in this condition. Primitive people are human beings, who work and labor for their sustenance, but these are not comprised within the objective value expression.—Moreover, objective value has its particular expression in civil society as exchange value, for exchange is the predominant form of distribution of the economic goods in that society; besides this, exchange value is the dominant form of distribution of the social surplus in it. The impact of these forms of social and economic distribution and redistribution distorts the consciousness, in such a way that another approach to the characteristic universal of the human kind is difficult to conceive concretely.—In the theory of socialism, value has another expression, for commodities, capital, exchange, and exploitation are eradicated, but social production goes on, and this is yet another reason for setting aside the quest for the universal characteristic of value. But the pure value expression which has social labor as its substance, and is freed of conditions of market, sale, commodity and price, profit and tax, leads to another theoretical consideration of the relation between form and substance, and between subject and object. Value theory is not liberated in this way. Here we consider only the relation between the theory of social labor and the theory of value, as its expression in civil society.

We have brought out a general expression of the value of social production in the reproduction of the human kind; the generality of this expression bears on modern civil society, in which the conditions of wage labor and the formation of capital predominate. This value expression is valid to the extent that the labor of reproduction, production, distribution and consumption is socially organized and quantified. It is abstracted and liberated in this sense from its ties to exchange value, for its ambit is broader than the condition of society in which exchange and exchange value predominate. The objective value of social reproduction and production has no immediate and intrinsic relation to subjective value or to the condition of social labor which is but modestly organized by its combination and division, or not at all, and it has not an immediate and intrinsic relation but a mediate one to subjective value. The universal characteristic of the value expression remains as a potentiality of the human kind.

There is no objective value which exists apart from a good. The good has some practical or theoretical, abstract or concrete, objective relation to our lives, whether it is useful, beautiful, interesting, or speaking negatively it eliminates an obnoxious, useless, ugly, boring, or noxious condition. Therefore we refer to value as being concrete in the good, and this is the objective relation of the value to the good. The good is concrete in that it meets a want of the human kind; the value placed on it is in this case an actuality in some human group. Or the value is the abstract expression of the potentiality of the worth of the good to all of us. The actual and potential value are relative to each other, and convert into one another. The relation of the subjective to the objective value is not an absolute difference between them, for the subjective value exists in objectivity to us; our desires have an object, real or fantastic, and we carry them out in objective reality; thus we transform our mystical and unreal thoughts into practical, concrete, objective reality by acting on them, acting them out, whether they are desired or undesired by others, willed or unwilled, willing or unwilling, on the part of the one or the other. The value in its objective and concrete expression, refers to the usefulness of the good in a system of values and goods.

Value in its objective and abstract expression of production refers to a quantity of a good produced, in a system of goods, values, and their quantitative expressions; thus the good, and its usefulness, are measurable in their objective value expression. The value is the form in its quantitative moment. The concrete, objective expression of the value is quantifiable, but in another sense. The objective abstract value expression has reference to a cumulative process, the objective cumulation being direct and immediate, mechanically direct and systematically immediate. The directness is a temporal process alone, the systematic process is at once temporal; as a system it is at the same time opposed to the temporal process. The concrete value is wiped out by its use. It is an all or nothing quantification.

Objective value has two constituents, 1) social labor time, and 2) quality or skill of work and labor, respectively the quantity and quality of labor. The quality is analyzed into the amount of time in learning, preparation and training of the social labor, and hence is a quantitative expression of another kind. Objective value is the form of which the constituents of social labor are the substance. The substance is not the essence or timeless stuff but a set of social labor processes. Work is a concrete immediate and discontinuous process, ending in the product; labor is mediate, and insofar as it is abstract, it is continuous; labor quantity and quality are abstract and concrete. The objective value of work expresses its concrete attribute, the objective value of labor expresses its abstract attribute; labor is both objective and subjective, hence the values which it expresses are subjective and objective. The objective value is a part of a system of value the related parts of which are the use value of labor and its product, exchange value and surplus value. These are the categories with which we deal under particular social and historical conditions. The exchange value and surplus are more immediately bound to the conditions of the market, commodity, price and exchange in the society in which wage labor and the formation of capital predominate, or the modern civil society; objective value and use value are more general variables, and serve as constants in the system of value. If we speak only of the human individual, then the subjective value is extrapolated from the objective; the extrapolation is provisional, and the expression is returned to its social context. Objective value is the form of particular human social relations.

Objective value varies according to substantive processes, which are the changes in the amount, skill, art and science of labor, and by the organization, combination and division thereof in society. The price varies according to the objective value of the good, and according to the market conditions, which are both formal and substantial. The good is an economic object, whether material or non-material, by which our thingly needs and human wants are met. The good is a substance, having the form of a commodity in the marketplace. The market is concrete at a particular time and place, or is abstract; it is an act of buying and selling goods in either case. The good is transformed into a commodity by the market relation of buying and selling; this act is a mutual relation between juridical or moral persons, in which reciprocity in exchange is conducted between them, whether of equal or equivalent goods. The social persons are groups, collectivities or individuals, whether formally or informally joined in the exchange. A material good is an object which we consume or can consume, in its given form, entirely, in the process of our human reproduction. A non-material good is a process of social labor, of a given amount and quality; the historical bent of the relations of civil society, in modern times, has been to develop the use.

Value is objective in consequence of its being the expression of the process of objectification of natural processes by labor. Objectification of the world by labor is both abstract and concrete, whereas value is the expression of the objectification process in its abstract side, whereby labor is given theoretical expression, abstracted from its concrete and practical relations. Thereby labor time is represented as an entity abstracted from the concrete tasks of labor as work. Thus objective value is the expression of only that part and condition of labor in which it has abstract expression as labor time and quality being abstracted from human activity and passivity in human space-time.

Economic exchange is objective and subjective, and exchange value is its expression. However in this process, form and substance are opposed to one another, as are the object and the subject. Subjective value is opposed to exchange value in civil society.

Objective and Subjective Value (*continued*)

Value is a phenomenon of the human order alone, and as such is either subjective or objective. We will consider subjective and objective value separately, first, and their conjunction later on. Taken objectively, value form is opposed to value substance, each being the expression of a relation, the notation of a regular combination of the two expressions constituting the law of objective value. The expression and the form coincide in this case; thus the law of value and the form of objective value are the same, objective value form and the law of objective value form being the expression of the relation of value to value substance under given circumstances of the history of human society.

The value substance in our society is both objective and subjective, for it is in actuality social labor; its potentiality, labor capacity, is immediately connected to it. The value form is solely objective, with respect to the objective and subjective value substance alike, but the objectivity of the form is not the same in the relations thereof to the objective and subjective substances. The law of value is the objective expression of the separability of value form and substance. This expression refers to an asymmetry however, for, given that objective value substance is at issue, it stands to the value form in a relation which is at once subjective and objective, whereas the value form stands to the value substance in a relation which is objective alone. Objective value form, and its law are the expression of the relation of social labor in the reproduction of the social whole. This value expression bears upon a human condition which is in its potentiality universal, hence the universality of the value expression within the human order is a possibility. The universality of the objective value expression is subject to a twofold restriction: it is restricted to the social processes in which labor time and capacity are quantified. The labor capacity is the potentiality of living labor developed in its social organization, by the combination and division thereof, and by qualitative specialization and variation, in which skills are applied in the process of reproduction of the social whole. Quantified labor time, and capacity, which are the aggregate of actual and potential skills and qualities of living labor, are the substance of objective value, the relation between them being an immediate one, and together constitute the measure of objective value, in a mediate relation between them. There is no other objective value than this.

Taken subjectively, value is both a human relation and the expression of the relation; it is at once the form and substance of a human relation; without difference, the form is one with the substance in this case. The expression of the preference is one with the practical act of valuing, choosing and expressing preference; the choice comprises subjective motive and outcome of the choice within itself, and is not further analyzable. The relation between form and substance of subjective value is in theory both objective and subjective, given that the relation between form and substance of all human matter is both objective and subjective. The relation between form and substance of subjective value is immediately and actively objective and subjective, the relation between form and substance of objective value is mediately, separably, diremptively objective and subjective, and both actively and passively in either mode. Therefore we speak of the law of value form as opposed to the value substance, value form and the law of value form being the same, value form and the expression thereof being without difference, in the case of objective value. Value form and value substance are non-diremptive in the case of subjective value, within the field of value theory. The motive of subjective value, the will and consciousness that underly it, are the matter of another field of theory than the theory of value itself. Value practice in the case of subjective value is constituted of the immediate unity of form and substance: every human being who is a fully recognized person within the social whole, is, in the subjective value practice, sovereign; to will is to command, being answerable to none. This is a fantastic practice of individuality, which, from the standpoint of objective theory of value is subject to criticism. Subjective value, being a matter of will, desire and consciousness, is the determination of the social person.

The objective value of any good is opposed in its form to its substance. Yet concrete and use value are systematically and historically the same in form and substance. In its objective mode, value as such is not a substance, but has a substance; thus objective value is a form, which is opposed to the substance of value, both in theory and practice. Objective value is determined abstractly by the process of social labor, which is its sole determinant.

Value judgment is a kind of value expression, and is either objective or subjective. It is sometimes associated with a subjective capacity of judgment, which by excluding the objective judgment implies a negative or diminished capacity, with a prejudice, and interest, a privilege. Judgment is a human capacity, and as such is neither objective nor subjective, but is both objective and subjective, whereby a privilege or a prejudice distorts the judgmental power by diminishing it, in which case we say that a given value judgment is predominantly subjective. An interest, which is objective or subjective, is associated with a value judgment, which is either. The exclusively subjective interpretation of value judgment, therefore, is a misunderstanding of the process of judging. The means of judging are given to us, internalized, made conscious in a tradition which is handed down, and by the variation under present conditions, the tradition, the process of variation, the present conditions, and the consciousness being objectively and subjectively determined. We judge, and express objective and subjective values, by means that are given, which are the social data and *facta*. The data are the givens over which we have partial control, but on varying them transform them into facta over which we have increased control. We do not control all of historical reality, but have some control over the recipient of the past of the material and human orders. The humankind has an interrelation with past potentiality which is variable both in respect of the human kind and of the past potentiality. The human kind is variable accordingly as it is organized in the various historical social wholes. Human historical process and judgment are objective and subjective. The human kind reproduces its history by reproducing itself; the reproduction being manifold, therefore the history is manifold. The history, however, is an externality in relation to the objective substance which is unitary. The objective judgment is therefore unitary in potentiality, in actuality it is manifold. The subjective judgment, for the reason that it has no distinction between form and substance, between internality and externality, or between actuality and potentiality, is one and many. The subjective judgment comprises both fantasy and reality, objective judgment comprises reality and actuality, without fantasy; abstraction is common to both objective and subjective judgment.

Historical judgment is not one but many. Thus, the reproduction of the human kind does not imply the reproduction of human history. The reproduction of the human kind being the process of variation with respect to the past, and variation and selection in relation to past and present self, therefore the past is not reproduced, being neither repeated nor recursive. We neither make nor remake our history, but remake only the historical record; historical reality is not affected thereby, but historical potentialities are labored upon and reworked, thereby becoming other.

Subjective value judgment is a part of the content and origin of the subjective value process, which has its source in the affections, consciousness, choice, judgment and will of human being. Thus subjective value and subjective valuation, or subjective value judgment, are at once the constitutive process, its content and expression immediately.

Value judgment, as a process whereby subjective and objective value is expressed, is determined by all the factors of the human order, both the data and *facta*, both the objective and the subjective. The objective relation in this process is at the same time a self-objectifying relation, which is variable. The humankind, being and self are materialized by a human relation to the material order and in the human order. The materialization is at once sensory actually, or potentially accessible to the senses, in that all material relation is ordered, some is organized, some of the organized is organic, living, and some of the living is human. Of the material relation which is ordered and organized, some is accessible to the senses; some material and human relations are not accessible to the senses, some accessible. The self-materialized process of the human kind is at the same time a self-materializing process; it is self-mediatizing and mediatized, it is self-objectified and self-objectifying. The process of labor is constituted of these relations of materialization, mediatization and objectification as activity and passivity in each case, and as self-relation in respect of each. These relations are both sensory and non-sensory, and bear on the relations of the human kind both to the material and human orders in that they constitute the process of labor.

Concrete objective value is the expression of the particular activities of human work and labor in the meeting of wants and needs.

Both abstract and concrete objective value are quantitative expressions of numerically measurable acts and relations. The measurement of abstract value in this case differs from that of concrete value, the former being cumulative, the latter not.

The objective value substance is that of labor; it is not all of labor, however, but only that labor which is socialized and quantified. The objective value form is the expression of the substance; the form is at once the expression and the form of the form, as we shall see. Abstract objective value substance is abstract labor, concrete objective value substance is human work.

The expression of the abstract objective value substance is the same as the expression of abstract labor; the expression of the concrete objective value substance is not the same as human work, or concrete labor. Abstract labor is brought forth in social conditions under which labor is socialized and the expression thereof is quantified; the development of the social conditions and of the quantified expression of abstract social labor coincide historically. Concrete labor extends over a broader range of human social relations than does the expression of the concrete objective value substance.

Subjective value is the expression of voluntary, aesthetic, judgmental and conscious relations of the human kind. The conscious relations and acts are sometimes identified with those of the subject, but this is an arbitrary and simplifying error, for consciousness and judgment are both objective and subjective. Consciousness and will are in their results, judgmental and aesthetic, are cognitive and affective. Consciousness and judgment are both subjective and objective, the subjectivity and objectivity of either being with and without differentiation, internally or externally. Aesthetic judgment is without differentiation of its subjective and objective sides. Opinions in sentences are the expressions of the judgments, and presuppose the activity of the consciousness; the judgments are the results thereof. Aesthetics is differentiated from aisthesis, which is the undifferential activity of sensation and perception; aisthesis is at the same time indifferently objective and subjective, but is not a thingly process. It presupposes the consciousness as well, but is not as such a valuative process. Sense perception is divided into the activity of the sense, which is thingly and objective, and the activity of perception, which is objective and subjective; perception is a valuative process, being inseparable from this process.

The will, desire and fantasy in the subjective expression of value lead away from the material order of nature, introduce the non-material factors of nature to account for them, and the abstractions of the consciousness; subjective value is the expression of the will and desire, and of the subjective consciousness. Subjective value is therefore in part an expression of an anti-anthropic principle, and in part of an anthropic principle; in the latter case it is articulated with the objective value expression immediately, and with the objective value substance mediately.

Subjective consciousness, judgment and feeling are valuative processes which are developed *pari passu* with objective consciousness, judgment and feeling, in interaction between the two sides, constituting an ill-fitting whole. The subjective element in these relations is willed, but the will is not free, for it is subjectively determined and bound by the general relations of the human kind in the natural and human orders and by the relations of the particular social whole to both. We proceed from the will to the judgment, feeling, consciousness in the subject. Objectively there is no difference in the order of the series, whereas subjectively there is the difference between that which is mediately and immediately determined. The will is the immediate determinant of the subjective cognition, affection and opinion; subjectively the judgment, whether cognitive or affective is mediated by the activity of the will. Sense-perception or aisthesis is objective and subjective, but that which is perceived by the senses, perceptive and conscious processes is objective; the object is then transformed into a subjective element by valuation, and into an objective element by objective valuation. Wish and desire, fantasy and illusion are subjective states which constitute the field of subjective value; to the extent that the subjective field is actively valuated, it is willed. This valuation is variable, for the unconscious wells forth in wish, desire and fantasy unwilled; we will and willingly suppress the distinction between illusion and reality. The will is the means of subjective valuation and of transvaluation of value; in that we regain lost ground in bringing forth the subjective element of the unconscious process of mind and of biological being we transpose subjective value, which is a transvaluation. The unconscious is the meeting ground of the human process of mentation and the biological process of *homo sapiens*.

The voluntary activity of human being is the means whereby we relate consciousness to judgment and feeling, feeling and judgment to consciousness. These are subjectively immediate processes, which are at once objectively mediated by human social relation. Objectively the human kind differentiates between feelings, and differentiates between affective and cognitive acts, acts of temperament, arbitrary and judicious acts, etc. Subjectively and mediately these distinctions are then hierarchized as better, worse, higher, lower. The affections and cognitions are more or less, for one wishes and desires more of that which one loves, less of that which is ugly and hateful. The hierarchization of the affections, their rank-order, is the mediate result of hierarchization of social relations. The internalization of social hierarchy of the human order is then represented in subjective processes and expressions of valuation.

Subjective value is the expression of the immediate relation of human form and substance to one another. In the process of objective valuation, the distinction between concrete and abstract value is introduced; this distinction is not made in the subjective value process; but by differentiating between the abstract and concrete objective value substance and thus between abstract and concrete objective value expressions, we differentiate between objective and subjective value. The differentiation between abstract and concrete objective value substance is the means to the distinction between abstract and concrete objective value form. The objective value substance and form are separated from one another and brought together in a relation which is mediate and active from the side of the substance and mediate-passive from the side of the form. The objective value substance is mediately differentiated as abstract and concrete by the process of self-objectification of the human kind, not in general but under particular conditions, which are brought forth in civil and bourgeois society. The objective value form is expressed in its abstraction as opposed to its concretion. Whether the historical order of appearance of these processes of differentiation is the same as the order of their appearance in the system is a problem apart, and will not be dealt with here. Subjective value in its concretion is not differentiated from its abstraction, or such differentiation as may be made in this connection is borne upon the subjective value by the objective value substance. The subjective value judgment, consciousness, feeling is indifferently abstract and concrete.

Subjective value is not concrete alone; while this may be the case in some instances, yet subjective judgment, will, fantasy are also abstract, and these are part of subjective value. Hence subjective value is abstract and concrete. Being subjective, the relations between the abstract and concrete are immediate, inward. Further, the I, the self, the subject, are both abstract and concrete in their relation and reference, hence the subjective value expressions are abstract and concrete. These expressions are not unfolded in their abstraction and opposed to their concretion, the expressions are not cumulative quantitatively; they are not abstracted from experience, hence we speak of them as immediate, intensive and qualitative. Although they are not objectively comparable to one another, yet analogies are made between them, and between objective and subjective value expressions; they are taken up in this way both abstractly and concretely.

The form of subjective value is immediately related to the substance, which follows from the non-differentiation between abstract and concrete subjective value; thus the form constitutes the medium of the substance, and the substance constitutes the medium of the form. What is form and what substance in regard to objective value is clear, as we have seen. No significant point is made by such a distinction in respect of form and substance of subjective value. It is by abstraction that the form is separated from the substance, yet if abstraction is separated from concretion in the case of subjective value, the form thereof is not separated from the substance. What is subjective value form and what is subjective value substance is subjectively and not mediately determined.

No value of any kind is placed on wishes, desires or fantasies unless they are related in form and substance to the will. The will is the subjectivity of teleology, which is a relation of the human kind alone. The teleological relation is both objective and subjective, both in the human transformation of matter and in the relations of the human order. The value in the process of transformation of the material order expresses this objective goal-relation and goal-activity mediately. The value expression of human relation within human society expresses this goal relation and activity; in this case the value expression is in its subjective side immediate, in its objective side mediate. By the voluntary action, wishes, desires and fantasies are made into the substance of subjectivity, the form of which is subjective value. Without the interaction with the will, our wish, fantasy and desire remain passive; the will humanizes these wishes, fantasies and desires, but only subjectively. They become the subjective substance of which aesthetic judgment, feeling and affection are the subjective value forms. All these relations are reversible, form becoming substance and substance form. The external is converted into the internal, and the internal into the external relation of the human subjective process. Thus desire is transformed, being transvalued into will, and will transvalued and transformed into desire. This is to be seen in primitive, archaic mythology and in the mythology, fantasies, wishes and daydreams of human beings in modern bourgeois society; thus time does not become space but space becomes time in Wagner's *Parsifal*; the mystical experience is here individualized. The new factor that is introduced into these processes is external to them, and is objective; it is the hierarchical relation of civil society, ancient and modern.

Natural doing is a non-separation of form and substance, human making is a condition for the separation of form from substance. Subjective value is the expression of the non-separation of human form from substance, objective value the expression of the separation of human form from substance; therefore the subjective value appears to be more "natural" than the objective. This was the case with the romanticist ideology of subjective value and with the modern economists who make subjective judgment the agency of choice, and hence subjective value into the constitutive factor in objective value. However, value, whether subjective or objective, is not natural but human. Subjective value in the market place is not the determinant of objective value, for relations of the human subject, although they are operative in the market, hence in exchange, are not determinant of relations of production, or of labor. Relations of labor and of production constitute the substance of value, relations of exchange the form. Subjective value is both form and substance in the subjective relations of choice, judgment, will.

Subjective value, in the matters of art, makes the form into the form and substance of human relation; choice is subjective selection, judgment is subjective decision, will is subjective transvaluation of value. Here the form is transformed and constituted as the substance of human activity and passivity, theory and practice. In artistry, in creativity, form is converted into human form and substance, and human substance into form and substance. Thereby art is made into an objective process of the human kind and submitted to objective value. The particular art is objective and subjective in origin; here technic, craft and science are the same; they are transformed into an objective process, the form which the transformation and its product take, upon their differentiation, being objective value. This is a new form in human history, and its activation is a new expression. The given form is an actual expression and is a potential element in a system of human communication. The arts, technics, sciences, however, have not lost their subjective form and substance thereby.

Human labor in the primitive condition may be said to have subjective value, but it would be idle to do so, for, lacking quantitative measures and estimations, it has no objective value expression; subjective value has meaning in human reference only in its distinction from objective value. Human labor in the primitive condition may be said to have concrete value, or use value, for it is practical, concrete, useful. (See below, Abstract and Concrete Value.) All value expression is relative, and the substance of the concrete value of an object is the property thereof, which potentially meets a want or need.

Subjective value is in an immediate sense the worth and the expression of the process of selection of the means to satisfy our desires. Worth is the estimation of an object and at once the product of that estimation. Subjective valuation is the process and product of estimation of worth and its expression. But value is objective and subjective, with and without difference between the two, for the objective substance of value enters into the subjective process of valuation, but is not differentiated from the latter in that process. Value therefore is subjective and objective, quantitative and qualitative, cumulative or not, with and without difference between them. If it is objective then it is quantitative and measurable, the measure being cumulative or non-cumulative, the result abstract or concrete, cumulative or not. Concrete measure is non-cumulative, abstract measure is either cumulative or not. Objective value is determined by the difference, either in actuality or in potentiality, between human form and substance; the actual difference between objective value form and objective value substance is brought out in the relations of civil society. Objective value form is determined by human relation, abstract or concrete, objective value substance is human labor, abstract and concrete. Subjective value is determined by the non-difference between formal and substantial, abstract and concrete relations of the human order. Subjective value is a qualitative relation which if quantified is so acted upon by measures which are willful, a matter of belief, subjective consciousness and judgment. Subjective value is the expression of implicit or explicit choice, and the ground of will, judgment and consciousness in the subjective sphere whereby the choice is determined. Objectively values are mediate, subjectively they are immediate, being expressions of processes in either case. They are not immediate objective actualities of the human relation of labor, but are made actual and are therewith realized under given social conditions. They are immediate actualities, without diremption from their potentialities in the subjective relations of practical activity and of the consciousness.

Value and valuation are both objective and subjective expressions and acts of choice and placement; subjective value and valuation are expressions and acts of choice and judgment, placement and estimation of the parts of our world according to our desire and will. The human individual judges this picture over that and chooses it, finding it more desirable and pleasing, in a wholly subjective act. We may make our choice for no reason, and for no reason withhold our choice; arbitrarily, we choose not to choose, make our choice for mysterious, hidden reasons, or we may make our choice for unutterable reasons according to our desire and will. The choice and placement of our belief or the picture we love are determined by traditional factors, arbitrary considerations, rational and irrational, in the world of subjective value.

Subjective value is both active and passive; it is at once the product and the process of its production; the process is the bringing to consciousness of the will and desire which is the subjective value content and expression; content and expression are one with the subjective value substance; the form in this connection is not opposed to the substance, nor to the expression. The expression is the activation of the subjective value form and substance; it is at once the conjunction and disjunction of subjective value judgment, will and consciousness. The abstract and concrete subjective value are not separate from one another; the transvaluation of subjective value is the exception to this. Transvaluation of subjective value is effected by the act of will and consciousness, of which the transformation of subjective value judgment is the result. The will is defined by the process of transvaluation of subjective value; subjective value is subjective determination, and is independent of the external world by an act of construction. The subject is the mediate relation of human being to the self. Subjective value is a qualitative relation and expression. Objective value is the same as objective human social value, and is abstract and concrete, the abstraction and concretion of objective value being opposed to one another; in this, objective value is other than subjective value. This is not the only distinction between them. Abstract objective value is the expression of the sum of human work and labor expended in the reproduction of the human order and of the human kind.

Individual and Subjective Value

The origin of all value, subjective and objective, abstract and concrete, is the relation of human beings, which is concretely embodied in the human individual. The latter has been made the seat of subjective value through the cult of individuality in modern society, civil and bourgeois. The confusion of individuality with the cult of the individual and the doctrine of individualism is a transitory problem, brought out in the commodity relation of capitalism. At the first height of capitalist power, during the 18th and 19th centuries, the individual capitalist was made into the hero in history, fighting off the insidious and crafty statesmen who sought to impose the power of the public sphere on the right of the private, which is the home of capital. Value is explicitly objective and private in origin, therefore. The private sphere of civil society is then identified with the subjective side of human being, and the subjective with the individual.

The Austrian school of value theory took the subjective act of will and choice as the determinant of market and commodity relations which it holds to be the predominant factor of economy and society. Objective processes of human labor and relations of which objective value is the expression are therewith set aside. Exchange, contract, commodity relations are made into the determinant of objective relations of economy and society, and the formal relations into the determinant of the human social substance. In this theory of value, the form is taken for the substance, the self-relation is taken for the individual, the subject is taken for the object, and that which is lesser is taken for that which is greater. The existence of subjective value as an element in value theory, and its importance in the economy and society are unquestionable.

Value as the act of subjective will and choice is no more a matter of isolated individual relation than is capital the matter of the private sphere. Capital is produced by social labor, both labor and capital appearing in commodity form. Therefore capital is external and objective to the human kind, being a product of the human substance, but transformed into a commodity by the exchange relation in civil society. The exchange relation is a formal one, which is expressed in the formal and objective law of exchange value; the subjective side of this relation is neither excluded nor is it determinant in this relation. The individual embodies and personifies social relations which are at once subjective and objective, separating the one from the other, the abstract from the concrete value expression, and the value form from the value substance. Capital is transformed into the matter of the private sphere by an act of preemption in the interest of those who set the agency of the public sphere as a barrier against the action of the social whole which seeks to control the exploiting and ruling class; the exercise of interest, however, does not hide the origin of capital at the hands of social labor, its immediate producer, and the conversion through the exchange of means of subsistence against living labor time and capacity of the product of social labor into a commodity. The disrupture of civil society into a public and a private sphere is not the source of power of the exploitative class, for that diremption comes about by another means, and is then applied by the exploitative and ruling class in its own interest. The participants in the exchange relation in capital production are social labor, which sells its labor time and capacity, and the owner of capital which sells the means of subsistence against the purchase of the time and capacity of social labor. Neither of the participants acts as a subjective mite alone, both are submitted to objective and subjective laws, systematic moments and historical factors. The individual is the concrete agency of the subjectivity of the same relation which the social whole, actual and potential, active and passive, has generated. The individual human being takes on the subjective side of the human social order in modern civil society for the reason that the public sphere and interest has coopted the objective side in its own interest. This co-optation, however, is a false objectivity, and the interest which has led to this falsification is the same as that which has been alluded to above: it is that of the exploiting and ruling class which has separated the objective from the subjective side of the value expression, and behind this, the subjective from the objective side of the process of production. The public agency serves the ruling interest, as before, and the consumer is driven into the private sphere, which is made out to be one with the subjective. Because the private sphere has been separated from the public, it is made into the shelter for the innocent from the depredation of the public sphere, a fiction that is intended to hide the fact that the agency of the state in the interest of the ruling class of civil society has its seat in the public sphere and is opposed to the private. But the agency of the state and the public sphere in civil society serve the interest of the social whole only in the self-serving propaganda of the ruling class. The private sphere is not the seat of that class in society, and is represented as such only by means of a fiction. The individuality has a relation to the subjective side of human life, but the subjectivity is also manifested in other human relations, general and particular; the subjectivity of the one does not exclude that of the other and of the many, taken together or separately. In the cult of personality and of individuality, the subjective side of the human being is located exclusively in the person and in the individual respectively. The subjectivity is located exclusively in the individual person in the private sphere of civil life, in the rites of that cult, and is opposed to the public sphere of civil society. In the capitalist system, the individuals enrich themselves in the private sphere at the public expense. The charge was made against Stalin that he made over the public sphere of life in the Soviet system into the sphere of his private interest, (in the cult of his personality). The Soviet system is no longer with us; the capitalist system is the most powerful branch of civil society at present. The relations of human society in general are at once objective and subjective. In civil society, the individuality, the private sphere and the subjective interest are brought together and opposed to the public interest and sphere, and the objective processes of the human order.

The relation of human substance to subjective value is an immediate one, the subjective being internal and external in its expression of value. The subjective is constituted of judgment, will and consciousness, but not by these alone; the affectional is a subjective relation, which is internal. Value judgment is the process whereby valuation is brought forth.—In some circumstances it is possible to find a law of subjective value, which may be determined by social and cultural factors influencing our choice, will, desire, and judgments related thereto. The expression of the subjective judgment is not different from its content, the external expression and the internal content being a continuous process. Form and expression are different modalities of the same subjectivity in regard to value, the form being the passive, the expression the active modality. The expression is not an agent, as such, any more than is the form, however; form and expression are active factors only in relation to the substance. The expression is a part of the content as well as the form of subjective value, hence it enters into the human substance mediately. The transvaluation of subjective value is a matter of the will and consciousness, and not of subjective value judgment, form and expression primarily. Thus the content and expression, in the matter of subjective value, come to be opposed to one another by the process of transformation of value, or the transvaluation of value; thereby form and expression are constituted as one, and are the passive externality of the subjective value content; the will and desire are its internality, and, as a part of the human substance, its active factor. In the absence of transvaluation of subjective value, value expression and content are one, active, and distinct from the form. Abstract and concrete value are non-different in the subjective value content, expression and form.

Objective value in production, abstract and concrete, is the expression of relations of the human kind both in the human order and to the material order. These relations are mediate, and the value expressed is therefore mediate. There is no value which is not an expression, objective value is a mediate expression of the relations which have been mentioned; the immediate relations of the human kind within the human order are thus excluded from the field of objective value, and constitute subjective value. Objective value is abstract and concrete, but these expressions are separate and opposed to one another, for the objects which they refer to are separate and opposed to one another. Subjective value is abstract and concrete without difference, in it there is an immediate relation of form to the substance of human being, and its immediate expression.

Subjective value exists because the human kind has subjective processes of which it is the expression. We have symbolic acts and meanings to which we assign symbolic value. At the stage of social development in which exchange in the market, combination and division of labor, wage labor and capital come to predominance, objective, abstract social value gains its expression.

Value, Exchange Value, and Use Value
Abstract and Concrete Value

If we hold an object to be a good, then we will seek its acquisition; the object is a good if it meets, in our estimation, our desire, or supplies a want. The estimation of the good is therefore subjective or objective, imaginary or real, actual or potential in its reality to us. We will speak of needs, which are thingly and material only insofar as they are transformed into wants, the latter being transformed either by our conscious action, or by our unthinking doing, as a traditional practice, for example. The object which we use to supply our objective want has in this way a utility to us, by virtue of which we consider it to be a good; the estimation of the utility of the good does not exhaust our relation to it, for it is objectified out of other considerations, theoretical and practical, aesthetic and affective as well. The utility of the object as a good is a practical relation to it, in that it will supply an objective want, abstract or concrete. The acquisition of the good is effected by taking it into our possession, or by establishing ownership of it. By possession of an object, whether we take it to be a good or not, we have an active relation to it, and the good suffers our act of possessing it. This relation of action and passion is observed in psychology, when we say that someone is possessed, presumably by a drive over which that one has no control; at one time it was thought that the possessed had lost his or her will, and was subject to the will of a demon, or spirit. Hegel, (*Rechtsphilosophie*, 54), who thought of the distinction between possession and ownership, made the act of possession into a tripartite process, of physical seizure, demarcation, and forming, working or shaping. He had concrete possession of land in mind. Our relation to a good, whether a piece of land or other, is not exhausted by possession or ownership, for these are privative relations; thus we also have relations of collective sharing, in which contribution and distribution by one person does not deprive another of the good. With regard to the appropriation in a privative way, whether by ownership or possession, this is again opposed to appropriation in a non-privative way. Thus we may possess an abstract instrument of labor, such as a scientific theory, but we do not own it as a property. By working with and on the theory, we make it our own, and appropriate it to our use, but not in a privative way. Again, we may apply a particular property of a thing, such as the light rays from Arcturus, to our use without taking the star into our possession, or establishing ownership of it. We invent a way to sight the rays of light, and to apply them in navigation, asserting ownership over the invention. Our relation to nature is not direct but mediate. The distinction between ownership and possession is useful with respect to property relations in civil society, and indicates a difference between individual and social relations therein. Possession is an individual privative act, and not a social act. Thus if one occupies a tract of land in an uncharted waste, which is no man's land, it can also be seized by another, without social, legal measures to support one claim or another. The distinction in question is particularly, not generally useful.

Property ownership, in the traditional Islamic *adat* law, in ancient Roman, or modern civil law, is a social act. The tract taken into possession and occupied, by being demarcated and worked, and registered at an official bureau by a juridical person, is then objectively acknowledged to be the property of its owner. It may be inalienable, being held in entail, or otherwise restricted by explicit covenant, by local custom or by popular tradition; we suppose that it is alienable, however. The sale of the piece of land is made if it is useful to another, and that other buys it if it is useful to her or him. The sale is made in consideration of the return of a good of an objective value, equal or equivalent to the one who sold the land; it is not equal or equivalent to the piece of land, which has no intrinsic value. The land has some utility in an objective sense, for house building or mining; we suppose that we have acquired the right to its subsoil and surface properties and qualities; the ownership is thus a bundle of rights of property in the land, its use, enjoyment, using-up and abuse, exploitation. The rights are variable; thus an attempt to mine the land in a residential district may be opposed by the district's residents. There are subjective or imaginary uses to which the good is put; thus one may acquire a tract of land for its beauty. Gogol wrote of a traveller in Russia who bought up dead souls. The souls were dead serfs and their purchase allowed him to say that he owned a dozen or a score of them, while admitting to no one that they were dead. This is a subjective value placed on them, which is falsely declared to be objective. A subjective value is placed on the Good, the True, or the beauty of the sunrise. Further to parse the subjective values is idle, for they are endless, or seem to be so.

We have referred to property in two senses; property is applied in one sense as the natural quality of a thing, the warmth of the sun, or the hardness of a stone. Property in another sense is formal in the history of civil society, as a kind of ownership. It is at once privative, an anti-social act.

The substance of labor comprises the relations of human reproduction, and these relations to nature and in society are abstract and concrete. The concrete process of labor is differentiated according to the relations to the nature of the materials, technics and product brought forth, and according to its social organization, the abstract process of labor is differentiated according to the relations of production, according to the organization of social labor. It is sometimes held that abstract labor is undifferentiated, concrete labor differentiated, but this is an unwarranted simplification of the process of differentiation and abstraction of labor. The concept of undifferentiated labor as abstract labor is set forth in connection with the theory of labor as a commodity which is sold and bought, the value of labor being materialized in its product. The concrete labor and product are abstracted from their concretion in order that a common valuation of both the living labor and its materialization in the product can be made. The abstraction of labor which is expressed as undifferentiated is applicable in connection with the expression of the exchange value of labor, for in this way living labor can be exchanged against another commodity, which is quite unlike it. But living labor, in order to carry through the sale of itself against another commodity, first transforms itself into a commodity, which it sells; the commodity in question is abstractly expressed as its labor power. That abstraction has a twofold concretion, labor time and labor quality, as we have seen. The abstraction, labor power is in turn twofold, labor commodity and labor capacity. The labor commodity is the abstraction of living labor as labor power in the wage labor relation, and it is expressed in terms of the exchange value of labor; this value and the commodity form which is expressed by means of the exchange relation refer to the abstract, undifferentiated labor.

Objective abstract value form and substance relate to the process of reproduction of the particular social wholes in the history of the human order. Relations of reproduction of the human social whole are those of production and consumption in their separation from one another, in which case they are connected by relations of equal or distributive reciprocation. If the social units of production and consumption are related by equal reciprocation in exchange, then that which is produced has an objective abstract social value in exchange, which is expressed as the exchange value of the product. This exchange value is not the same as the abstract objective social value for two reasons. First, the abstract objective social value is the expression of a relation of production, whereas the exchange value is the expression of equal reciprocation in exchange. Second, the social relations of production and consumption are not those of exchange alone, but are also those of distribution and of distributive reciprocation. The social conditions under which production is related to the consumers, in exchange relations, are opposed to those under which they are related by distribution and distributive reciprocation. Thus, production and consumption relations, which are connected to exchange are different from the same that are connected to distribution. The relations of exchange and production differing for those reasons, the respective value expressions will differ.

Exchange value is an abstract expression of the relation of equal reciprocation in exchange. But the relation of equal reciprocation in exchange is a formal relation; it is a form of human relation predicated upon formal equality and freedom of the exchanged. Thus exchange value is the form of a form.

Objective social value as an abstraction is the general value form; it is the same as the general value expression. The abstraction is the same as the general value form. It is a form, and not the form of a form. The exchange value is the particular expression of the general value form. Value, exchange value, objective value, concrete and abstract value are expressions; they produce nothing. Use value is the expression of the capacity of products of human social labor to meet human wants and needs. Being an expression, it produces nothing, but is a measure of a product's capacity to act in a socially useful way, when activated by labor. Objective social value, abstract and concrete, is produced by human labor in its combination and division in society, that product being the expression of a measure. The value is therefore an abstract product that is produced in the process of making concrete, useful objects, which meet human wants and needs. These useful products, and the wants and needs themselves, have another value expression, which is also an abstraction; both the abstract and concrete products are *quanta*, for they exist in some amount, but their quantification differs in either case. The product of labor, and the labor itself are valued, the expression of both is the same, being the quantity of value. This expression is not a single quantitative term, but is a complex one, made up of the differential labor processes in many branches and fields of the process of human social reproduction. The value produced is quantified, which is a kind of social labor, and that which is produced by socially quantified labor is expressed by value *quanta*.

Exchange values are complementary expressions of relations in society of diremption between labor and its product, and between producing and consuming social unity, and or alienation of the product from the producer, which presupposes the dual relation of diremption. The exchange value is the expression of the relation of alienation of the product with equal, equivalent or proportionate reciprocation in exchange. Abstract value arches over relations of civil society in practice and of socialism in theory, but is not relevant to relations of the primitive-communal condition of the human kind.

The abstract objective value expression in civil society is exchange value, the concrete value expression is use value. Use value satisfies no earthly want or need of the human kind, but expresses the capacity of the object and of the self-object to satisfy such a want or need. Abstract value and exchange value are measured. Abstract value is not the same as exchange value, for abstract value is the measure of a process of production in society, not of exchange.

Exchange value and objective social value are not the same, for the substance of exchange value is the exchange relation, whereas objective social value has another substance, of which it is the expression; that substance is social labor time and capacity. Labor power as labor capacity is the abstraction of differentiated social labor, the abstract labor capacity and the concrete labor time and quality varying according to the objectified and cumulative time in preparation for the given process of reproduction and production. This preparation is not congealed but is objectified and self-objectifying qualification through learning by labor. The time and quality of the preparation is an active relation of labor in its self-reproduction and has a multiplier effect on the process of value accumulation. The process of cumulation of labor qualities has sometimes been referred to as a storing-up, but this storage has only a part of the process of cumulation in view, for the stored up is then drawn upon in the process of reproduction of the social whole. The individual in this process is the juridical person selling labor power against a wage, the entire process is constituted of a mass of such transactions; this refers to another concept of abstract labor, as the undifferentiated, and plainly contradicts it. It is to be distinguished from the process of differentiated, abstract social labor which is cumulative in the process of social reproduction, and is expressed as value.

The differentiation of concrete living labor is immediately related to the production and reproduction of useful objects, social goods and services whereby the concrete wants and needs of the social whole are met, the differentiation of abstract living labor is mediately related to the foregoing, and is related mediately as well to the process of learning, variation, cumulation and transmission of the qualities of social labor in the process of its self-objectification and self-reproduction. The abstract differentiation of labor, as labor capacity, is then given a differential value expression.

Exchange value is the expression of the value of commodities and this includes living labor as a commodity, both as wage labor and as unfree labor. Exchange value coincides with value under particular social circumstances, in which living labor is a commodity, whether the juridical power over it is held by wage labor, or by another person. The identification of exchange value with value is an expression of the distorted form and substance of labor in civil and bourgeois society, and hence the distortion of value expression and value theory under these circumstances. Value theory has been brought out during the history of civil society, with regard to the distinction between value form and substance, but without regard to the distinction between value and exchange value. Value has no connection with the commodity relation, exchange value has this connection; value is the form in which social labor is given abstract expression in the process of social reproduction of the human kind. The predominance of the relations of exchange, contract and of the commutative principle which is related to these has determined the formulations of the laws of value and of exchange value, in such a way that they have not been distinguished from one another. This determination is a concrete process, but the laws themselves are abstract, as is the distinction between them.

Subjectively, use and use value are with and without difference between them; a dream castle may have subjective use, subjective reality, and subjective use value. Subjectively you may identify use and use value, or what you please.

The use value is an expression of the concrete value of a product of labor or the labor itself, the goods and services of labor to meet our wants and needs. The use value is not the usefulness of the product or the labor time in making it; it is therefore not concrete in the object or in the human being, but is abstract relative to either and to both. The usefulness of the good or the labor process in bringing it forth is concrete in either, whereas the use value is the expression, which is an abstraction relative to its use. The water in the stream is potentially useful in meeting our thirst; the work of carrying it to the place where we drink it makes the potentiality into an actuality in quenching the thirst. The usefulness of the water in quenching the thirst is concrete, its use value is the abstract expression of that concrete act; the use value is at once the abstract expression of the concrete state of being sated, which is a judgment relative to the act. The use value of the good or service is immediately relative to the usefulness of the good or the act. It is mediately relative to the exchange value and to the objective value of either. The water in the bucket and the bucket in the hand are the substance of the use value, which is concrete and objective.

The system of objective, social value, to which reference will be made in the following pages, bears on civil society alone. Some foreshadowings of this system may be found in primitive society, but it makes its appearance only in the various periods of the history of civil society; its system is best exemplified in modern society, civil and bourgeois; but throughout the history of human society, wherever exchange is well developed, this system of value obtains. Its foundation is in the relations of exchange of socially useful goods. It has come to its present position by one new factor, the expansion of the relations of wage labor and capital. The relation of exchange adds this new factor of labor which is free *pro forma* to the exchange process; theory of exchange, value, market and price relations is not altered in substance.

Concrete work, or work as such has no value expression, save as we may value it subjectively. Only when we relate it to labor time and capacity does it receive an objective value expression.

The abstract labor has an objective value expression in general, without particular connection to the historical circumstances of civil society in which it is found; the objective value expression is determined in this case by the capacity of labor to determine itself as an abstraction; here labor relates to itself as an abstraction immediately for the reason that it has already objectified itself, the act of objectification having been made concrete and is accomplished. The accomplishment is posited as the actualization of a potentiality which lies not in the material but the human order, hence it is real in connection with potentiality, and is opposed to past possibility. It is contingent and abstract, having been posited under determinate circumstances that have brought about its abstractness; this cannot be made into a universal of necessity, for the discerption of abstraction from concretion, which is brought by human social relation into being, is relative; it does not proceed from external nature as such, but is introduced solely within the human order; it has no determinate being and no possibility in the material order of nature; save as it is made real by relations in the human order. The relation of abstraction is an asymmetrical one in this case. The human kind has abstracted itself by its labor from the material order. The act of abstraction is an objective one, for the material order becomes the object of human activity; it is the object again for the reason that the object exists only on the human side and from the human standpoint, there being no other object in nature than that. The objective value expression is in this case determined by the objective relation of the human kind to the material order, in the dual sense given, whereby the latter is transformed by human labor, the labor determining the natural field as its object, thus determining itself as the means of self-objectification of the human kind; by introducing the self-relation the human kind thereby determines itself as the subject, and objectifies itself doubly, in relation to the material and the human orders.

Abstract labor has a objective value expression in particular with reference to exchange value in civil society. The two objective value expressions have no necessary connection with one another, the generality of the value expression as abstract in the given circumstances of human history being concretely realized in civil society as the particular abstract expression, exchange value. What is abstract from the standpoint of one circumstance is concrete by virtue of its particularity and mediacy from the standpoint of another. Abstract value is the expression of the value substance where labor is measured and thus quantified. This is not universally the case, nor is it quantified always, in the case where it is quantified, in the same way, for labor may be quantified in reference to production in one way, in reference to exchange in another, and in reference to the meeting of concrete wants and needs in a third way.

The calculation of the value of use differs from the calculation of objective social value, or value of production, from exchange value, price and surplus value. The use value of a good has a qualitative and a quantitative expression, the qualitative expression being concrete; thus the use value and concrete value are in this sense the same. The use value of the good is particular to the good, and is not abstractable from it, or otherwise transferable. The use value of the loaf of bread is the expression of its ability to satisfy our hunger, the bread being of no use in warding off the rain, or in quenching our thirst. The use value of the bread is therefore an expression of a quality of the bread which is concrete and particular to it. We estimate what the bread is good for, to what use it is or may be put, and act according to our estimative judgment. Either the bread in this amount satisfies our hunger or it does not, it has met our hunger or not, or it will do so or not. This is a quantitative, non-numerical calculation; it is additive, in the sense of being calculated, plus or minus; either our hunger is satisfied by the food or it is not. The process is not cumulative, for the hunger comes again, and food is eaten again, in a finite process, until death, the disappearance of the society or of the human species. The use value is the expression of this quantitative, non-numerical estimation.

The use value of a good has a quantitative expression as plus or minus, or zero-sum. The good, in meeting our needs, is useful; food meets our needs in one way, clothing in another; thus, goods are always needs-specific; the best clothing will not satisfy our thirst. The goods are also in a zero-sum relation in another sense, for the meal satisfies our hunger today, but tomorrow we are just as hungry;

the good is in this sense also time-specific, for the needs for food, drink, warmth are never permanently satisfied.

There is an abstract relation between the theory of use value and the calculation of needs-specific and time-specific usefulness of goods. These needs, and their specific qualities of goods to meet them are concrete; the abstract calculation of their needs, or the wants, and the specific qualities of goods to meet them is one of the triumphs of civil society, particularly in the modern age. Thus, if we pawn a coat to buy food, we convert a concrete good into an abstract one, money. We also take into account the social problem which has led the poor into the pawnshop and forced them to leave their clothing behind. The needs mentioned are concrete, the means to meet them, in this case, concrete and abstract. We also presuppose a scale, in which the want of food is more urgent than the want of protection against the cold.

The product of labor in civil society has use value, concrete value, in that it meets a human want, but that value expression is not relative to exchange value, for in the primitive condition of human society there is no social exchange, in determinant and predominant amounts in the social relations, hence the corresponding exchange value expressions are lacking. Concrete value is relative to abstract value on the one hand, and to the meeting of wants on the other, both these relations in potentiality or in actuality. Abstract, objective value, is relative to concrete or use value in the system of value on the one hand, and to social relations of labor on the other. Exchange value is relative to value, objective, social, abstract, under particular conditions of civil society, in which equal or equivalent reciprocity in exchange is predominant; this reciprocal relation is the immediate substance of the exchange value, the concrete, practical utility of that which is exchanged is the mediate substance of the exchange. Value in civil society is exchange value in actuality, for it is determined by the predominance of exchange relations therein.

Value, insofar as it is objective, is an abstract expression of the amount of time expended in human reproduction of the humankind; it is a form, therefore, in relation to the labor substance. Value is a form among other forms, in which the human substance thus expended is not given this temporal, quantitative expression. The labor substance and the human substance are in this case not the same; objective and subjective relations constitute the human substance, abstract and concrete, mediate and immediate relations of the human kind, active and passive practices thereof, constitute the labor substance. In the value expression of labor which we are considering, the subjective element is diminished, and will be taken up in another relation.

The value expression is variable, being the objective expression of a regularity that is observed and demarcated under differing social conditions. It is the expression of a particular organization of practices whereby human wants and needs are met, the law of value in civil society taking the form of a quantitative expression of labor time expended in the process of human reproduction. The value expression is an abstraction, the law of value is an abstraction of an abstraction. The form of labor, which is the value form, apart from its substance, is constituted by an abstraction, and is expressed as another abstraction; thus it is constituted by its abstract value expression, is opposed on the one side to the form of labor as a concretion, such as is brought out in its concrete value expression, and on the other hand is opposed to the labor substance. Objective value and social value are abstract and concrete, but they are not concrete in the same way. The abstract value expression is the form of abstract labor, and presupposes the differentiation of abstract from concrete labor. Therefore, in order to grasp the abstract value expression, we first turn to the difference between abstract and concrete labor. Concrete value is, under the condition that labor time is measured and reckoned up in producing the good to which that value is attributed, the expression of concrete labor; the measurement of the labor time is its abstract expression.

Concrete labor is labor in an immediate relation to the process of meeting human wants and needs, and is in an immediate relation, therefore, to the concrete product which is consumed in that process. The concrete value of that product, under the condition that the concrete and abstract labor processes have been separated and opposed to one another, is use value. Use value is not a concrete property of the object produced, by which human wants are met; use value is the expression whereby reference is made to the given property. Use value is the means of reference to the property in question, which is in this sense an attribute, for it is transformed by human work and labor, and that which is its property is attributed to it by the meeting of a want or need in the human order. The property of a thing in the material order, such as that of water to quench thirst in animals, is then transformed into an objective human attribute of the material relation of the thing by human work and labor. The drinking or absorption of water by animal or plant organs is variable according to the different species, whereas the conveying of water to the human organs is variable according to the customs of the peoples, the hands being cupped by some people, by others it is drunk from vases or bowls; lapping of water is forbidden by some religions; the meeting of a need, the quenching of thirst, is modified by control of amount, quality, purity, by cyclicity, when or where water may be drunk in the day. The property of water has a human property attributed to it, which is determined by economic, ceremonial, juridical, or political factors; the natural property thus becomes a communal or social property, and in the latter case is further differentiated as public or private, in civil society. Water is then bought and sold as a commodity, and its distribution controlled by weighing one want against another, whether for cultivation of the soil or for drinking, for animal or human use, for hydroponics, fishing and fish farming, or for industrial applications. The purification of the water is a matter of priorities, availability of water and of funds, technology of conduits, desalinization. The need becomes a want, and comes to be modified in the system of human wants, for a human group will make do with less water, and redistribute its uses, as its system of wants changes, or give up another want for more water, of greater or less purity, or availability at different times. Water becomes a matter of value, and has a use value attributed to it under these conditions, which it did not have when communally distributed.

Use value exists in relation to abstract value, and is the expression of the concrete property to meet a human want and need. Use value is therefore the property of the human labor product, thus its attribute in the human order. But this attribution of the capability of the given property to meet a given want and need is not found throughout human society; it is present only under particular circumstances. [The quality of water is variable, and its ability to quench thirst depends on its chemical constituents within a given range of temperatures and pressures. Water as such therefore does not meet a want, but some of its qualities are applied to meet that want.] The use value of water therefore varies, being developed relative to value, the concrete want being variable, and therewith the labor to meet it is variable. Use value is found in potentiality in communal, archaic, primitive society, but objective, abstract value, of which use value is apart, is not found there in actuality. Only social labor has objective, abstract value for its expression; communal labor has the expression *in potentia*. The abstract is not separated from the concrete labor, and the abstract expression thereof is not separated from its concrete expression in the communal condition. Use value, moreover, has a separable, not a necessary, relation to exchange value, having been brought together in the relations of civil society, which are historically limited. Exchange value and objective value are not the same.

The good, whether a concrete product, activity, or service, is a social good insofar as it meets a concrete want and need of a particular human group. The good has potential value by virtue of its usefulness in this sense. The good is not a good as such, but is variable according to the changing relations of the human kind both to the material order and within the human order. The good is not the natural thing but is the natural thing transformed into the human object, whereby a property, quality or attribute of the thing is determined, concretized and objectified, being abstracted from the material order and converted into an object of the human order.

Concrete labor is labor expended in preparation of a product in immediate relation to its consumption. Concrete labor is, however, other than labor measured by use value. Use value is sometimes held to be the real, concrete quality of a good which meets a want. This is a mistake, for the use value is the measure of the utility or other quality of the good in meeting the given want or need. It is not a cumulative value, but is wiped out when the need or want is satisfied. In this the calculation of use value is feasible, but the calculation is not the same as the calculation of abstract value, which is cumulative. The use value is therefore an expression of a form of value, just as exchange value, or value as such, but its substance is not labor time. The substance of use value of a good is its capacity to satisfy our wants and needs. Concrete and abstract labor makes the expression and calculation of use value possible, but there is more to concrete labor than the production of means whereby concrete wants and needs are met. The utility of concrete labor in this respect is but one aspect of labor, whereas the premise of utilitarianism, according to which human activity is measured in terms of meeting wants and needs, and thereby happiness is measured, is a reduction by simplification of human activity and passivity.

Concrete labor is the means of meeting concrete human wants and needs and thus of maintaining the human kind in its materiality. It is an element of the process of self-reproduction of that kind, and indeed without concrete labor there is no means of securing the animal or human reproduction of the human kind. Concrete labor enters not only into the production of that which is measured by use value, it enters also into the production of that which is measured by abstract value, objective value of production as such, and by subjective value. The value form of concrete labor is limited to those social conditions in which concrete labor is measured, either by use, concretely and non-cumulatively, or by abstraction and cumulation. Concrete labor extends beyond these social conditions of the human kind, and is developed under circumstances in which it is not measured at all; save by an estimation of the amount of living human skill and force of a traditional kind, and an estimation of human capacity to vary that skill, concrete labor is not measured under archaic primitive conditions. The measurement as a cumulative and a non-cumulative process under these circumstances rests as a potentiality of those conditions, such as are realized and made actual under others.

The utilitarian principle of happiness as the measure of human activity has a partial relation to the theory of use value and to concrete labor and value. The utilitarian principle is limited, however, for happiness, by which is meant the state resultant from the meeting of wants and needs, is a field which is restricted to one kind of activity alone. There are other fields and kinds of activity beside those relative to happiness, and hence other measures of human activity relative to use value. We may work and labor for our happiness, or make the work and labor into their own end, without regard to our happiness. Labor in the latter sense is a means and end unto itself, and work is conducted without regard to recompense or happiness. If it is then argued that the happiness in the work is the reward, then the inducement of happiness is a circular explanation. The explanation of work and labor by the motivation of happiness bears in part on its onset, but does not thoroughly explain why we work; and it does not bear on the process of work and labor itself.

Use value is a theoretical formulation relative to the concrete products of work and labor whereby they are given non-cumulative expression. The satisfaction of wants is in this sense non-cumulative; concrete labor has a practical form and substance which is other than use value, that practical form being in immediate conjunction with its practical or theoretical substance. The form and substance of the concrete labor is its product, which is consumed. (See below, on Form and Substance.)

To think of the use value of a good as the actual good which meets our wants is to hypostasize the value expression, and to tear it from the use to which the good is or will be put; in another sense it is a reification of the value, or the representation of the abstraction as a concrete object or thing, which it is not.

The use value or concrete value of labor time is the expression of the capacity of our work and labor to meet wants and needs under given circumstances, being an abstract form relative to a concrete substance, which is inseparable from the capacity of the product of human labor to meet a want, to enter into relation with abstract, objective labor, with our concrete, theoretical and practical human activity, and with our subjective relations.

The form of concrete labor has therefore an abstract and concrete expression; that expression is at once practical and theoretical, and is both subjective and objective, being the outward manifestation of substantive relations of these kinds.

The contradiction between the determination of the production process both as abstraction and in its abstract relation by the exchange process, and the determination of exchange value by the abstract expression of the amount of labor expended in the production process, is brought about in the following way. The determinant, abstract labor, and the determinate, abstract value, are separated from concrete labor on the one side, and concrete value on the other. These separations do not take place by an internal process, but by a given historical moment, the development of secondary social relations of exchange, which is a factor external to the production process, and which brings about its secondary socialization.

Abstract labor is concretely expressed in one sense as wage labor, in the society of the production of capital, as the commodity of social labor in the same social condition, and as the exchange value of labor in that condition. Abstract value is historically expressed as exchange value in these historical circumstances; the two expressions of value coincide in this case, but they are not intrinsically the same: value, abstract value is the expression of the relation of production in society. Theoretically and practically, abstract value is determined by the quantity of labor time and capacity expended in the production of socially useful objects, and thereby meets social wants and needs. The abstract value is the expression of a quantity independently of any and every exchange relation. It coincides with exchange value in a particular historical circumstance, in which the product is exchanged in society as a commodity, the labor time and capacity that is expended in its production being likewise exchanged as a commodity. Abstract value is thus historically determined as exchange value in the circumstance in which the processes of production and consumption are interrelated predominantly by the process of exchange. Abstract value is thus concrete historically as exchange value.

Use value is an abstraction, but it is not abstract value in the system of economic relations of production of civil society. The use value, we have seen, is the expression of the quality of the product to meet a human want. The use value is not the quality itself, but its expression. The concrete value and the use value coincide with one another both historically and systematically. Concrete labor and concrete value coincide, just as abstract labor coincides with abstract value. The organization of concrete labor is not to be analyzed in terms of levels; it is linear, the linearity being expressed as a plus-minus, or zero-sum relation. The concrete labor is work expended in the production of concrete goods, the usefulness of which is brought out in their capacity to meet concrete wants and needs in human society; use is not measured in natural social but in human social terms. The expression of the usefulness of the good produced is its use value, which is quantitative, being measured as a whole unit that is wiped out on being consumed. The concrete product is eliminated not in the production process but in the process of consumption in connection with the process of social reproduction. The work is comprised in the concrete product and is eliminated with the consumption of the latter. The concrete organization of work in this sense admits of no residue; it is a simplex that is immediately connected to the process of production, consumption and reproduction, being with out branching or ramification. The quantitative expression of the organization of work is a one-dimensional or linear program. The quantitative expression of the organization of abstract labor is in all societies three-dimensional and in modern civil society is an n-dimensional system.

The concrete value or use value has work as a part of its substance, and the quality of the good produced as another part of its substance. The use value is the expression of the combination of the two. The work is the means of actualization of the potentiality of the quality of the natural materials to meet our wants. Thus the water in the well has the quality in potentiality to quench our thirst; this potentiality is fulfilled by the work of carrying it in the bucket to the house, where we drink it. The capacity is the quality of the water and the amount. Abstract labor stands in a mediate relation, through the concrete work, to the usefulness of the good produced, and hence in a mediate relation to the use value of the good.

Labor which is constituted as the substance of objective value is not all of labor, for private labor is excluded. Objective, social labor is the abstract and concrete object of its own relations in the human order, and therewith to the material order. The labor time which is expended in production, distribution, consumption, and thus reproduction is not the value substance as such; it is the value substance only insofar as it objectifies itself abstractly and concretely. It is constituted as self-objectifying human effort in this way, which is the capacity of the human kind to reproduce itself. The labor capacity which is organized, combined and divided in society is that of living labor, which is expended in the process of reproduction of the social whole by the transformation of itself and of natural materials into a socially useful object in the process of meeting human wants and needs. Labor capacity is both subjective and objective in its potentiality; in actuality, in the process of meeting given human wants, it is objective. The labor time that is expended is both abstract and concrete; living labor thus contains within itself the relations of labor and work, being the objectification of the natural material, and at once the process of self-objectification of the human kind.

The concrete value is the expression of living labor capacity, whereby the latter is transformed from its objective condition into one which is at the same time objective and subjective. The reason for this is that concrete value or use value is the expression of the actual satisfaction of the want and need that is realized in the social production process, that want and that need being a part of the human substance and these are in themselves objective and subjective, both abstractly and concretely in the matter of the wants, concretely in the matter of the needs. (See Krader, *Treatise of Social Labor*, Chapter I, Section IV.) The concrete value expression, just as concrete labor with which it is mediately connected, is quantitative but not cumulative, nor is it relative, for the want that is met is eliminated by being met and arises again in undiminished form, both as a material and as a human process: hunger, thirst, biological reproduction, etc., for however well we have eaten yesterday, today we hunger again.

The use value as such is abstract and meets or satisfies no want; it is the theoretical expression of the capacity of the bread, etc. The algebra of the use value computation is a quantitative, additive, but non-cumulative expression. Thus, the quantity of bread is 1, the hunger it meets is -1; $1 - 1 = 0$, in a given day. The quantity of food eaten on that day is of no use in satisfying the hunger felt on the next, in which case another quantum of food is eaten, and another additive, non-cumulative expression of the want in relation to the product, bread, is computed.

The process of consumption is cumulative or non-cumulative. It is abstractly cumulative as a part of the process of human reproduction, production, consumption. Consumption *in concreto* is non-cumulative, for the product is used up, whether immediately or mediately. It is consumed immediately in the case of food, which we eat in a short time, at table; or it is consumed mediately in the case of an axe, which wears out more slowly and over a longer time. The cumulative and non-cumulative operations of our consumption processes are given expression in various algebras.

A thing is not a good as such; it is transformed into a good according to our estimation of its capacity to meet our material and non-material, concrete and abstract, practical and theoretical wants. The estimation of the capacity of the good to meet our want is qualitative, in answer to the questions: is there a want? of what kind? is this object a good, of a kind to meet it? The estimation is quantitative, in answer to the questions: how great is our want? how much of it can this good meet? and how much of this good can meet it? We give the cases of hunger and bread, thirst and water. There is a specific relation between the want and the concrete product. The bread does not meet the want of shelter against rain; only in fairytales are houses made of gingerbread. The goods which meet our wants are concrete, particular, non-transferable. We do not alter our wants to suit the goods available.—The product is the concrete outcome of our concrete labor, or work. The act of discovering a wild plant which meets our hunger is a kind of work; pounding it in a metae, and cooking it is work of this kind, as well. The use value of the product or the find is objective, the good as such is objective and subjective; the concrete labor which, until the achievement of its transformation in the product is objective, on its material embodiment in the product and on being consumed thereby becomes an objective and subjective social good, which is a part of the objective and subjective process of social reproduction. The material form of labor is objective; labor time and capacity, the human substance in its relation of labor in society, which bears within itself the determination of all human process, relation and product is objective and also subjective. The relation between the subjectivity and objectivity of labor time and capacity and the subjectivity and objectivity of human wants and needs constitutes the human substance; it is mediated by the means of production and product, the mediation is transformed into the system of self-objectification of the human kind, and this system is active and passive both in its subjective and objective aspects; potentially it is universal, actually it is particular. The relation of subject to object in the process of production is universal, actual and potential, as such immediate, leaving no residue, and is coextensive with the human order as a whole in this sense. The relation of subjectivity to objectivity in the process of particular social reproduction is mediate, both actively and passively so.

The production of a good varies simply and primitively as the want varies; the greater the hunger, the more food we produce; the converse is not the case. However, if the appetite grows as we eat, then we no longer speak of the simple and primitive case, but of a complex and advanced one. In the consumer society, the appetite for food, clothes, display is spurred on, and the production determines the appetite for the product. The production is in turn wantonly excited by those who profit from the exploitation of the induced appetite. We attribute a use value to the wantonly consumed goods as we do to the goods meeting our concrete human wants and animal needs.

That which the use value measures is quantifiable, being additive, but it is not cumulative, as has been shown. The wants and needs which are met by the usefulness of the materials of the natural order are as such not cumulative, hence the usefulness of material in meeting them is not cumulative, for the relation between usefulness as a property of the material is concrete and immediate; thus there is a useful quality in meeting wants and needs of the human kind, and this in severability is not altered by the operation of human labor upon the materials in order to transform them and make them available to the meeting of the wants and needs. This concrete process of utilization of natural materials and qualities is additive in the sense that a drop of water added to another will attain a quantity that is needed to satisfy thirst, and the process as such is both subjective and objective. The objectivity of the process works backward from the want-satisfaction to the act of meeting the want, whereas the subjectivity works forward from the estimation of the amount of natural material to be transformed, transported, etc., in the process of meeting the want and need. The ancient conundrum, how many grains make a heap?, is answered by tradition and convention. The notion of the dimensionless points which are piled up to make a dimensionless heap is a paradox. We determine objectively what is a heap when we think we have enough of a good to meet our want of food and our animal need of it. The heap is in this case an expression of an estimation, which is objective. The grain is objective in its existence, having dimension, weight and size, and the qualities or capacities of which in their sum will meet our want and need. The sum is not in the grain, but in its heap, and is an abstraction of a concrete form and substance. The process of meeting the hunger by consumption of the nutrient qualities of the heap of grain is an additive one, being moved from plus to minus when the hunger returns, as it will so long as we are alive, healthy, and normal. The heaping of the grain is a cumulative process, and is independent of its additiveness and subtractiveness, which bear on the process of its satisfaction of the want. The monads, having neither external nor internal relations, are not cumulative; henads, having these are cumulative.—The cumulativeness or non-cumulativeness of the material, such as grains of wheat is not immediately determined by any intrinsic property thereof, but by the mediate relation between the human want, our estimation of the amount required for its satisfaction. The additiveness is an expression of the process of meeting the want, and not of the cumulation of the grains. The cumulation and the addition are both objective processes.

The human wants and needs are as such variable, for some are met by the accumulated, mediate, objectified and self-objectifying labor; they are, in this sense, both cumulative and additive, whereas some are only additive within the process of meeting immediate and concrete wants and needs. Those wants that are met by cumulative and additive processes are both abstract and concrete, those that are met by additive processes alone are concrete. The usefulness is therefore an expression of a relation that is throughout concrete, and is in part abstract, the use value is the expression of a relation that is solely concrete, for an abstract want, such as substantive freedom, substantive equality, distributive as opposed to equal reciprocation, has use, being wanted, in theory, but has no use value whereby it is expressed. The abstract expression of the want and need is both additive and cumulative, the additive, cumulative expression being objective and subjective. Labor both concrete and abstract, bears upon both objective and subjective relations of the human kind.

The relation between concrete value and concrete labor is mediated by the relations of the system of wants and needs; it is mediated abstractly by the value system. Concrete labor by its additive quantitative expression mediately and abstractly determines the additive, non-cumulative, quantitative expression of concrete value, or use value; the additive, quantitative expression of use value is the mediate determinate of the concrete wants and needs. The concrete value system is the mediate expression of the relation between concrete labor and its product, on the one side, and the concrete social want on the other, the concrete want constituting the substance of the use value, the use value constituting the expression of the want; work and its concrete product from this standpoint constitutes the mediation between the concrete value form and substance. Work is quantitative in its expression, which is either additive or non-additive, cumulative or non-cumulative; but not all work is constituted as a concrete value substance. Concrete or use value is constituted as such only within the objective value system as a whole, and forms the concretion of that which is abstractly expressed as value, in the particular case of civil society as exchange value.

Use value, concrete value, abstract value, and exchange value are developed in the history of civil society; exchange value is coterminous with that society and its history with the history of that society. Value, abstract and concrete, does not end, either in history or in theory, with the termination of civil society, for the reason that abstract and concrete labor, abstract and concrete living labor capacity, and their quantitative expression do not come to an end with the termination of civil society in history. Exchange comes to an end as the means of relating social production, consumption and reproduction, and therewith its expression as exchange value, and the connection between value and exchange value therewith is severed.

Concrete, use value as the concretion of value does not come to an end, but continues to be applied as the expression of concrete, useful labor and its product in the meeting of human wants and needs. The opposition between the product and living labor capacity and the product of social labor is generated within the system of civil society potentially and implicitly, actually and concretely in the system of modern civil society, that opposition extends in theory beyond the limit of the history of modern civil society.

The subjectivity of the living labor capacity exists not in itself nor yet in opposition to the product and its use, but in relation to the self-objectification of living labor, therewith to the objectivity of living labor, its time, skill and capacity. The use value is the expression of the concrete, objectified past labor, the form in which it meets a present want and present need. The use value as an expression is objective, the form of the past labor in the product at present is at once objectified and objective, objectified and therewith objective.

Social labor is abstract and concrete; it is the means of human reproduction, and the substance of the human kind in general, and in particular of the given, historically reported social wholes; social labor in abstracto is a continuum. The form that this substantive process takes is the given human society. The entirety of the human order is at once actual substance, concrete form, potential substance and its mediate abstract expression, whereas the particularization of the entirety, the generality of the human order is concrete in the particular social whole in history. The abstract continuum of labor is mediately interrupted by its momentary concrescence, the mediation being systematically introduced by the production process itself in its product. The product is the concrete discontinuity of the abstract universality of the continuum of labor, such as is necessary for the reproduction of the concrete social whole, concrete social labor and the concrete and abstract human individual. The concretion of the continuum is effected by the constitution of social labor in the organization of the archaic social wholes; this organization is the undivided capacity of all those who are capable of work and labor. The concretion of the continuum of labor is dirempted, being internally opposed and alienated in society, social labor here being embodied in the class of social labor. Social labor is concrete in its form in relation to the abstract continuity of social labor. The class of social labor in civil society is at once abstract and concrete, in which its abstract relation is expressed as value in general, exchange value in particular, its concrete relation expressed as use value.

Value Form and Substance
Value in Production and Value in Exchange

The abstract value substance is abstract social labor. Abstract social labor is the expression of the quantity of labor time and skill expended by the social whole in the process of its self-reproduction. Social labor is constituted of the relations which can be analyzed quantitatively and qualitatively within the given social whole and the relations to the material order, whereby both the human social whole and the particular field in the material order are transformed. In its relation to the material order, labor is as such theoretical and practical, mediate and alien. Labor in its relation within the given social whole, whereby it is constituted, organized, combined and divided, is mediate and immediate, abstract and concrete; it is alienated in human society not in general but in a particular set of circumstances. Objective abstract value is the expression of the quantity of and quality of social labor expended in the process of meeting particular wants and needs in the process of human social reproduction. The objective value expression is opposed to the objective value substance abstractly and concretely.

Abstract value is measured objectively, separately from subjective value, quantitatively and cumulatively. Abstract and concrete value are at the same time subjective in the substance; the objective expression of the substance implies the separation and mediate relation of the substance and the form. The objectivity of the value lies not in the formal expression, but in the labor substance.

Abstract objective value in its formality is historically variable. Exchange value as an expression coincides with abstract value under particular circumstances of the history of human society in its civil condition. In the relations of civil society the expression of abstract value as exchange value follows from the unwarranted assumption that the market and commodity relations are determinant of both abstract and exchange value. Exchange in the commodity and market relations of equal reciprocation, as opposed to exchange in the archaic, symbolic and ceremonial practices of human society, is a relation between the units of production and consumption in the process of social reproduction of the humankind.

By equal reciprocation in exchange a standard measure of equality is posited as a formality in society. This standard is labor time, living and present, in which it is self-mediatizing and therewith self-objectifying, or past labor time that is materialized and therewith objectified, that is expended in production; the labor time comprises in this case the skills, qualities and capacities of social labor, and the science and technology of the social whole. The exchange relation presupposes the establishment and acknowledgment of the difference between producing and consuming units in society, which undertake the exchange. The production is measured both in cumulative qualities and in plus-minus, additive, non-cumulative quantities. The exchange takes place on the presupposition that the product of the one producing unity meets a want of the other, which becomes the consumer, and conversely, the product of the other meets the want of the one. It is the amount of labor in production, not the degree to which wants are met that determines the equality of the exchange, and its continuation, recognition, development, systematization and prolongation under these circumstances, practical and theoretical; the exchange becomes social exchange; the objective, economic relation is socialized to begin with, and is given a formal expression as exchange value. The exchange relation is a determinant of the formation of civil society. The production relation continues to be practical; the labor of production is now divided into two parts, abstract and concrete. The concrete part is the meeting of human wants and needs; social labor in production in the concrete sense is nothing other than labor expended in the meeting of these wants and needs. In order to bring into existence the equality between products of concrete labor exchanged, the products must be divided within themselves into a concrete part which continues to meet human wants and needs, and an abstract part. The abstract part is separated from the concrete context and thereupon is theoretically represented and practically applied in various contexts. The abstract part is the objective value expression. In the exchange process it is the exchange value expression, or exchange value, objectively and abstractly considered. Production and exchange are thereby separated; distribution, consumption, production and exchange are no longer in a continuum.

The abstraction, value, is mediately determined by the relations of labor in the production process; the relations of labor in this process constitute the substance of value, the value is its expression; the value is the form and is the formal expression of the substance. The substance is measured, being expressed in quantities. The quantities are independent of their measurement; both are human *facta*, being made, produced, and brought together, once in social practice, and again in value theory. The theory and practice form one system, but they have separate historical courses, the practice having been introduced long before the theory made its historical appearance. The formal side of the relations of production is expressed as abstract value, given that the theory of value and the mathematical theory are developed and clearly grasped. Before this, labor in society had been organized, objectified and quantified, both in the relations of production and exchange.

Abstract labor has a value form and expression, and insofar as it is inwardly dirempted from concrete labor is brought forth under those social circumstances in which it appears only in a given variation of value form. The abstraction of labor from its concretion, and its abstract representation and expression, presupposes the constitution of social conditions in which value as such is given expression, abstract value separated and analyzed apart from concrete value, and use value, exchange value and surplus value are known. These expressions, analyses, separations and cognitions may be present or past, explicit or implicit, actual or historical. The value form has a plurality of expressions; that form is a variable and is plural relative to the value substance, which is labor. The relations of labor in human society and to the natural order are multiple and variable. The relations of plurality and singularity between form and substance are relative and variable.

The abstract expression of the value form differs from its concrete expression in that the abstraction is potentially one, the concretion is both actually and potentially many. The abstract expression of value is potentially one in that the human kind has the potentiality of unification of the entire labor process in a single social whole, whereby all the parts thereof are interrelated in a common mediative process. This is a prospect which is not actual, at present, but is not fantastic and utopian. The concrete value form bears upon processes of labor which are plural, and in that concrete wants are plural and variable, subjective wants individually variable, is determined as actually and potentially multiple.

The abstract and concrete value forms constitute a system, but this system is not an independent entity, for it is dependent on the process of labor and work and is the expression of that process. The process of social labor, and its concretion in work, makes up a system in that it is internally related, articulated and concomitantly variant. The work process is the means whereby concrete wants and needs are met; the social organization of the labor process, its division and combination, the development of labor skills and technics, the materialization thereof in the given technology, are determinant of the relations of work.

The abstract value has the same relation of form and expression as concrete value, even if the substance of abstract value differs from the substance of concrete value. The expression of both concrete and abstract value is in either case an externality in relation to the substance, as is the form; the expression is in either case an activation of the form. The form as activated by the substance is given human expression, and is then abstract or concrete value expression respectively. It is acted upon by the substantive value relations, and it is as though the form were active in its expression, but it is not. The form of value, both abstract and concrete, is abstract, mediate expression of the substance, passive until acted upon by the latter, cumulative in respect of abstract value, non-cumulative in respect of concrete value. The expression is separable from the substance in its appearance, but is inseparable in actuality. The substance of value takes on many expressions and has a plurality of forms; as we have said, it is itself variable. The form is separated from the substance, for it has a different historical course from the historical process of the value substance. Yet the value substance has some form or other, and the form a substance.

The abstract expression of labor in the production process as an abstraction is

186 / Lawrence Krader

value, its law is the law of value. It is opposed to and is the determinant of exchange value within the value system. The value system as a whole is determined by relations of labor, production, consumption, reproduction, distribution, exchange and circulation in historically existent societies. Systematic determination is a mental process in this case, and is opposed to the determination of mental processes by relations in human society and in nature. We are therefore faced with two relations of determination. The system of value, abstract and concrete, value in use and exchange, is a human construction, in which theory is abstracted from and applied to practice; the practice is the economic and social relationship. The relation of concrete labor to concrete value will make this clear: concrete value is use value, which is the expression of the product in its given form that is consumed in the process of meeting human wants and needs under given circumstances of civil society. Concrete value, or use value, is an expression as another value expression. It is the result of human labor in concrete form. The abstract flow of the labor process is arrested, the product excerpted, or abstracted from the continual process, and applied to consumption, whereby the reproduction as a continuum is brought about, and the product is given, as concretion. The given is a *poiesis*, that which is made. The concrete form of labor has in this case the expression as use or concrete value. The concretion of labor as a product consumed in the meeting of wants and needs is not the same as its concrete expression: the concrete product has a value expression, concrete value, or use value. The form is in this case dual: that which is accessible to the senses as visible, tangible form, which is in conjunction with the substance consumed, and thereby meets a want, is not the same as its theoretical expression. The form in the first place is thus made practical, materially concrete, useful, a sensory object. In the second sense it is the formal expression in which it is entered as a part of the theory of value. The separation of the two concrete forms has a different history from the separation of abstract labor from abstract value. The separation of the abstractions, labor and value, was begun in the work of Aristotle and carried forward in the 19th century, by Marx, whereas the separation of concrete product from concrete or use value was carried through later. (Krader, *Treatise of Social Labor*, Chapter 2; *Dialectic of Civil Society*, Chapters 3 and 4.)

The objective value form is constituted by the abstract expression of the objective labor substance, which is both abstract and concrete, in the process of human social reproduction, and by another formal relation. The value form is an abstraction, and its expression presupposes that there is abstract labor of which that form is the expression. Thus the further prerequisite of the value form is the distinction between concrete and abstract labor. Concrete labor has as its expression concrete value, or, under particular social conditions, use value, which measures the ability of a given socially produced good to meet a concrete human want.

Abstract labor has abstract value as its expression; the value form is at once abstract and concrete in its reference, thus corresponding to the abstraction and concretion of labor.

The labor substance in civil society is constituted of abstract and concrete relations of labor, the labor form is the dual value form, abstract and concrete value. The abstract value in this condition is expressed as exchange value, the concrete relation of social reproduction as use value. The value expression is not universal in human society, but is brought out only under particular conditions; in this process, labor is abstracted from the social substance, and is expressed as labor time. The labor time is a combination of present living labor time and capacity which is expended in the process of meeting human social wants and needs, and past labor time and capacity which has been expended to the same end. The past labor time is abstract in that it is the time spent in training, whereby past labor processes are handed down, learned and mastered, and is abstract again in that what is past is immediately varied in the present; the past labor time is concrete in that it is the materialized product of past labor made available to the senses and to other human body organs, and applied in the process of reproduction of the given social whole. These relations of labor time expended in social reproduction represent the labor capacity, which is the limit of the value expression. This limit is approached, but is not reached in the objective value form, being further determined and therewith limited by another formal relation in the social relation which is given objective value expression.

Value in production is an abstract quantity whereby a substantive relation is expressed, relative to another substantive relation, whether like or unlike the one. The objective value of a given good, product or service is determined by the amount of labor expended in bringing it forth, and is expressed in units of labor time; the expression brings together the amount of present and past time expended in the process of bringing it forth. The time in the past is the time expended in mastering the organization and technics of the given labor process, in working with others, and in preparing the materials and instruments applied both in the learning and in the actual labor process. The abstract quality of the value is independent in its expression of the good as such; the abstraction is thereby made educatable with another concrete good, which otherwise could not be so equated with the first. The objective value of the good is its abstract form, which is reckoned up independently of its substance.

The substance of the good is the amount of labor time expended in bringing it forth, the labor being both abstract and concrete. The abstract labor does not go wholly and immediately into the abstract value expression, but the latter is made possible and brought into being by the activity of labor, its capability of self-representation as an abstraction, and its analysis of labor time by classifying it, reckoning it up, dividing and adding it, calculation, by constants and variables. There is abstract labor, therefore, and abstract value. Abstract labor is labor which is separated from the immediate, practical and concrete tasks of social reproduction; abstract labor enters into these processes mediately by theoretical activity, by theoretical and practical sciences, and by the concrete and abstract relations which bear upon learning of the technics and arts of the reproductive process of the human kind, mastering them and varying them. In this way we distinguish the mediate process of human reproduction from the direct, biological reproduction of *homo sapiens*. The human medium is constituted of these relations of preparation, mastery, abstract and theoretical in relation with concrete and practical activity, whereby the medium as such is worked on, expended, maintained and varied, both quantitatively and qualitatively. In this process learning and mastery are in the relation of a potentiality and actualization of the potentiality.

The concrete relation of production and of reproduction, distribution and consumption determines the concrete value expression, use value. There is no concretion of exchange, in the sense of equal or equivalent reciprocation as measured quantitatively and objectively. The concrete or use value stands in opposition to the value expression immediately, therefore. It stands in a mediated way thereby in opposition to the exchange value expression. It is sometimes held that use value and exchange value are bound together, and form a pair, but this is a misconception. Abstract value and concrete value constitute the systematic determinants of exchange value. Without the production of that which is expressed as concrete value, or use value, exchange cannot take place, hence no exchange value can be expressed. Without the relation of abstract labor, whereby abstract production takes place, exchange cannot be undertaken. The existence of abstract labor and of abstract production is called forth by the exchange relation, in the secondary sense given above; abstract labor and production are in this sense determined by exchange.

The relation of value and exchange value is one of mutual determination, each of the other, under the given circumstances in which exchange is a predominant relation in society, which is that of modern society. Under these circumstances, exchange by living labor of its labor capacity against the means of subsistence, exchange of commodities and of living labor time and capacity as a commodity, and market relations, together with the relations of alienation of the social surplus, are the determinants of the social relations, both primary and secondary; exchange value and value then coincide, value expression determining exchange value expression. The reason for this is that the relation of self-objectification of the human kind by means of its labor in society is a human generality, and continues unchanged, whereby the relations of the social whole and its reproduction in the human order, as opposed to the process of natural reproduction, are maintained. Exchange determines social relations under particular historical circumstances, as opposed to the universal relation which continues throughout human history, and in this sense exchange value as the expression of exchange, is a determinant of abstract value; exchange value is not a determinant of use value, but is, as we have seen, mediately determined by the latter within the value system of the given society. The freeing of the relations of labor from the bondage of exchange, commodity and market relations, is the radical requirement of social labor in actuality, and of the social whole in potentiality. The form of freedom will then coincide with its substance. Human freedom substantively is at present constrained by the exchange relation; the form of freedom determines the substance of unfreedom. We will see what this means by examining it from the standpoint of value theory.

The value form is opposed to the value substance. The form in this case is the expression, the substance is that which is expressed by the form. Value form, law of value and value expression are the same, the substance is mediately related to them and determines them, whereupon they determine the substance.

The value substance has a formal relation of two kinds, external and internal. The value substance is the relation of the social whole in its self-reproduction, it is the self-objectification of the human kind in its concrete form, whereby wants and needs are met. The form in this case has both an external and an internal relation without separation into constituent parts. The substance is formed and concretized in the process of self-reproduction of the human kind, distributed, shaped, organized, combined and divided, under particular conditions; in the modern era of civil society the predominant form of distribution is exchange. The substance is constituted of relations which are abstract and concrete, and are given a value form, whereby they are expressed as abstract and concrete value; the internal and external relations are now separated. These relations are the external relation of the substance and the internal relation of the form. The internal relation of the substance is divided into labor of hand and head, practical and theoretical labor, which is activated by an external relation to the form, without which it remains a potentiality, without actualization. The form is the mediate relation whereby the substance actualizes itself. The substance has first internalized the external relation of the form, which gives the substantive relation a particular and concrete shape, determined by the going conditions of a given social whole. Only when endowed with a formal existence, having determinate being and particular attributes, both as sensory phenomenon and abstract relation, can the substance be activated. It is made concrete in tools and instruments, stored in granaries and bins, and stored up in the head, abstractly stored and retrieved in the computer, in production, and it is made formal and abstract in the exchange process. In its concrete form the consumer is one with the producer, which is the internal relation of the form to the substance; in its abstract form the consumer and producer are separated from one another, the product being abstracted from the hands of its producer; it is thereupon freely given away, distributed in a reciprocative relation, alienated in equal or equivalent exchange by formal contract, and alienated without reciprocation in exploitative relations. The substance in relation to the form is subdivided in inner and outer relations, the form in relation to the substance is subdivided into different inner and outer relations, which the substance internalizes; the form is not an internalizing agency; for internalization is a relation of the substance alone, which externalizes itself through its form. The form is variable and appears under given social conditions in different, connected ways. The most readily apparent external relation of the substance in modern civil society is that of exchange; but exchange, formal relation of reciprocation by contract in the strict sense, is not universal in human society, and has only recently come to predominance. In its universal relation the human kind has the same relation of form to substance whereby the latter is activated, and its potential actualized, as it has under particular social conditions. In its universal relation, the production process is one with the process of consumption, the consumer and the producer are the same human being, and the form in its internal and external relation is without differentiation. This universal relation is abstract, actual, active at any given time, but it is without concretion. The producer and consumer in the process of social reproduction of the human kind are divided from one another in modern civil society, and are related by formal exchange with reciprocation, and by alienation of the product without reciprocation.

The producer has internalized form and substance alike in the process of self-reproduction; the human kind has objectified itself concretely in this process. While self-reproduction and self-objectification overlap, they do not coincide. The process whereby the human kind reproduces itself is the totality of activities of the human order whereby concrete needs and wants, together with the abstract wants are met, activities which bear mediately on the material order. The needs are of biological provenience and are concrete, including food, warmth and the like. They are the same needs in the human and material orders, being met by the human kind through the social organization of labor, that is, mediately and objectively. In their biological provenience they are met concretely and directly, neither objectively nor subjectively, but in a thingly way. The wants are social, human in provenience and in the way they are met; they are mediate in relation to the natural order, being the work of the human subject. These wants are the social organization of human activity, the reciprocative distribution of the product, the substance and form of freedom and of equality. The meeting of these wants calls for the radical reorganization of civil society. They are both abstract and concrete, and are a part of the process of self-reproduction and of self-objectification of the human kind. The wants are immediately objective, the needs are material processes which are transformed into human processes and are objectified. In meeting these wants and needs in the process of self-reproduction, the human kind objectifies itself. The wants do not lose their concrescence by becoming increasingly abstract in modern bourgeois society. The subject in the process of self-reproduction has desires, which are opposed to the objective wants and needs, and are opposed to the process of self-objectification, and are the means whereby the latter exceeds itself. The subjectivity is expressed in desires, which are abstract fantastic, theoretical, willful, conscious and unconscious, arising in dreams, wishes, temperament, being given form in painting, poetry, music, sculpture and other arts. This subjectivity enters into the process of self-reproduction of the human kind, and therewith into its self-objectification. The utopian vision of humanity arises out of the subjectively desired possibilities, entering thereupon into the scheme of reorganization of the human social whole, and into the system of objective human wants and needs. They are internalized by the human kind in the process of its self-objectification marginally, not with respect to the present, but with respect to the future. The process of self-objectification has an abstract and theoretical aspect, which is introduced mediately into the process of self-reproduction of the human kind. The objectification of the material order is practical in the process of meeting human wants and needs, theoretical in relation to the practical process, and theoretical abstracted from the practical process. Our theoretical relation to the material order *in abstracto*, apart from its praxis, is part of the process of objectification of the material order and of self-objectification of the human kind in actuality; it is potentially a part of the process of self-reproduction as the theoretical side of scientific activity is related to the practical side; after having been abstracted from the latter, the theoretical is recombined with it, to be abstracted again.

The product has internal form; the producer having internalized the form and substance of past production externalizes them in the product. The substance is made concrete in the given form, which is determined by a particular social tradition and varied within that tradition. The product, while it and the act of producing it remain within the tradition and its recognized variation, has an internal relation to the production process, and is the concretization of the relations internal to that process, which is the internal relation of the form to the substance. The product is the past activity which is borne upon the present, and reactivated, the past in concrete form to which the producer stands in an objective relation; the past product is objectified by being present in a concrete form to the act of living labor, which is not the same as the act of past labor whereby it was produced. The past activity is not present to living labor because it is objectified, it is present to living labor because it is made concrete. The objectification of human determinate being is a general and not a particular relation between the past and present in the process of self-reproduction of the human kind; the concretization of past activity of production and reproduction is the particular relation in this regard. Concretization, mediation and self-mediation, objectification and self-objectification, which constitute the labor process, have been taken up in the past in terms of a congelation process. The result of past activity, which is made concrete in the product, is varied, reactivated, repotentialized, and these processes are not implicit in the senses of crystallization or congelation.

The congelation or crystallization of past labor in a product is a way of referring by a figure of speech to the reification (itself a figure) of the process of work and labor, and of the workers and laborers in civil society; to the extent that living labor is alienated in the process of social reproduction as a whole, the reference is accurate. The relations of labor to the means of production are reified, and the products themselves are made concrete. The congelation or crystallization is the trope which expresses the human-inhuman condition of labor in modern industrial society, in which the control over technics and initiative in social organization of production, combination and division of labor, are taken away from living labor and given into the hands of others. But those who control the production process do not constitute a class in society, for they formally include both the elements of the ruling class, and substantially include the elements of the mediate producers. The latter elements out of false interest have in some cases allied themselves with those who have a substantial opposition to the class of social labor in its immediate production capacity. The class of social labor in modern industrial society, however, is constituted in its substance of those engaged in immediate and mediate production processes.

The history of the form of social labor and that of the substance are severed from one another under these circumstances, and they proceed separately. Moreover, a part of social labor as a whole has come into opposition to the immediate producers, and has formally allied itself to the controllers of the production process, and this opposition between form and substance in the process of reproduction in modern civil and bourgeois society has led to a further stultification and reification of social labor as a whole. This reification, however, is a momentary matter, and has a potentially restricted future. The relations of labor in the process of reproduction of the social whole are potentially those of its self-concretization, self-objectification and self-activation of the human kind, in which the congelation as a metaphor is eliminated. Labor freed from external controls and superimposed power is labor which frees itself in its substance as well as in its form. The concretion of the past is tangible, visible, generally available to the hand, mouth, being manipulated, reworked, consumed. Being available to the senses, it is perceived in an old and in a new way, old and new potentialities of the past product as instrument in present production and reproduction being applied by the producer.

The form of the product is the externalized and concretized form of a past substance, which is internalized by the producer in the process of production. The producer is the human kind, the consumer is the same, and the process of production is that of human reproduction. The form is past, objectified and concretized labor, the substance is present, self-objectifying living labor, the activity of which is objective and subjective, its relations both abstract and concrete, whereby the form, which is passive as such, is activated and reactivated variably. The active process is only in the present, the activity of the past or future having only a ghostly existence. The past is activated by being concretized, the future has no concrescence, but has an objective relation which the present activity of the human kind bears to it. The substance is the human substance, which is throughout determinate in space-time of the material order. The past is transformed into a concrete object and is present to the producer as concretized, objectified relation in a given form. The formal in the relation is an internal bond linking the past to the present activity, whereby the living labor in the present communicates with the past in a mediate relation by working upon the past concretized substance and varying it. The medium in which the communication takes place between the present activity and the past is the human order, the instruments of which are the human organs and the concrescence of past activity, the products of labor and the objects of the human field. The mediate communication has language as one of its aspects, among others: the given social whole is an expression and medium of communication; labor is a means and medium of communication, of which language is a particular kind.

The medium is transmitted from the past as a tradition, varied in the present relation, and in the present relation to the past; the tradition in the present stands as a variable in relation to other traditions, past and present. The medium is an objective relation, and is independent of living labor, which reproduces and varies it both as product and expression. The form and variation of form are the objectification of living labor in the process of self-reproduction, self-objectification, of reproduction of the social whole and the objectification thereof. Form and variation are the mediate communication between present living labor and the past, the means whereby the process of self-objectification of the human kind in the present is the medium of communication as mediate, traditional, new. *Vetustatem novitas, umbram fugat claritas, noctem lux eliminat.* (The new drives out the old, shadow and night flee before the light, according to the old Rouen Ritual.) The old remains and is the burden on the present; it gives the present weight, it is a necessary burden. We vary not anew but with themes handed down from the past. The old is the form against which we apply force, without which the force is unrealizable; the force remains as potential without actuality.

By means of the exchange relation the consumer is transformed, and is now other than the producer. The consumer is the social whole, living labor in social form the producer, as before, but the product has a new form in the exchange relation. This new form is continuous with the old substance; the new form is externalized, separated and abstracted; it only enters into the production process anew as an abstraction, in the form of that which it has been exchanged against, concretely the consumed enters into the production process in being reprocessed by natural and by human operations. The used up, inorganic and dead go into the respective natural and human economy, and enrich the atmosphere which we breathe, or fertilize the soil, providing the amalgam for new production, and energy for its fires. The abstract form is a relation between human beings, who are now opposed to each other, the one as producer in relation to consumer, the other as consumer in relation to producer. Each stands to the other in an inverted way, which is righted by an abstract expression of value.

The exchange value is a form which differs from the form in production; the latter is independent of the exchange process, just as reproduction and consumption are independent of the exchange process. The form of value, in this case exchange value, does not exist independently, but is the expression as an abstraction for the exchange. The exchange is not necessary to the economy, for it is a mediate and historically determinate relation, without immediate participation in social production, distribution, or consumption. There are other mediations between production and consumption in the process of social reproduction, than exchange, therefore it is not a necessary part of human reproduction. Exchange being a condition of the system of civil society in that it is there predominant, exchange value is brought forth as its expression in that condition. The value form, however, is determinant only of the law of value in the given form, and of nothing else. Exchange value is the form of a form, for exchange, to which exchange value refers, is a formalization of a relation of equal, equivalent and proportionate reciprocation, which is a predominant and determinant process in civil society, ancient and modern; that process is a formal congeries of contractual right and obligation, in accordance with the principle of commutative justice and right.

The substance of objective value, being social labor time and capacity, as such is not other than the human substance, subjective and objective; it is active and objectified only in immediate relation to the form. The form of the form is separable from the substance, and appears to have movement and life of its own. It is still an expression of a relation, formal and substantial, between human beings; this expression is formal, and separable from human form and substance. The formal expression of value as exchange value in civil society is the translation of the commodity relation of human social labor as living and as product. The formal expression is not a thing but an object of the social relation of production, which is expressed as a product, and is itself a construction, which is a human factum as a mental production. The formal expression is therefore not a relation, social or otherwise, between things. It appears to be an object, but is in its reified form the object separated from the subject, or from the human subject-object, and has entered into the mythology of civil society as a thing. It is the reification or representation of the object as a thing, as matter.

Objective value form and objective value substance are sometimes confused, the form being taken for the substance, and less usually, the substance for the form. The form of objective value is separable from the substance. The substance is the self-objectification of the human kind, the form of value is its expression. After many millennia of internal development, the self-objectification is given quantitative measure; the quantitative expression of the value is then adapted under particular historical conditions of exchange, commodity and market relations as exchange value. Exchange value, however, is not the eternal form of value; it is not the whole of the historical objective expression of social value. Exchange value is the objective expression of value under the particular conditions of economic exchange as equal, or equivalent, reciprocation, in the historically concrete circumstances of civil and bourgeois society, with reference to its modern period, and thereupon with a more general reference to its historical course over the past three or four millennia; this is to be extended back in time by two millennia in various parts of ancient Asia and North Africa, Peru, Mexico, and perhaps other parts of the world. Value in its objective social substance has no necessary connection with the given historical form, having come into being under other circumstances than those comprised in the exchange relations; the value substance will pass out of being under other circumstances than those that regulate and determine the passing away of the given value form as exchange value. The historically momentary coincidence of the given value substance and the given value expression is falsely internalized as a necessary connection between the two. Human form and substance generally, value form and substance in particular, are mediately and socially connected; there is no necessary connection between the two in human history.

Value is defined in terms of the attributes of objectivity, sociality and abstraction because labor has these qualities, for labor constitutes the value substance. Labor has another form than value, however, that form being labor power. Value is, therefore, not the form of labor immediately but mediately; it is the form of the form. Value is the abstract expression given to labor power in the relations of social labor whereby the social whole and therewith labor itself is reproduced. That labor power is an abstract right of disposition over labor time, and that abstraction has as its concretion the quality and quantity of social labor itself.

Periodization of the Value Process

Value in the primitive, archaic condition of human life is without difference between form and substance, and without difference between abstract and concrete labor, hence without difference between expression and content. The relations of labor determine the relations of value, for they stand to value as substance to form, hence as content to expression thereof; the value form and substance, abstraction and concretion, subjectivity and objectivity, expression and content, process and product are in an immediate relation to one another; they are non-mediate for the reason that the formal and substantial relations of labor are not differentiated to any great degree. The relative non-difference of these processes is determined by the communal relations of labor, which are without great differentiation in their combination and division, without specialization of technics in the process of work and labor, and without significant differentiation between production and consumption. These differences are thus without determinative influence in society, for they exist in low degree, hence have no predominant influence in archaic forms of primitive life. The relation between production and consumption in this condition is that of sharing, sharing out, distribution, with little exchange.

In the process of transformation of communal into social labor, abstract value is differentiated from concrete value, value form from substance, quantitative expression from qualitative, and subjective from objective value. The relation between form and substance is mediate, and an opposition between them is then generated. The relations of labor are general, throughout the human order, but are now divided in their expression into subjective and objective value. On the objective side, value is divided into abstract and concrete value by differentiation of qualitative and quantitative relations of labor; and these are differentiated and connected in virtue of the divisions of the process of reproduction of the human kind.

The subjective value process is less developed in its differentiation than the objective; the relations of objective value are more developed with respect to the differentiation and connection of the abstraction and concretion, and of quantity and quality of value estimations than are the relations of subjective value. These differentiations and connections are then developed as mediate and oppositive relations of form and substance in civil society.

Objective value is the expression of the active relation between the human kind and the natural order, and the activity in the human order of the human kind whereby the matter of the natural and human orders, and the human kind therewith, are transformed in the process of meeting human wants and needs. The matter which is transformed in this process is both that which is accessible to the human senses and that which is not, thus material relation concrete and abstract; the process of meeting human wants and needs is that of reproduction of the human kind, the wants being abstract and concrete, and the needs concrete. The process of human reproduction goes on whether it is endowed with a value form or not, the value form and expression being limited to those relations of society in which labor is quantified in the process of human reproduction in society. The measure, qualitative and quantitative, of labor presupposes a particular organization, combination and division of a given social whole, which has been historically limited to civil society. The usefulness of the process and product of labor in meeting human wants and in transforming the physiological needs into these wants thus lies at the base of human reproduction immediately, and of the given value form and expression mediately. The utility of the process is concrete, and constitutes a part of the human substance, concrete and abstract. This concretion is general, substantive, the value expression is particular and formal. This formality has a further restriction, for the value expression does not appear as such in human history, but in conjunction with a formal social relation of exchange by equal, or equivalent reciprocation. The equality of the equivalence in the exchange is an estimation, which, if it is objective, is determined by the quantity and quality of labor expended in the process of the exchange, and in the process of production of the exchanged. This is the relation of self, diremption of the self-relation, relation of self and other, diremption of the relation between self and labor, self and product, self and other. The relation of the self to the other, to the product, to the labor process and to the self is that of an alien under this condition, and the continuum of self-relation of the primeval community is transformed into an alienation of this relation. The product of labor being alienated to another person in exchange, the producers are alienated in relation to themselves. The self-relation is that of the community, tribe, clan, village, and therewith the individual, whereas the other is of the same kind, but another community; the opposition between them is a construction which is projected onto the earlier epoch by an observer later in time, in modern society. The projection is not without objective validity, but is also artificial.

In that later period the expression of value in exchange is sometimes mistaken for the value expression as a whole, and value in use is often mistaken for use as such. Thus the lesser part is taken for the greater, and the form for the substance. The self-relation is mistaken for the individual relation of the self in modern society, which repeats the same errors. A subjective factor comes into opposition to the objective in the exchange relation, if those engaged in the exchange feel that they depend on their respective internal, individual, and therewith subjectivized judgment in estimation of the value of the commodities exchanged; in this relation the three mistakes are recapitulated in one; thus the subjective feeling of fairness, which is the psychological or moral expression of the outcome of the exchange, is taken to be its objective substance. The satisfaction of the exchangers in mutuality is not a matter of choice, however, for the selection, critical and non-critical, has been introduced by a factor extrinsic to the objective valuation process and its outcome. The subjective value is a relation unto itself, and is separate from that of objective value in civil society.

Objective valuation is a process, the expression of the process, the principle, and act. Objective value is a form, and as such is mediately related to the substance as the expression thereof, hence it is an active relation of the human kind in its various forms, value as such, exchange, use value, and value abstract and concrete. Subjective valuation and subjective value are less far removed from one another than are objective valuation and value; the processes are relative, valuation and value being related as process and product, thereupon as product and process, for the one is transformed into the other both objectively and subjectively.

Human history is a process from the archaic primitive condition, to the modern bourgeois conditions of social life, in which the relations of wage labor and the formation of capital prevail. There is no absolute cleavage between the two conditions, for all human beings in all circumstances engage in acts of estimation and valuation in their lives, whether sporadically or regularly, and systematically. The attribution of an objective value to the products of social labor, and to the time and capacity of the labor itself, is systematically, regularly and pervasively carried on in modern civil society, taking the form of exchange value in that society. It is found in earlier eras of the history of the human kind, both in the society with and without social classes, with and without the state. The attribution of objective value to goods, products or processes of labor, as time and capacity, depends not on these relations and constructions of society, but on the calculation of the amount of time and preparation spent in production. The calculation, or estimation, of the time spent in this way is the basis for the objective value expression, and its substance. The regularity and system of the objective value as the form of social labor are determined by the system of social labor in the estimation and exact calculation of labor time and capacity in production. In the earlier eras of society and modes of production, the estimations of labor time were cruder than they are at present, often sporadic, or were not made at all. Objective value in production is expressed as exchange value under particular social circumstances, and is expressed as price in the condition of market relations, commodity transactions, and capital formation, the condition in which labor for wages prevails.

Symbolic and Economic Exchange. Symbolic and Economic Value
Exchange in society has its history and prehistory, its development in society, civil and bourgeois, having been preceded by another kind of exchange, and the development of the predominance of economic exchange preceded by the sporadic and infrequent undertaking. Social exchange is of two kinds, symbolic and economic.

The symbolic exchange is found in all kinds and conditions of human society, being an exchange of objects having symbolic value. It is practiced in conjunction with ritual and ceremonial, and is usually connected with the symbols of the ritual or ceremony, both religious and secular. There is but little difference between the symbolic exchanges practiced by the peoples in a communal, primitive social condition, and by those in the civil condition. Exchange, either symbolic or economic, is a relation of reciprocity between human beings, whether individual or in a group. In symbolic exchange no particular opposition of interests is present in the reciprocation, whereas in economic exchange there is such an opposition between the different sides engaged in it. Marcel Mauss referred to symbolic exchange as the archaic form of exchange; it is not only archaic but current among us in the exchange of birthday presents, and other ceremonial ritual exchanges. Symbolic exchange is also informal, or occasional, in spur of the moment gift and counter gift. Symbolic exchange involves certain objects of symbolic value, but certain others are untouchable, and are not subject to symbolic exchange.

By economic exchange is meant a material process between human beings in a relation of equal or equivalent reciprocation. This material process has both concrete and abstract labor as its substance, hence is both material and non-material. The reciprocal relations of exchange of equal or equivalent objects is practiced in communal and primitive social conditions, but is found there sporadically, infrequently, and in this sense unsystematically. It is systematic in modern society, civil and bourgeois, hence we see that it undergoes an internal development. Symbolic exchange undergoes little change or development of this kind. In the following, by exchange is meant economic exchange, unless otherwise qualified.

An exchange is made between two parties who have a use on either side for the goods exchanged; the use is objective and subjective. The exchange in civil society is a process between human beings as juridical persons; it takes place not as an isolated event, but under social conditions which serve as the concrete circumstance and abstract system in which the process occurs. The social relations in the exchange, with reference to the use of the goods exchanged, were brought out by Aristotelian, Marxian, and neo-classical, marginal utilitarian theorists. Aristotle pointed out that we first meet our concrete, practical wants, by the supply of useful goods, and then apply ourselves to theoretical tasks. The exchange is effected between persons capable of making it, in a relation between different sides to meet their respective ends; the various sides to the exchange are analyzed into a set of dyadic relations. The same model, *do ut des*, give and it will be given, obtains for an *n*-adic exchange process. It is a relation between two persons, respecting two goods, of which each is the respective owner, and which the other holds to be useful in meeting some want, objective or subjective. If we expend all our earnings in acquiring dream castles, then our civilization will go under; this is not unknown in human history.

The quality, objective or subjective, of a good, which is useful in meeting our want is expressed by its use value, or its value in use; the value in use is not in the good but apart from it. The exchange of unlikes in bourgeois society is made by reference to an abstract expression of the exchange value of goods exchanged; the exchange value is not apart from its concrete expression in the use value of the good. The exchange value is not the same as the good exchanged, and the use value is not the same as its usefulness in meeting our wants. Sometimes the good which meets our want is called a use value; this is done for shortness; but unless it is explained that a step has been skipped, it is faulty practice to take the good and the use value to be the same. A good is not a use value; its use value is the abstract expression of our estimation of its use in meeting our want, or of some attribute which it possesses in doing so; the estimation is objective or subjective, so is the want, and the means to supply it by violence, expropriation or peaceful exchange. In that the use to which a good is put is objective or subjective, its expression as a use value is objective or subjective respectively. Objectively, the use of a good and its use value are not the same. The coat which is worn for protection from the cold is useful to its wearer; its capability of warmth supply is not its use value, but is expressed thereby, for the capability is concrete, either in actuality or potentiality, whereas the use value is an expression of the capability in potentiality, or the supply of warmth in actuality, and is abstract. The coat has a use value, which is related to an exchange value. The supply of warmth by the coat is to its use as its exchangeability is to its exchange value. Without the usefulness of the coat there is no exchange with reference to it; without the use there is no use value in potentiality, and without the anticipated use there is no concrete exchange; without the use value there is no exchange value, which is another abstraction.

The exchange is a material interaction between the parties to it, which is completed by the process thereof. Thus it is a plus-minus, or zero-sum relation, which is renewable, in a series, and the series in a matrix of these processes, but the exchanges as such are not a cumulative process, for the exchange stores up nothing, accumulates nothing, and is wiped out without residue on completion. Thus it is a symmetrical process which is concrete and abstract, but is not a transitive process concretely; it is, however, a transitive process abstractly, having been made such by other factors which enter into the exchange. These factors are the repetition, duration, continuation, perpetuation and specialization of exchange, not in regard to the particular, concrete exchange, but in regard to exchange in the given society in general, or in human society in general, as an abstraction. Goods having economic, not symbolic value are the objects of economic exchange.

A factor in the development of exchange which is extraneous to it, but which by its development undergirds it and contributes to its systematic extension, is the process of mutual acknowledgment by the parties to the exchange as social, and in this sense juridical or moral persons. This factor is extraneous to the concrete, particular exchange, but is connected to the system, and its perpetuation and generalization. In the exchange practice, each side acknowledges both the exchangeability of the objects in the exchange and the social capacity of the other to engage in the exchange. In the case of the silent trade of the Chukchis, Inuits and other peoples of the North Pacific, in traditional times, the exchange was both a material interaction and a means of mutual objective acknowledgment and subjective recognition. Exchange is therefore impersonal or personal; in the latter case the personality of the opposed party there is taken into account. But the person is juridically as well as psychologically defined; in trading it is juridically defined, whereas in symbolic exchange it is psychologically, culturally and traditionally defined. There are religious and juridical elements in such traditions. Symbolic and economic exchange may both be rational.

In the process of exchange, the product, whether material and non-material labor, or abstract and concrete labor, the materialized and concretized form thereof, or the combination of these in commodities, is brought forth and separated from the human process of labor as such, in a reciprocal relation between the different sides in the exchange. The exchange therefore presupposes the relations of labor in society, social relation, the material and concrete substance and their abstract, immaterial transformation. The social relation is that of mutual acknowledgment and recognition as persons participating in the exchange, the persons having rights and obligations, in a system, implicit or explicit. The persons are constituted and acknowledged in the interaction of the exchange, either within the given social whole, or between the social wholes, cross-culturally, inter-regionally or internationally. The relation between the persons in the exchange process, at the moment of the exchange, is that of immediate equality and freedom *pro forma*. This relation is objective, and is acknowledged as such by both sides. But away from the moment of interaction in the exchange, the immediate relations of acknowledgment, recognition, equality, freedom and formality disappear; the disappearance of the relations, however, does not affect their actuality at the moment of the exchange, even given that the exchange systematically and frequently recurs.

Exchange presupposes a relation of one and other, and further, the relation of difference and connection between them. The difference and connection is of the human kind, being mediate and oppositive in respect of an interest, and the interaction in the exchange is therefore, in its developed form, not communal but social. Therefore the human relation of the one and the other implies the mediate relation of one, other and many, for the social relation is a complex process, in which labor and its product are alienated from one another, and the labor is dirempted in its self-relation. This process is asymmetrical, for whereas labor is self-diremptive, its product is not; the latter is alienated in the process of exchange.

A further presupposition in the process of exchange is that between internality and externality, whereas labor, in the reproduction of itself immediately, and of the human kind mediately, generates an internal situation as the subject, which is the self-relation of labor, and an external situation of the alien object, which is the self-field relation of labor. In the communal and primitive condition of human society, there is no difference between the internal relation of the social whole and the internal relation of labor. The silent trade, which has been mentioned, is not an exchange between individuals, nor between social wholes, for the two are not opposed to one another in their interests; this trade is a relation between discrete internalities of labor in their external relation to one another. The discrimination between internality and externality is presupposed in this case; the discrimination between individual, communal and social interest is not.

In consequence of the interactive moments of separation and opposition between labor in its relation of self, other, medium and field, a social relation of labor is constituted, which is that of exchange, whereby labor generates a mediate relation to itself and its product. The labor of reproduction of the human kind then works on itself as the field of its activity, objectifies itself in relation to its field, objectifies its field in relation to itself, and transforms itself into a field, thus making itself into a medium of its labors practically and theoretically. This process is the self opposition of labor in general, which is subjective and objective, and in particular the opposition of labor to itself as object. The self-objectification of labor in this process is then developed by a second opposition in particular, between labor and the product thereof. By means of the processes of human reproduction, of self and field, of one, other and many of diremption, opposition and mediation, objectification and mediatization, internality and externality, labor transforms itself actively and passively into social labor.

The product of this process of internal diremption, between labor and its product and between labor and itself, is then alienated to another person in the exchange; and in this process labor becomes alien to itself, having opposed, dirempted and alienated itself and its product. The labor time in relation to itself and to its product, is no longer its own, but is the property of the other person; the relation of one's own, another's own, and of ownership is then constituted, together with that of alienation between the one person and the other. The continuity in the process of human reproduction between labor, the self-relation, and the product, is thereby disrupted, and the property, individual, communal, own and other is generated in society; property is the expression of the relations of opposition and alienation, and is not a social relation of the human kind as such.

Exchange is a relation which is simple or complex. Simple exchange is a dyadic relation; complex exchange is *n*-adic and transitive. The system of exchange in society is *n*-adic. Exchange which is in a series of dyadic interactions is nevertheless simple exchange. The dyadic process is traditional in primitive and archaic societies, and is formalized in civil society. The social form is separated from the social substance, and the labor form is opposed to the labor substance in either case, for the exchange process presupposes this separation and opposition.

Exchange is a disruption of the process of human, social reproduction; it is abstractly the diremption of the process whereas it is concretely continuous. Yet the concrete social labor internalizes the abstraction and its diremption; this is a diremptive process at the basis of civil society, generating further oppositions within it.

Social labor, by virtue of its diremptive, mediate, abstract and objective relations quantifies itself and its product. In the process of its reproduction, it separates the unit of production from the unit of consumption; reproduction in this case is the process of production and consumption and the mediate relations between the two. Exchange is the form of one of these mediate relations in civil society. The quantification and abstract expression of labor and its product is a formal condition of exchange, and of the abstract expression thereof by objective social value.

Exchange is momentary and sporadic or it is regular and durative. If it is regular and durative it is trade. Commerce is a further variant of exchange, which is developed by specialists, traders, merchants, comerciantes, etc.

Exchange has a mediate relation to production and consumption, and hence a mediate relation to the process of human reproduction, in its formal aspect. Exchange has a further relation to the usefulness of goods or services exchanged, the usefulness being objective or subjective, formal or substantial, economic or symbolic.

By economic exchange, as opposed to symbolic exchange, concrete and material wants are met in the process of human reproduction. This exchange is an inverse relation, in which the producers are opposed to one another, and each producer has an internal relation of self-opposition as actual or potential consumer. It does not matter if the exchanger immediately consumes the object acquired in the exchange, or exchanges it further and thereupon consumes the object in exchange. In the economic exchange the immediate process, whereby human wants are met, is opposed to the mediate process whereby needs of a physiological kind are met. The human want of food, warmth, and other sustenance of life is immediately and the animal need of the same mediately presupposed in the economic exchange. The meeting of needs is at the same time a direct relation of the material order; immediate process of exchange in this connection is mediate in another, in that exchange of any kind is a mediate relation, among others, between production and consumption, and between producer and consumer in general.

The particular mediation in exchange, in civil society, is that between buying on the one hand, selling on the other, and in greater particularity, between buyer and seller. Money is a means and medium in the exchange process. It has both economic and symbolic value among the Yap Islanders and in modern bourgeois society.

Symbolic value has been the subject of a rich literature, particularly in ethnology of religion. A beginning of this study has been made by Marcel Mauss, *Essai sur le don,* who showed that the gift giving in archaic societies is an act of exchange. It is an act of symbolic exchange, to which symbolic values are attached. These values are not individual expressions, but are socially determined, according to the traditions of the peoples, having ceremonial significance, religious meaning, or celebratory intent; one group may seek to outdo another in the sumptuousness of its gifts to the other, and force itself on the other into penury in doing so.

Symbolic value is the expression of symbolic exchange, in ritual processes, where the expression, substance and content are one. The subject, object and act are without difference in respect of form and substance, quality and quantity. Symbolic value, expression and content are differential in respect of their abstract and concrete substance. They are connected as subject and object in their difference, but as abstraction and concretion are differentiated in the ceremonial acts. These are as such not differential either abstractly or concretely, and are not differential objectively and subjectively; objectively we know the difference and the nexus between the one and the other. The object of veneration is in actuality one with the subject, and there is no difference between their form and substance. As the abstract and concrete are not differential in the ceremonial act, the subject and object are not differentiated in the symbolic value expression.

As in the case of subjective value, the form and substance of the symbolic exchange are not opposed to one another, nor is the subject opposed to the object, or the subjective to the objective relation. As in the case of subjective value, form is substance, and substance form, the subject is the substance and the object in the symbolic exchange. Symbolic exchange is in all cases a communal and social relation. The exchange of prisoners, wounded and dead between the parties to a peace treaty is symbolic; it is humane, and for the living it is practical and useful.

Whereas economic exchange is reciprocal in equality or equivalence, symbolic exchange is not, or is not of necessity so. We give in a symbolic act and are given, or we give and do not receive. The giving is in some cases symbolically valued in the act, not the amount of the gift and counter gift, the object given, the ceremonial occasion or any combination of these. Symbolic value, which is its expression is communal and social, whereas subjective value is communal, social or individual. There are other cases, however, in which the amount of the gift and the counter gift is reckoned up. Further, the two sides vie with one another in the amounts exchanged, even if the exchange as such is only a symbolic one. Some symbolic objects have an absolute value, some a relative one. The objects with an absolute value are symbolic, and their value is purely symbolic; they may not be exchanged. The objects having a relative symbolic value can be exchanged.

Thus we further distinguish between symbolic value and symbolic exchange, the former being in given circumstances of civil society the greater, the latter the less extensive category. Symbolic and economic exchange presupposes relations of producer and consumer, diremption between them, and valuation. The objects of symbolic exchange are not useful in meeting concrete wants and material needs. We thus distinguish symbolic use from economic use; use value is attributed to the latter, not the former. Symbolic value is attributed to the objects of symbolic use. Not all objects of symbolic value are exchanged, whether by symbolic or any other kind of exchange. The most sacred objects of a religious community have the highest symbolic value, and will not be exchanged under any circumstance. Such objects are the Hebrew Ark of the Covenant, the Buddha's Tooth, the True Cross of the Christians and the Kaaba of Islam, having absolute value, there being none like them; they are not exchangeable.

The lesser objects in that system are relative to one another, and are the subjects of symbolic exchange; they are relative to the holiest, which is not relative to them. Secular objects, such as Magna Carta or the Declaration of Independence are of the highest symbolic value, and are not subject to exchange. The relative symbolic value of the lesser objects of symbolic exchange will be evident to those engaged therein, but will not be immediately evident to outsiders. Ceremonial occurrence of exchange and the exchange of ceremonial objects are of use in a subjective and abstract process between those engaged in the exchange. This subjectivity is an immediate relation which is then, in some cases, mediately related to an objective process, e.g., the constitution or affirmation, reconstitution, or reconfirmation of the social bond between the parties in the symbolic, ceremonial process. The conclusion of peace after hostilities is an occasion for a symbolic exchange of gifts.

An economic exchange may be conducted in a ceremonial way, and a symbolic exchange may also have an economic substance. Symbolic exchange is a condition in the development of economic exchange, but the latter is not a factor in the development of the former.

The traffic in objects of fine art has an equivocal place in this regard. Some of these objects circulate freely, being subject to private sale and public auction. Others, however, are accounted national treasures, and may not be sold. Nevertheless, they are often put into circulation by military conquest, confiscation, seizure or theft. Those that are exchanged at auction or sale may have the same repute, artistic worth or fineness as those which are accounted national treasures. At this point, historical accident and subjective or symbolic values make an objective judgment of their merits impossible. The definition of a national treasure is, moreover, historically variable. The Greeks demanded the return of the Elgin Marbles, which are on display at the British Museum, on the grounds that they belonged to Greece, having been acquired by Lord Elgin when that country was still under Turkish rule. The terms of the acquisition by the English peer were held to be irrelevant because the Greeks were not a party to the transaction. The British protested that once these returns were started there would be no end to them. For example, the return to Greece of the Winged Victory which is now in the Louvre might also be called for. But the Greeks were indebted to the French for support of their membership in the European Common Market at that time; they felt no such obligation to the British, and defined what is and is not a national treasure accordingly.

Economic and Symbolic Exchange, Historical Note
Social labor is expended in the process of human social reproduction, as opposed to biological reproduction. Social labor thus expended is also opposed to communal labor. By communal labor is meant labor in which the unity within the given social whole that produces that by which its human existence is sustained consumes what it produces; the communal unity is the unit which produces what it consumes, and consumes what it produces, whereby it is sustained. The product is still the human social product, the reproduction process is still human social reproduction, but the social relations of reproduction are communal relations, the organization of labor is determined by these communal relations within the self-sustaining and self-reproducing community, and the unit of production and consumption are the same. This is a limit which is approached but not reached by the archaic social wholes which are of a primitive kind in human history. Where the unit of production is not immediately the same as the unit of consumption, and a mutual dependence is introduced in the relations between the two unities, they then form part of an expanded process of social reproduction. In this case the relations of production and consumption are of two kinds: either they are distributed by sharing out or they are exchanged; the relation of reciprocation is present in either case, but in the former it is a distributive reciprocation, in the latter it is an equal reciprocation.

The distinction made by Aristotle between equal and proportionate reciprocation is formal, without substance; proportionate and equal reciprocation are two different methods of reckoning the same relation of equivalence of objective value in accordance with the principle of commutative right and justice; they are distinguished with reference to specializations in the production process, whereby qualitatively unlike goods are subjected to equality in exchange. Thus the physician's services are reckoned up in terms of a unit of value and exchanged against a shoemaker's or baker's product. The relation of equality in reciprocation subsumes the differences of social labors which are made proportionate to the unit of value which is abstractly applied throughout. (Aristotle, *Nicomachean Ethics,* Bk. 5, ch.5.)

The exchange relation is developed in the archaic and primitive society, but it is not developed to a degree in which it is determinant of social relations of equal reciprocation. There is very little exchanged, since the units of consumption are predominantly the units of production, hence while there is reciprocation, that which is reciprocated is not reckoned up in units of equal value; the reciprocal is not abstracted from its unit of production, which is the autarchic, or self-governing and self-sustaining community. The exchange that takes place is to a small degree the reciprocation in equal amounts, and is to a large extent symbolic exchange, which is exchange that affirms the social bond between the parties to the exchange, and the principle of moral, human, solidary, functional unity of symbolic exchange replaces the commutative principle of equal exchange or exchange of value equivalents. The social unity of symbolic exchange is mediate and concrete, and the social relations which are thereby constituted are the same. These are the relations of society which is not divided into social classes. Symbolic exchange is not abstract but concrete, for it is not reckoned up in abstract units of any kind, and is not abstracted from the social process in which it is brought forth. Symbolic exchange is mediated by the relations of the social whole in which it is generated, and not by particular, analytic relations within that whole.

The symbolic exchange is part of the preparation for economic exchange, and is a part of its history, early and late. Nevertheless, symbolic exchange and value have their own process, apart from economic exchange and exchange value. Symbolic exchange and value are related both to commutative and distributive right and justice. Symbolic exchange has the element of exchange of gift and counter gift, or of act and counteract in common with economic exchange; it has the element of giving without respect to an accounting of the value received in exchange, and in some respects without the expectation of receiving anything in exchange, but to distribute as an end in itself.

The potlatch of the Kwakiutl and other Indians of the Pacific coast in traditional times had elements of economic and of symbolic exchange in it. In the exchange ceremonies, an account was kept of how much goods were distributed or destroyed on one occasion, and it was expected that a greater amount would be destroyed on the next, in a contest between rival chiefs, the challenger and the challenged.

Market Relations. Purchase and Sale, Supply and Demand

In the analysis of market relations, we presuppose that the human process of re-production has been broken up into different parts, with a mediate relation between them. The human reproduction process is that of production and consumption, and distribution between producers and consumers. Where there is a mediate relation between production and consumption, the distribution is in the form of exchange, equal, equivalent, unequal, symbolic, coerced, regular, irregular, systematic, etc. The market is a meeting place, abstract or concrete, in which the purchase and sale of goods takes place with regularity and in a systematic way. It is in this sense a place of trade, which is a kind of exchange, being regular and durative, orderly and systematic. The market is further developed into the kind of exchange which we call commerce, having specialists who are engaged in the market activities of exchange in trading, and perform these acts in which they are engaged to the exclusion of others, whereby they get their living. The market place may be a physical, concrete locality in which people meet and engage in their acts of purchase and sale of goods, or it may be abstracted from any particular locality and exist quite generally, varying according to the available technics of communication in the act of exchange, whether by telegraph, telephone, radio, etc. The market moreover varies accordingly as it is organized on a daily basis, weekly or annually as a fair; or it may vary in space, meeting here on Monday, there on Tuesday, and so forth.

The act of buying and selling, for which the market place provides the facilities, is a single undertaking which is conjoint between persons each of whom acknowledges the capacity of the other to engage in the exchange. The exchangers, traders and commercial specialists are juridical or moral persons of civil society who have the right to engage in the transaction of buying and selling. The act of sale and purchase is single, conjoint, for there is no sale without a purchase, and no purchase without a sale; neither is possible or real without the other. The act of buying and selling constitutes a joint, single transaction in the market. The right of buying and selling is at once an obligation to provide a good in exchange, according to the economic, juridical, political and other (e.g., ritual) practices of the market place.

The good which is exchanged in the market is exchanged against another good, both goods being of equal or equivalent value in civil society, in theory. In practice, servile labor, wage labor, salaried labor and other forms of labor in that society exchanges the labor time and capacity against a quantum less than it has provided in the exchange. The quantum of difference in this transaction is not the value of production but the value of a social surplus which is produced by the various forms and kinds of social labor mentioned. The goods exchanged are concrete products or the processes, services, labor time and capacities of living labor in civil society. The goods of various kinds are objective in relation to those who provide them in the exchange. The goods in question are in this sense objects which meet a human want of one kind or another. In order to supply this want in our society, we buy a good which is sold, and sell another, or the same, which is bought. One worker sells his labor time and skill against the means of subsistence; or a specialist in commercial transactions sells a ton of corn against a sum agreed on with another. Again a specialist in the market transactions sells a dollar today against the return of a dollar tomorrow; it is not the same dollar, for it is ever appreciating or depreciating, rising and falling in price relative to some other good; money and credit are civil goods, in actuality or in potentiality.

In order to supply a human want in civil society we buy a good which is offered for sale, and find a buyer for the good which we offer in exchange. The want is acknowledged to exist on both sides in the transaction, the want of the good offered by the one side in the transaction is acknowledged by the other, in mutuality. The want is the absence of some mediate and objective condition of human existence, not in general, but under given social circumstances, such as a particular food, shelter, or a source of warmth. The wants are also the presence of some pain or burden, such as too much heat or cold, or some pestilence, or danger. These wants may be material, such as those which have been just mentioned, and which differ little from our animal needs, with which they are closely connected, or the wants are the absence of some non-material good, such as cooperation, fellowship, social interchange and common understanding.

The good whereby the want is met is the process of human labor of one kind or another, whether communal, social, cooperative, servile, wage labor, etc., or a product of such labor. By the market relation we convert goods into commodities, the latter being defined as goods bought and sold on the market, and nowhere else. The market transaction is a relation of equivalent reciprocity in exchange; equal, symbolic, and unequal reciprocations being ruled out. The act of selling meets a demand for the particular good, and the act of buying on the market supplies its want. The relation of buying and selling and of supply and demand are both abstract and concrete, for the wants supplied are both abstract and concrete. These are differentiated as relations of actuality and potentiality; the process of buying and selling is an actual one in relation to the wants, the process of supply and demand a potential one in that relation. (The good exchanged in the market transaction is thereby transformed into a commodity; this will be discussed in the next section; the result of this transformation will be considered in *Value and Price*, below.)

The usefulness of a good is its capability of meeting a want, and the human practice of applying it in such a way is the use we make of it. The use is therefore twofold, the usefulness of the good in supplying the want, and our usage of it in this connection. The use of the good is not inherent in it; it is our relation to it that makes it useful. The use is at the same time our regular and systematic usage in relation to it. The use of the good, such as food, clothing or housing, congeniality or collegiality is its utility and usage. In both respects it has the quality of being systematic and orderly, repeated, and in this sense usual; it is a social, customary practice, and has a location in time and space. The place is denoted by our common and usual practices, in the annual fair or the local and international market, which are the means of realization of these regular, systematic and durative relations relative to the goods, wants and their supply. By regularity of the market relation we mean the continued return of both sides in the market transactions; by systematic relations is meant that both sides bring the same goods, or the same kinds of goods, in a known quantity to the market, and that either side counts on the other to meet these quantitative and qualitative relations. The market is a durative relation of trade and commerce, in which commercial specialists and money, credit and financial processes are generated. The theory of use, use value, commodity exchange, market relations and their development in commerce is opposed to haphazard or sporadic social and economic relations.

Exchange as a Formal Relation. Commodity Exchange

The mutuality of cooperation and interdependence of the human kind is both a formal and a substantial process. The organization of social labor, by the combination and division thereof, is found in all human societies, and not in the society of the formation of capital alone. It is found in ancient civil society, in Asia, in the classical antiquity, in the period of transition from the primitive to the civil social condition.

Considered in the abstract, primitive society is a human condition in which immediate relations predominate in the process of human reproduction; in this condition, there is no difference between mediate and immediate relations of production, distribution and consumption. Concretely, this means that the social group which produces its means of living is the same as the social group which consumes the product in the process of its self-reproduction. The producers are the immediate consumers in the village, tribe, clan, the village clan community, and the like. There is little or no economic exchange, and each social unity is self-maintaining, and autarchic; there is an immediate distribution between producers of the product for consumption and self-reproduction; thus the adult, normal, healthy members of the community produce and distribute their product to one another, to the children, the aged, and to the infirm in mind or body.

Where exchange is extended over time and space, systematized, and socialized, the exchange relation determines the production relation, and the exchange expression determines the value expression as an abstraction. Exchange is a social relation in another sense, regardless of its systematic development; for production is a social relation, in view of the social organization by the combination and division of labor.

The exchange relations are systematized in the concrete relation of exchange that is developed in conjunction with the exchange value, which is its abstract expression; here we speak of a secondary socialization of the exchange relation, which is now abstract, systematic, and durative as a relation, and objective and abstract in its expression. Since the production relation is social to begin with, and socializes the exchange relation, production then is socialized in conjunction with the systematically, secondarily socialized exchange relation. Value in its objective, abstract form, is the expression of the amount of labor of a given degree of skill, quality and capacity which is expended in social production, and in this sense determines value in exchange; it is not the same as value in exchange, or exchange value, just as production and exchange are not the same. The production process is determined in its abstractness, in its objective diremption from the distribution and consumption process, and in its alienation from the reproduction and redistribution processes, that is, in its alienation from the hands of the immediate producers by relations in a given historical exchange process of civil society.

The exchange process is the means of bringing this abstraction, internal diremption and external alienation about. The abstraction is taken in a twofold sense, as physical taking away and as abstract representation. Sublating is a particular form of abstraction, raising up and bearing off, in history. The exchange process, both as primary and as secondary social relation in the sense given, abstractly determines, in civil and bourgeois society, the production relation. The abstract production value determines the abstract exchange value under particular historical circumstances. Concretely, the production relation is determined by the entire process whereby labor is expended to meet wants and needs of the social whole; this relation, expressed in civil society as use value, is the same throughout history; it is indifferently use value and concrete value; it does not change its form; its function remains the same, however variable the content of the relation may be, which is the particular, concrete wants and needs. The substance, concretely taken, is in this sense made up of constant function, variable content, and constant and variable production relations. The relations of constancy and variability in this case are both theoretically and practically determined.

Economic exchange is a formal relation between producers and consumers who are strangers to one another, members of different producing communities, bound by their mutual dependence, each on the product of the other. The justice in the exchange is sought between those who stand to one another as aliens, without intimate contact between them. The relations of economic exchange between those who have a substantive relation of mutual dependence is safeguarded by formal relations of equal, proportional or equivalent reciprocity; these are expressed by just price, contract, written or unwritten, between buyer and seller, and juridical practices in support of the exchange system.

Each side in the economic exchange has a product which can meet the want of the other. Each side alienates to the other the product of the one, and takes in exchange the product of the other. The alienation in this case is an objective one, between the producer and the product; it is presupposed in the alienation of the product of the one to the other, and of the other to the one, in equal or equivalent reciprocation. That each side in the exchange is alien to the other is a subjective relation, each side appearing as a stranger, unknown to the other, coming from another village, clan, community, tribe or people. They have no mutual relation of trust and good faith; they stand to one another as outsiders, and their mutual dependence is established only at their place of meeting, which is the market, abstract or concrete. Therefore in the absence of close interdependence of a communal, neighborly, consanguineal or collective kind, they count on the safeguards of justness in the exchange which are in the market and juridical systems. These are formal relations, dirempted from the substance of the relations of reproduction by production and immediate distribution of the products, such as the process within the kin group or the community. The safeguards of the justness of the distribution in this case are both formal and substantial, and are unquestioned, as between parents and children, in a normal relation between them.

The safeguards of the market in the exchange relation are positive in the affirmation of the justness of the quality and quantity of the products on either side in the exchange; they are negative in the prevention of adulteration or falsification of the product, or cheating on either side. A negative safeguard is the nonrenewal of the exchange procedure, in the case of mistrust or betrayal, and the search for another exchange partner. Multilateral exchange is analyzed into the bilateral processes as a formality.

In the exchange process, there is a multiple diremption, of one human being from another, of the product from the producer, and of the human form from the human substance. The first diremption is that of human beings who meet one another in the market, in their mutual estrangement, as nonbelligerents. The second diremption is the alienation of the product, as such a multiple process, general and local, mediate and immediate, objective and subjective. The third diremption is the development of a mediate relation of the market, and the further formalizations of contract, and of commodities in the process of the economic exchange. In these relations, the substance of human reproduction, the good, is transformed into a commodity, and has another form than that which is usually encountered in the primordial human condition. The form and the substance each appear to go their separate ways, and come together only after long periods of human time, as measured in generations or centuries. The commodity is a formal expression, which is the outcome of the exchange process. The commodity fetishism is the belief in the existence of the commodity, apart from the social substance of its production; this is a development which has no foundation in reality. Yet it is a belief which has within it the diremption of the form from the substance in the exchange and distribution process.

By virtue of the alienation of the product of social labor from its producers, a bifurcated social relation is introduced, and therewith a bifurcated value expression. In the relation of exchange by equal reciprocation the product is alienated from the producer thereof, who receives the product of another in return. The equality in the reciprocative relation in the exchange is determined by an act of translation from the amount of concrete labor, or work, expended in the process of social reproduction, to the abstract expression. This translation is the relation between concrete value, which is the expression of concrete labor, and abstract value, the expression of abstract labor. Under given social conditions of human history, the abstract labor is expressed as exchange value, whereby the formal equivalence between the different materials of the exchange is ascertained and denoted. The material difference is that of the object wherein labor is concretized in the process of its reproduction, and therewith objectified, the same being the process of its self-concretization and self-objectification. This combined process of concretization and objectification is the means whereby the substance of value is brought into existence. The value substance therefore is not labor, nor is it labor time or quality, skill or power; the value substance is the self-organizing concretization of labor, its objectification, self concretization and self-objectification. The product is the material result of the expenditure of labor time and skill or quality in the process of its self concretization and self-objectification. The self-concretizing process stands in opposition to the self-abstractive process, which is brought out in the meeting of concrete wants and needs, and their abstract value expression; the self-objectifying process stands in opposition to the self-subjectifying process, and is the social as opposed to the individual relation of human being. The product exchanged is the concretization of material relations of human social reproduction and therewith its objectification. The concretization of the process of reproduction is not the sufficient condition for exchange, however, for the product of this process must first be made into an object; being objectified, opposed to its producers, it is then distanced and alienated from them, its concrete, material substance being endowed with an abstract formal expression which is then exchanged in equal reciprocation against its like. The form in this case is separated from the substance, the latter being the concrete, objectified relations of human work; the substance is borne into the exchange process by its formalization and abstraction. The exchange value is thus immediately the expression of the formal and abstract translation of the substantive relations of work and labor, which are the concretized and self-objectifying processes of human self-reproduction. Labor, abstract and concrete, is both passive and active, being passively concretized and actively objectifying itself. The abstract value is the expression of both relations, active and passive, the exchange value, which is the historically more limited particularization of the same, is the expression of the formal and passive side of the abstract relation of reproduction.

Exchange is a mediate process of abstraction and alienation of the product from its immediate producer, in the relation of equal reciprocation against another. Equivalence in the exchange is ascertained abstractly by the expression in the product of the amount of objectified labor concretized in it; exchange value is the mediate reference to the process of abstraction, abstract relation, alienation, formal equality and its formal expression. Exchange value is the abstract expression which enables the alienation of dissimilars between the one and the other in an equivalent reciprocation. The dissimilars exchanged may be abstract or concrete, living or dead, human or inhuman; their common term of reference is the objectification of the natural order and of labor itself by labor, and the quantification of both processes, that of objectification and of self-objectification by living labor. The process of objectification proceeds from the transformation of the concrete thing into the object, both abstract and concrete, the self concretization of living labor and its transformation into the equivalent object, both abstract and concrete, to that which is alienated from the natural order and objectified in the human. The exchange process is a social relation between human elements by virtue of its equality in reciprocation; it is a reified human relation by virtue of its formal and abstract character, in which the form of equality is opposed to the substance of human relation. Living labor is formally equal to its exchange partner in the process of alienating its objectified quality, time and power to another against an amount of value which in turn is equal to the necessities for its social reproduction.

The alienation of the object of labor and of the self object of living labor is in actuality a formally reciprocal social act, hence a formal social relation between human elements, beings, classes, social wholes. The abstraction of the object and of the self object by living labor makes feasible the abstraction of the object of exchange, in which living, self-objectifying labor is an active participant. Exchange value is the abstract expression of both objectifications and at the same time the abstract expression of a given amount of concrete, useful value of the object.

Exchange is a formalization of a kind of distribution, with equal, equivalent, or proportional reciprocity in the economic process. Exchange is a particularity, of which distribution is the generality. Economic exchange is not original to the relations of civil society, but is more highly developed therein, historically, than in any other. The market, contract, commutative justice and right, exchange value are developments of the relations of economic exchange; these are all formalisms, in particular of modern society. There are yet other relations of equal or equivalent reciprocation than those of economic exchange in that society. Contract is a formal relation of civil society bearing on reciprocations of various kinds, economic and non-economic, symbolic, subjective, combinations, and others beside these.

Distribution, Exchange and Exchange Value

We have distinguished between exchange of the same and of different objects, labors, etc. Exchange of the same objects is a kind of equal exchange, and is effected by the exchange of like goods in equal amounts; these are objective differences. Equal exchange is also effected in respect of differences of a subjective quality. Objectively, the same bushel of rice is exchanged today against its return tomorrow, or it is exchanged in this place against its return on the same day at some other place.

In the exchange transaction we buy and sell one good against another. If it is the same good to be sold and bought, this is an exchange of equals; it is an exchange of equivalents if the goods exchanged are not the same in kind. That we engage in the sale and purchase of equivalents in social, objective exchange has been known to the theorists in this subject from Aristotle to Marx. The equivalents are, accordingly, goods which are abstractly equal in value to one another, but of different kinds, having connection to one another in a common system of social production, value and exchange. The exchange is thus denominated the exchange of equivalents, or values. Exchange is undertaken both in respect of equivalents and equals, or the same good, against the same good, whether as product or as service. Aristotle considered the services of the physician as a part of his system of exchange; the exchange in such a case has objective and subjective parts to it. Thus if the physician has a child who is ill, objectively he may be capable of treating the illness, but subjectively may feel too distraught to undertake the treatment, and will engage the services of a colleague to cure the child of its illness, performing the same service in exchange for the other. The same factors, mutatis mutandis, will hold if we think of the saying, the lawyer who pleads his own case has a fool for a client. In these instances there is an exchange of the same good against the same, in equal reciprocity, for the same service is exchanged by the physicians. The motivation for the exchange may be set aside as subjective, but objectively, an equal exchange takes place. It is a fair exchange, abstract or concrete, or both, and therewith an equal reciprocity in exchange. The services exchanged are equal; their respective use values are equivalent.

But the exchange of different labors, or of different goods, or of labors against products, is not an equal exchange; this is the exchange of equivalents in respect of the dissimilarity between them. The labors of the rice grower and of the physician are concretely different. The exchange between the product of the one and the service of the other is effected by an abstract equivalence between them; the dissimilars have an equal objective value expression. The amount of labor of the rice grower in producing the bushel of the grain is estimated against that of the physician's services, and if an equivalence is brought forth, then the exchange between them is effected. The products of the two are concretely different, but abstractly the same if a value expression can be generated to comprise the two sides in their difference. The monetary unit which is applied in the value expression is a useful means in making the value quantities precise. Other uses of money, in respect of prices, marketing, credit, differ from the value expressions in view of the subjective factors of will and desire of the human kind, variable conditions of the market place in respect of supply and demand, and in view of scarcity and abundance of the products wanted, or desired.

Equal reciprocity in exchange is other than equivalent reciprocity; the equivalence in the reciprocal relation, given that it is objective, is the expression in terms of value, of the abstract, objective equality in the exchange. The factors of price, market, commodity, credit, in the value expression are particular to exchange in civil society; the relations of exchange, equal and equivalent, are historically particular to the same social condition as that of the market, commodity and prices. The relations of value, objective and subjective, are not historically particular in this way, for they are in theory those of the theoretical socialist system as well.

Equal exchange is concrete or abstract; in barter it is concrete, as it is traditionally practiced, but in respect of the objects exchanged it may be concrete or abstract if the objects are concrete or abstract in the exchange. Equivalent exchange is abstract alone, for that which is exchanged is given an abstract value expression, and this bears on the objects, whether concrete goods, or living labor, and the products thereof, which are exchanged. The objects of the equal exchange are like, whereas the objects of the exchange in equivalence and of equivalents are like and unlike. Equal exchange is a reciprocation of objects, products and labors which are alike in quality and quantity. Exchange of equivalents and in equivalence is a reciprocation of objects which are quantitatively like, insofar as they are commensurable, and qualitatively unlike; if they were qualitatively like then the exchange would be an equal exchange, even if expressed in abstraction as equivalence. The quality is abstract or concrete; the quantity is an abstraction alone, being an expression of a human relation.

Equivalence is established in a system of reference, in which the equality of likes and unlikes is expressed by objective values which are abstract in the given system; the equivalence is concrete in the quantities of the goods, products, labors exchanged. The concrete exchange generates a system of exchange values, which are constituted in an abstract and objective exchange system. The exchange system is a process of reciprocity in equality between the exchanging parties; the exchange equivalence is the abstract expression of this process. The equivalent is literally the equality of values, objective and abstract, in a system of exchange values.

Exchange, if it is economic and not symbolic, is a means to meet objective wants and needs, and is concrete in meeting them. The wants and needs are different and many in the human kind. Being different and many they are met by the mediate process of economic exchange in particular, as a kind of distribution in general. The exchange of likes is concrete and is concretely met by a like in return for what is offered, a pound of wheat in exchange for a pound of wheat, or the service of one physician to heal the child of another in an exchange for a like service in return. An exchange of unlikes has generated within it an abstract expression for the satisfaction, objective and abstract, of the different sides to the exchange. The equivalence, or equality of values, abstract and objective, is generated to effect the exchange of unlikes, for instance, a pound of honey against a quart of wine, or a day's labor against the means of subsistence for the laborer. Exchange is concrete in the case of that which is like in quality and equal in quantity; it is abstractly expressed in the case of the exchange of unlikes in quality, with differing measures of quantity. The exchange, whether of equals or of equivalents, is expressed in the law of exchange value. The exchange is abstractly expressed as a law, and is abstract again in relation to the concrete use of the social good, labor or product, exchanged. The concrete use is not equal on either side in the exchange, for the meeting of the hunger of the one is not the same as the clothing against the cold of the other. The principle of exchange value is on the one side a means to express these unlikes by an abstract equivalence between them in the quantity and quality of the labor in meeting the different wants. The principle of exchange value is at the same time an abstract value expression as a commutative right; this abstraction has another abstraction which it denotes; the latter is expressed in the form of a contract. The society in which this principle, the law of contract, and the abstract expression of exchange of unlikes by their equivalence in exchange value are brought forth, is civil society. Here we are conscious that we interpret the Aristotelian system of justice and right in exchange in the view of Grotius and Hobbes, Barbeyrac and Adam Smith. The concrete utility of that which has exchange value as its abstract expression is fundamental to the relation of equal or equivalent reciprocity in exchange, it implies the exchange value as law and abstract expression, but is not limited to the relation of reciprocation, formal contract, and the principle of commutative right and justice. The concrete use is expressed as use value in civil society. Although use value is the means whereby reference is made to concretion, namely, the particular quality or attribute of an object, whereby a given human want is met, nevertheless the use value is as such an abstraction whereby formal expression is given to the object, its attribute or quality. Thus it is not the use value of water that quenches thirst, nor is it. Water as such, but fresh water at a temperature above frost and below boiling. Reference to use value as a real existent in a concrete object has been made, but this is an error.

Exchange value presupposes use value, in which a want on the side of either party to the exchange is expressed; further, exchange value presupposes a reciprocal exchange by parties to the exchange. If that which is exchanged is unlike that which it is exchanged against, then the objects of the exchange are given an abstract expression whereby they can be exchanged by a relation of equality in reciprocation. In the case of reciprocation of like objects, memory or a concrete record assures an equal reciprocation, which is just. The case of geometrical reciprocation adds nothing to the exchange, for it involves two parties, three, four, or more, who have unlike objects to exchange. The principle of commutation, the law of contract, and the abstract expression of equal reciprocation in exchange remain the same, whether two or n parties are related in the exchange process.

Exchange value is a part of the system of abstract value which includes both exchange value and use value within it, and not only these, as we shall see. Exchange value and use value are particular value expressions, which are brought out in civil society, that is, under limited circumstances in the history of human society. The value expressions are developed under the circumstances in which the market, exchange and contract relations, commutative right and justice, that is, *synallagmasi diorthotike dikaion*, in Aristotle are developed, but they are not limited to these relations.

Aristotle, Locke, Petty, Franklin, Steuart, Adam Smith, Hegel, Ricardo and Marx, have brought out the laws of value with regard to a particular relation of ancient and modern civil society. They were formulated by Aristotle in respect of practices in ancient civil society; the law of exchange value was formally grasped by him, but its substance was not. Locke grasped the substance, and not the form; he had been preceded in this by Luther, Machiavelli and Botero. Only in the 18th and 19th centuries were the form and substance of the law of value brought together, in the writings of Ricardo and Marx, but with many problems left over. (See Krader, *Dialectic of Civil Society*, 1976, ch. 3.)

The value expressions are localized historically in the laws of value in use and exchange, which bear upon civil society both ancient and modern, in which the market, exchange, commodity and contract relations are developed. They were developed to a limited degree in ancient and to a fuller degree in modern civil society. The value expressions differ in their quantification and measurement, for exchange value is measured by abstract labor time, the amount of the exchange value of a given good being determined by the quantity of labor time abstracted from the concrete labor process expended in the production of the given social good; whether in the form of a service by living labor or in the form of a concrete product, that good is a commodity in the labor process in modern civil society. The abstract labor time and the exchange value which is thereby determined and measured are cumulative quantities; the usefulness which is measured by the use value expression is non-cumulative; the use value is nevertheless quantitative and abstract as an expression, such as is programmed in a computer.

The usefulness of the good in meeting a want is the substance of a reciprocative process, of which the use value is the form. The usefulness of the good and the labor expended in its production, or the equivalent as a service, constitute in turn the substance of the social relation, of which the exchange value, being its expression as an abstraction, constitutes the form. The concrete labor expended in production enters into the meeting of a want, therewith into the substance of the reproduction process of the given social whole, whereby social labor and the social whole are maintained and developed, but it does not enter into the substance of the exchange value immediately. Concrete labor enter into the substance of the exchange mediately by the process of maintaining social labor and the social whole. The relations between form and substance in respect of value are therefore variable and relative, for what is substantive in one respect is formal in another, and what is immediately and determinantly substantive in one relation is mediately and determinately substantive in another. Thus exchange is the result of the determination of usefulness of a product, mediately of production and of alienation of the product from the producer; exchange is the product of abstraction of the product and the abstract expression thereof, which is exchange value. Exchange is the determinate of these relations, being the result thereof. The usefulness of the product is expressed as its use value, the use value determining the exchangeability of the product immediately, and the exchange mediately. Use value is in this sense abstract in the exchange relation, but is concrete relative to exchange value and is a determinant, among others in this process. Relative to the use of the product, use value is a form; relative to exchange value, use value is a substance of which exchange value is a form.

The exchange value formally expresses the amount of abstract labor expended in production of the product exchanged. The abstract labor is measured by units of labor time which bring together the actual time expended in production and the labor capacity, or cumulation of past skills, technics, arts, the time spent in their mastery, variation, and the concrete work instruments that have been produced. The abstract labor is not immediately the substance of the exchange value of the good, nor is the abstract labor time and capacity in an immediate sense the substance of the value in exchange of the given good, product or service. Abstract labor is not as such a substance, but is a form, of which concrete labor and its product are the substance; abstract and concrete labor together constitute social substance. Abstract labor constitutes mediately and actively the substance of the exchange process, and mediatively the substance of the exchange expression, or exchange value. The intermediation between the abstract labor expression and the exchange as such is effected in civil society by the formalization of the exchange relation, by the structure of the market, by the law of contract and by commodity expression and transaction. These intermediations between abstract labor as substance and the exchange value as abstract form are summed up in the principle of commutative right and justice.

> To speak properly, commutative Justice is the Justice of a Contractor; that is, a Performance of Covenant, in Buying and Selling; Hiring and Letting to Hire; Lending, and Borrowing; Exchanging, Bartering, and other acts of Contract. (Thomas Hobbes. *Leviathan*. 1651. I, 15.)

The formalization of social relations by the market structure, by contract or covenant, commodity expression, and commutative justice and right is a development of a process whereby the social form is abstracted from its religious mystical expression, secularized, and given a laic, quasi-independent expression of its own in civil society. This formalization is mediately related to the process of formation of the state, the ruling class, and of the law of surplus value. (The order of introduction of the formalized terms into the system is not always the same as the order of appearance in history of the processes to which they refer.) The law of contract and the exchange value expression presuppose a formal and abstract expression of the labor process, by means of its cumulative quantification, which is carried through by the commodity and market structure. This formal and structural process is developed by transformation of barter into monetary transaction, the money form being the abstract expression of the concrete circulation process. Money is the means, by virtue of its abstract form, whereby concrete circulation is effected; circulation of goods is a concretion, the abstract form of which is the commodity in civil society; money is an abstract, determinative moment of the commodity relation in particular and of the circulation process in general. The process of circulation thus has both an abstract and a concrete moment in its constitution. The commodity relation has a formal moment alone, money an abstract and particular moment therein. Money, market, contract, commodity are formal moments of the relation of exchange by equal reciprocation, which constitutes the determinate and mediate substance thereof; the exchange relation constitutes a form, the substance of which is constituted by abstract labor, which stands to the form as the mediate determinant thereof. Abstract labor in turn is a formal moment of which concrete labor is the immediate, active determinant.

Exchange in primitive, archaic, social conditions is formalized as symbolic exchange, and has both moral and juridical sanctions which pertain to 't. The moral sanction of exchange is at once a religious, mystical process, with the expression of the just and right as moments within it, which is bound together with the relations of the social whole, whereby the latter is maintained. The economic and symbolic exchange are not separately unfolded, but are interrelated and mutually supportive. The economic exchange, to the end of meeting the practical wants and needs of the respective parties to the exchange is developed under these circumstances as an aspect of symbolic exchange.

> The kula ring of traditional Melanesia is a symbolic exchange process which accompanied economic transactions. The latter were of minor significance both with respect to the practical sustenance of the Melanesians of old, and with respect to the symbolic significance of the kula exchange cycle. In the history of civil society, fairs and weekly or annual markets, are economic structures in a secular sense, which are held in conjunction with a cycle of holy days, and are determined by symbolic considerations in their periodicity. Fairs have a historically determinate relation to holy places. The loosening of the relation of exchange, market and commodity expressions to the religious, sanctioned and sanctuary locus of trade and merchandise is a process of the history of early civil society. Secularization of exchange, contract and trade is fully developed only in modern civil society. The trader in ancient civil society was the stranger, thus the enemy who had need of sanctuary, under the laws of hospitality, on the one hand, and of religious sanctions on the other. (B. Malinowski, *Argonauts of the Western Pacific.* 1922.

The human kind reproduces itself in a human way by producing and consuming the goods it produces. The relation between production and consumption is the sharing the labors and sharing out their products in archaic and primitive social conditions, in which the unit of production and the unit of consumption closely coincide. The participants in the sharing and sharing out of the products of the group which produced them are those who are subjectively recognized and objectively acknowledged to be its members. The relation between production and consumption by sharing and sharing out in this case is distribution in an immediate sense. In modern civil society, the principal relation between production and consumption of goods produced is the exchange process, which is formal and mediate. There are many gradations between the immediate distribution by sharing and mediate distribution by exchange in human history. The reproductive process of the human kind has the three chief divisions of production, distribution and consumption of goods and labors; we subdivide the process of distribution into an immediate and a mediate part. The immediate process of sharing and sharing out precedes the mediate relation of exchange in human history. In our society, the participation in the distributive process is a right which is determined not by membership in a communal or social whole, but by contribution of labor time and capacity of the members, or of its value equivalent in goods. The right of participation in the latter case is a formalization of social processes which is pro-

222 / Lawrence Krader

jected back to the earlier ones.

The establishment of the right of participation by contribution of labor time, capacity, and products is a rational as opposed to a traditional relation. The rationalization is the theory, not the practice of exchange.

The house community or *zadruga* of the South Slavs in traditional times was organized on the basis of membership in it by right of kinship, and participation in the distribution of the product of the community was determined by this right independently of the work or labor contributed to the whole by those to whom the distribution was made; the distribution was thus a sharing and sharing out of the communal product. The traditional Germanic Genossenschaft, Genootschap, and fellowship, and the Russian mir and artel', were in intermediate gradations between the olden zadruga and modern exchange; they were organized on the basis, one, of kinship, fellowship, or other means of admission into the membership of the community; two, on the basis of contribution of work, or of the product of the work to the community. Participation in the distribution of the product is thus both an inherited and an acquired right, there being several surrogates for the foundation of the right of participation in the distribution beside the hereditary right; latterly, in the history of the mir, a contribution of money was accepted beside the contribution of work or its product. The right of participation in the distribution is a return against the obligation of contribution, in a contractual relation, whether explicit or implicit.

We distinguish between immediate and mediate distribution of goods and services, the immediate distribution being practiced without regard to an equality or equivalence in return for the outlay; this is the case in the archaic community and in the family, ancient or modern. On the contrary, generosity and self-sacrifice of the older for the younger generation, or the converse is often practiced. Mediate distribution of the social product and of labor by equal or equivalent reciprocation is brought about by the formalization of the exchange practices. Distributive right is the principle of immediate distribution, commutative right the principle of mediate distribution.

The relation between production and consumption is established by means of distribution, both immediately as a sharing out among the members, and mediately by a determinate contribution. The principle of distribution, whether immediate or mediate, is that of distributive reciprocity. The determination by contribution in the relation of distributive reciprocity is *pro forma* an act according to the principle of distributive right and justice; substantively it is an act according to the principle of commutative right. The distribution among those who have contributed work, labor or a product having an equivalent value expression, in the traditional Genossenschaft, Genootschap, fellowship, mir or artel' is made according to a restrictive covenant, which has a twofold stipulation: the acknowledgment of membership, and the contribution of work or labor. The covenant is effected between those who have by their contribution established their participation in the distribution of the social product as a right; it is restricted to those whose right to participate in the distribution by virtue of membership in the given social form is acknowledged by the other participants therein. Distribution of goods according to the principle of membership in a group is therefore also a practice of commutative and not of distributive right, insofar as it is based on a contribution made by the members to the common product, which establishes a right to share in its distribution in an equal or equivalent way.

We proceed not from immediate but from mediate distribution to formalization of exchange. Economic exchange is the formalization of relations between the producing and consuming unities, whereby the product is separated from the producer, alienated therefrom, abstracted in an objective relation, submitted to contractual obligation and right, and exchanged in the relation of equal reciprocation, whereby an equivalent is alienated from the consumer, who becomes the oppositive producer in relation to the first, who becomes the consumer in the exchange process. The abstraction is twofold, taking away and giving abstract value expression to that which has been exchanged. The exchange process is twofold, diremption and alienation. The diremption is twofold, being a separation from consumption and a discerption of the product from the producers, which is undertaken by the producers themselves, exchange value being its abstract expression. The alienation is twofold, being the objective abstraction and the formal reciprocation, replacement of the abstractly represented object by its abstractly acknowledged equivalent. The formalization of exchange relation is undergirded by official, public sanction, which is demystified in the history of civil society. Civil society is the expression of the development of oppositions between public and private, objective and subjective, producing and consuming relations in the process of social reproduction. Exchange is the development of formal and mediate relations in human society, the form of the relation of exchange being developed as the medium therein. This medium is an abstraction which is concretely expressed as the market, contract, commodity, money, credit; these concretions are in turn abstract in relation to concrete labor and concrete products which are consumed. The exchange relation of equal reciprocation is an abstraction relative to concrete relations of civil society, and is abstracted from them; the appearance of this abstraction apart from its concretion is a hypostasis, which is made into a fetish.

The relation between production and consumption is constituted in theory either by distribution or by exchange, in practice by exchange whereby the distribution relations are determined. The distribution by its subordination to exchange is a mechanical process of securing the physical allocation of items, objects, goods, services in the commodity process, which are not as such bought or sold. Within the production process, before the completion of the production process, and before the exchange of the product as a commodity, the materials and relations of labor are distributed in the producing unit. On being bought, the commodity is distributed within the consuming unit, and is then consumed. Distribution is carried through, ancillary to the exchange process, the commodity being physically distributed to the purchaser who has acquired ownership of it. The distribution in conjunction with sharing and sharing out takes place within the unit of production, which is one with the unit of consumption; the relation of distribution in this case is a communal and not a social relation, being a social relation which is reduced to a communal one. The distribution in conjunction with the association, fellowship or Genossenschaft, is the same in substance with that which is practiced in conjunction with the commodity transaction; this distribution is determined by relations of equal reciprocation in exchange, according to the principle of commutative right.

Distribution according to the principle of distributive right is a social relation, presupposing the non-diremption and reunification between the units of production and consumption; the unit of production distributes that which it produces to the unit of consumption, and receives that whereby its wants and needs are met. The producing and consuming unities are not particular human groups, still less are they individuals, but are the human kind in general, without further qualification, the relations thereof being determined mediately by natural processes, and mediately and immediately by social processes of distribution within the human order. Distribution in respect of distributive right is therefore established not by virtue of membership in a human group, association, or a particular social whole, but by virtue of being human and having human wants and needs, which are met by labor of the human kind, which is all of our kind, and all of social labor. Distributive right, *dianametikon dikaion*, is etymologically related to *dianemesis*, distribution; *nomos*, law, or bounds of common (pasture); but now it is distribution of that which is common to all, and is the opposite of exchange, which is the formal relation of equal or equivalent contribution and reciprocation. The practice of distributive reciprocation between production and consumption according to the principle of distributive right is socialism. There is in the statement of this principle a complex program: one, emphasis is placed on the factor of distribution, and therewith on the principle of distributive right and justice; two, the de-emphasis on the factor of contribution; three, the elimination therewith of the factor of a contribution by each, that is, by an individual; four, the elimination of the factor of a distribution to each, that is, to individuals; five, the elimination of a formal relation of exchange and the development instead of a substantive relation of distribution which is formalized in many ways. We note in passing that the original thought in this regard is Aristotle's.

The practice in civil society, whereby exchange value is the expression of the form of that of which use value is the expression of the substance, determines the value expression as exchange value. The relation between the exchange value expression and the value expression is extrinsic and not intrinsic to either, for exchange value is the formal expression of an exchange relation immediately, and has a mediated relation to the process of social production, whereas value as such has a mediative relation in the exchange process, and is the immediate, formal expression of the relation of social production, which constitutes its substance. It is under the conditions of exchange and social reproduction in civil society that the expression of value and of exchange value coincide; they do not of necessity coincide under other social conditions.

The process of exchange is systematized as commerce and trade. In the primitive archaic condition of social life, exchange for economic purposes is found, but it is not systematic; it is rather sporadic, when on occasion the proper conditions are fulfilled. Among these conditions is the personal relation between those engaged in the exchange. This exchange is a relation between persons known to each other as kinsmen, and neighbors, later between companions, compagnons, compagni, compañeros, Genossen, tovarishchi, comrades. Exchange is distantly related to the customary law of hospitality.

The trader often comes to the community as the stranger, or foreigner; as such he is without a personality, for he is not recognized or acknowledged as a member of the village, clan, community, band or tribe. Only when a member of the host group vouches for the foreigner as one known to him, is the stranger endowed with a personality, subject to the protection of the law. Insult or injury done to the person of the newcomer is the same as insult or injury done to the person of the host. Exchange is then systematized in terms of the law of hospitality, which then enters into the terms of trade. These are further extended and systematized in international commerce, according to the customs between the nations. In medieval Barcelona, the customs, *usatges*, formed a part of the terms of commerce; Catalan *usatges* and English *customs* are related terms, with reference to corresponding practices between nations. (Communication of my late friend, Angel Palerm.)

Exchange value and objective value are sometimes confused with one another. To be sure, they are joined, objective value having but one form in modern civil society, and that is exchange value; but in their substance they differ from one another. The substance of objective value is objective, social labor; objective value is the abstract expression of the abstraction of this substance. The substance of exchange value is twofold; mediately it is the same abstraction of objective, social labor; immediately it is the capacity of the object, product, good, or labor, to meet a human, social want. Labor which has value as its expression has the meeting of such wants mediately in relation to its substance; hence objective value has a mediate relation to the meeting of these wants. Thus value and exchange value have an inverse relation to the substance, labor on the one side, and the meeting of wants on the other, for what is mediate in one respect is immediate in the other.

In the exchange process between buyer and seller of the labor time and capacity, the standpoint of the two sides to the exchange is the same, objectively considered. Each party in the exchange is *pro forma* free, and *pro forma* equal to the other in the system of law and polity of civil society; each party is a seller and each a buyer. Each alienates a social good, or its equivalent, to another. The system of law and polity, of contract and of political rights, legal and civil rights, has been made to conform to this exchange process. The conformability of the system of law and right to the exchange system is a recent development of civil society, effected during the capitalist period; the economic exchange which it regulates, however, is an ancient one, thousands of years older. The difference between the two is the degree in which wage and salaried labor is the predominant form of the exchange of the labor, its time and quality, against the means of subsistence. The system of equality in the exchange process of wage and salaried labor is that of an objective and abstract equivalence between the two sides in the exchange; if they differ it is in their subjective relations. For the seller of the labor time and quality alienates to another the substantive labor power; it is the living and working time that is being sold and bought, the skill and knowledge, cumulated and present. This is a loss of the human substance to the individual human being, for which one gets one's daily bread in return. The buyer of the labor time and quality in the system of capital converts the substantive labor power thus obtained into product and profit, into exchange value and surplus value. Wage and salaried labor gets only its means of subsistence out of the exchange, regaining its human substance during the free time, in leisure and sleep, after it has fulfilled its part of the contract for the sale of its substantive labor power. The free time is quantitatively complementary to the substantive labor time in the living day; it is marginally productive. The substantive labor power which is purchased by the employer, public or private, is centrally, qualitatively and quantitatively productive.

System of Objective, Subjective, and Symbolic Value

Objective value. Objective value is a form of value, that is, of social value, or of value of social labor in production. Objective, social value and the value of labor in production are the same; it may be called value for short. It is a form, having objective social labor as its substance in the transformation of material and other natural processes, whereby the human kind reproduces itself by human means.

The social relations of labor are the organization by their combination and division in the transformation process. Labor is determined and reckoned up in these relations with respect to its quantity and quality, or time and capacity, mode of social organization, technics and productivity. Labor quantity is determined and expressed as the amount of time expended in social production and consumption, thus of social reproduction of a given human group, society, or a like historical entity. The labor quality is the amount of preparation, training, or schooling of social labor for the process of human social reproduction.

With respect to objective value in the given sense, we distinguish between abstract value, concrete value, in general, and between the value of labor in production and value in exchange. These forms of value are distinguished from surplus value.

1. Abstract value is a form having abstract labor as its substance. Social labor is in the abstract continuous, having abstract labor quantity and quality as its expression. It is constituted of various kinds of labors in society, both of likes and unlikes, all of which have labor time and capacity as their common expression. Abstract labor is not completed in a particular product, but is ongoing, incessantly. Abstract value is the expression of qualitatively like and unlike social labors in a common system of quantities of labor time.
2. Concrete value is use value. It is a form having a value substance of two kinds, the one immediate, the other mediate.
The immediate substance of the concrete value is the capability of a labor process or product to meet a human want or need.
The mediate substance of the concrete value is concrete labor or work. Labor is in general of two kinds, ongoing or completed in the product. Abstract labor is of the first kind, concrete labor of the second.
Objective social value, abstract value and concrete or use value are general value forms, appearing in various social conditions, whether practical or theoretical, historically reported, or not; the formal expression of the substantive process of social labor is general in as much as social labor is a general process of the human kind, in various social conditions.
3. Exchange value is not a general but a particular formal expression of the human kind, bearing on the process of human reproduction in which exchange is prominent or predominant.
In complex social conditions of the human kind there is a mediate relation between social production and consumption. The complex mediate relation between the two economic processes in human reproduction we call distribution; the simple, immediate relation between human production and consumption we call sharing.
Exchange is a formalization of the distribution process in society, being con-

ducted by an exact reckoning between the opposed parties in the exchange. Exchange is a social process which presupposes two or more parties in a relation of give and take. Particular to the exchange relation in the history of civil society is an economic process, in which the parties to the exchange reckon up as exactly as they are able, the objective value of the good, social labor or product which each side gives to the other and takes from the other.

The reckoning up is a twofold process in the exchange of this kind, with respect to the exchange of goods of like kind, or exchange of goods of unlike kind.

The exchange of goods of like kind is expressed as equal reciprocity in exchange; the exchange of goods of unlike kind is expressed as equivalent reciprocity in exchange.

The exchange value is the expression *pro forma* of the relation in exchange of equals or of equivalents between the parties. The goods exchanged are concrete labors or their products, which are converted into commodities by the economic exchange.

The exchange value is a form having a substance of two kinds, the one mediate, and the other immediate.

The immediate exchange value substance is the use of the goods exchanged in meeting human wants and needs; the formal expression of the goods' use in civil society is concrete or use value.

The mediate exchange value substance is the amount of concrete labor expended in the production of the goods exchanged.

Subjective value. The subjective value of a good of any kind is what we please, according to our will and desire. The value is the expression, which is the form of our subjective judgment; the form is non-different from the substance. The form and substance of the subjective value are in an immediate nexus with one another; yet subjectivity of the judgment, the value, will and desire are not the same, but are in a common, immediate process with one another.

Symbolic value. The symbolic value is the formal expression of the worth of a ritual or ceremonial good, object or labor. It is indifferently subjective and objective. The potlatch of the Kwakiutl is an example of symbolic exchange. The symbolic value is shared, being handed on across the generations, or among contemporaries. The subjective value is shared or not. Objects, goods, labors of symbolic value are given and taken in mutuality among those who share them. There is no objective measure of these values, nor is there an objective measure of subjective values. Some items of symbolic value may be exchanged against others; in such cases the reckoning of the values in the exchange relation is symbolic. Other items of symbolic value may under no circumstances be exchanged, having religious, nationalistic, historical or personal sentiment attached to them, as a fetish, a charm, or *memento mori*. There is no objective expression of symbolic value in exchange or otherwise.

The subjective value is not an expression of an exchange process, but is a part of the market, commodity, and price relation. In this case, the subjective value enters into the objective value process in exchange.

Form and Substance of Symbolic and Subjective Value. In neither case is there an opposition between form and substance; in respect of the tokens of symbolic and of subjective value alike, the form is the substance, and the substance is the form.

Objects of symbolic and of subjective value are not the same, nor is the human relation to them the same; the objects of subjective value, and subjective value judgments are of all kinds, idiocentric, ethnocentric, among others, but they are not nomothetic. Objects of symbolic value, and symbolic value judgments are shared and not individual, but common among many; they are capable of being nomothetic, but are nonobjective.

Value Form and Distribution

If there is distribution which is not exchange, then theoretically there is a distribution value form relative to the substance of the distribution process. This may be computed or otherwise reckoned up apart from the value of labor in production, and apart from the exchange value of a good, etc., being more general than the exchange value.

There is a requirement of formalization in equal or equivalent reciprocation in exchange by the expression of exchange value; this formalization is not necessarily the case in respect of the value of distribution, for social justice and equity are then determined by other means.

Value, objective, subjective, or symbolic is an expression of human judgment or estimation; value in production, exchange and use, as well as surplus value, abstract and concrete value in general are objective forms of value. In theory the objective and the subjective value forms or expressions are separable. Our will and desire are both the form and substance of subjective valuation and expression. Will and desire are subjectively inseparable, but objectively separable. Objective selection and criteria for selection of this kind, whether mediate or direct in nature are further analyzed; subjective selection or choice and the criteria for choice of this kind are not further analyzed, given that the analysis is an objective process. If the analysis is subjective, then it is whatever you please. The subjective value is an expression, not a law. Objective value is expressed as a law, and is not altered according to our pleasure, will and desire.

By separating the unit of consumption from the unit of production, new relations of a mediating kind are introduced into the social whole. The distribution is made systematic and is measured objectively. The production is conducted according to specializations of function, and combination and division of labor. The consumption is comfortingly related to production and distribution; it is systematic, henadic, and is opposed to a dyadic relation between producer and consumer; it is objective, equal, and is a kind of reciprocation. The reciprocation is within an age group, or between the generations. The exchange, if it is symbolic and ceremonial, is not an equal reciprocation. The distribution conforms to the rule of equal reciprocation and is no longer distributive reciprocation.

Reciprocation in exchange presupposes the establishment of an objective measure of equality in the reciprocal relation. The symbolic reciprocation in the exchange of ritual objects presupposes the subjective expression of value of the social whole, in which form and substance are non-different from one another: the form is the substance, and conversely, the substance is the form, in the symbolic exchange relation. The non-difference between the substance and form of the subjective value of the social whole is the expression of difference between the symbolic value form of one social whole as opposed to that of another. Symbolic exchange is the presupposition for economic exchange, not its historical forerunner.

By symbolic communication in exchange, a social link is established between human beings. In economic exchange there is a diremption between the producer and the product, and between two producers, each of them an exchanger.

Value, Essence and Reality

The interposition of a mediate relation between the human and the material order of nature is a human process, and is opposed to the direct relations of the material order, which include its relations to the human order. The mediate relation is human, in an asymmetrical process with the material order. The mediate relation in question is our labor, and is a twofold process. It constitutes the means whereby we work on the material world, transforming it into the objects of our processes relative to that world; and it constitutes an objective medium on which we work. Both the material world and the medium of our relation to it are the objects of our labors. In the latter case we transform the medium itself, which is our labor, by working on it. The material and human orders have a direct, concrete relation to one another only from within the order of matter. The human relation in the material order is mediate, objective, abstract and concrete; it is not concrete alone, and it is not direct, or thingly, either in the archaic primitive condition, or in the modern civil condition of the human kind. The concrete relations of space and time are mediate, abstract and concrete in the human order. Time is separated from space and made abstract in any human condition; days, seasons, and years are dealt with mediately and separately from one another and from space; they are concrete in the human condition, and reckoned in an abstract way. It is not the concrete relation alone, but its mediate relation and reference which are the conditions for the abstraction of time.

Time is a natural concrete relation, which is transformed into an objective, measured relation in the human order; there it is mediately and variably quantified, the means and ends of the measurement being socially determined. These means are historically variable, being abstract and concrete, at first predominantly concrete, and latterly increasingly abstract; they are throughout both subjective and objective. Time is directly a relation in the natural order, and is immediately a quantity in the human order, in the sense that time has no substitute; time as such, in the relation of succession, is a concrete relation. In measurement of a sequence of occurrences, in the human order, we say that the amount of time is equal to the distance divided by the rate of speed, in a given direction; we must first find out the system of coordinates, and the movement observed in its time and space relations.

C. F. Gauss distinguished between space in external nature and in our minds. Time is likewise twofold; first, it is there, in nature, and external to us. Second, it is in the human order; it is our labor time, and is objective to us in that our labor is objective; time in this sense is an objective construction of the human kind; it is also subjective.

Objective human time is mediately quantified in the sense that it is measured by instruments, concrete and abstract; mechanical and electronic clocks, day and night, and the seasons are applied as instruments in the measurement of temporal quantity. Time is valued in consequence of its being measured. There is no valuation of time objectively without its measurement. The objective value of time is the social relation thereof. With the social relation of time there is no objective value, and conversely, in consequence, without objective measurement of time there is no social valuation. Objective value is not constant but variable immediately as historical relations change, it is variable mediately within the changing historical relations in society and it is mediatively and concretely variable, being the means whereby variation is introduced in the history of society. Without concrete and in this sense direct temporal variation, there is no variation from one social whole to another, and no variation within the given social whole from one time to another. The mediate variation of the social whole with respect to its historical course is other than the variation within the given whole from one individual to the next, and other again than the concrete variation of the individuals within their own lifetime. The individual variation is as the variation upon a theme. The variation of the social history of the human social whole is not thematic; thus it would be circular to argue that the social whole serves as its own theme, which varies in relation to itself, for this would explain nothing. The variation in the group is a relation of constants and variables, the constants being relative and not absolute and fixed, but variable more slowly than other variables, insofar as they refer to the objective world.

There is no value essence. The only value there is exists as a form, the substance of which has been set forth. Karl Marx held that all science would be superfluous if the apparent form and the essence of things coincided directly ("alle Wissenschaft wäre überflüssig wenn die Erscheinungsform und das Wesen der Dinge zusammenfielen"). (Karl Marx, *Das Kapital*, III. Marx-Engels *Werke*, Bd. 25. Berlin 1972, p. 825). External things have no essence. Their only existence is that which is given to our senses, or to scientific instruments; it is their phenomenal form. We distinguish between form and substance, not between form and essence. Had the great materialist lived to see his work through to publication he might have corrected this formulation, which is metaphysical as it stands. There is a deeper misconception in Marx's position. Sciences arise not from some supposed gap between essence and appearance, but from our mediate relation to the objective world, from our transformation of things into objects, and from the interrelation of theory and practice In our mediate and objective processes with regard to the external world and to the human self.

Value and Price

Objective value is an expression of the quantity and quality of labor time expended potentially in all human reproduction, and in actuality in civil society. The labor time is applied both practically and theoretically to the transformation of materials of the natural and human orders in this process of reproduction; concretely therein the material and nonmaterial wants of the human kind and the physiological needs, converted into human wants, are met. Value is an abstraction and expresses the abstraction of labor in the said process of reproduction; the process as such is concrete and is the result of concrete labor, or work. The process of human reproduction in its immediate relation is that of production and consumption of its product; the relations of production and consumption are mediated by the process of distribution, in general, and in civil society by processes of distribution and exchange. The processes of labor in civil society are abstract and concrete in the activities of production, consumption, distribution and exchange. In considering objective social value in production as the expression of the quantity and quality of labor expended in human reproduction in civil society, the society in question is both ancient and modern. Value in its system and in the theory of that system bears on social labor, abstract, objective, concrete, combined and divided, in other social conditions as well, including those which exist only in the theory of socialist society.

At one time it had been held that the want of a good is subjective, and the value expression of that want subjective as well, whereas the labor of supplying the want and its expression as price, real or just, or as value, are objective. This dichotomy was attributed to Albertus Magnus and Thomas Aquinas, theorists of the just price, who had the economic theories of Aristotle in view. Aristotle applied the term *chreía* to the objective process of exchange in the non-natural economy of the polis. *Chreía* has the meanings, use, traffic (exchange), and want; some uses and some wants are objective and some subjective, and this variety of meanings has caused some confusion in regard to the interpretation of the meanings of Aristotle and his 13th century followers. The want of warmth that a coat meets is objective, hence the use and use value of the coat are objective; our feeling of cold or warmth may be objective or subjective. The objective use value is mediately related to the objective value of the labor in its production, distribution and consumption, and immediately related to the exchange value of the coat. The labor time and quality or capacity in production of the coat, as of any good to supply our wants, are immediately related to the objective value of the good, and mediately related to its exchange value. The demand for a good is in accordance to the use to which it is put, and is subjective or objective; the demand as such is neither objective nor subjective. We work back from the use to which the good is put, be it objective or subjective, practical or theoretical, to determine whether the good, its value expressions in use and in exchange, are objective or subjective, practical or theoretical. The value expression of the labor in human reproduction is objective, but is not intrinsic to the labor; the objectivity is determined by its outcome, or by what we make of it.

Price is not the same as value, but is the expression of a common term in an exchange under particular conditions of supply and demand in a market, popular taste, religious sanctions, legal and political restrictions, and factors of tradition and innovation. It is not the accidental relative to the substantial factor, for labor time and capacity together with their value expression are variable according to factors of tradition and innovation, legal and political restrictions, religious sanctions, peaceful and belligerent contacts. The just price was at one time thought to be a safeguard against excessive price fluctuations or stagnations through monopolies or extra economic factors in the exchange. The just price for a good was to be safeguarded by a vigilant authority, ecclesiastical or secular, in the marketplace.

Exchange is a kind of distribution in which the distribution, which is mediate, symmetrical and asymmetrical, formal and informal, is narrowed down. Exchange is in this sense a variant of the distribution process, being the formal, symmetrical, and reciprocal side of it. The exchange process is formalized and therewith institutionalized by the development of a market relation, which is its location in a particular place where the exchange transactions are conducted. Of late these locations are generalized, and take place in a system of communication which is not anywhere in particular. The market relation is further formalized by a system of contract between juridical persons, bearing on buying and selling of commodities, and by the development of a systematic means of converting human labor and its product into commodities, separating the product from its producer, and alienating it to another. The systematic means of commodity transaction, market relations of selling and buying, contract and commutative rights in general is institutionalized by concrete, immediate exchange *in natura*, or barter, and by abstract and mediate exchange by price expressed in money.

Price is not an accident, and value is not a substance; both are variable in space and time. Value is not a timeless essence, but an abstraction existing in reality. In modern bourgeois society, the value is abstracted from the conditions of the market, from factors of supply and demand, from tradition and innovation, and from the extra economic factors which determine the price. All these factors are in operation in the same space and time of the human world. Substance and essence in some philosophies and theological doctrines are made out to be timeless, and to be opposed in various ways to the accidents of nature and of human life. The abstract and concrete factors of value and price, on the contrary are all in nature, in human space and time which are in nature. The factors of price in modern bourgeois society cover a wider range of variables than those of objective value and of exchange value; the factors of all of these are in interaction, those of value being more durative and less locally determined than those of price. The factors of value and price are not causes of anything, but are expressed as the variables, in this case of value and price.

Price is a concrete expression in the market of value, hence is an expression of an expression, and an abstraction of an abstraction. As an expression it is a form, and as the expression of an expression, price is the substance of a form, which has the appearance of movement apart from its form. The form in fact moves for a time, by virtue of its institutionalization in the relations of the market, commodities and contracts, independently of the substance. Money and price have, in this process, the mediate relation of a form to a substance, which is the good as a commodity. Thus the value, which is a form in relation to the process of labor, becomes a form in relation to price, which is its substance. Price is mediately determined by the process of value, which in turn is mediately determined by the process of labor. Price is immediately determined by the relations of the market, supply and demand for products in the form of commodities, for the meeting of wants and needs. A local and momentary scarcity of a given product in commodity form will effect a change in its price, apart from its value substance.

The system of market price, commodities, and contracting for purchase and sale is conducted by the expenditure of social labor; this labor is mediate and formal, whereas labor of production is mediate and immediate, formal and substantial. The two kinds of labor are momentarily and locally independent of one another in their movement and changes.

The movement of the value substance and of its expression as value is objective, and movement of the prices of commodities in the system of market exchange is mediately objective, whereas in its immediate relations subjective factors are introduced.

The relations of social labor in civil society are determined immediately by the system of exchange, and mediately by that of production. In the exchange process, labor gets the means of its subsistence in return for the sale of its labor time and capacity or quality in the process of human social reproduction. The exchange process, in the condition of civil society, in which the production of capital predominates, is that of wages in particular, which is generalized as that of salary. The question of the lowering of wages, and of the purchasing relation of salary has been raised under the heading of the increasing pauperization of the working class. This question bears on the movement of prices, cost of living, supply and demand, market, money and commodities, their fetishism and the movement of wages and salaries. These movements have a general bearing on the process of value, not a particular one, and are in theory a separate question from the latter. In practice, and in history, there is an interaction over a long term, measured in generations, between prices, the rising and falling of costs of living, on the one hand, and of the movement of value on the other. The theoretical difference between the two is determined by the factors, objective in the case of value, objective and subjective in that of price, mediate in the case of value, immediate and mediate in the case of price, substantial in the case of value, formal in that of price. The question of the movement of price is an epiphenomenon and a historical one in relation to that of the movement of value, which is a concrete phenomenon and the substantive determinant of prices. In practice, both economic and non-economic factors are at work in the marketplace, and determine prices, and their movements. Since objective social value has labor quantity and quality as its substance, for this reason, as well as the others which have been mentioned, value and price differ from one another; their difference is formal and substantial, both in history and in the system thereof.

The economic factor of the exchange relation in the market is a mediate one, in which needs and wants are met by both sides in the exchange. The medium, however, has its own history, into which non-economic factors are introduced; these are matters of the superstructure, or external to the economy, and apart from the exchange relation in the market. The non- or extra-economic factors are those of political and military forces of the society, ethical and psychological considerations. The good has a mediate and objective value expression, the commodity has an expression as a price, which is mediate and immediate, objective and subjective. The price is concrete in a barter of concrete goods and services, and is abstract in terms of money, including credit and other financial instruments. The objective scarcity or abundance of a good at a particular time and place will drive it into undersupply and overdemand, or oversupply and underdemand, thus determining the price as higher or lower than otherwise it would be; and the good is made dear or cheap to the purchaser. The value, objective, social and mediate, is not altered. The price is variable in this way, it is variable in others as well, which are factors of tradition, fashion, and technical innovation. Novelty of fashion is a subjective factor, whether of food, clothes, or entertainment, in buying and selling, whereby a momentary glut of a desired commodity and a momentary rarefaction of another of the same kind are brought forth. By our subjectivity, will and desire, the prices are then moved down or up. Technical innovations in the movements of commodities and of their prices are objective factors in these movements; traditional factors are both objective and subjective. The public or private hand can control prices regardless of whether the commodities to which they are related are in glut or scarcity, in the one case by the action of government, police, civil agencies and other officers of the law; in the other by formation of cartels, monopolies, monopsonies, and the like. Adam Smith deplored the action of the statesmen alone; reformers, radicals of the left deplore the action of the cartels of private interests in the manipulation of prices; both sides, public as well as private, hold that their acts are in the interests of the many, of society and the process of our reproduction by our labor. Price, commodity and market are the formalization of mediate relations between production and consumption which are hypostases of our human relations. Exchange of goods is a formal means of control by legal and other means over the process of reciprocation in mutuality between human beings; it is developed in the relations between aliens, in overcoming mistrust and the potentiality of being cheated.

The distribution of goods in the relation between producers and consumers is required and called for: the economic exchange, as it is historically developed and controlled, whether by public or private hands, in civil society, is a diremption of the human social form from the substance thereof, and is an artificial, distorting factor in the process of human social reproduction. The alternative to exchange in the process of distribution is the relation of distributive reciprocity. (See L. Krader, *Treatise of Social labor*, 1979, chapter 4, On Distributive Justice and Right.)

In the history of the theory of price, the notion of the just price was brought out in ancient and modern times. This price is a formal expression of traditional factors in the determination of commodity exchange; it is recognized and acknowledged to be an ethical relation between buyer and seller. Traditional means of determining the just price include the adjudication of differences under abrupt changes of historical circumstances in the exchange and market relations.

The price varies about the objective value; the latter is the substance relative to the form, which is the price of the good. The good is transformed into a commodity by the form of social labor under market conditions; the transformation is not one of substance. The value is transformed into a price by another formal, insubstantial relation; the value in question is objective social value. This value in turn is a form which has objective social labor as its substance. The market is the formal medium in which the processes of diremption of the human form from the human substance take place.

Price is the expression of exchange value in the market; thus it is a reformulation and new expression of an expression, or its deformation and reformation. Profit is the expression of surplus value in relation to the exchange value of commodities. Profit is the new expression of surplus value under market conditions. The different value expressions, exchange value and surplus value, are given the forms of profit and price in money terms in the economy of civil and bourgeois society. Price, profit and money are given particular, not general expression, being subject to local market conditions. Thus there is no universal market, nor is there, as K. Polanyi thought, one big market. Money varies in the quantitative and qualitative relations between nations, between the rural and urban sectors, and between different branches of production between nations and groups of nations, and blocks over periods of time. The treatment of rates of profit is therefore historical, and not systematic; it is local in time and space, and not general. The prediction of the doom of the bourgeois society is not an economic but a social and political judgment. The economic process is that of exploitation by extraction of a social surplus from the social class of labor, without an equivalent reciprocation for it; the social process is that of the consciousness of this extraction by the exploited class.

The market is a concrete place or an abstract process of economic exchange. The market, exchange in relations of buying and selling, and commodities bought and sold are abstract and concrete; the process of the market relations are historically variable, both qualitatively and quantitatively more so with the introduction of money and credit in capitalist society. The process of exchange and of exchange value are therewith variable, both qualitatively and quantitatively in the history of society. The exchange value is in theory separated from market and price relations in modern society, civil and bourgeois. Surplus value is given a clear expression, separate from the concrete process of exploitation.

The process of exploitation in society is relative. The peasants in a village are exploited by the exploiting class there; the village, both exploiters and exploited, is then exploited by the government, industrialists and bankers of the nation; the nation is then exploited by foreign interests, the multinational concerns, banks, foreign nations, and combinations thereof. This has been the case in countries such as China, Mexico and India, with traditional peasant economies which are still carried forward (in the 1990s), and with industrial centers within the national territory. The exploitative relation is relativized, and a process of double, triple, etc., exploitation is brought to bear on the different elements of the working class in these countries.

Marx discussed the falling rate of profit under capitalism. This is a local and momentary problem, which bears on particular, historical relations of capital formation; the question of the falling rate of profit is a practical and concrete matter. The process of abstraction, concretion, objectification, self-objectification and alienation as an active relation of labor in society is developed together with another process constituted of the same relations, in which labor is a passive element, being objectified, exchanged, itself and its product as object abstracted and alienated by another. The power to exchange living labor which rests in other hands than those of living labor itself is the power over living labor by another, which is the master over it, and is indicative of the unfree condition of labor, the unfreedom bearing both the form and substance of labor.

Value, Objective and Subjective, and Price
The objective value of a good is the expression of the amount of time and quality of the labor expended in its production. The good is concrete in the product, and abstract and concrete in the labor, its organization in society, its production relations, and its technics, or the immediate relations of labor to the instruments of work. The good is expended in the process of production, distribution and consumption of a means to meet a social want; social labor is expended in this process. A product, such as food and clothing, housing and means of transportation, is as such a good, as is the labor of bringing them forth. Therefore we speak of the labor not only of production, but also of distribution and consumption, in the process of social reproduction of the human kind. We have the means to express the values of the goods and labors, both in theory and in practice, of the materials of our human, social reproduction, but given the variability in the preparation, education and formation of social labor, a general value expression which is applicable to all mankind is excluded on practical grounds, even though the theory of it exists. Apart from the variability of the quality of labor, the general value term is excluded, also on practical grounds, in view of the variability of the relations of human reproduction. The variability in either case is a qualitative expression, whereas we seek the quantitative factors in the determination of objective value.

In the primitive condition the relation between social production and consumption is an immediate one, for the product is shared out in the community between the actual and potential producers, the adults and the children respectively, and the aged and infirm. These communities are predominantly if not entirely autarchic, hence the system of their reproduction is predominantly if not entirely an immediate one. The process of immediate social reproduction is transformed by the development of exchange between the communities; the immediate relations are then made into mediate ones. The relation of sharing out is a process of distribution of the communal product; the relation of exchange between the producing communities is a developed form of distribution between them, the development being a mediation in their mutual processes. The producing communities which are engaged in the exchanges between them are no longer primitive, but are mutually dependent, in reciprocity between them, whereby the product of the one meets the wants, needs and desires of the other, and conversely, the product of the other meets the wants, needs, and desires of the one. The product of either is no longer consumed internally, but is externalized by the medium of exchange between them. The three moments of the transformation, from immediate to mediate human social reproduction, from the immediate internalization of the product, and distribution by sharing and sharing out, in consumption, mediate relation of externalization and internalization of the product, and from immediate distribution by sharing and sharing out to mediate distribution by exchange, are processes in the transformation of society from the primitive to a more developed condition.

Money is sometimes reckoned to be the medium of exchange, which is partly a valid judgment. Money is part of the medium of exchange in trade and commerce, not in barter. All of these are mediate relations.

Among the Trobriand Islanders of the south Pacific, in traditional times fishing and yam raising were practiced in separate communities, coastal and inland. The communities were mutually dependent, the fish of the one side being exchanged against the yams of the other. The two sides in the exchange had not a primitive but a more developed economy, distribution having the form of exchange by trade not commerce between them. The exchange was regular, durative over a long time, when measured in human generations, and was systematic; therefore it is not simple exchange, but a kind of trade. The equivalence between the products traded was worked out in concrete and not in abstract processes between the parties in the exchange.

In the more developed relations of exchange by trade, market relations, sale and purchase, commodity transactions and price in abstract terms of money are introduced. Thus, trade is a system of development out of the exchange relation as a medium between the parties to the exchange. Barter is a concrete form of trade. In the different forms of distribution by exchange, trade and barter, the product is separated from its immediate producer and alienated to another against the return of a like, equal, or equivalent product moving in a contrary sense. The process of exchange of products is twofold in its internal relations; it is a self-diremption, voluntary or involuntary, of the labor time and capacity of the immediate producers, and an alienation to another of the product in a mediate and objectified relation between the parties to the exchange. The labor time and capacity are then abstractly put up for sale and purchased as is its product.

The exchange process is developed as a medium between buyer and seller; it is perfected by an elaboration of the mediate relations of exchange. The e laboration which is internal to the medium is developed by specialists in the exchange and market processes. The product, labor time and capacity, are controlled in their sale and purchase not by labor itself, but by others. The specialists in the exchange and market processes are the merchants. The merchants as a group in ancient Asia, Europe and Mexico transformed trading practices into commerce. In this case a complex alienation is effected, that of the labor time and capacity and of the product from the producer.

The market, whether as a concrete place of distribution, or as an abstract and unlocalized system of communication, is the relation of exchange, trade and commercial transactions in concrete form; the commodity is the expression of the product of distribution in alienated form; capital is the expression of the means of production, actual and potential, in commodity form.

Labor is a form of capital in modern civil society; it is self-mediating, offering itself for sale on the market as free wage labor, and self-objectifying, turning its time and capacity into a commodity which is the object purchased by the employer. Whereas labor is self-activating, capital is not. By our labors, products, skills and units of labor time, instruments of production, both abstract and concrete, are produced. They are converted into commodities in the medium of exchange, which is the market; that part of the product which is not consumed but is distributed in further production, is capital, fixed or circulating, if that which is produced thereby is a commodity. This is the case with respect to the self-objectifying labor, or its objectified product. The objectification presupposes a medium in which the labor time is exchanged, the medium presupposes the objectification both of labor and its product. The medium, we have said, is the market, the object is both the labor and the product which are sold in socially accountable units. The entire human field is subject to quantification and direction of movement, expressed in vectors of motion.

The process of commodity transactions is expressed in abstract form as a contract of purchase and sale.

The medium of exchange as a concrete field of activities of marketing is made into an abstract medium in money form. The process of transformation has its history. The exchange appears as a movement of the marriage partners, either of the one, or of the other, or of both, from one group of kin to another. It is accompanied in some cases by a movement of bride wealth, or, as it is sometimes erroneously termed, bride price, the *kalym* of the pastoral Turks of Central Asia, and the *lobola* of the pastoral Bantus of East Africa, in traditional times. In these movements of those who could afford it, hundreds of heads of stock changed ownership. Prestige and ceremony accompany the economic movement, which are inseparable in these transactions. It is not a process of circulation, for it is without an abstract medium of exchange; there is a kind of market for the arrangement of marriages under these circumstances, whereas there is no means of establishing equivalence in movements of the actual or potential spouses, of ritual and economic, or symbolic and social wealth. The symbolic wealth is abstract, the social wealth concrete.

The Mongols in traditional practice had an exchange in which an equivalence was established between a standard unit and other products in the exchange. The various kinds of cattle and other pastoral products, which they traded with the neighboring Chinese and Russians in past centuries against tea, rice, cotton, and silk, were measured by them against the value in exchange of a healthy four year old horse. This was the unit of account, called *bodo* (in modern Mongol; from *bodoqu*, in classical Mongol, to count, calculate, reckon). The term bears not on the animal, but on the abstraction, the standardization of the unit, and the measure of other valuable goods against it in a system of reference to all of them. In one variant of this system, six sheep were equal to one *bodo*, five camels equal to six *bodo*, etc. The system varied in time and place. The Mongols in olden times had trade, without commerce, for whereas they had regular and systematic exchange, covering many useful items which were exchanged in commodity form, they had no class of merchants; merchants and merchant caravans came to Mongolia mainly from China and Russia during the 17th to the 19th centuries.

The development of specialist fellowships, organized in companies of commercial venturers in Europe during the Middle Ages, was closely related to their stock in trade. The fellows laid out an investment in a commercial venture; their investment was a fee in money or goods, one form of which was cattle; *fee* in its etymology is a term for cattle; cf. German *Vieh*. Companions are those who share bread, *pan*, in a commercial or military venture. German *Genosse*, companion, comrade, has a related history of merchant venturers, and the Russian *tovarishch*, companion, fellow, is a borrowing from Turkic *tavar*, "good, cattle, stock, commodity;" (perhaps from Armenian *tvar* "sheep"); Latin *societas* meant a group of venturers who retained their individual rights over their property in the venture, and did not pool it in a common fund, as did the *collegium*, or the companions, in a company. A participant in the societal venture was a *socius*, associate.

These different movements in the development of exchange, trade, and commerce are not to be summed up in a single historical movement, for the long distance commerce of the rulers of central Mexico before the Spanish conquest was conducted on behalf of the official royal, priestly and political interest, and not on behalf of the special class of merchants by whom it was practiced, extending over great parts of ancient Mexico.

The capitalist practice of commerce in its proto-history is a development out of the European practice. The *wergeld* was instituted in medieval Europe as a compensation of one social group by another for physical harm, homicide, or theft of property. The *wergeld* (*wer*, man; *geld*, money) was constituted as a standard unit of wealth and therewith price of a man, in which an abstract system of social status and reference was put together, according to the rank of the one who suffered the harm or wrong, and the one who did the harm or wrong, whether noble or common, servile or free, and according to the age and sex of either.

The objective value of the good or service is abstracted from the economic process, whether of production, distribution or consumption, in a third relation of alienation, and appears as exchange value in civil society, ancient and modern. Thus objective value in civil society is transposed into exchange value. The commodity in the transactions of the society of capital exchange and production in the form of money and credit is additive, subtractive, cumulative and accumulative; it is an abstraction.

Social production has objective and subjective factors in its constitution, and its product has these as well in its manifestation as a good. The subjective is not diminished or excluded by virtue of the abstraction of the product from the producers by being exchanged. The market has therefore both objective and subjective factors operative in it, for it is the medium as the field in which the exchange of products and labor as product takes place.

An exchange in the economic sense is concrete in the reciprocation between the parties to the exchange of like against like, A puts out a bushel of wheat today against the return of a bushel of wheat tomorrow; or expends a day's labor in the field of the neighbor against the return of a day's labor in A's own field. In this exchange relation there is equality but not equivalence; the equality is the expression of the relation of reciprocity in a system in which they are reckoned up; it is presupposed that in the social condition there is the capacity to identify a unit in the exchange and a system of reckoning with this unit; it is additive, that is, posited and wiped out, or subtracted, when the exchange in mutual reciprocity is carried through, but not as such cumulative. Cumulation and accumulation are practices in another system of reckoning than addition. The reckoning of equality in exchange, although it is an abstraction, is in an immediate relation to the concrete exchange. The processes of cumulation and accumulation are methods of calculation, which together with the addition and subtraction are mediate and abstract, as well as immediate and concrete.

The positing of equivalents in the exchange is a means of relating unlikes to one another, having an equal value as an abstract and mediate process between them. In this relation between equivalents, the concrete relation of exchange of a good, product or labor, which is similar in quality and equal in quantity is presupposed. The labor is undifferentiated, whether rude or qualified and skilled, therefore we lay out a day's labor against another. The introduction of differentiated labor into the system of reckoning presupposes the social organization, combination and division of labor, and the technical specializations; the differentiation and connection of social labor are processes of the development of mutual dependence and reciprocity in the social relations thereof. The equivalents of labor time and skill, and of the products thereof, presuppose the generation of a medium of exchange, its abstract expression, its calculation by additive, cumulative and accumulative processes, and the system of the mediate, abstract, and calculative matrix of processes. Equal value, or equivalence, is the expression of these processes in a particular way in the exchange; the particularity is generalized in the system of exchange in the market. The qualitative relations of likeness are expanded to a variety of qualitative unlikes, and the quantitative relations of equality and equalization are developed further in the new methods of calculation of value. The values are objective, having reference to our labors in the process of human reproduction of the human kind and to the products of those labors.

The value expression of the good produced remains objective in the product of our labors. It is made into an abstraction by the generation of the system of value equivalents. As an abstraction, it is capable of being moved about from one context of calculation to another. In the market conditions, which are posited by another means, as we have seen, it appears as a commodity. The conditions of the value expression of objective labor and product in the relations of exchange in the market are those of a commodity. The commodity is an abstraction, mediate, passive, objective, abstract and symbolic; it is concrete in the labor and in the product thereof. Money is a kind of commodity; whereas the commodity by its abstraction is given symbolic capacity of movement, money has further development of this symbolic independence of its concrete form in the labor and social product. Commodity and money are a form in the market relations of society, of which social labor and its product are the substance. The market is the medium of exchange in the economy of a given society, money is the concrete medium of exchange in this exchange medium. Money is the concrete expression of the abstract medium of commodity movements in exchange. Credit is a means of expansion of the money supply in the relation between present and future transactions of market exchange. In modern bourgeois society credit is a faithful contract between buyer and seller, and between the present and future processes between them. Credit and interest on the credited outlay of capital are subject to the expansion and contraction of labor capacity, materials and products; in this relation capital, being a commodity, is passive.

The traditional Mongol exchange, which had the standard of value of a horse as its expression, was a concrete measure of equality between objects exchanged; it was not applicable to the outlay of labor time and capacity, but only to the social product of the pastoral activities, the beasts, and the goods against which they were exchanged. Thus the *bodo* was not generally exchangeable, hence was concrete in one respect, and abstract in the exchanges of different kinds of goods in the traditional Mongol community in another. In one respect it is a kind of exchange equivalent, as money, and in another respect it is not. World money, *Weltgeld*, is generally exchangeable at a given time.

The product of human labor, as the labor itself, is objective and subjective in its substance; the subjective appears both together with the objective substance and apart from the latter in the relations of exchange between buyer and seller of a good. The subjective substance is not expressed in the objective value, which remains the determinate of the labors in the production of the good which is sold and bought, and expressed in bourgeois society in the value in exchange. The substance as subjective is expressed in our choice, when there is one, between this good and that, or between an attribute of this kind or that with respect to the good which we intend to purchase. If the purchaser has a choice, in buying a coat, between this color and that, the quality of protection against the cold being equal, then the choice is subjective. The subjectivity has a value expression, which is other than the objective value expression, the former being a matter of pleasure, will and desire.

The local market conditions of scarcity or abundance of coats of the quality mentioned, in green or blue, do not influence the objective value of the product; the objective values of the coats are in all cases expressed by the quantity and quality of the mediate, abstract and objectified labors in their production. These market conditions do not influence the exchange value of the goods, which expresses the capacity of that which if offered meets that capacity in another good to meet a concrete human want, which is the same or other. The market conditions of the varieties of wills and desires, and of relative and concrete abundance and scarcity of the goods which meet our wants are subjective and objective. The market conditions determine not the value of the good or labor, but its price; to the local market conditions are to be added the general market conditions, which are concrete in the traditions and history of the prices, and of the goods to which they are related. The price is a variable expression, which is determined by objective factors, expressed in objective value form, made concrete in civil society by their expression in the form of exchange value, and by the subjective factors, expressed by subjective value form and substance. The choice is the act according to our will and desire, and is expressed in the offered and accepted purchase price, in mutuality between purchaser and seller.

The price is relative to the objective value, and is variable relative to the latter in consideration of subjective and of further objective market conditions, such as the concrete abundance and scarcity of a good. The price thus varies about the objective value, and is a determinant of the latter, not a determinant thereof. The determination of the price of the good by the objective value of it is a general and not a particular determination. At any moment and at any place the price may vary widely or narrowly from the objective value; the price of the good or labor time is expressed in our civil society in terms of money and its relations. The science of pricing and of prices in its historical and current expression therefore has objective and subjective market factors as its concern, and thus differs from the science of the factors which determine the objective value.

Price is not a universal expression, for it is determined in major part by traditional and subjective factors, is concrete and localized in its currency. Value in its objective expression is more general than price, but whereas in theory it is a human universal, in practice it is not.

The objective value of a good or of the labor in its production in society is a particular form of its substance; the form is variable in human history, and appears under given social conditions as exchange value. Yet the objective value form in relation to the production process continues to exist under the changed circumstances of its historical expression, for the production process continues to exist apart from exchange and the market. The substance, production relations and process, in this case has a general form, objective value, and a particular form, which is the exchange value. Thus, exchange value as the form and expression of the expression is a particular phenomenon of society, there is nought that is universal about it, and it disappears from view when the conditions of exchange as a predominant relation between producer and consumer is eliminated; it is found in the practice of archaic economic relations, and in the theory of socialist relations of production, distribution and consumption. The objective value is not eliminated but remains, whether explicit or implicit, for the relations of labor remain in force in the process of human social reproduction. The objective value is abstracted from the production process by the further distribution of the good, in a mediate relation, which is increasingly extensive, between its production and its consumption. Exchange, we have seen, is but one form in which this distribution takes place. Exchange is in one sense a concrete distribution relation, under particular social and economic circumstances. Exchange in practice is a means of abstraction of the product from the producers, often by the producers themselves. Thus exchange is an abstraction of an abstraction, and exchange value is the abstract expression of this double abstraction. Distribution is an abstract relation in general, under non-primitive conditions of human reproduction, and exchange is an abstract relation in particular under these conditions. Price is a further abstraction in relation to value and exchange value; it varies about the two objective value expressions, but does not necessarily coincide with either. The price differs from the value expression and from the exchange value expression in that subjective as well as objective factors enter into the determination of the price. The price diverges from the objective value not because the exchange value intervenes between the two; it should be borne in mind that value, exchange value and price are all forms, expressions, and are not independently active in human affairs. The private or public determinations of price, or what is more usual in civil society, their combination, are brought about by the introsusception of the exchange process into the relations of human reproduction. This process is the substance of the exchange value, which is the form, and the form of social labor as the commodity which is made out of wage labor. The price is the form, under particular, local and historically variable market conditions, of a value expression, which is the substance of the price. But the value expression, objective or subjective, is another form; objective value is the formal expression of the labor time and capacity expended in the product of our labor; subjective value is the expression of what you will. All forms are abstractions.

Abstractions are abstract in relation to a concrete subject or object. The abstractions are in actuality or potentiality further abstractive, thus there are abstractions of abstractions, and abstractions of abstractions of abstractions, *ad infinitum*. The *concretum*, concrete thing or object is concrete as such; there is concretion of an abstraction, but no concretion of concretion. All things are concrete as such, being in space-time; fantasies, mysteries, speculations and paradoxes are in this sense concrete things, being in the human system of space-time. All form is the form of a substance. There are forms of forms, but no substance of substance. A form is a substance of another form, and a substance is a form of another substance. The value of a good is the form of which the good is the substance. The price of the good is the concretion which the value takes in the market and commodity system. It is also a form of a form, for the price is a formal expression relative to the commodity having the price put on it. The commodity is in this case the substance relative to the form. But the commodity is a form relative to a good which is the substance having the abstract and formal expression as a commodity. Form, abstraction, estimation, value in exchanges, and commodity prices are a human construction. The forms and abstractions are real in the same sense that the things and objects which are their substance and concretion are real.

Calculation of Value

Value in its objective sense is the expression of the quantity of labor, time and skill or qualification which is expended in the process of human reproduction under local social conditions. The expression is an abstraction, and includes the entire quantum of labor time and quality expended without regard to the differences in that process between labor in production, consumption and distribution, without regard to differences between practical and theoretical labor, or between mediate and immediate labor. Finally, in the calculation of the value quantum, an abstraction is made whereby a social unity, such as a nation under particular historical conditions, is set forth; the unity in question comprises all the branches of social labor; independent of the extra, non-social, or private and subjective labors.

The calculation of objective value in production presupposes our capacity to determine the unit of account in the various labor processes in production, distribution, and consumption, and the capacity to reckon the additive and cumulative relations of the unit.

The expression of value is an abstraction, in theory applicable everywhere in the human order. It is in fact an expression of local relations of labor in production, and a general value expression is an abstraction of an abstraction.

The calculation of value has two processes within it, the one organizational, the other technical. The organization of labor in society is that of its combination and division. This process is the relation between mediate and immediate production. The mediate and immediate labors are in this sense relative both to one another and to the organization of production in the economic branches and sectors of the given social (e.g., national) whole. The mediate labor is relatively more highly qualified, educated, trained, abstract, and theoretical; the immediate labor is relatively more concrete and practical, and is less qualified, educated in general and trained in particular.

The technical question concerns the relation of labor to the means of production. Means of production are abstract and concrete, theoretical and practical. The concrete and practical means of production are those which are accessible to the senses, and material in form. The concrete and practical means are tools of work and instruments of labor; the instruments are also abstract and theoretical.

In the calculation of value, the labor time and quality in the organization, combination and division of labor in a given time period is introduced.

Next, we turn to the relations of production. These are, in part, the technics, which are the immediate relations of labor to the instruments, practical and theoretical, abstract and concrete. The instruments are the products of past labors. In the calculation of value all the past labors, materialized in the instruments, and in archives of production, reference works and manuals, are included. The materialization includes the original plans and construction of the instruments as means of production, and their maintenance and repair, modernization, powering and fuelling to keep them serviceable and running.

In the calculation of value, the amount of time expended in social reproduction in a given social unity is first summed up; this summation is additive and cumulative. It is qualified according to the amount of time stored up in the labors of social reproduction. The storing up is the time spent in education and training of the social labors in the reproduction process. The third term in the mathematical expression is that of the amount of time expended in the production of the means of production of the social labor. For these calculations, quantitative and qualitative, a kind of space called Leibniz space, is then constructed.

The calculation of the social labors as the quantum of labor time is expressed as the labor time in production, and this is an arbitrary expression which includes the process of consumption, distribution and exchange. The labor time in the production process in this sense comprises all the social labors, at the given time, this process being calculated as an annual unit of account; these labors comprise the rural and urban, industrial, agricultural, mining, transportation, communication, in the public and private sectors, wage and salary, home and external services, health, sanitation, food processing, clothing and other personal services.

The calculation of the labor time thus specified has two components, the calculation of the amount of social labor in the given nation, and the calculation of the quality thereof.

The quantity is the expression of units of social labor time. The quality of each unit of labor time is the expression of the amount of time spent in the training, education, qualification and preparation of the social labor, by all means, formal and informal, traditional and modern, practical and theoretical. The branches of rural and urban material production of goods for immediate and mediate consumption, service industries and professions have several partial differential equations; they are not summed up in a three-dimensional space. Services are goods, as any other.

All objective value comes from labor in production, but it does not come forth immediately from its source, for value is an expression which implies the labor of expressing the objective value. Value is a human making and not a natural doing, and as a process of making it is not a concrete relation, but an abstract form which is mediate in the human order. Value is the universal expression of labor not in actuality, but in potentiality, for value is the expression of social labor, and not of all labor, in the process of self-reproduction by the human kind. Value is the system of reference of social labor and not the relation of labor, but the system is not unitary, save in a simple social formation of the economic life. Value is the expression of the quantity of abstract and concrete labor expended in the process of social reproduction of the human kind; it is not exhaustive of that expression alone, the practical and concrete expression having reference to the meeting of wants and needs. We will take up only the objective value of labor in production, setting aside the subjective value of meeting subjective wants. Value is an expression of the process of producing and its product, it is not a doing, the activity of producing and its product is a process of social labor, and its object.

The relations of the material order are a process of doing, which is practical, and concrete; those of the human order are a process of making, wherein the practical is converted into an activity which is practical and theoretical, the concrete into a relation which is abstract and concrete; the thing is made into object and subject. There is no opposition in the material order, the practical activity being developed as a concrete relation, and this relation is developed and unfolded as practical activity. The relation between random occurrence and processive order, variation, and external and internal relation is not an opposition but a concrete development.

The relation between the human kind and the material order is an ongoing process of evolution. At the same time the relation of internality and externality in nature is developed into the relation of opposition in the human order; the opposition is the development of a potentiality in the natural order which is then made explicit in the human, in which it is realized. Material processes and results stand in a direct relation to one another, without distancing. The process of production and its product are separated from one another in the human order; the direct relation between the process and its result in the material world is transformed by human activity into a mediate relation, for in the latter case the process is worked upon, apart from its product, and the medium of production, the means and instruments are elaborated, together with the product. The relation of process and product while developed together is nevertheless a separate development, the means and result being worked upon in distinct processes. The separation of the human process into distinctive fields of activity is the working out of an alienation between labor and its product, which is the expression of the human activity of working upon the medium of production. This relation of labor to the means and instruments of production is developed as a primary relation of mediation and alienation, whereby the human kind removes itself from the material process, develops a human variation on the natural order in the human process of reproduction. The relation of opposition which is developed by the human kind is the combination of these differences between material and human processes. The past is worked on anew in the present, the relation between past and present being in the process of change and repotentialization.

The relation becomes the *differentia specifica* of the humankind in its relation to the material order and to itself. The human reproductive relation is other than the material reproduction of life, the two reproductive processes being developed in the human order *pari passu*.

The difference and nexus between the human and material orders are relations of substance and of form, in reference to the processes of reproduction of life processes and of the human kind. The natural relation of variation of the human kind in relation to the material order and the continuity between the two are demonstrated. The system of formal and substantial difference and nexus between the two orders is made into the basis for opposition on the part of the human order in an asymmetrical relation to the material order. It is at once a diremptive relation between the two, which is another asymmetrical relation, for nature does not dirempt the natural; yet the human order, being natural, not having left the natural order, is dirempted from it. The human kind and order are diremptive, alien, self-alienating and alienated only from the standpoint of the human order in relation to the other orders of nature. The difference between the social wholes within the human order is one of form, the substantive human relation being common to them. The formal difference, however, is internalized, and enters into the human substance; the difference is false but nonetheless real. It is as though there were substantial differences between the social wholes of the humankind, and as though each were absolutely other in relation to one another. This intussusception of the form is expressed by the false consciousness of difference and supposed superiority and inferiority between the social wholes, nations, empires, and political systems, whereupon wars of conquest, colonization and enslavement are fought.

Within the history and structure of civil society divisions are introduced with substantial difference, relative to the process of human social reproduction, for in this division, two classes of society are constituted, one having both a formal and substantial relation in the given reproductive process, the other only a form alone. The substantive relation of the material order is thereby submitted to a twofold transformation, within the human order, by separation of form from substance in the latter, and by separation of a part of the social whole from the substantive process of reproduction of the whole. The opposition between part and whole is developed in the latter case, which is the actualization of an implicit and potential opposition of other forms of human social relation; this opposition is not a necessary one, for it has no objective basis, being introduced by substitution of a subjective relation for the objective one in human history, together with the false consciousness thereof, taking the subjective interest for the whole, subjective and objective, and the part for the whole therewith, as before.

Value which is objective is the expression of opposition between the mediate and immediate process of labor in a given social whole and the result of that labor, which is the objectified product. The dialectic of labor process is that between the self-objectification and the object, and hence between the self-relation of labor as the object and the product of that relation; it is therefore the opposition between the self-relation of labor as the object, and labor as the subject of the process of human reproduction. The process, labor, in this sense is that of opposition between the actuality, which is the relation of social labor as the part to the whole, and the potentiality, which is the relation of unity between social labor and human social whole. Out of this opposition between part and whole, as between actuality and potentiality, the dialectic of the system of reference of value to the labor process is developed in respect of abstract and concrete value, abstract cumulative and concrete non-cumulative value, in respect of equal and equivalent reciprocity and distributive reciprocity of value, and in respect of value of reproduction of part and whole. The expression of social labor by the value thereof is brought out in the abstraction, labor, and in abstract value; concrete value is in this case the expression of the quantity of wants and needs that are met by labor. Abstract labor and abstract labor expression are both cumulative, the former as relation, the latter as reference; concrete labor and concrete value are both quantitative and non-cumulative, the one as relation of work, the other as reference which is expressed as use value. The relation of equal or equivalent reciprocation is the exchange relation and is expressed by exchange value; it is opposed to abstract value, both mediately and passively; it is opposed to concrete labor and its expression as use value both immediately and passively. The relation of abstract labor to exchange is asymmetrical with the foregoing, be in mediate and active; the relation of exchange or equal/equivalent reciprocity to distributive reciprocity is the active relation of social labor in the process of its self-reproduction on condition that the potentiality of unity between social labor and the social whole is met. The opposition between form and substance of value presupposes the opposition between exchange and self-reproduction of social labor, for the self-reproduction of social labor is the substance of value, whereas the form of value is variable, appearing-historically either as abstract value or as exchange value.

The human kind by its labors reorganizes and reorders the material order of nature, the world in which it is generated, but not systematically. The material order is sensible, concrete, being in space-time, orderly, systematic, incomplete, open and variable. We internalize the material world abstractly and concretely, whereby our system of order is determined and mediately conditioned to be open, incomplete, relative, changed and changing. The orders and systems of nature are manifold, whereby the human systems of order are multiple abstractly and concretely. We construct in abstraction many systems which are absolute, invariant, timeless, immobile, perfect and complete, in themselves. The motivations and reasons, psychological and philosophical, for these constructions are many, varying from one people to another, from one historical epoch to another, and from one individual to another. The absolute is made into an object of adoration, as though it were independent of those who made it, and of those who acquiesce in its cult. It is then held that this being, conceived to be absolute, is the creator of its creators, and of all things. The world is changing, and we change in it. Some recognize this changefulness, and live by it. To others, the shakiness of our foundation in the world is a reason to attribute a positive subjective value to the absolute systems, in the hope that they be made real. Our fears create the gods, which then allay our fears. We think that our own time is especially beset with uncertainty, and express not only our own hope of salvation, but our inner despair that it is beyond our reach. This hope and despair are thousands of years old, and are new, and appear in the nightmare figures painted by Hieronymus Bosch and Fuseli. They are the expressions of old, subjectively received values, and their doubt.

The subjective value itself of the creativity of the person then becomes an object of our self-affirmation. The value of subjective value of the person then takes on the same brazen constitution as the law of the Medes and the Persians, which altereth not. The subjective value and the value of the person appear to be the same, they seem to be fruitful and to multiply out of the same reasons and motives, providing affirmation against self-doubt where no other certainty is forthcoming. These formulations find in subjective value the firm foundation where its quest in other directions is given up. This value of subjective value is a part of the problem of value; in it the objective value is not accounted for, and the lesser part is taken for the greater, or for the whole. The subjective value is not unrelated to the objective, for the human being is subject and object. Neither the subjective nor the objective is all of the problem of value; the result of mistaking the one for the whole has been the construction of a theory of the value of subjective universal value. The objective value theory is no more universal than the subjective.

The practices which bear on subjective value are those of will and desire, which are made concrete in acts of choice. Choosing is a subjective act, which follows from our subjective judgment, through will and desire. The act is without further appeal, and is the responsibility of the individual or legal person.

Labor Time and Space in Relation to Value
Our labors bear on the various orders of nature, without being in a direct relation to them. The abstract expression of our labors in society is that of value. In primitive society, the value may be given subjective expression, because choices are made. In civil society, the objective value expression is brought out, and dirempted from the subjective, and the abstract from the concrete. Objective value under these conditions is defined as the amount of labor time expended in the production of a good whereby our wants are met. The labor time is analyzed in terms of the organization of labor, its combination and division, the skills, capacities, arts, technics and sciences which the labor masters or is at its disposal. The labor time

is the objective, abstract productive value substance; the form of the labor time is its value expression in the given human social condition.

The labor time is time in the human order, and is abstracted from space. The labor space is the concrete, material space of our work and labor; that space is transformed from the material to the human order by our labors, and becomes what it is, the concretization of labor time, the working and laboring place of the human kind. The objective, abstract value expression is a quantity which is reckoned in terms of time, and not of space, and not of concrete space-time. The reason for this is that the model for our apprehension of the labor process and the work product is that of our relations to the material order. This model was developed in ancient and further developed in modern times, having been internalized by the human kind very deeply, so that we can scarcely perceive and comprehend ourselves apart from this model of nature as matter. That the human kind is other than matter, having been generated in the material order, by material processes, living and non-living, was grasped in a general way only in the past century. We are material and non-material in our constitution. Our theories and practices with respect to value and labor, human time and space, were worked out with respect to matter and the sensory order of nature. In this order, time and space are concrete in relation to one another, whereas in the human order we abstract, dirempt and distance them from one another. Extension and direction of matter, time and space remain objects of our work and labor. In theory time and space are distanced from one another, whereas in our practice they are concrete, continuous and direct in their mutual relations. The relations of matter are those of extension and direction, which are concrete. Human relations of space and time are material and concrete in this sense, and they are non-material, abstract; the non-material, abstract relations of space and time of the human order are those of distance. These relations are mediate; the direction, extensive magnitudes, or dimensions of these processes of the human order are imposed on them as projections from our perceptions of space and time of the material order.

The material space-time has the direction, and directional-magnitude of time. Since the fields taken from this order are the most important, being the most objectively productive and valuable fields of our work and labor, the quantity measured in determining the value of labor is that of time. Labor space is then measured in the human fields as the material and concrete form of labor time, and labor time the substance, material and nonmaterial, concrete and abstract, of labor space.

Labor time and capacity are treated as a problem of algebra, in which a manifold of n dimensions is posited. They constitute a space called Leibniz space, having the attribute of homogonous relations between the parts. The homogonous relation is not a qualitative but a quantitative one, which can be treated numerically but also, characteristically, non-numerically. The parts are mapped onto one another in either a continuous or discontinuous process between them. The parts are henads, having difference and nexus between them, and are not monads. As henads, they have both inner and outer relations to other parts of the manifold, which is a system, and to other systems.

Social Labor and the Laws of Value

In the early history of civil society, Mencius and Aristotle were conscious of these processes, of their sources and history. The relations of exchange, of social labors of production and reproduction, and of exploitation, were present in the ancient Oriental, classical, medieval and modern bourgeois forms of society. There is a difference of degree between the ancient and the modern forms of civil society. Wage and salaried labor is a predominant form of labor in modern society; these relations of labor are found in a modest degree in the ancient forms of civil society. Labor converts itself, its time and skills, technics and science, into a commodity as wage labor. It is converted by another into a commodity in the ancient and medieval economic formations of society. The labor in any form, servile or wage labor, which is converted into a commodity is subject to the laws of exchange and their expression by exchange and use value. The laws of exchange value and use value are valid in the different eras of civil society, ancient and modern in that commodity exchange takes place. Labor itself is a commodity throughout the history of these economic formations of civil society; the difference between them is that labor time and capacity is sold by itself in the capitalist mode of production, and is sold by another in the condition of slavery and serfdom. This is a formal not a substantial difference between servile and wage labor. The law of objective, social value of production is valid wherever the class of social labor produces and reproduces itself and the social whole. Given that exchange disappears, exchange value will be eliminated as its expression. But the objective, social value of labor in production will not disappear, for it accords with exchange and exchange value only in modern civil society.

The laws of exchange and exchange value are valid not only where wage labor and capital predominate in society, and in the relations of production; they are valid wherever trade and commerce are found. These relations are present to a more modest degree, and in different forms in earlier eras of society, in the various economic formations. These eras are found in ancient Asia, Africa, Inca Peru and Mesoamerica, the servile, slave and serf societies of ancient and medieval Europe, and modern civil society.

The difference between wage labor and servile labor is one of formal freedom and unfreedom. Servile labor is unfree both in its form and substance; wage labor and salaried labor is free *pro forma*, but unfree in substance. The value expressions, objective, social, and formal, bear on the substance of the relations of labor in society, both civil and socialist. The labor substance is common throughout the history of society in its non-primitive, civil condition. The value expressions bear on the common substance through their changed and changing forms. The changes in the forms of this society are determined by changes in the formal relations of social labor, whether unfree or free. Where there is predominance of commerce and of social exploitation there is the expression of objective, social value of labor by exchange value and surplus value. The proportion and amount of commodity exchange in the process of social reproduction in modern civil society are greater than they were in past eras of civil society. The validity of the laws of exchange value and surplus value is not determined by changes in these proportions and amounts but by the fact of commodity exchange.

Appendix I. Aristotle, Marx, and the Theory of Exchange Value

Aristotle represented economic exchange as a dyadic relation of nexus between persons, unlike and equal, who transfer, each to the other, goods unlike and equal. The one demands of the other the good which will supply a want, each differing in the want from the other. Thus a baker exchanges the product, bread, against the shoemaker's product, shoes. The bread supplies the want of the shoemaker, and the shoes the want of the baker. Shoemaker and baker are equals, the amount of preparation for their tasks, the costs of setting up shop and the costs of acquiring the materials for their respective trades being the same; or if there is a difference between them, it is not detectable by the given state of the techniques, practical or theoretical, of measuring it. The exchange is transacted according to the commutative principle of justice and right. It is a contract between buyer and seller, in which, if five loaves of bread equal one pair of shoes, then their value is translated into money as the unit of account, such that the shoes, worth a number of drachmas, are not exchanged against the bread, worth a number of *obols*, but the drachma against the shoes, by the baker, who has exchanged the loaves of bread in order to meet the shoemaker's price. The price being just, the exchange of unlikes is equalized. The relation between buyer and seller is not immediate but mediated by the money in the transaction. In this process, abstraction is made from the two remaining principles of particular justice.—It is presupposed in this doctrine that the parties to the exchange are juridical persons, who are formally free and equal, and thus capable of making the exchange of their property in their respective social goods. The slave may engage in an exchange, but only if empowered to do so by the slave-owner, or by a more general provision of the civil law in force, in which case, the slave acts as the surrogate of the juridical person.

The product, by means of the exchange process, is converted into a commodity; the attribute of the product as a commodity then determines that the labor of the producer, free or bound, is a commodity.

The exchange of the labor time and capacity against the means of subsistence, in the process of human reproduction is expressed as the sum of the social labors in a given society, and the sum of its products. This is reduced to a private transaction in the exchange of the substantive labor powers against the means of subsistence by the social labor in modern society. The market relations are social relations, whether just or unjust, private or public, exploitative or not; the market relations are subjective and objective, abstract and concrete, formal and substantial, mediate and immediate. The labor time expended in production has a qualitative and a quantitative element in it; it is represented as an abstract space.

Marx (*Das Kapital*, I, ch. 1, sect. 4) wrote that the producers, in selling their labor time and capacity, convert the latter into a commodity. To the producers, he wrote, "the social relations of their private labors appear as what they are, that is, not as immediate social relations of persons in their labors, but rather as material relations of persons and social relations of things." The material relations of the persons are their substantive relations to one another, they being related in their social reproduction in that the processes of the material order are converted into goods which are used to supply human wants. The relations are at once nonmaterial, being thought, taught and learned, transmitted and humanly varied. The process of human reproduction by human means, of which the material supply of material wants is a part, is therefore abstract and concrete; in either case it is a social process of the human order, which is carried through by our labors; these labors are the substance of our reproductive process, varying in their form as bound and free; in the latter case they appear as labor hired for a wage and salary. Marx brought out the first of these conditions, the material and formal side; to these are to be added the nonmaterial conditions, which are both formal and substantial, in the process of human reproduction. Thus the greater the amount of training and other preparation of the producers in the reproduction process, the more mediate is their relation in production. Formally, the exchange of their labors against the supply of means to meet their wants is the same; yet the greater the degree of their preparation, training and education, the more intensive is their exploitation. That the mediate producers are highly paid does not alter the fact of their exploitation, or its qualitative augmentation.

The quality of unlike participants in the economic exchange is the result of the social organization, combination and division of labor; these processes are not relations of production alone, but of all the relations of human, social reproduction.

Marx criticized Aristotle's theory of exchange, saying that there is no concept of value to be found in the latter's writings on economics. This is imprecise, for the concept of value form is found there, but not the concept of the value substance, which is labor time and capacity. The value substance which Aristotle imputed to the value form is, in our modern nomenclature, indicated by use value; it is the capacity of the good exchanged to supply our want which provides its value substance. This is its exchange value substance, and is its usefulness. The objective value substance is the labor time and capacity expended in the production of a good; the exchange value has a twofold substance, the useful capacity of the good to supply our want and the labor time and capacity spent in producing it. The exchange value of a good is its concrete capacity to supply our want by our act of acquiring it in exchange for a good having an equal amount of the labor time and capacity, or substantive labor power, in its production. Marx, although he made an advance over Aristotle's theory of value, did not distinguish between the objective value of the production of a good and its exchange value. The two value expressions are brought together in practice in the capitalist economy which he had as the subject of his analysis. However, the theory of value is not limited to a particular economic and social condition. The law of objective, economic value of production extends over all phases of civil society and over all the history of the social economy, in ancient Asia, in classical antiquity, in feudal Europe, and in capitalism. Marx's contribution to this discussion was his distinction between value form and substance, with respect to exchange value. We undertake the investigation of the system of this form and substance, and examine it in reference to the exchange value, form and substance, the use value, form and substance, and production value, form and substance. (Marx, ibid., ch. 1, sect. 3).

The exchange value substance is, as we have seen, twofold; unless a good supplies the want of the one who acquires it, an exchange for it does not take place. The want may be imaginary or have objective existence. This is the part of the exchange value substance which Aristotle brought out. It has been held to be subjective by some, but this is imprecise. The exchange value substance is objective; those who purchase a good acquire it in view of a want which it supplies. In some cases, this want is subjective, the will to possess it, or desire for it. The want maybe imaginary. These motives for acquisition of a good by purchase are normal; usually buying and selling are undertaken to supply an objective want in civil society; we allow a part of our wealth for the acquisition of goods to satisfy our subjective desires and imaginary wants. It is the mark of abnormal persons, that they expend a great amount of their wealth on goods which are intended solely to satisfy their subjective or imagined wants.

The use value is a form, the substance of which is the capacity of a good to supply a concrete, objective want. The usefulness of a concrete value substance enters mediately into the exchange value substance, and thereby into the exchange relation. The labor power has a form and a substance; wage labor sells its substantive labor power, or its time and productive capacity, capacity of distribution, and consumption, which make up its human substantive power of human reproduction, against a wage, and mediately against the means of its subsistence. Wage labor does not sell its formal labor power, but retains it. Marx formulated the concept of labor power and distinguished it from the concept of labor. The labor power has a form and substance, which are to be distinguished. In Aristotle's criticism of the economy of classical antiquity, the marketplace was denounced; he made an error of historical judgment in this case; the economy of the household, held to be natural by Aristotle, was set forth as an already outmoded model for human relations. His judgment of slavery is an error of another kind. He made the distinction between human and natural processes, but he did not carry through this distinction systematically, holding some men to be by nature slaves. But then they are not men; this is a formal contradiction in Aristotle. Men, women, barbarians are potentially or actually citizens of the polis, and in this sense political animals, in that they are human beings. This was recognized by many subjectively in classical antiquity, and was acknowledged objectively in the Code of Justinian.

An economic exchange takes place in civil society between parties having the formal power to engage in the purchase and sale of the goods exchanged. The exchange is therefore a relation of buying and selling between juridical persons in this sense. There are other senses in which the term, juridical person, is applied, for example in the political sense of citizen in civil society, but these fall outside our present discussion; the buyer and seller may or may not be citizens, but have an acknowledged power or right to buy and sell economic goods under given circumstances, which are socially and historically variable. Thus, the right or power of the stranger to come to a community and engage in selling and buying there may depend not on a civil right, but on the right of hospitality practiced in that community. The law of that community is particular and local; the peace of that community, or the right to sojourn there in peace and under the protection of the customs of the place is extended to those who are accepted by its inhabitants, and enjoy their neighborhood and society. The stranger has no such right, unless a representative of the group of local inhabitants extends to him a formal relation, in which the former is acknowledged to be as a friend, kin or neighbor of the one who extends the ceremonious relation. Thus, an injury done to the person or property of the stranger is as an injury done to the hospitable one, his kin or neighbors. The rights of these parties, community and stranger, are local, customary rights; they are not civil rights. The extension of a common law to many communities, cities, tracts and ways between them in a nation is an undertaking of civil society, right and law. It is universal within the national extent of the civil right and law of the given form of society, and the local, particular, customary right of hospitality to the stranger is made superfluous. The stranger under the law of hospitality comes as a merchant to trade, selling and buying; the goods he brings are useful to supply the wants of the receptive community, and the latter provides goods in exchange to supply wants in foreign parts; therefore the right of hospitality to the stranger is particularly useful, the extension of the human right of protection against inclemency of the weather, or the predatory beasts is generally so. The right of hospitality is generated on the margins of civil society, among communities which are in the process of developing trade relations, processes of mutual dependence for subsistence, mutual social relations and political relations; or else these communities are in the process of being comprised by powerful neighbors in the formation of the state. The stranger as trader is active in both processes of kinds as a marginal agent. With the transition to civil society, whether by internal or external means, the right of hospitality is then transformed, and the particularity disappears, being replaced by the universalized, civil right of protection. The human right in general remains.

The relation of mutuality is both general, as in the case of exchange, and particular, as in the case of hospitality, in human society. Exchange in the economic sense is an objective relation of reciprocation, in general of useful goods between persons. The reciprocation in this case is concrete in the meeting of concrete wants, and abstract in the meeting of the abstract ones. The goods exchanged are either like or unlike. If they are like, then a concrete and equal reciprocation is made in the immediate relation of exchange between the parties to it; if they are unlike, then in order to express their equality, an abstract measure is introduced. The reciprocity in this case is either that of concrete or of abstract equivalents in the exchange. The abstraction in this case is expressed by an equivalence of goods and services, and is applied both to concrete equals, abstract equals, or both, to likes and unlikes, concrete and abstract. The exchange is a formal relation, the substance of which is twofold, in respect of the use of goods in the supply of wants, and in respect of the time and capacity of labor in the production, distribution and consumption of the goods. The goods in question are social goods, either objectified in the product, or the self-objectifying labors of the human kind.

Mutuality came to be used for reciprocity in the early history of civil society, but here the distinction between the two is made; exchange is a kind of equal reciprocation in mutuality, or of equivalence. The mutuality is an n-adic relation, concrete reciprocation a dyadic one, in its formal side; in their abstraction and in their substance, mutuality and reciprocation are n-adic. The mutuality is extended reciprocation, the latter is the formal relation of mutuality in exchange. The economic exchange is a substantive relation between human beings in a formal relation between persons, in an objective reciprocation between them, which is abstract and concrete. The exchange as an abstraction has the formal expression of exchange value.

The exchange has a form and a substance; its form is expressed in the law of exchange as a reciprocation in mutuality of equals or equivalents, in the latter case of likes and unlikes, in the former of likes; the reciprocation in exchange in this process is objective and concrete in the supply of respective wants, either like or unlike, either abstract or concrete, between the parties to the exchange; the wants, their supply, and the exchange are objective; the exchange in question is not symbolic exchange, not ceremonial or ritual. The economic exchange is a substantive reciprocation of goods in mutuality between human beings, in a formal process between persons. The ritual and ceremonial goods supply no concrete want, but provide symbolic expression to another social relation between them, by their exchange. The symbolic exchange in the kula ring of the Trobriand Islands in traditional times was carried through without respect to social hierarchy between the parties to the exchange; the symbolic exchange of the potlatch of the Kwakiutl and other peoples of the Pacific Coast of North America in traditional times was carried through with social ranking, whereby the parties were placed in a hierarchy according to the amount of social wealth destroyed by each side in this form of exchange: the greater the amount destroyed, the higher the rank.

The law of exchange value, with respect to its form, was expressed by Aristotle as the relation of person A with respect to good a, in exchange with person B for good b. A is the owner of a, B the owner of b, and the exchange is of an economic kind, in equal or equivalent reciprocation between them. The commutative principle of exchange and the commutative law of arithmetic are applicable to the same relation. This relation holds for equal and for equivalent reciprocation, for the latter is the same principle applied both to likes and unlikes in economic exchange, for which an expression of an abstraction is called forth. The exchange value is a form, in a mediate relation to two substances, the usefulness of the goods exchanged, and the labor time and capacity embodied in them; the use value of the good is the immediate and proximate substance of the exchange value. Objective value in production and reproduction is cumulative and additive; use value is non-cumulative; exchange value has both elements as its substance, the additive and cumulative, and the non-cumulative. In its form, exchange value is the same as objective value in production, being additive and cumulative.

We distinguish in this respect between addition and cumulation. Addition is cumulative or not, whereas cumulation is additive, and not non-additive. In the Aristotelian theory of exchange, the exchange is equal if the want on one side is supplied by the other in reciprocity. This is an additive, non-cumulative process and is an expression of an equality between the parties to the exchange, not in relation to the goods exchanged, but in relation to the want which is met by the exchange. If A does not meet his want by his own labor or product, then he turns to B who supplies what A wants, and conversely, B turns to A to supply B's want.

The relation of production and consumption is abstract and concrete with respect to the wants and their supply in the process of human reproduction. The abstract relation is ongoing; its substance is abstract labor, and its form is abstract value in civil society. The concrete relation of production and consumption is work, whereby the product which is consumed is produced and given in exchange for another product, abstract or concrete to its consumer. The product which is consumed, whether theoretical or practical, is concrete in that it is consumed; the concretion of its consumption is independent of whether that product is abstract or concrete in its substance; formally it is concrete in that it is consumed in the process of human reproduction. The production of a concrete good which is consumed is human work; the production of an abstract good, which is furtherance of the process of production is abstract; it is abstract labor. The supply of the good which meets our want by being consumed is non-cumulative, for it disappears in consumption; it is a concrete act of supplying the good, regardless of whether it is a loaf of bread, or the enjoyment of a work of art. The good is variable, consumed or not; its supply is non-cumulative. The want is non-cumulative, for it disappears on being supplied. Our organic being continues to bring forth the same wants daily, and we learn also new wants, but their daily supply is non-cumulative in either case. If we move from the tropics to the polar zone we learn the want of warmth and how to meet it daily. The Inuit came to the polar zone from a warmer climate, and so did the peoples of the Tierra del Fuego. The concrete want and its supply are therefore concrete and non-cumulative, and the work of supplying the want is concrete and non-cumulative. The concrete processes in this case are additive, with a positive and negative valence; the negative is the want, and the positive is its supply, not in general, but in particular, in the individual case. The good a supplies want of it, a, and a zero state is provisionally achieved. This achievement is not final, for our human life goes on. The achievement is final and concrete with death, which is a physiological and not a human condition. The wants are human, variable and objective. Thus A's hunger is met by the loaf of bread which B supplies; but if B's hunger is greater than A's, then the amount of bread which A supplies him in return will not satisfy it; the want on either side is objective, and each will sicken and die if it is not met.

Plato held that the polis is constituted by the process of meeting the different wants of the human kind by many different kinds of labors. (*Republic* 369CD). No one is self-sufficient. The discussion of the means to establishment of just exchange in antiquity, and in the medieval period, led to the theory of value, and to the theory of prices, just, current, and other, unjust in various ways. For it was agreed that there can be no social intercourse if there is no exchange of economic goods with which the different parties to the exchange are satisfied. Aristotelians in the Middle Ages, Albertus Magnus and Thomas Aquinas, held various theories of the just exchange. They dealt with price, and only with the form and not the substance of the exchange; yet the medieval theorists had a clear idea of the exchange value form in relation to use value, and the relation between exchange and utility of goods in the process of economic exchange, which they developed out of the Aristotelian theory of exchange.

An explanation of the value of a good, apart from its substantive relation to the supply of a want has been attributed to Aristotle and to his medieval followers. If the formal expression of the value is relative to the capacity of a good, the value of which is being expressed, to meet a given want in equal measure to the capacity of another good to meet another want, then a theory of the exchange according to the commutative principle is brought out. We have not gotten an expression of the value substance in this respect. If we exchange unlikes, such as bread against shoes, or a house against a physician's services, then according to Aristotle we have taken up a proportion, bread to baker, shoes to shoemakers, and conversely, bread to the shoemaker, and shoes to the baker. Various forms of the exchange process are elicited by the expressions, arithmetic and geometric proportions, but they remain formalities, and do not bear on the value substance. The relation of the combination and division of labor by its social organization is brought out thereby; the difference between the autarchic community and civil society was expressed by Plato and Aristotle; but the geometric and arithmetic ratios and the principles of the kinds of particular justice, respectively distributive and commutative do not explain the difference between value and price, nor do they account for the difference between value form and value substance in economic exchange.

Albertus Magnus and Thomas Aquinas rendered Greek *chreía*, want, as *indigentia*. In either case, ancient Greek and medieval Latin, a particular want is held in view. Want or indigence are abstract and general; we also speak of particular wants as well as general want, but indigence and poverty both denote a general state. To meet a particular want, we exchange a particular good, which we have. In a condition of general want or indigence we can engage in no such exchange, for it is implied in theory that we have no goods to exchange. In practice we engage in the exchange poorly having insufficient goods to exchange. The good is a substantive labor power, or a product, which is the value substance.

The establishment of an equivalence between goods in an economic exchange is not effected by confirming their mutual capacity to meet the respective wants of those engaged in the exchange. The confirmation is objective, but the equivalence is established by another means, and the price by yet a third means. All those who partook in these discussions mentioned both objective and subjective factors in the exchanges; but only the ones which are objective and have been brought out by them have been developed here.

The equality of the exchange with respect to the meeting of wants is a concrete relation of equals. The want is an absence of some good, expressed as a negative factor on either side; the supply of the want of the good by the supply of the good is a positive, the presence of the good on the other. The result is a neutralization, or zero, by the cancellation of the positive by the negative. This is an addition of a positive and a negative, but it is not cumulative. For the want of food returns when the food is consumed, or shortly thereafter; however well we ate yesterday, we suffer hunger today; the meeting of the want is a non-cumulative process. By extension of the principle of additive, non-cumulative supply of wants, the commutative principle is then applied: A's want of good b is met by providing its owner, B, with good a, which B wants. Both the wants and the goods are cancelled out, the wants by their being supplied, and the goods by being consumed, that the want be supplied. A is not reduced to zero, but the want is, and this is the same for B. The production of goods is both additive and cumulative, the addition being positive and negative; multiplication is reduced not to the additive but to the cumulative process. Cumulation is additive serial addition. In addition without cumulation a + a = a; in addition with cumulation, 1 + 1 = 2, or a + a = 2a.

Accumulation is in theory a means of storing up the added and cumulated goods in a suitable concrete warehouse, and in an abstract system of units of account. Capital is accumulated in that it is concretely expressed in the exchange of goods, and abstractly expressed as a commodity, money. Abstractly, capital as a commodity is separated from the concrete good or ware, which is cumulated in the warehouse. It then appears to have a life of its own, undergoing self-valorization. This thought was expressed in reference to Marx's theory of accumulation of capital, "Capital is thus, by definition, value looking for accretion, for surplus value. But if capital produces surplus value, surplus value also produces additional capital." This is a fallacy of misattributed agency. Capital, value and surplus value are not agents or active factors, but forms of goods produced by labor; they produce no goods, and supply no wants, being passive states of the substance and qualities of labor, of exchange, and exploitation. Alice in the looking-glass world discovered that the King, Queen and members of the court were nothing but a pack of cards.

Subjective and objective factors are active in our exchanges. Thus in buying food, we may choose bread or potatoes or spaghetti, all of which have carbohydrates useful in our diets, and do not make our purchases of food or of any other goods without choices. The objective factor at work in this case is the want and need for sustenance of some kind; in buying in our supplies to meet our wants traditional, objective and subjective factors at work lead us to choose peas instead of carrots, or the search for novelty may lead us to choose blue cloth over green. The Austrian school has given prominence to the factor of choice in the market for the purchase of our supplies in exchanges; no doubt the factor singled out by that school of thought is at work in the world of commodities, market, price, exchange and exchange value. The Marxists have analyzed the exchange value in the world of commodities and exchange, and single out the objective factors of labor time and use value. Concrete exchanges in bourgeois society take place with all these factors at work. The freedom of choice in the exchanges is a formal, not a substantive freedom. This matter is examined elsewhere in our work. The practice of exchanges is an objective fact, which is analyzed into objective and subjective factors and moments, and theories to account for the practices and their motives are then erected, which account for one or another aspect of the process of exchange and value. These are here brought together, and the subjective motive in the exchange is separated from the objective value determinant.

Things are active and passive in nature; objects apart from human beings are active in the human order, and are at once the recipients of human actions; their activities as material things take place in another order of nature than the human order. The social relations of the human kind are the relations of human beings, who are subjects and objects, or the subject-object. Economic exchange in civil society, both in ancient times and modern, is a formal relation between persons, the substance of which is the goods they exchange. The form is separated from the substance in this transaction, the form being the juridical and political relation of freedom and equality between the parties to the exchange and the power to engage in the exchange as a right. The formal exchange is not a social relation between human beings in their labors, for this implies that the form is not separated from the substance; the social relation of exchange takes place between juridical persons. We distinguish between human beings and persons, and between goods and things. If we alienate to another our labor time and capacity as a commodity, then it is as though these, our substantive labor power, are the same as a material good. They are in fact in the form of an object sold and bought. But the substantive power is not an object alone, for it is part of our living human substance, of our wakeful and conscious day; it is therefore subjective and objective in its substance. It is handled as a material object, but it is both material and non-material. Hence we make a part of ourselves into an object, in commodity form, and separate within ourselves the object from the subject, the material from the nonmaterial, and the form from the substance. Marx wrote in this sense that commodity fetishism, which includes wage labor, is a material relation between persons, which covers a part of the ground; to this he added that it is a social relation between *Sachen*, materials, or things. This is an imprecise formulation, and is superfluous. Wage labor is not material or thingly. They who sell their labor time and capacity for a wage may subjectively feel that they are treated as things, and that it is a thing which they sell, but it is not so. Objectively, wage labor is not a tool, an instrument, a work animal, or another means of production; not even the ancient Roman slave was such. The slave was a defective juridical person, and at once a human being, for all that he or she was deprived of the rights of a citizen. As a human being the slave had the powers of speech, thought and revolt.

In the analysis of the exchange of substantive labor power by wage labor we affirm that exchange is a social process between human beings who are in a formal relation of juridical persons. The substance of the relation is the human reproduction of the human kind; the human beings have relations to one another, which are material and non-material, an objective, a subjective, a concrete and an abstract relation, a human relation, also an inhuman one, a social and anti-social relation. The process is productive and the productivity is augmented and diminished; we are diremptive and self-dirempted, and both immediately and mediately alienated from our products and from ourselves. The inventiveness of the workers is diminished, in the process of capital formation by wage labor, and the workers' initiative deformed. That which contributes to the greater productivity, humaneness, comfort and health is routinized, bureaucratized, and generated from without, or from above down. Labor becomes banal; it is *pro forma* free, hence objectively free; but it is in its substance, hence objectively and subjectively unfree. While it is a human activity, it is dehumanized. Hence to many labor in all its forms is opposed to freedom, which is false. The substantive unfreedom of labor is twofold. It is unfree in its substance in that it is exploited, and is unfree in that it is routinized, divided and combined in a way that is separate from the will and consciousness of the working class. Perhaps for this reason, the theorists of the division of labor in society talk only of the division, and not of the combination and division of labor. The division is striking to the observer, and the effects on the workers no less so. When we speak of the combination of labor we have not only the communal combination in mind, for labor is social in its organization, combination and division in civil society.

Marx opposed the private to the social labors in production, whereas all labor is social in class society, civil and bourgeois, insofar as it supplies a social want. The social relations of producers in their labors to this end are mediate and immediate; the exchange of the labors for a wage is the exchange of the substantive labor power for the means of subsistence in a mediate relation between them. This is a formal privatization in the capitalist economy, yet in its substance, the social character of the labors is not thereby lost. Labor in the process of capital formation is opposed to communal labors. This condition of labor, not the labor itself, is social, therefore. Its condition is social in two senses; one, in an immediate sense, that labor is engaged in an individual transaction for the sale of labor time and capacity against a wage; and two, in a mediate sense, in which all wage labor enters into the formation of capital, hence is exchanged, alienated and exploited. Exchange as such is not anti-social.

Private labor is a particular, formal category of social labor under the historical condition in which wage labor and capital predominate. There are other forms of labor in this condition than the private. The material object continues to be active in the material order of nature, while it suffers human transformation and action on it; the action of the first kind is direct, and of the other kind mediate. The social labor by being privately sold and bought as labor time and capacity continues to be what it was, social labor in its immediate and substantive relation in production, while it is sold in a mediate and formal relation to the process of social production, and therewith of human reproduction. The formality and substantiality, mediacy and immediacy in these processes are relative, that being formal and mediate in one relation which is substantive and immediate in another. Whether the sale is private or public is irrelevant in this connection, for the exchange and commodity relation of labor and capital obtains in either case. In either case, private or public, labor time and capacity are sold in exchange for a wage which is then converted by the seller into the means of subsistence. The means of production are held in a formal and mediate relation between the owners and controllers thereof on the one side, and social labor on the other; the means of subsistence are held in another formal and mediate relation between the owners and controllers on the one side, and social labor on the other. Ownership is but one means of control over the means of production and subsistence, among others. Private ownership over both is predominant in the capitalist mode of production, and public ownership was predominant during the history of the Soviet system; these are both social modes of the formation of capital, or the means of conversion of the means of social production into capital, which is the same. The social processes of capital formation and of industrial production in either case are determined by the relations of social labor which sells its labor time and capacity, or its substantive labor power, immediately against a wage or a salary, and mediately against the means of subsistence.

Sometimes it is said that a good is supposed to meet a demand for it; the demand is then held to be subjective, and the supply in relation to the want objective. Yet we see that the relations of demand and supply are formal, and of want and supply are substantive; all are subjective and objective.

If it is labor that is supplied, then it is unfree or free *pro forma*. Unfree labor is labor which is bought and sold by another person. There is a condition in which free labor may sell itself, and that is by selling itself, its formal and substantial labor power into slavery, in which case it cancels its freedom, and is unfree in form and substance. The owner of the labor in this case is other than the laborers themselves, and the relation of the owner to the unfree labor is without stint, being bounded only by physiological processes of fatigue, infirmity and death. The labor then takes its objective revenge, for its productivity is less than that of labor which is *pro forma* free; this was already known to Adam Smith. The product of unfree labor may be consumed within the social unit in which it is produced, without further distribution or sale, as it was on the slave plantation or feudal barony; or it may be sold. If it is in its socially predominant amount sold then it is a commodity; this was the case in the American south, down to the Civil War. The product was converted into capital, for the plantation as the means of production was a form of capital, and the slaves were capitalist slaves. This is a contradiction without sense, a formal contradiction which was obliterated by the victorious northern armies. As in the case of wage labor, the substantive labor power of the slave or serf is a commodity if the product thereof is a commodity; the formal labor power, or the right of disposition of the social substance thereof, is in the control of its legal owner, the slave master or feudal lord.

Wage labor sells its substantive labor power as its owner; the substantive labor power is then a commodity; this is the labor time, skills and knowledge of the laborer. The formal labor power is not sold.

The equality of the exchange then takes on a new form; it is the formal equality of the formally free juridical persons who sell to, and buy from, one another. The labor time and quality bought and sold are not equal, nor is their materialization in their respective products. They are rendered into an abstract equivalence in the system of abstract, objective social value. The seller and purchaser of the labor quantity and quality are each *pro forma* equal and *pro forma* free, juridically, and therefore socially and economically. The juridical freedom and equality have been appropriated and internalized by social labor in the capitalist mode of production. By making them its own and internalizing them, social labor then is able to overturn the mode of production of capital in all its forms. The relations of the superstructure of society then determine the relations of the economy, the form determines the mode of production. Or, to put the same thought in another way, the consciousness is the determining factor in the social relations of production, and not the determinate of these relations. Exchangeability of the labor quantity and quality is determined by the social factors of formal freedom and formal equality of wage and salaried labor with the purchaser of the labor quantity and quality, or the substantive labor power.

The labors of human beings are social processes between them. If we make the time and capacity of these labors into commodities then we separate the form from the substance thereof. A is then *pro forma* free to sell good a to B, in exchange for good b, both being owners of their respective goods. In the process of capital formation, a is the substantive labor power, b is the means of human reproduction of A and B. This is the exploitation of A; the difference between the social product of A and the amount thereof which is set aside for the maintenance and reproduction of B, which is other than A, is expressed as alienated surplus value. Surplus value is the expression of the social product which is not consumed or immediately reproduced in the social economy; it is in part an expression of the process of capital formation, but not all of the excess product is taken away from production, some part being returned. The alienated surplus value is an expression of the portion of the social product which is neither immediately nor mediately reproduced in the social economy.

Aristotle, *Nicomachean Ethics*, Book V, ch. 5.
Karl Marx, *Capital*, 2nd ed., Book I, ch. I, sect. 34.
————, Ibid. Book III, ch. 48.
————, *Grundrisse der Kritik der politischen Oekonomie*, Berlin, 1953, pp. 354–374.
————, *Theorien über den Mehrwert*, Vol. 3, ch. 21.

Appendix II. Value and the Mental Process

If we assign a value, whether in the objective or the subjective sense, to a thing, we give meaning to it doubly; first, the act of valuing it is meaningful, and second, the thing becomes an object which has meaning for us. The thing enters our human world, and is no longer a foreign piece of matter. The act of valuing it may be subjective; in this case it is a mental process of all the human kind, for subjectivity includes our will, desire, and aims, which all people have, whether in the primitive or the civil condition of human society. Objective valuation by measurement of the amount of labor time and capacity in the production of a good, and ascertainment of its use in the expression of its use value are processes of mental effort in civil society; we give meaning to the objects valued thereby, and give meaning not only to the fact of our labors but also to their quantitative measure; we give meaning to a thing by expressing its use value, which is to objectify it in yet another way. The ascertainment of its usefulness is a general process which is found in all societies, primitive and civil alike; its expression as use value is particular to civil society, for it connects to exchange value.

The assignment or discovery of meaning in the thing and in our relation to it is a complex mental act; it bears on the purpose it will serve us, with which it is now endowed. For the only purpose it serves is that which we attribute to it; otherwise it has none, purpose and aim being human acts alone. The meaning bears on our estimation of its significance, great or small, to us. Aside from intention and signification, the two chief acts in relation to meaning, we may assign many more; intention and signification are attributed to sense and reference in meaning. We do not always mean by subjective value what J. A. Schumpeter, P. Sweezy and L. v. Mises mean by the term, and do not mean by objective value what Marx always means. In all cases, however, the writers mentioned perceive or imply that valuation is a meaningful act, and that meaning is a valuative one. The terms, meaning and value, overlap, although they are not identical. We state what we intend in these matters.

Valuation becomes a mental process through the meaning, intention and significance, which we attribute to labor and the products of labor. Meaning is a mental process to begin with which is concretely and particularly applied, among others, in the valuative processes mentioned above.

Appendix III. On the Market Economy in Russia and China

The draft of this formulation of value theory was completed in May 1983, at a time when the Soviet economy appeared to be unshakable. This notion was overtaken by the events of August 1991–October 1993, when two separate but interrelated processes, the one national and political, the other economic, took place in Russia. In the national and political sphere, the Baltic republics and the Ukraine have broken away from Russia, and the Soviet rule over Poland, Bulgaria, Hungary, Czechia, Slovakia and east Germany has come to an end. After a period of indecision, Russian domination has been reimposed over Belarus, Armenia, Georgia, and Azerbaijan. The future of Moldova is uncertain. The central Asian region is in flux; Kazakhstan, Uzbekistan and Turkmenistan are seeking a way out from the Russian sphere of influence, but Tajikistan, under the menace of the Afghan Tajik Uzbek attacks from the Afghanistan side, has returned to the Russian sphere. Kirgizstan remains outside, and is now independent. Chechenia, the Ingush region and Tatarstan present potent problems of national sovereignty in both respects, the economic, and the political. The Chechens and Azerbaijanis are centers of Mafia activity in Moscow and other big cities. The large Russian populations of Kazakhstan, Ukraine and Moldova threaten the national sovereignty in those countries.

The Marxists ignored the national problem, Luxemburg having declared that Ukrainian nationhood was an invention of a few poets, journalists and schoolteachers. The Ukraine is a nation under siege, being forced to buy gas and oil from the Russians at world market prices. But now, if in exchange for an agreement on the partial destruction of atomic weapons, the Ukraine can purchase fossil fuels at prices internal to the Russian economy, this will ease the Ukrainian economic strain, and lower the inflation rate; but it will chain the Ukrainian economy for the present term to the Russian, and cast doubt on Ukrainian aspirations to national sovereignty. The two tokens of Ukrainian sovereignty, military, meaning the questions of the atomic weapons and control over part of the Black Sea fleet, and territorial, meaning control over the Crimea, are already problematical, although the Crimea still is nominally in Ukrainian hands. In the long term, Ukraine will break permanently with Russia; the long term is measured in generations or centuries.

The headlong drive of the Russians to privatize their economy has been slowed by two chief and entirely foreseeable factors. The first of these is the actions of the ruling class in controlling the rate and direction of privatization; the second is the fate of the military-industrial complex, which is, of course, bound to the first, as the tail to the dog; in this case, the tail is big enough to wag the dog. The ruling class of higher party ranks, industrial managers, and regional overlords consents to the transition from public to private ownership and control over industry, finance centers, transport and communication, agriculture, and the markets for consumers, on condition that it is able to ride out the stormy period of transformation. The depredations of the Stalin period, and stagnation of the Brezhnev period were followed by the first two stages of transition, one, the stage of *glasnost'* and *perestroika*, leading to the putsch of August 1991, and two, the stage in which shock therapy of unbridled privatization alternates with pity for the pensioners.

The privatization has let loose the dogs of the Mafia, who are the new entrepreneurs. Criminality was first hidden by lies, but now is publicly recognized. This is but a stage in capitalist development. The criminals will seek the protection of the law, will gain acknowledgment by the government of their ill-gotten gains, will be able to bequeath their fortunes on their passing to their heirs and assigns, and will be legitimized in their status as capitalists and members of the ruling class. Russia recapitulates the history of capitalism in Europe and America. Russian privatization has been limited to the spheres of distribution and exchange of consumer goods; whole regions, as Nizhny Novgorod, have gone over to private enterprise, but the record of privatization is generally sporadic, because banking and finance are still in the public sector, agriculture has scarcely been touched, and the military-industrial complex not at all; the big employers and big centers of capital, such as the railroads, air transport and communications will continue to be owned and controlled by the State, supported by grants and subsidies; they will be placed in private hands only as and when the ruling class figures out a way to move safely into the new period, with its control over the private industry, finance and the military-industrial complex reduced but still intact.

During the transitional period which has just now begun, the way is open for adventurers, such as Zhirinovsky, briefly to flourish. Zhirinovsky has put a welcome weapon into the hands of the marshals, generals, and industrial managers in the military complex. His boasts, threats, and appeals to wounded national pride provide the excuse the marshals need to force Yeltsin's hand; thus, Poland is at present disappointed in its hopes for acceptance as a full member of NATO; Russia at the marshals' instigation has vetoed the Poles' aspirations in this regard; Russia declares that it feels threatened by a line drawn by NATO which excludes it. Russians and Ukrainians in Moldova are given support by the military, who avow that Tiraspol is Russian forever. Georgia pleads to be allowed to join the SNG as the price paid for Russia's help in ending internal strife and the war with the Abkhazians. The Azerbaijanis beg for Russian support to end the war with Armenia over Nagorny Karabakh. The Russian army is active in defense of the frontier in Tajikistan, Turkmenistan and Azerbaijan; the army is an internal defense against warlordism; the country has no need of a new Petlyura or Ungern Sternberg. The losers in this upsurge of influence in the hands of the military-industrial complex are: 1. Internal to Russia, the private interests and the Russian people as a whole, who seek to better their standard of living; the Russian economy does not merely stagnate, but is temporarily deteriorating. The army and the weapons industry continue to tax the Russian economy heavily; Yeltsin raised the officers' pay shortly before the election of December 12, 1993; his effort was, however, vain, for they voted in large numbers for Zhirinovsky, who has a fraction in the new Duma. 2. External to Russia, the losers are the republics of Lithuania, Latvia, Estonia, Poland, and Ukraine, who feel the undiminished Russian threat. Yeltsin rediscovers his social conscience, declaring that the poor, the beggars, the aged, and the sick have suffered too much from the impetuous race toward privatization; the pace must be slowed. Decoded, this means that the ruling class in Russia gains temporary relief from the pressure of foreign bankers to introduce a market economy, and to place banking and industry in private hands; the industrial managers and Russian bankers will move more slowly to privatize certain industrial sectors, such as soap and cosmetics, textiles, shoes and household furniture manufacture, while postponing privatization of heavy industry and finance, as they hope, forever. Gaidar is an honest man, for he states that the inclusion of Belarus in the Russian ruble zone will further tax the Russian economy, industry, consumer and taxpayer alike. Belarus is an economic disaster zone, poor, and entirely in the hands of the former Communists, now the partyless rulers of the country; they will not privatize their economy.

We do not conduct an international class analysis, but an analysis by country. The Ukrainian nationalism is undoubtedly existent, and so is the nationalism of the Lithuanians, Latvians, Poles, and Estonians; nationalism is bound up with nationhood, sovereignty and independence. Ukrainian nationhood is not based in history on Khmelnitsky, Shevchenko and the ribald letter of the Cossacks in answer to the Turkish Khan. It is founded on nothing like the sentimental feelings of the intelligentsia ridiculed by Luxemburg. Ukrainian nationalism has real roots in the forced famine of 1930–1933, purges, executions, incarcerations and exile, from the 1920s on, numbering in the millions, in every family, and every village. In its ideological expression, L'vov leads the way, but Kiev, Odessa, Zhitomir and Vinnitsa are not far behind. Khar'kov, the Donbass, and Crimea are dubious participants in this assertion of Ukrainian nationalism because of the large proportions of

Russians there.

Nationalism, nationhood, sovereignty and independence are real, existent, and profoundly felt among the Israelis and the Palestinians. The European left derides the Israeli nationalism as the invention of western imperialism, first English and now American; the left in Europe and in the Japanese leftist scene merely show how little they understand of history, society, humanity, psychology, and politics. The peoples of the Near East, as the peoples of Eastern Europe, have a national identity as the result of positive feelings stemming from their historical traditions, and religious creeds, and of negative feelings stemming from persecutions, genocide in the case of the Jews, wars, incarcerations and exile on both sides, Israeli and Palestinian. The European left has at the same time produced great figures, such as Karl Liebknecht, who in 1914 voted against the war credits in the German Reichstag, standing alone, a noble gesture of a deep and great character, equal in stature to his commiliton, Rosa Luxemburg.

The American left has its own heroic figure, Eugene Victor Debs, who fought against the American entry into the European war in 1917. The Germans now honor Liebknecht and Luxemburg in an attempt to grasp their own past. The Americans have not yet achieved this level of historical consciousness. But the activity of Debs proves that Sombart was wrong in asking why there was no socialist movement in America. The action of Debs shows that there was no *corrupt* socialist movement in America, 1914–1918; this is added to the freedom from corruption on the part of Liebknecht and Luxemburg. They all fought against the war carried on by the military-industrial complex which brought death into the world and all its woe. But they did not act in concert. The actions of Luxemburg, Liebknecht and Debs against the war were practical, and concrete, but isolated. The antiwar conferences of the socialists at Zimmerwald and elsewhere were internationally represented, but they were abstract and theoretical. They did nothing to arouse the Russians, the English, the Germans, the French, the Austrians against the slaughter motivated by mindless patriotism and hunger for profits of the military industrial complex.

Karl Marx was the most brilliant and profound social thinker, critic, economist, and philosopher of his time. His system of value was not original with him, but was developed in an original way out of the earlier contributions by others, some of whom have been mentioned. It is erroneous in many respects, and one-sided in others, but its critique represents a good point of departure for further development. There is nothing to criticize since then, for his followers simply repeat dogmatically what he wrote, and his enemies reject his theory out of hand. Its inadequacies are evident, as are its strengths; we have considered both; he carried forward objective value theory up to a point, which we have stated. After a century, we have begun not anew, but have taken up the theory of objective and subjective value, once again, in consideration of what Marx, Schumpeter and Sweezy, Böhm-Bawerk and L. v. Mises had to say. Marx made difficulties for himself as a social theorist. His view of society was reductive, for he considered only objective factors, the subjective being set aside by him, and the sole objective factor he considered was class consciousness of the proletariat; the conflict between the public and private spheres of civil society was ignored, national consciousness was scorned by him. Society was reduced by him to the social classes, popular tradition, religion and national identity counting as nought; the social classes were reduced to class oppositions within the political arena, and politics to party politics by the Marxists and their opponents. The European left does not realize that it is the captive of the very political system it seeks to overthrow. The party system is the product of political battles in England and France in the 18th century, aristocratic and bourgeois, its scope and methods being determined by those battles and by the political institutions erected to carry them on. More exactly, the political party is the offspring of the beginnings of industrial capitalism, arising in England in the middle and late 18th century, then spreading to America, together with the new form of capitalism. It is not the offspring of mercantile capitalism of the 16th, 17th and early 18th century, but arose only out of the consciousness of the incipient industrial capitalist class in opposition to the aristocrats. The European left has not considered critically how it is that a party system, socialist, or communist, arising out of the history of its class enemies, should serve as a model for the construction of socialist society and world, or provide the leadership for such a society, and the left in America has shown no more critical acumen in this regard. The party system everywhere is corrupted by the lust for money, power, glory; it attracts people to it of this sort, on the right and on the left, who have no other motives than these, and who win out over the noble characters I have mentioned. Those who do not know their own history are not condemned to repeat it, for nothing repeats itself; there is no return to the past. But they will continue to act vainly, destroying the very means to the ends they seek. The past has meaning to us for the symbols it provides, which guide our actions. At last a monument to the brave sailors at Kronstadt who fought mightily for freedom will be erected in Russia.

Private capital and wage labor now rule the world. The word *now* does not mean "forever." Russia and China have joined the capitalist economy, while the ruling class in each case does what the ruling class in the other countries seeks to do, namely, to preserve itself and to retain control over the state power; the ruling class in Russia and China has the further problem of presiding over the transition from public to private capitalization of industry and finance, which is contrary to the prognoses of Marx and Schumpeter.

We do not take Marx's formulations on value theory as the first word on the subject, nor the last, but as a contribution to value theory. His conflation of value in production with value in exchange can perhaps be accounted for by the immense power of exchange and contract, and the expansive might of capital in his time. With the eradication of slavery in the American south, all capitalist countries became countries of wage labor from the 1860s on. Whereas the beginnings of industrial capital are found in the late 18th century, its full development was undertaken in the mid-19th century; the setback of private capital in Russia and China now has been made good, for the market economy is fostered not only in Moscow, St. Petersburg and Nizhny Novgorod, but also in Canton, Shen Zhen and Fujian; Deng Hsiaobing has declared that his great mistake was to delay the opening of Shanghai to private investment until 1993; this means also the opening of the Yangtze river ports of Wuhan and beyond, to Sichuan, to private investment. Marx interpreted exchange value as though it were the same as production value; production and exchange are distinct processes, and their value expressions are distinguished from one another. It is only under given historical circumstances that they coincide. When these diverge, the value expressions separate.

There are two processes to be taken up, privatization and exchange; thus, privatization has come to predominate over public ownership, and exchange value has swallowed up, in practice, not in theory, value in production. Gerashchenko and Zaveryukha are fighting a rearguard operation on behalf of State control over banking and finance in the one case and over agriculture in the other. We are not concerned with these power struggles, but with the theory indicated; the chief elements of the theory before us are the oppositive relation between the public and the private spheres of civil society and the distinction between production and exchange, together with their respective value expressions. We eschew all schemas of their conflation. Further, we have presented in outline the theory of objective and subjective value, the theory of value, in relation to price and to the market, and the difference and nexus between value in production, value in exchange, and value in use. There is no necessary connection between privatization and the conflation of exchange value and production value, but only such a one which occurs under particular historical conditions. By referring to capital, exchange and contract we do not personify them, but use a shorthand in reference to capitalists, exchangers, and contractors, including wage labor in the last two categories, as opposed to the first.

Notes

Note 1

Our task is to present a theory of value. We cite Marx with regard to value theory because he has contributed more than anyone else to its social, objective side. He did not present a rounded theory of objective value, and he did not take up subjective value theory. He did not formulate the theory of use value well, and he did not distinguish between exchange value and value in production. Yet he made great strides forward over Locke, Petty, Smith and Ricardo, who were his forerunners in this field of theory. Since his time, objective and subjective value theory alike have become caught in the toils of political antagonisms, Marx's followers having engaged in dogmatic assertions and fulminations against their enemies, who in turn have hurled vile words and arguments with little substance against the Marxists.

Some of these difficulties are owed to Marx. In the *Grundrisse*, Einleitung, 2 (MEGA², II. 1.1., p. 26) Marx wrote of the general relation of production to distribution, exchange and consumption. However, to this it is to be added that exchange is a kind of distribution, and that the general term for this process is reproduction in civil society, in which the chief form of distribution is exchange with the use of money. Marx proceeded (ibid. p. 27): production is immediately consumption of two kinds, objective and subjective; and consumption is immediately production. "The product receives its last finish in consumption." A railroad is only a railroad *dynamei* if it is not travelled on, not used up, not consumed; it is not a railroad in reality. Production is potential and real. His argument is incomplete, because the pair with potentiality is actuality; these two together make up reality. Marx then wrote: without production no consumption, but also no consumption without production, which would then be purposeless. "Consumption produces production doubly: 1. In that the product becomes a real product in consumption. E.g., a dress becomes a real dress only by the act of wearing it." Here Marx's argument has lost its course. The act can exist *actu* or *in posse*. Actuality and activity are not the same, for whereas the existence of activity *dynamei* is posited, the existence of actuality *dynamei* is not. Thus there is the dilemma in Marx: Suppose for a moment that a woman owns two dresses. Only one of them would be a real dress; it is the one she is wearing; for while she is wearing it, the other fades into unreality. Marx would have served his own purposes better by not equating actuality and activity. Marx continues, "for product is production not only as objective activity, but also only as object for the active subject. 2. In that consumption creates the need for new production." (Ibid, p. 28). Marx has only objective consumption in view, for both types, (1) and (2) are of this kind, even though in the first case he speaks of the active subject. For the subject does not act as the subject save in the formal sense, as e.g., the legal subject. The subject does not act subjectively according to our desires, volitions, arbitrary choices, and on other subjective grounds in Marx's conceptualization. Had Marx added the subjective act in the latter sense to his theory, this would not perhaps have forestalled the attack against him by the Austrian school of subjective value, but he would have prepared a broader foundation for value theory. As it is, we have incorporated a part of his formulations in the system which we here present, bearing in mind both the changes we have indicated; and the addition of subjective value theory.

E. v. Böhm-Bawerk, *Zum Abschluss des Marxschen Systems*, 1896, represented the school of subjective value, or marginal utility. He found a contradiction in value theory between volumes I and III of Marx's *Kapital*. The contradiction is examined in terms of four arguments (Böhm-Bawerk, op. cit., ch. 3): the sum of production prices of the commodities produced equals the sum of their values (MEW 25, p.169); the law of value controls the movement of prices (MEW 25, p.189 and 186); the law of values controls the exchange of commodities; the law of value regulates at least indirectly and ultimately the production prices. In relation to the last point, the total surplus value regulates the average profit and the general rate of profit. (MEW 25, p. 189.) Further, total profit and total surplus value have identical magnitudes. The average profit and the total surplus value are the same, (MEW 25, pp.182f.), distributed through the mass of capital in each sphere of production according to their relative magnitude. The contradiction between v. I and III of *Kapital* derives from the definition of value as labor capacity or labor power; the value of the labor power is directed like any other commodity by the working time necessary for its reproduction. (Böhm-Bawerk, op. cit., ch. 1.)

We distinguish production and exchange. Production in civil society is expressed in terms of production value and is measured by labor time and labor capacity. The labor capacity is an expression of labor skill, which is developed by training, and preparation, both formal and informal, in the public school system and on the job, in higher education, in the sciences, in technical training, etc. Exchange is a relation of buying and selling, whether by barter or the use of money and credit, of equal or equivalent amounts of goods. Value in exchange expresses a relation of economic, not symbolic exchange; this economic act presupposes the production of useful goods. The exchange value of goods is the expression of two value formulations, value in use and value in production. Each of the formulations expresses an act in the economy of civil society; value in production expresses what it says it does; use value is the expression of the usefulness of goods, among which labor time and capacity are numbered. A good is by definition socially useful in meeting a want or need, as food, drink, clothing, etc. A good is converted into a commodity by the exchange process which normally occurs in the market place where the exchange is transacted. Exchange value is there converted into a price, whether in terms of a concrete good or an abstraction, money. One house may be exchanged against five beds; the price of the house is then five beds; the price may be expressed in money terms, $500, and the price of the beds, $100 each. The price may vary in a general way around the value in production of a good, but it is also determined by supply in excess, scarcity, fashion and other subjective moods of the public, changes in technology, such as ease or difficulties of transport and communication, etc.

The school of objective value begins with value in production, and seeks to account for exchange value and price thereby. This is erroneous on two counts, first, exchange value is an expression of use value and production value; exchange value is not the same as the latter alone; second, price is determined by market conditions and by production relations, but may vary sharply from the latter by fundamental market effects, such as oversupply or scarcity; government controls and lack of them have a strong influence on market conditions. The Marxists, beginning with Marx, have failed to distinguish production from exchange, production value from exchange value, and value from price. The subjective school of value has eliminated all thought of objective value, or labor value in production, and deals only with market and price; their approach to value theory is one-sided, as is the Marxist.

Profits and costs are not terms in value theory, but are expressed in money terms, as are prices; we set barter aside. Prices, profits and costs of goods and labors differ from the practices in economics as well as in value theory. The factor of costs has been erroneously introduced into the labor theory of value by Ernest Mandel, Introduction to Karl Marx, *Capital*, vol. 1, 1976, p. 73. L. v. Bortkiewicz sought to distinguish the mathematical calculation of value and price, not their theory, as here set forth. Paul Sweezy, Introduction to Böhm-Bawerk, op. cit., 1975, p. xxiii, equated surplus value and profit, another error in theory. Sweezy, however, then wrote, op. cit., p. xxiv, "C + V + (C + V) p = price of production where c represents the investment in plant and materials, v the investment in wages, and p the average rate of profit." He held that this method is flawed in Marx. Input is here measured in values, output in prices of production. "Obviously this is not right. A large part of today's output becomes tomorrow's input, and it is clear that, to be consistent, they must be measured in the same terms." This is correct as far as it goes; Sweezy failed, however, to distinguish production from market relations, and value terms in the former from money terms in the latter.

Use value is the expression of the usefulness of a good. Production value, or value for short, is objective value in social production, which is measured in the amount of labor time and capacity expended in production of useful goods. Exchange value is a complex expression of the use values of goods in an exchange relation and the production values of the goods. Social reproduction has the parts of production, distribution and consumption in it; exchange, we have seen, is a kind of distribution; in civil society, the circulation of money is part of the exchange process, in which subjective factors, expressed by subjective values have their place.

Market relations are particular to a market economy, in which money, prices, buyers and sellers, and contract for buying and selling are present; this kind of exchange relation is sporadically found in primitive society, and is systematically developed in civil society. Production value is applicable to the latter; it is also applicable to a socialist economy in theory, without the market, price and contractual relation.

These terms of reference are not set down dogmatically nor are they motivated by political considerations. They are what they say they are, definitions of terms, no more and no less. They have been presented to audiences in Berlin, Canada, India, and Mexico, on repeated occasions in all these places, to people who were heartily glad to hear them. I am deeply grateful for the chance to present them and for the response to them.

The whole of the social product comes from labor alone, and is the work of social labor; the value expression is the form of social labor in civil society, and in that expression there is nought but labor. John Locke said, "For 'tis Labour indeed that puts the difference of value on every thing."—Here it is presupposed that labor is social labor, is objectively valued, and is the expression of relations historically limited to civil society. Labor is not the same as the class of immediate producers, and these do not constitute a social class. The whole of value is the expression of the relation of labor in society, and this expression comprises the form of activity in social reproduction by the classes of mediate and immediate producers, who make the class of social labor. Excluded thereby are those engaged in exchange alone, consumption alone, or who fall outside the reproduction process. Those engaged in distribution are partly within the production, partly within the exchange process in civil society. Labor indeed puts a value on itself and all our products; the system of value has the difference and the nexus of the quantity of values for its parts.

Note 2

Albertus Magnus, *Commentaries on Aristotle's Ethics and Politics*.

Aquinas, Thomas, *Commentaries on Aristotle's Ethics and Politics*.

———, *Summa Theologica*, II, II.

Aristotle, *Nicomachean Ethics*, Book V. Idem. Politics, Book I.

Baldwin, J. W., The medieval theories of the just price. *Transactions American. Philosophical Society*, n.s., vol. 49, pt. 4, 1959.

Berle, A. A. and G. C. Means, *The Modern Corporation and Private Property*, 1933.

Böhm-Bawerk, E. v., *Karl Marx and the Close of his System*, R. Hilferding, L. v. Bortkiewicz. P. Sweezy ed. 1949.

Borkenau, F., Zur Soziologie des mechanistischen Weltbildes. *Zeitschrift für Sozialforschung*, Vol. I. 1932, pp. 310–335.

Bortkiewicz, Ladislaus v., *Wertrechnung und Preisrechnung in Marxchen System*, (1906f.) 1976.

Brentano, Lujo, *Der wirtschaftende Mensch in der Geschichte,* 1923.

Cannan, Edwin, *A History of the Theories of Production and Distribution in English Political Economy, from 1776 to 1848,* 3rd ed., 1917.

Commons, J. R., *Legal Foundations of Capitalism,* 1924.

Dobb, Maurice, *Theories of Value and Distribution Since Adam Smith,* 1978.

————, *Studies in the Development of Capitalism,* Rev. ed. 1963.

Freyer, Hans, *Die Bewertung der Wirtschaft im philosophischen Denken des 19. Jahrhunderts,* 1921.

Gelesnoff, W., (V. Zheleznov). Die ökonomische Gedankenwelt des Aristoteles, *Archiv für Sozialwissenschaft und Sozialpolitik,* vol. 50, 1923.

Grossmann, Henryk, Carl Grünberg. *Anarchismus, Bolschewismus, Sozialismus,* 1971.

Grossmann, Henryk, Die gesellschaftlichen Grundlagen der mechanistischen Philosophie und die Manufaktur. *Zeitschrift für Sozialforschung,* Vol. IV, 1935, pp. 161–231.

Haguenauer, S., *Das "justum pretium" bei Thomas Aquinas*, Stuttgart 1931.

Hayek, F. A., *Collectivist economic planning,* 1935.

————, *The Constitution of Liberty,* 1960.

————, *Law, Legislation and Liberty,* 1982.

Hegel, G. W. F., Jenaer Systementwürfe III. Hamburg 1976. (Der Geist nach seinem Begriffe.)

Heilbroner, R. L., *The Worldly Philosophers,* 3rd ed., 1967.

Hicks, J. R., *Value and Capital,* 2nd ed., 1946.

————, *A Theory of Economic History,* 1969.

Johnson, E. A. J., *The Predecessors of Adam Smith,* 1937.

Kaulla, R., *Die geschichtliche Entwicklung der modernen Werttheorie,* Tübingen, 1906.

————, *Staat, Stände und der gerechte Preis,* 1936.

Korsch, Karl, *Karl Marx,* 1938.

Krader, L., *Treatise of Social Labor*, ch. 2. Cf. ch. 4, pt. 1, discussion of Aristotle, theory of commutative justice and right as a theory of contract and exchange in civil society. Geometric proportionality is a theory not of exchange but of the combination and division of labor in civil society. Distributive justice and right is a theory in Aristotle of the relation of human whole and human part; it is as such a statement of the theory of the potentiality of socialist society.

————, *Dialectic of Civil Society,* 1976, ch. 3, 4.

Lange, O. and F. M. Taylor, *On the Economic Theory of Socialism,* B. E.

Lippincott, 1937.

Locke, John, *An Essay Concerning the True Original, Extent, and End of Civil Government*, (Second Treatise), 1698. On Labor, §40.

Luxemburg, Rosa, *The Accumulation of Capital,* (1913), 1951.

———, *Imperialism and the Accumulation of Capital. (Anti-critique).*(1921). Contributions by R. Luxemburg, N. Bukharin, K. Tarbuck ed., 1972.

Mandel, Ernest, *Marxist Economic Theory,* 1968.

Marshall, Alfred, *Principles of Economics,* 8th ed., 1974.

Marx, Karl, *Das Kapital,* vol. I–III. 1867–1894. = Marx Engels *Werke,* Bd. 23–25. (MEW).

———, Grundrisse der Kritik der politischen Ökonomie (1857–1858). 1953. = Marx Engels Gesamtausgabe, 2. Ausgabe. 2. Abt., Band I, Teile 1–2. 1976. (MEGA²).

———, *Zur Kritik der politischen Ökonomie,* 1859.

———, *Theorien über den Mehrwert,* 3 vols., 1965.

———, (Zur Kritik) (Manuskript 1861–1863), Marx Engels Gesamtausgabe. 2. Ausgabe. 2. Abteilung. Band 3. Teile 1–6. 1976 ff. (MEGA²).

Die Marx-Kritik der Österreichischen Schule der Nationalökonomie. E. v. Böhm-Bawerk, "Zum Abschluss des Marxschen Systems." (1896). R. Hilferding. "Böhm-Bawerks Marx-Kritik." (1904). J. v. Komorzynski, R.Rosdolsky, E. Lederer, 1974.

Mauss, Marcel, *Essai sur le don: Forme et raison de l'échange dans les sociétés primitives.* 1923–1924. Exchange in the archaic societies is symbolic exchange.

Meek, R. L., *Studies in the labour theory of value,* 2nd ed., 1973.

Mises, Ludwig v., *Socialism,* New ed., 1951.

Mitchell, W. C., *Types of economic theory.* 2 vols, 1967–1969.

Morishima, Michio, *Marx's economics,* 1977.

———, and G. Catephores, *Value, exploitation and growth,* 1978.

Osnovnye problemy politicheskoj ekonomii. Sbornik statei. O. Bauer. L. Boudin. N. Bukharin. R. Hilferding. K. Kautsky. H. Cunow, K. Marx. A. Pannekoek. Conrad Schmidt. G. Eckstein.— Sh. Dvolajckij, I. Rubin (eds.) 1922.

Pribram, Karl, *History of Economic Reasoning,* 1983.

Ricardo, David, *Works,* P. Sraffa ed., 1951– .

Robinson, Joan, *An Essay on Marxian Economics,* 2nd ed., 1966.

———, *Economic Philosophy,* 1962.

———, *Economic Heresies,* 1971.

Roscher, Wilhelm, *Geschichte der National-Oekonomik,* 1874.

Rosdolsky, Roman, *Zur Entstehungsgeschichte des Marxschen 'Kapital',* 1969.

Rozental', M. M., *Dialektika "Kapitala" K. Marksa.,*1967.

Rubin, I. I., *Essays on Marx's Theory of Value,* (1928) 1975.

Schilling, O., *Die Staats- und Soziallehre des hl. Thomas,* Paderborn 1923.

Schreiber, E., *Die volkswirtschaftlichen Anschauungen der Scholastik,* (Just price in Thomas Aquinas, and down to the mid-15th century.) Jena 1913.

Schumpeter, J. A., *History of Economic Analysis,* 1954.

———, *Capitalism, Socialism and Democracy,* 3rd ed., 1950.

———, *Economic Doctrine and Method,* 1954.

Sewall, H. R., *The Theory of Value before Adam Smith,* 1901.

Smith, Adam, *The Wealth of Nations,* R. Campbell, A. Skinner and W. Todd (eds.) 1976.

———, *Lectures on Jurisprudence,* R. Meek, D. Raphael, and P. Stein (eds.) 1978.

Soudek, J., "Aristotle's theory of exchange," *Proceedings American Philosophical Society,* vol. 52, 1952.

Sweezy, P. M., *Socialism,* 1949. (See Böhm-Bawerk.)

———, *The Theory of Capitalist Development,* 1970.

Thompson, E. P., *The Poverty of Theory,* 1979.

Weber, Max, *Wirtschaft und Gesellschaft.* 5th ed., 1972.

Zheleznov, V., *Ekonomicheskoe mirovozzrenie drevnikh grekov,* Moscow 1916, (i.e., Gelesnoff, above.) (Use value is here conceived to be subjective.)

Note 3
Elsewhere in this work, the distinction is made between two kinds of quantification, numerical and non-numerical.

Numerical quantification is further divided between addition and cumulation. The process in digital computers of adding bits of information, in a plus-minus relation is additive, non-cumulative, unless another algebraic system of relations is introduced. This additive relation is applied to the theory of use value, whereby the capacity of a good to meet a human want is expressed.

Another algebra is introduced in the quantification of value in production, which is abstractly cumulative; this value expression is objective; it is other than the objective expression and computation of use value.

Note 4
Hugo Grotius and Thomas Hobbes in the 17th century, Jean Barbeyrac and Adam Smith in the 18th, interpreted the theory of commutative justice of Aristotle as the basis of the theory of exchange and contract, the importance of which was recognized by the theorists in the florescence of capitalism and bourgeois society. Aristotle's theory of commutative and distributive justice is interpreted in another way in the 20th century, and Smith's editors have thought that he misunderstood Aristotle. But Smith set his interpretation of Aristotle in the context of his time. There is no eternal verity in the matters of hermeneutics. F. A. Hayek has ex-

pressed his repugnance toward Aristotle's theory of distributive justice. The modern theory of socialism, which he opposes, is mediately derived from Aristotle's theory. The fate of the theory of commutative justice is determined by varying historical conditions; the outcome of the theory of distributive justice is determined by systematic conditions. I propose that there is a systematic relation between the two theories, of commutative and distributive justice; I do not propose that there is a chronological sequence; that would require the services of the fortune teller.

Grotius, Hugo, *Laws of War and Peace*. Jean Barbeyrac, ed. 1743. (1625)
Hobbes, Thomas, *Leviathan*. 1651.
Smith, Adam, *Lectures on Jurisprudence*.

Note 5
An exchange takes place by stipulating, offering, bargaining, haggling, negotiating, sticking. (Ben Jonson. *The Staple of Newes*): The exchanger in the marketplace scorned the gentleman who did not haggle, and the latter scorned the former, who did.

J. Tropfke. *Geschichte der Elementarmathematik*. 4. Aufl. Bd. 1. K. Vogel et al, ed. Berlin 1980. p. 522. Item es sein 2 gesellen, dy wellen untereinander stechen.
    p. 522, 523. Es sind zwei Kaufleute, die zusammen tauschen wollen.—It is always a relation between 2 who come together.
    p. 527. Luca Pacioli. baratare non e altro se non commutare una mercantia ad un altra con ani[m]o de megliorare conditione.

In the Middle East and in Italy bargaining is an honorable procedure. In Aristotle and in aristocratic circles it is not.

L. Pacioli recognized that exchange, *commutare*, stick, *stechen* is a relation between two persons. They acknowledge that they are capable of conducting an exchange, and that each has a good which can be exchanged against the good of the other. Each acknowledges the right of the other to sell and buy. The point is that they meet to conduct the exchange of goods with one another. The goods exchanged are the same or different, but that is not essential, important or even interesting. The one buys a clock today from the other, and sells it back at some other occasion. Each has the same (or another) time piece when it is wanted and needed. Whether the good exchanged at the different times is the same or not is irrelevant to the transactions. I cannot exchange with myself, for that is not an exchange, but is thinkable only in another way.

Johannes Tropfke, *Geschichte der Elementarmathematik,* 4. Aufl. Bd. 1. K. Vogel et al (ed.) Berlin 1980, pp. 522–524.

Note 6

"By means of the value relation, the natural form of commodity B thus becomes the value form of commodity A, or the body of commodity B becomes the value mirror of commodity A." "In a certain way it is the same with the human being as it is with the commodity. Since one comes into the world neither with a mirror nor as the Fichtean philosopher: I am I, the human being mirrors himself at first in another human being. Only by the relation to the man Paul as one of his own kind does the man Peter relate to himself as a human being. Therewith Paul also with head and hair, in his Pauline corporeality, serves for him as the form in which the genus man appears." "In that commodity A is related to commodity B as an embodiment of value, Wertkörper, as the materialization of human labor, it makes the use value B into the material of its own value expression. The value of commodity A, thus expressed in the use value of commodity B, possesses the form of relative value." The given quantity of value contains a determinate quantity of human labor. "The value form thus has not only value in general, but quantitatively determinate value, or the magnitude of value, to express." Karl Marx. *Das Kapital,* 3rd ed. Book 1, Ch. I, Section 3, A. 2.

Marx here ridicules the notion of the mirror or reflection as a human act. The mirror is not born in us, nor is there an identity, I am I to begin with. Only by relating to another human being as one of our own kind do we relate to ourselves as human beings. The mirror is figurative; Engels and Lenin took a literary trope for the reality. See the discussion in the chapter, *Consciousness.*

We deny that any commodity has a natural form; it has only a value form, and is nought but that form. Commodities are forms, the substance of which is two-fold: the capacity of a good to meet a given human want, and the quantity and quality of labor which are concrete in it. The only form it has is the one given to it by a human device, there being nought of nature otherwise in it.

The value form of commodity A and B is an abstract expression, which is common to them, and to all commodities in the given value system. Commodities A and B are both Wertkörper, embodiments of value, but they are not the value proper, the materialization of human labor, or any other object, good, etc. The commodity is a body of forms.

The value in question is objective, social value; it is only relative, there being no absolute value of this kind. This value is only a form, which we dirempt from the value substance. We are the human beings who have taken up a given objective social value system in the processes of exchange, commodity, market, price, and related processes in the history of civil society.

The quantity of value, Wertquantum, is an expression or form, having a determinate quantity of human labor as its substance; the exchange value has this substance, and another, which is the capacity of the good, of which it is the form, to meet a human want. The exchange value is the realization of the objective social value in general under particular social, historical conditions, which are those of our society, civil and bourgeois, given the relations of exchange, commerce, money, credit, the market.

The objective social value, or value of social labor, is quantitatively determinate value; it has no existence, no apparent or other form, than this; it has not a value form "in general," but only this form, which is at once the expression of quantity and quality of labor, or the amount of preparation, training, previously acquired skill of the human labor which has gone into the making of the good. The good is apart from its commodity existence; in order to make this clear, consider the good as a loaf of bread. It meets our human want of food, and animal need (hunger) whether we have bought it as a commodity or baked it ourselves. The want of food and the animal need are not the same, for some things which Peter will eat gladly and meet his want and need will be abhorrent to Paul, who will die before he eats them.

The value is a form which expresses a determinate value quantity and quality under particular social and historical circumstances; it has a value magnitude under these conditions.

Marx begins not with the individual human being, but with one in relation to another. We begin not with a dyadic relation, but with a henadic human relation among many human beings, who are one and other in their relations, with difference and nexus between them.

Aristotle, *Nicomachean Ethics,* V, 4–5, (On justice), VIII, 10–11, X, 6.

———, *Politics* 1252–5, 1259, 1278, 1330 (on slavery).

Darwin on Man, H. Gruber, ed, New York 1974, p.169.

Hegel, G. W. F., *Philosophy of Right*, 182–256 (civil society). 261 (Rights and duties). On civil society, see also his *Phenomenology of Mind*, C. (AA). Reason. V.C. a. The spiritual animal kingdom and deception, or the matter itself.

Krader, Lawrence, *Dialectic of Civil Society*, pp. 257–267 (on Marx and Darwin), Chapter 3 and 4 (on value, history and theory).

———, *Treatise of Social Labor*, Chapter II, Section XII, (on value theory), Chapter IV (on Aristotle).

Marx, Karl, *Das Kapital*, (*Werke*, vol. 23) On Aristotle, p. 74, Indian weaver caste, p. 360, relation to Vico and Darwin, pp. 392f. note.

———, *Theorien über den Mehrwert*, III. *Werke* 26.3, p. 289.

————, *Ethnological Notebooks*, p. 183 (on castes. See also there, Introduction, pp. 14–16.)

————, *Selected Correspondence*, Jan. 16 1861 (to F. Lassalle, on Darwin and teleology), p. 123, June 16, 1862, (to F. Engels, on Darwin and teleology; on Hegel), p. 123.

On the history of value theory:
Meek, R. L., *Studies in the Labour Theory of Value.*
Schumpeter, J .A., *History of Economic Analysis.*
Mauss, Marcel, *Les formes archaiques de l'échange.*

Note 7

Hegel wrote, against Kant, "Could one ever have thought that philosophy would deny the truth of intelligible essences because they are lacking in the spatial and temporal matter of the senses?" Lenin commented on this passage: "Also here Hegel is in essence right: value is a category that does without the stuff of the senses, but the category is truer than the law of supply and demand." In Hegel, the truth of the essence is either affirmed or not, but is not relativized. Value, according to Lenin, is a category, and so are exchange value and use value therefore categories. Exchange is a concrete process, exchange value is a measure whereby the exchange in human society is effected, the measure is not that which is exchanged, but is a category whereby unlike objects are abstracted from their concrete form and substance, and are related to one another by an abstract property which they share; and that property is the time and quality of social labor expended in the production of the given object. The exchange value is then the expression of the measure, the expression being a form which is related to a substance; the value form is relative to the value substance, which is the social labor, of a given amount and quality. The use value is not other than the exchange value in this connection, for it expresses the usefulness of a given object of exchange, without which the exchange does not take place. The use value is then the expression of a substance, which is the usefulness of the object exchanged in meeting a human social want and need, and stands in relation to that substance as the form thereof. The value in either case is the category into which the expression of the use or the equivalence of exchange falls. The relation between form, substance and expression is separable and variable, hence they may be treated separately in human society. The concrete property of the thing in the material order is transformed by labor into a human relation, whereby a concrete and abstract quality is attributed to it; the concrete attribute is the usefulness of the thing transformed into the object in meeting human wants and needs of a particular kind, the abstract attribute is its exchangeability against another object with an attribute which can be given an equivalent expression; on exchange it is given that expression in fact. The value is the form of the two concrete substances of the object of the human order, the usefulness thereof, in respect of its use value, and the labor time and quality, in respect of its exchange value, both value expressions standing as forms in relation to the respective substances. The value expressions are abstractions and in this sense categories. The value is an abstract attribute of a concrete property of the object, moreover, being made into a law, which is an abstraction of the afore mentioned abstraction. The law of value is the abstract expression of the many exchange and use relations, hence it is a form of forms, the forms into which exchange value and use value are set, being the respective laws thereof. The set of laws of value are distinguished as the law of exchange value, use value and surplus value, being particular to civil society, the law of abstract and concrete value being applicable both to civil society and to other forms of human society. The laws of value have reference only to those human social wholes in which the self-diremption of form and substance takes place in actuality. Now use value was treated by Marx not as a category but as a material object: "Der Gebrauchswert verwirklicht sich nur im Gebrauch oder der Konsumtion—Use value is realized only in use or in consumption. Use values make up the material content of wealth, whatever its social form may be." But value has the same reference in regard to use value and to exchange value; it is not a concrete material itself, but is the expression of material content of wealth. The use value is not material, but is a formal expression, as a form; this form is not as such a substance in relation to another form, but has a function of bearing another form along, use value bearing exchange value abstractly, as use bears exchange concretely. Use value is therefore an abstract category, just as exchange value is, whereas the referent of the use value is concrete, the referent of exchange value abstract. It is possible that use value is different from other value, but this would be so not by virtue of its usefulness, but by virtue of its value, which is absurd, for in this case it is not use or exchange that changes meaning, but value in respect of either. That the category changes the world insofar as it is a category is an idealist doctrine. When Marx wrote, "Es ist also ein besondrer Gebrauchswerth, ein bestimmter Artikel, den der Kapitalist vom Arbeiter anfertigen lässt. It is thus a particular use value, a determinate article, which the capitalist has the worker prepare. The production of use values, or goods, does not alter its general nature by being carried on for the capitalist and under his control." (Marx, *Kapital,* I, 4th ed., 1914, pp. 2 and 140.)—If a good is a use value then it has an intrinsic virtue, to apply the term of Nicholas Barbon. In this case, it does not *have*, but *is* the use value, which is its intrinsic quality. But if this use value is the expression whereby we refer to the quality of the good to supply a want, then the relation between the good and the use value is not intrinsic, but extrinsic, for the use value is attributed by the user to the good. The want of warmth is supplied by the fur of seals or bears in the Arctic, whereas the want is not supplied thereby at the Isthmus of Tehuantepec. The fur may supply some other want, for instance, as a rug or door mat, but not as a body garment, as a coat, in the latter case. The use value is the expression of the respective supplies of the given wants. In this case the fur of the seal has not one but many uses, and not one but many use values, whereby the different uses are expressed. Hence there is no intrinsic virtue of the fur in its usefulness; the use value is not intrinsic either to the use nor to the thing in its objective use, as an object transformed into a good. The fur as such is not a good, but is a natural thing, a part of the seal's body. It is transformed into a good by the hunter or huntress, by skinning the carcass, scraping and softening the pelt, cutting and shaping it. The argument against the intrinsic exchange value of a good, and against the intrinsic value of good in the production thereof, also bears on the argument against the assignment of an intrinsic use value of a good, and against the identification between use and use value. Use values are therefore not produced, but expressed. To be sure, our expression is a kind of labor, but it is not labor in the same sense as the labor of transforming the natural thing into a good useful to us in some particular way. (Nicholas Barbon, *A discourse on coining the new money lighter*. London 1696, p. 6.)

Note 8

Hegel, G. W. F., *Wissenschaft der Logik*, vol. 2, Meiners 1963, p. 228.
Lenin, V. I., *Werke*. 6th ed., Berlin, vol. 38, p.162.
Lukács, G., Die Erkenntnistheorie Lenins und die Probleme der Philosophie. *Existenzialismus oder Marxismus*. Berlin 1951. Ch. 4, section 3.
Marx, Karl. *Kapital*. Marx Engels *Werke*, Berlin, vol. 23, p. 50.

Here the theory of value is taken up as an epistemological problem, without criticism of the difference between abstract reference and concrete substance of value, use value, exchange value and surplus value. The thesis is advanced that there is an absolute knowledge which is such if it reflects objective reality correctly ("wenn sie die objektive Wirklichkeit richtig wiederspiegelt"), and that the absolute and relative states of knowledge constitute an inseparable dialectical unity. (Lukács, *Schriften zur Ideologie*. P. Ludz ed. Luchterhand 1967, p.489: "Die absolute und relative Beschaffenheit der Erkenntnis bilden eine untrennbare dialektische Einheit.") The postulation of an absolute and a relative knowledge state arose in Lukács' formulation in connection with the contradiction regarding value as abstract and value as concrete (ibid., p. 488). Absolute knowledge would be the attribute of a deity, but is beyond the mortal ken. It is not consonant with a materialist doctrine, old or new. The judgment of correctness of reflection of the world in the consciousness is not objective alone, but is subjective as well.

Note 9

Descartes, in distinguishing between *res cogitans* and *res extensa*, applied the term extension to material body, excluding it from thought. The thinking thing is active, *res cogitans*, whereas the extension of material body is not. That body is *res extensa*, *l'étendu*, which is the extended, in the passive state. (*Méditations*, II. Adam, Tannery, ed., vol. IX, p. 24.)

Thought and matter are both in space and time, but are not in the same space and time. In the space-time of the material order of nature, space, time and matter all have extension of the same kind. The extensive magnitudes thereof have the same natural properties, and are expressed by the same quantitative processes by the human kind. Space and time of the material order have not only extension, but also direction, and material body, or matter, has motion, extension and direction of the same kind as the space and time of the sensory and material order. No matter is without motion in space-time; matter, motion, space and time have direct, concrete, continuous relations to one another in the sensory order of nature. They are not the same, yet their relations of extension and direction are the same. Dimension has the constituent relations of extension and direction. Extensionality of space has three directions in the sensory and material order of nature, height, breadth and depth; each of these directions is reversible in respect of the motion of a material body, which moves up and down in the dimension of height, right and left in the dimension of breadth, and forward and back in the dimension of depth.—The wind rose is not a direct dimensionality of matter, but is a mediate one, being a construct of the human order. The directions of the compass are infinite *in potentia*, the plane of the compass being infinitely divisible, but is not actually so divided.

Time in the material and sensory order has one dimension, having one extension and direction. The direction of time, and thus its dimensionality, are irreversible.

Extension, direction, and dimension, of the material order are direct, concrete and continuous in relation to one another, passing into one another without interruption, and with nothing between them. Hence time and space of the material order, which has these relations of extension and direction, and of directness, concreteness and continuity with respect to one another, pass into one another without interruption, and with nothing between them; these are the same relations of passage of material body and its motions, which pass directly, concretely and continuously into one another, and into space-time; conversely, space-time of the sensory system and the material order passes directly, concretely and continuously into the material body of that order and into the motions thereof.

Yet space, time, matter and motion of the sensory and material order are not the same, for, whereas space and time are continuous and pervasive in the material order, matter and its motions are not. Hence the extensionality of space-time of the material order is not the same as the extensionality of matter and motion of that order.

Time and space of the material order differ in respect of the number of their dimensions, which is a quantitative difference between them. They do not differ in the quality of their extensional relations; it is the same extensionality of space as it is of time in the sensory system. The directional relations of space of the material order differ from those of time, with connection between them, the spatial relations of direction being reversible, the temporal relations of direction irreversible, in the given order.

The dimensions of space-time of the material order, hence of matter and its motions, has the same number as that of the extensional relations of that order, three of space and one of time. The direction of space-time is the direction of time in the material order.

Time and space apart from one another are abstract. The humankind abstracts space from time, time from space, and either from material body and its motions. Locke called "the extension of space, the continuity of unsolid, unseparable, and immovable parts." (*Essay Concerning Human Understanding*. Bk. II, 4, 5.) The abstractions of space and time are non-material, in the human order of nature. These non-material and abstract processes nevertheless have relations which are both practical and theoretical. While they are abstract, they have a mediate relation to one another; it is not that they have no relation, but rather that they have no direct relation, to one another.

The relation of space and time in the human order being mediate, there is some process between them; or they are in another relation to one another than that of direct, concrete and continuous relation to one another, passing into one another in some other way than that in which they pass into one another in the material order.

In one sense the human kind has aggrandized itself, acting and thinking as though it were the center of all things, and that everything was created for us, a childish vision of nature. The self-aggrandizement at the same time was accompanied by a false humility, which expressed the notion that although we are weak and unworthy, yet we have been singled out to be the means whereby the mystical creator of all exposes his wonderful ways.

Res extensa and *res cogitans* are not exhaustive of nature. Both are real, having place, being, form and substance in the space-time manifold, but there are other orders of nature than the material order and *res extensa* of that order, and the human order, and *res cogitans* of that order. The quantum order of nature, the order of gravitational process and of light are regular and durative processes of nature; these orders are not exhaustive of natural relations.

In another sense, the human kind perceives that it is in and of nature, and has constituted, manufactured and mentifactured another order of nature than that in which it is generated. The human kind, being and order are real in space and time; this space and time differs from the space-time of the material order, it has a system which differs from the system of sensory and material space-time; there is a connection between them. The connection is threefold: 1. The human kind has a concrete relation to the order in which it is generated; it is a variation by natural evolution of that order. 2. The relation of the two orders is concrete in relation to one another in that both are contained in the manifold of space-time, both are parts of that manifold, both are imbedded in that manifold, both are internal to that manifold, both are lesser in relation to that manifold, which is greater than either and both. 3. The two orders, material and human, are articulated with one another; their articulation is asymmetrical, although systematic. The relation of space-time of the material order to the space and time of the human order is direct, concrete and continuous, whereas the space and time of the human order are mediate, concrete and abstract, continuous and discontinuous in relation to the material order and the space-time thereof. Space-time of the material order is concrete and indisseverable, in this sense one and not other, nor yet many. Space and time of the human order are abstractable and abstracted from their concretum; they are not one but henadic, concretely, and n-adic abstractly, in relations of one, other, and many, *ad infinitum*.

Extension of the material order is continuous in the human order, and direction of material processes are the same. But the human kind generates discontinuities, mediacies, diremptions as well as continuities, immediate and non-diremptive, in the human order.

Distance is a relation of space-time which is other than extension, for it has no extensive magnitude, and its quantification is other than that of extension. It has no direction in the same sense of direction of material space-time and the processes thereof. Distance relations are direct or mediate. The quantum jump of atomic particles is direct, concrete, discontinuous. It is in space-time, hence it is concrete, but not in the space-time of the material order or in that of the human order. The jump has no relation to the extension, extensive magnitude and direction of material body, yet the quantum jump is a change of space-time relations between particles, and in this respect distance of the space-time relations is in being. The distance of the quantum space-time relations is the expression of discontinuities thereof. The particles and their energies pass through these distances; the passage is carried through with something between one state of particulate being and another, or with interruption of their space-time relations, and discontinuity of the endo-atomic, quantum space-time.

The abstract space-time relations of the human order are continuous and discontinuous. The discontinuities and the distance processes thereof are mediate. In this case there is not something but some object, some objective relation between space and time, between this process of space and time and another, both being of the human order. The various processes of the human order pass into one another, mediately, abstractly, concretely, immediately, with material dimensional, continuous, extensional and directional magnitudes between them and with discontinuity, distance between. Both the processes of continuous and direct passage and of discontinuous, mediate passage are objective to us, either in actuality or in potentiality. They are some what, either as thing or object, and are as such knowable in potentiality or known in actuality.

Labor is a relation of the human kind which bears on the material, human and other orders of nature. It is a mediate, concrete and abstract, material and non-material, differential and nexal process; it is immediate, objective and subjective, practical and theoretical, manual and mental. It is the means whereby we transform our natural, material, non-material, luminiferous, gravitational surroundings, and ourselves, in the process of human production and consumption, thus of our human, self reproduction. In the process of reproduction of the human kind by labor we meet our objective wants, thingly needs and subjective desires. The means of meeting them, and of our self reproduction are the transformation of the natural surroundings, material and non-material, as far as we are able. Our abilities are circumscribed by our practical and theoretical capacities. We transform material bodies, inorganic, organic and living; we transform the material and non-material processes of atomic particles, light beams and electrons by the use of lasers, and linear accelerators; and we transform the human being and order, which is material and non-material, but in another way than the atomic particles. We do not transform gravitation, but apply it in practice, depend on it passively, and, in our theories, comprehend it in part.

The relations of the human kind are mediate in respect of space-time, body and motion of the material order; our relation to extension and direction of body and motion is therefore mediate in this order. The relations of the human kind to the quantum order are mediate, abstract, and concrete. Both these orders and their processes are objective to us, in practice and theory; they are not immediate. Our relations to the human order are immediate and mediate.

Bibliography

Albertus Magnus, *Politicorum Aristotelis commentarii*, Borgnet, 1951.

———, *Super Ethica*, Borgnet, 1951.

Aquinas, Thomas, *In Decem Libros Ethicorum Aristotelis ad Nicomachum Expositio*, R. M. Spiazzi (ed.) 3rd ed., Marietti, 1964.

———, *Summa Theologicae*, T. Gilby et al (eds.) Blackfrairs, Eyre and Spottiswoode; McGraw-Hill, 1964–80.

Aristotle, *Metaphysics*, G. P. Putnam's Sons, New York, 1933.

———, *Nicomachean Ethics*, G. P. Putnam's Sons, New York, 1926.

———, *Poetics*, Clarendon, Oxford, 1978.

———, *Politics*, W. L. Newman (ed.) 4 vols., Oxford University Press, Oxford, 1887–1904.

Baldwin, J. W., "The medieval theories of the just price," *Transactions American Philosophical Society*, n.s., vol. 49, pt. 4, 1959.

Berle, A. A. and G. C. Means, *The Modern Corporation and Private Property*, Macmillan, New York, 1933.

Böhm-Bawerk, E. v., *Karl Marx and the Close of his System*. R. (Ed. P. Sweezy), A. M. Kelley, New York, 1949.

———, "Zum Abschluss des Marxschen Systems," *Staatswissenschaftliche Arbeiten: Festgabe für K. Knies*, Otto von Boenigk (ed.) Haering, Berlin, 1896.

Boole, George, *Laws of Thought*, Dover, New York, 1958.

Borkenau, F., "Zur Soziologie des mechanistischen Weltbildes," *Zeitschrift für Sozialforschung*. Vol. I. 1932, pp. 310–335.

Bortkiewicz, Ladislaus v., *Wertrechnung und Preisrechnung in Marxchen System*, Achenbach, Lollar/Giessen, (1906f.) 1976.

Brentano, Lujo, *Der wirtschaftende Mensch in der Geschichte*. Felix Meiner, Leipzig, 1923.

Cannan, Edwin, *A History of the Theories of Production and Distribution in English Political Economy, from 1776 to 1848*, 3rd ed. P. S. King, London, 1917.

Coleridge, Samuel, *Biographia Literaria*, Dent, London, 1975.

Commons, J. R., *Legal Foundations of Capitalism*, Macmillan, New York, 1924.

da Vinci, Leonardo, *Notebooks*, Jonathan Cape, London, 1977.

Dobb, Maurice. *Theories of Value and Distribution Since Adam Smith*, Cambridge University Press, Cambridge, 1973.

——, *Studies in the Development of Capitalism*, Rev. ed., International Publishers, New York, 1963.

Freyer, Hans, *Die Bewertung der Wirtschaft im philosophischen Denken des 19. Jahrhunderts*. Gg. Olms, Hildesheim, 1966, (1921).

Gelesnoff, W., (V. Zheleznov). "Die ökonomische Gedankenwelt des Aristoteles," *Archiv für Sozialwissenschaft und Sozialpolitik*, vol. 50, 1923.

Grossmann, Henryk and Carl Grünberg. *Anarchismus, Bolschewismus, Sozialismus*, Europäische Verlagsanstalt, Frankfurt-am-Main, 1971.

Grossmann, Henryk, "Die gesellschaftlichen Grundlagen der mechanistischen Philosophie und die Manufaktur," *Zeitschrift für Sozialforschung*. Vol. IV, 1935, pp. 161–231.

Grotius, Hugo, *Le droit de la guerre, et de la paix / par Hugues Grotius; nouvelle traduction, par Jean Barbeyrac [3e éd.] De jure belli ac pacis libri tres. [Laws of War and Peace]*. A Basle: Chez Emanuel Thourneisen, 1746. (1625).

Gruber, H. (ed.), *Darwin on Man*, E. P. Dutton, New York, 1974, p.169.

Hagenauer, Selma, *Das "justum pretium" bei Thomas Aquinas*, VSWG Beiheft 24, Stuttgart, 1931.

Hayek, F. A., *Collectivist economic planning*, G. Routledge, London, 1935.

——, *The Constitution of Liberty*, University of Chicago Press, Chicago, 1960.

——, *Law, Legislation and Liberty*, Routledge & Kegan Paul, London, 1982.

Hegel, G. W. F., *Jenaer Systementwürfe*, Felix Meiner, Hamburg, 1976.

——, *Grundlinien der Philosophie des Rechts*, Frommanns, Stuttgart, 1928, (1821).

——, *Phänomenologie des Geistes*, Ullstein, Frankfurst-am-Main, Berlin, 1970.

——, *Phenomenology of Mind*, Humanities Press, New York, 1964.

——, *Philosophy of Right*, Oxford University Press, New York, London, 1967.

——, *Vorlesungen über die Aesthetik*, Werke. Bd. 15.Suhrkamp, Frankfurt-am-Main, 1970

——, *Wissenschaft der Logik*, vol. 2, Meiners, Berlin, 1963.

Heilbroner, R. L., *The Worldly Philosophers*, 3rd ed. Simon and Schuster, New York, 1967.

Hicks, J. R., *Value and Capital*, 2nd ed. Clarendon Press, Oxford, 1946.

——, *A Theory of Economic History*, Clarendon Press, Oxford, 1969.

Hilferding, Rudolf, "Böhm-Bawerks Marx-Kritik," *Marx-Studien*, Bd., 1, 1904.

Hobbes, Thomas, *Leviathan*, Penguin, Harmondsworth, 1968 [1651].

Johnson, E. A. J., *The Predecessors of Adam Smith*, Prentice-Hall, New York, 1937.

Jonson, Ben, *The staple of news*, Manchester University Press, New York, 1988.

Kaulla, R., *Die geschichtliche Entwicklung der modernen Werttheorie*, Vaudz/ Liechtenstein: Topos Verlag, 1977, (1906).

————, *Staat, Stände und der gerechte Preis*, J. Springer, Wien, 1936.

Komorzynski, J. v., *Die nationalökonomische Lehre vom Credit*, Wagner, Innsbruck, 1903.

Korsch, Karl, *Karl Marx*, Chapman and Hall, London, 1938.

Krader, Lawrence, *The Asiatic Mode of Production*, Van Gorcum, Assen, 1975.

————, *Dialectic of Civil Society*, Van Gorcum, Assen, 1976.

————, *Treatise of Social Labor*, Van Gorcum, Assen, 1979.

Lange, O. and F. M. Taylor, *On the Economic Theory of Socialism*, B. E. Lippincott, New York, 1937.

Lederer, E., *Grundzüge der ökonomischen Theorie. Eine Einführung*, J. C. B. Mohr (Paul Siebeck), Tübingen, 1922.

Leibniz, G. W., *The Monadology*, Thomas I. Cook (ed.) Hatner Publishing Company, New York and London, 1966.

Lenin, V. I., *Werke*, vol. 38, 6th ed., Dietz Verlag, Berlin.

Locke, John, Two Treatises of Government (ed. Peter Laslett) Cambridge University Press, Cambridge, 1960.

Lukács, G., "Die Erkenntnistheorie Lenins und die Probleme der Philosophie," *Existenzialismus oder Marxismus*. Aufbau Verlag, Berlin, 1951.

Luxemburg, Rosa, *The Accumulation of Capital*, Yale University Press, New Haven, 1951, (1913).

————, *Imperialism and the Accumulation of Capital*, (*Anti-critique*).(1921), (ed. K. Tarbuck) Allan Lane, The Penguin Press, London, 1972.

Mandel, Ernest, *Marxist Economic Theory*, Merlin, London, 1968.

Marshall, Alfred, *Principles of Economics*, 8th ed., Macmillan, London, 1974.

Marx, Karl, *The Ethnological Notebooks of Karl Marx*, Lawrence Krader (ed.), Van Gorcum, Assen, 1972.

————, *Grundrisse der Kritik der politischen Ökonomie* (1857–1858), 1953. = Marx Engels Gesamtausgabe, 2. Ausgabe. 2. Abt., Band I, Teile 1–2. 1976. (MEGA²) Berlin: Dietz Verlag.

————, *Das Kapital*, vol. I–III. 1867–1894. = Marx Engels *Werke*, Bd. 23–25. (MEW) Dietz Verlag, Berlin, 1968.

————, *Kritik der Hegelschen Rechtsphilosophie. Marx Engels Werke*, vol. 1. Dietz Verlag, Berlin, 1968.

————, *Marx-Engels Selected Correspondence*, Progress Publishers, Moscow, 1968.

————, "Resultate des unmittelbaren Produktionsprozesses," *Arkhiv Marksa i Engel'sa*. V. Adoratskij ed. Vol. II, 1933.

————, *Theorien über den Mehrwert*. Marx-Engels Werke 26.1–3, Dietz Verlag,

Berlin, 1968.

———, *Zur Kritik der politischen Ökonomie*, 1859.

———, (Zur Kritik) (Manuskripte 1861–1863). Marx Engels Gesamtausgabe. 2. Ausgabe. 2. Abteilung. Band 3. Teile 1–6, 1976 ff. (MEGA²).

Mauss, Marcel, "Essai sur le don: Forme et raison de l'échange dans les sociétés primitives," *l'Année Sociologique*, seconde série, 1923–4.

———, *The Gift: Forms and functions of exchange in archaic societies*. (Trans. by Ian Cunnison, with an introduction by E. E. Evans-Pritchard), Cohen & West, London, 1954.

Meek, R. L., *Studies in the Labour Theory of Value*, 2nd ed., Lawrence and Wishart, London, 1973.

Milton, John, *Samson Agonistes*, Cambridge University Press, Cambridge, 1977.

———, "On Shakespeare, 1630," in Merritt Y. Hughes (ed.) *John Milton: Complete Poems and Major Prose*, Macmillan, New York, 1957.

Mises, Ludwig v., *Socialism*, New ed. Jonathan Cape, London, 1951.

Mitchell, W. C., *Types of Economic Theory*, 2 vols. A. M. Kelley, New York, 1967–1969.

Morishima, Michio, *Marx's Economics*, Cambridge University Press, Cambridge, 1973.

———, and G. Catephores, *Value, Exploitation and Growth*, McGraw-Hill, London, New York, 1978.

Plato, *Republic*, Dent, London, 1976.

Pope, Alexander, *Works of Shakespeare*, Preface, 8 vol., C. Hitch & L. Hawes: London, 1762.

Pribram, Karl, *History of Economic Reasoning*, Johns Hopkins University Press, Baltimore, 1983.

Ricardo, David, *Works*. (ed. P. Sraffa), Cambridge University Press, Cambridge, 1951 ff.

Robinson, Joan, *An Essay on Marxian Economics*, (2nd ed.) Macmillan, London, 1966.

———, *Economic Philosophy*, Watts, London, 1962.

———, *Economic Heresies*, Macmillan, London, 1971.

Roscher, Wilhelm, *Geschichte der National-Oekonomik*. Königliche Akademie der Wissenschaften, Munich, 1874.

Rosdolsky, Roman, *Zur Entstehungsgeschichte des Marxschen "Kapital,"* Europäische Verlagsanstalt, Frankfurt-am-Main, 1969.

Rozental', M. M., *Dialektika "Kapitala" K. Marksa*. 1967.

Rubin, I. I., *Essays on Marx's Theory of Value*, Black and Red, Detroit, 1975, (1928).

———, Osnovnye problemy politicheskoj ekonomii. Sbornik statei. O. Bauer. L. Boudin. N. Bukharin. R. Hilferding. K. Kautsky. H. Cunow, K. Marx. A.

Pannekoek. Conrad Schmidt. G. Eckstein.— Sh. Dvolajckij, (ed. I. Rubin) 1922.

Sanders, Thomas Collett (ed. and trans.) *Institutes of Justinian*, 8th edition, Longmans, Green, London, 1885.

Schilling, O., *Die Staats- und Soziallehre des hl. Thomas*. F. Schöningh, Paderborn, 1923.

Schorkowitz, Dittmar, (ed.) *Festschrift für Lawrence Krader*, Peter Lang, Frankfurt-am-Main, 1995.

Schreiber, E., *Die volkswirtschaftlichen Anschauungen der Scholastik*. G. Fischer, Jena 1913.

Schumpeter, J. A., *History of Economic Analysis*, Allen & Unwin, London, 1954.

———, *Capitalism, Socialism and Democracy*, 3rd ed. Allen & Unwin, London, 1950.

———, *Economic Doctrine and Method*, George Allen & Unwin, London, 1954.

Sewall, H. R., *The Theory of Value before Adam Smith*, Macmillan, New York, 1901.

Smith, Adam, *The Wealth of Nations,* (ed. R. Campbell, A. Skinner and W. Todd) Oxford University Press, New York, 1976.

———, *Lectures on Jurisprudence*, (ed. R. Meek, D. Raphael, P. Stein) Oxford University Press, New York, 1978.

Soudek, J., "Aristotle's theory of exchange," *Proceedings American Philosophical Society*, vol. 52, 1952.

Sweezy, P. M., *Socialism*, McGraw-Hill, New York, 1949.

———, *The Theory of Capitalist Development*, Dobson, London, 1970.

Thompson, E. P., *The Poverty of Theory*, Monthly Review Press, New York, 1979.

Tropfke, J., *Geschichte der Elementarmathematik*, 4. Aufl. Bd. 1. (ed. K. Vogel et al) Berlin 1980.

Weber, Max, *Wirtschaft und Gesellschaft*, 5th ed., J. C. B. Mohr, Tübingen 1972.

Zheleznov, V., *Ekonomicheskoe mirovozzrenie drevnikh grekov*, Moscow, 1916.

Index